D0855450

PHYSIOLOGY AND GENETICS OF REPRODUCTION

Part A

BASIC LIFE SCIENCES

Alexander Hollaender, General Editor

Biology Division
Oak Ridge National Laboratory
and The University of Tennessee
Knoxville
and Associated Universities, Inc.
Washington, D. C.

A Continuation Order Plan is available for this series. A continuation order will bring delivery of each new volume immediately upon publication. Volumes are billed only upon actual shipment. For further information please contact the publisher.

PHYSIOLOGY AND GENETICS OF REPRODUCTION

Part A

Edited by

ELSIMAR M. COUTINHO

Department of Maternal Health and Child Care
Federal University of Bahia Faculty of Medicine
Salvador, Bahia, Brazil

and

FRITZ FUCHS

Department of Obstetrics and Gynecology
Cornell University Medical College
New York, New York

WARNER MEMORIAL LIBRARY
EASTERN COLLEGE
ST. DAVIDS, PA. 19087

PLENUM PRESS • NEW YORK AND LONDON

5-28-87

Library of Congress Cataloging in Publication Data

International Latin American Symposium, 13th, Salvador, Brazil, 1973.
  Physiology and genetics of reproduction.

  (Basic life sciences, v. 4)
  Includes bibliographies.
    1. Reproduction—Congresses. 2. Genetics—Congresses. I. Coutinho, Elsi-
mar M., ed. II. Fuchs, Fritz, 1918-   ed. III. Title. [DNLM: 1. Genetics
—Congresses. 2. Reproduction—Congresses. W3BA255 v. 4 1973 / WQ205
I617 1973p]
  QP251.I647   1973   599'.01'6   74-17494
  ISBN 0-306-36591-X (v. 1)

QF 251 .I63 1973
International Latin America
  Symposium (13th : 1973 :
Physiology and genetics of
  reproduction

First half of the Proceedings of the Thirteenth Latin American
International Symposium held in Salvador, Bahia, Brazil, December 3-7, 1973

© 1974 Plenum Press, New York
A Division of Plenum Publishing Corporation
227 West 17th Street, New York, N.Y. 10011

United Kingdom edition published by Plenum Press, London
A Division of Plenum Publishing Company, Ltd.
4a Lower John Street, London, W1R 3PD, England

All rights reserved

No part of this book may be reproduced, stored in a retrieval system, or transmitted,
in any form or by any means, electronic, mechanical, photocopying, microfilming,
recording, or otherwise, without written permission from the Publisher

Printed in the United States of America

Contributors

C. E. Adams
A.R.C. Unit of Reproductive Physiology
  and Biochemistry
University of Cambridge
Cambridge, England (Part B)

Pekka Ahonen
Department of Medical Chemistry
  and Steroid Research Laboratory
University of Helsinki
Helsinki, Finland (Part B)

A. Arimura
Veterans Administration Hospital
New Orleans, Louisiana;
Department of Medicine
Tulane University School of Medicine
New Orleans, Louisiana (Part A)

G. Azadian-Boulanger
Centre de Recherches Roussel-Uclaf
Romainville, France (Part A)

J. M. Bahr
Departments of Animal Science
  and Physiology and Biophysics
University of Illinois
Urbana, Illinois (Part A)

Aimée H. Bakken
Department of Zoology
University of Washington
Seattle, Washington (Part A)

C. Barros
Department of Biology
University of Houston
Houston, Texas (Part B)

G. Bartsch
Department of Urology
University of Innsbruck
Innsbruck, Austria (Part A)

Etienne-Emile Baulieu
Laboratoire de Chimie Biologique
  Faculté de Médicine, Paris, France
Unité de Recherches sur le Métabolisme Moléculaire
  et la Physio-Pathologie des Stéroides de
l'Institut National de la Santé et de la Recherche
  Médicale (Part A)

R. A. Beatty
A. R. C. Unit of Animal Genetics
Department of Genetics
Edinburgh, U.K. (Part A)

J. M. Bedford
Departments of Obstetrics, Gynecology, and Anatomy
Cornell University Medical College
New York, New York (Part B)

Rubén Belitzky
Centro Latinoamericano de Perinatologia
  y Desarrollo Humano
OPS/OMS
Montevideo, Uruguay (Part B)

Claudio Benech
Instituto de Investigación de Ciencias Biológicas
Departamento de Ultraestructura Celular
  and Laboratorio de Biofísica
Montevideo, Uruguay (Part A)

Lars Philip Bengtsson
Department of Obstetrics and Gynecology
University of Lund
Lund, Sweden (Part B)

Kurt Benirschke
Department of Reproductive Medicine
University of California, San Diego
La Jolla, California (Part A)

Pierre Borgeat
MRC Group in Molecular Endocrinology
Centre Hospitalier de l'Université Laval
Quebec, Canada (Part A)

William T. K. Bosu
Primate Laboratory for Research in Reproduction
Department of Obstetrics and Gynecology
University Hospital
Uppsala, Sweden (Part B)

A. Boué
International Children's Centre
Groupe I.N.S.E.R.M. U.73
Château de Longchamp
Paris, France (Part B)

J. Boué
International Children's Centre
Groupe I.N.S.E.R.M. U.73
Château de Longchamp
Paris, France (Part B)

Mario H. Burgos
Instituto de Histología y Embriología
Facultad de Ciencias Médicas, U.N.C.
Mendoza, Argentina (Part A)

Roberto Caldeyro-Barcia
Centro Latinoamericano de Perinatología
  y Desarrollo Humano
OPS/OMS
Montevideo, Uruguay (Part B)

W. H. Carter
Veterans Administration Hospital
New Orleans, Louisiana;
Department of Medicine
Tulane University School of Medicine
New Orleans, Louisiana (Part A)

Cornelia P. Channing
Department of Physiology
University of Maryland School of Medicine
Baltimore, Maryland (Part B)

J. Rodrigo Cifuentes
Centro Latinoamericano de Perinatología
  y Desarrollo Humano
OPS/QMS
Montevideo, Uruguay (Part B)

David E. Comings
Department of Medical Genetics
City of Hope National Medical Center
Duarte, California (Part A)

E. M. Coutinho
Maternidade Climério de Oliveira
Universidade Federal da Bahia
Salvador, Bahia, Brasil (Part B)

Jean Coté
MRC Group in Molecular Endocrinology
Centre Hospitalier de l'Université Laval
Quebec, Canada (Part A)

D. H. Coy
Veterans Administration Hospital
New Orleans, Louisiana;
Department of Medicine
Tulane University School of Medicine
New Orleans, Louisiana (Part A)

E. J. Coy
Veterans Administration Hospital
New Orleans, Louisiana;
Department of Medicine
Tulane University School of Medicine
New Orleans, Louisiana (Part A)

Horacio B. Croxatto
Universidad Catolica de Chile
Santiago, Chile (Part B)

J. Carlos Cuadro
Centro Latinomericano de Perinatología
  y Desarrollo Humano
OPS/OMS
Montevideo, Uruguay (Part B)

L. Debeljuk
Veterans Administration Hospital
New Orleans, Louisiana;
Department of Medicine
Tulane University School of Medicine
New Orleans, Louisiana (Part A)

Egon Diczfalusy
Swedish Medical Research Council
Reproductive Endocrinology Research Unit
Karolinska Sjukhuset
Stockholm, Sweden (Part B)

M. E. Drets
Laboratory of Human Cytogenetics
Instituto de Investigación de Ciencias Biológicas
Montevideo, Uruguay (Part A)

Alan B. Dudkiewicz
Department of Zoology
University of Tennessee
Knoxville, Tennessee (Part B)

A. Eberhard
Department of Obstetrics and Gynecology
Universite de Paris Val-de-Maine
Centre Hospitalier Intercommunal
Créteil, France (Part A)

G. M. Edelman
The Rockefeller University
New York, New York (Part A)

Louise Ferland
MRC Group in Molecular Endocrinology
Centre Hospitalier de l'Université Laval
Quebec, Canada (Part A)

J. Frick
Department of Urology
University of Innsbruck
Innsbruck, Austria (Part A)

Anna-Riitta Fuchs
The Population Council
Biomedical Division
The Rockefeller University
New York, New York (Part B)

Fritz Fuchs
Department of Obstetrics and Gynecology
Cornell University Medical College
New York, New York (Part B)

W. E. Gall
The Rockfeller University
New York, New York (Part A)

Roberto B. García
Instituto de Investigación de Ciencias Biológicas
Departamento de Ultraestructura Celular
and Laboratorio de Biofisica
Montevideo, Uruguay (Part A)

J. P. Gautray
Department of Obstetrics and Gynecology
Université de Paris Val-de-Maine
Centre Hospitalier Intercommunal
Créteil, France (Part A)

Alvaro L. Gimeno
Instituto de Neurobiología
Buenos Aires, Argentina (Part B)

Martha F. Gimeno
Instituto de Neurobiología
Buenos Aires, Argentina (Part B)

P. Grippo
CNR Laboratory of Molecular Embryology
Arcofelice (Naples), Italy (Part B)

Carlos Gual
Department of Reproductive Biology
Instituto Nacional de la Nutrición
México, D. F. (Part A)

Nobuyoshi Hagino
Department of Neurophysiology
Southwest Foundation for Research and Education
and
Department of Anatomy
University of Texas
Health Science Center at San Antonio
San Antonio, Texas (Part A)

Barbara A. Hamkalo
Departments of Molecular Biology and Biochemistry
and
Cell and Developmental Biology
University of California, Irvine, California (Part A)

J. Hib
Centro Latinoamericano
de Perinatología Desarrollo Humano
Hospital de Clínicas
Montevideo, Uruguay (Part B)

Rufus Ige
The Population Council
Rockefeller University
New York, New York (Part A)

Robert B. Jaffe
Department of Obstetrics and Gynecology
University of California
San Francisco, California (Part A)

Elof D. B. Johansson
Primate Laboratory for Research in Reproduction
Department of Obstetrics and Gynecology
University Hospital
Uppsala, Sweden (Part B)

A. Jolivet
Department of Obstetrics and Gynecology
Université de Paris Val-de-Maine
Centre Hospitalier Intercommunal
Créteil, France (Part A)

Fernand Labrie
MRC Group in Molecular Endocrinology
Centre Hospitalier de l'Université Laval
Quebec, Canada (Part A)

W. Ladosky
Department of Biodynamics
Federal University of Pernambuco
Recife, Brazil (Part A)

Robert Landesman
Department of Obstetrics and Gynecology
Cornell University Medical College
New York, New York (Part B)

Jørgen Falck Larsen
University of Copenhagen
and
Department of Obstetrics and Gynecology
Gentofte Hospital
Copenhagen, Denmark (Part B)

Florence Ledwitz-Rigby
Department of Physiology
University of Pittsburgh School of Medicine
Pittsburgh, Pennsylvania (Part B)

F. Leygonie
Department of Obstetrics and Gynecology
Université de Paris Val-de-Maine
Centre Hospitalier Intercommunal
Créteil, France (Part A)

G. C. Liggins
Postgraduate School of Obstetrics
and Gynecology
University of Auckland
Auckland, New Zealand (Part B)

A. C. Vieira Lopes
Federal University of Bahia
Bahia, Brasil (Part B)

Tapani Luukkainen
Department of Medical Chemistry
and Steroid Research Laboratory
University of Helsinki
Helsinki, Finland (Part B)

Mary F. Lyon
MRC Radiobiology Unit
Harwell, Oxon, England (Part A)

H. Maia
Federal University of Bahia
Salvador, Bahia, Brasil (Part B)

H. Maia, Jr.
Federal University of Bahia
Salvador, Bahia, Brasil (Part B)

H. Marberger
Department of Urology
University of Innsbruck
Innsbruck, Austria (Part B)

Luigi Mastroianni, Jr.
Division of Reproductive Biology
Department of Obstetrics and Gynecology
University of Pennsylvania
Philadelphia, Pennsylvania (Part B)

Anne McLaren
Agricultural Research Council Unit
of Animal Genetics
University of Edinburgh
Edinburgh, Scotland (Part B)

O. L. Miller, Jr.
Department of Biology
University of Virginia
Charlottesville, Virginia (Part A)

C. F. Millette
The Rockefeller University
New York, New York (Part A)

Daniel R. Mishell, Jr.
Department of Obstetrics and Gynecology
University of Southern California
School of Medicine
Los Angeles, California (Part B)

A. Monroy
CNR Laboratory of Molecular Embryology
Arcofelice (Naples), Italy (Part B)

Takaaki Murata
Department of Obstetrics and Gynecology
University of Southern California
School of Medicine
Los Angeles, California (Part B)

Yukihiro Nagata
Department of Obstetrics and Gynecology
University of Southern California
School of Medicine
Los Angeles, California (Part B)

Robert M. Nakamura
Department of Obstetrics and Gynecology
University of Southern California
School of Medicine
Los Angeles, California (Part B)

A. V. Nalbandov
Departments of Animal Science
and Physiology and Biophysics
University of Illinois
Urbana, Illinois (Part A)

J. G. L. Noronha
Department of Physiology
Catholic University of Paraná
Curitiba, Brazil (Part A)

E. F. Oakberg
Biology Division
Oak Ridge National Laboratory
Oak Ridge, Tennessee (Part A)

Benedito Barreto de Oliveira
Medical and Public Health School
Catholic University of Bahia
Bahia, Brazil (Part A)

E. Parisi
CNR Laboratory of Molecular Embryology
Arcofelice (Naples), Italy (Part B)

Henning Pedersen
Laboratory of Reproductive Biology
Department of Obstetrics and Gynecology
Rigshospitalet, University of Copenhagen
Copenhagen, Denmark (Part A)

Cora de M. Pedreira
Laboratory of Human Genetics, Department of Biology
Institute of Biology, Federal University of Bahia
Bahia, Brasil (Part A)

Lucy I. S. Peixoto
Institute of Biology, Federal University of Bahia
Bahia, Brazil (Part A)

Georges Pelletier
MRC Group in Molecular Endocrinology
Centre Hospitalier de l'Université Laval
Quebec, Canada (Part A)

B. De Petrocellis
CNR Laboratory of Molecular Embryology
Arcofelice (Naples), Italy (Part B)

D. Philibert
Centre de Recherches Roussel-Uclaf
Romainville, France (Part A)

Kleyde Mendes Lopes Ramos
Laboratory of Human Genetics, Department of Biology
Institute of Biology, Federal University of Bahia
Bahia, Brasil (Part A)

J. P. Raynaud
Centre de Recherches Roussel-Uclaf
Romainville, France (Part A)

T. W. Redding
Veterans Administration Hospital
New Orleans, Louisiana;
Department of Medicine
Tulane University School of Medicine
New Orleans, Louisiana (Part A)

J. J. Reeves
Department of Animal Science
Washington State University
Pullman, Washington (Part A)

Valeria Rettori
Instituto de Neurobiologia
Buenos Aires, Argentina (Part B)

Rafael Rios
Centro Latinoamericano de Perinatologia
y Desarrollo Humano
OPS/OMS
Montevideo, Uruguay (Part B)

M. Rossi
CNR Laboratory of Molecular Embryology
Arcofelice (Naples), Italy (Part B)

B. Sanborn
Program in Reproductive Biology
and Endocrinology
University of Texas Medical School
at Houston
Houston, Texas (Part A)

A. V. Schally
Veterans Administration Hospital
New Orleans, Louisiana;
Department of Medicine
Tulane University School of Medicine
New Orleans, Louisiana (Part A)

Sheldon J. Segal
The Population Council
Rockefeller University
New York, New York (Part A)

H. Seuanez
Department of Genetics
Facultad de Humanidades y Ciencias
Montevideo, Uruguay (Part A)

C. Alex Shivers
Department of Zoology
University of Tennessee
Knoxville, Tennessee (Part B)

R. V. Short
M.R.C. Unit of Reproductive Biology
Edinburgh, Scotland (Part A)

J. Roberto Sotelo
Instituto de Investigación
de Ciencias Biológicas
Departamento de Ultraestructura Cellular
and Laboratorio de Biofisica
Montevideo, Uruguay (Part A)

Richard Stambaugh
Division of Reproductive Biology
Department of Obstetrics and Gynecology
University of Pennsylvania
Philadelphia, Pennsylvania (Part B)

A. Steinberger
Program in Reproductive Biology
and Endocrinology
University of Texas Medical School
at Houston
Houston, Texas (Part A)

E. Steinberger
Program in Reproductive Biology
and Endocrinology
University of Texas Medical School
at Houston
Houston, Texas (Part A)

C. Tachi
Zoological Institute
Faculty of Science
University of Tokyo
Bunkyo-ku, Tokyo, Japan (Part B)

S. Tachi
Zoological Institute
Faculty of Science
University of Tokyo
Bunkyo-ku, Tokyo, Japan (Part B)

Ian H. Thorneycroft
Department of Obstetrics and Gynecology
University of Southern California
School of Medicine
Los Angeles, California (Part B)

J. Vilchez-Martinez
Veterans Administration Hospital
New Orleans, Louisiana;
Department of Medicine
Tulane University School of Medicine
New Orleans, Louisiana

Gorm Wagner
Institute of Medical Physiology B
University of Copenhagen
Copenhagen, Denmark (Part B)

Mårten Wikström
Department of Medical Chemistry
and Steroid Research Laboratory
University of Helsinki
Helsinki, Finland (Part B)

Foreword

The broad areas covered in the annual Latin American International Symposia have included much emphasis on genetics. It was, therefore, a logical development to hold a symposium in Salvador da Bahia on the relation of reproduction to genetics, especially since a strong group working in the area of reproduction is located at the University of Bahia. The idea for the symposium was first considered as a result of discussions with Dr. Sheldon Segal, vice president of The Population Council. An open discussion of the biological basis for reproduction, its genetics, and its scientific implications appeared to us to hold potential of great value. At Dr. Segal's suggestion we contacted Dr. Fritz Fuchs of Cornell University Medical College, New York, who immediately took vigorous leadership, and in cooperation with Dr. Elsimar Coutinho of the Federal University of Bahia, planned the program and organized the symposium.

The symposium turned out to be of great importance not only for Brazil but for many other areas in the world. Modern industrialization has created problems of a complicated nature, particularly in population growth. The large attendance of investigators from all over the world demonstrated the widespread concern about these problems. There were many important discussions with probable long-term implications.

I especially want to express my thanks to Drs. Coutinho and Fuchs and to the groups (listed on p. xii) who supported the symposium.

As with the previous symposia, Plenum Publishing Corporation has done an excellent job in bringing these volumes out. Previous symposia in this series are indicated in an appendix to this volume.

Allexander Hollaender
Oak Ridge National Laboratory,
The University of Tennesse,
and
Associated Universities, Inc.

Acknowledgments

Conselho Nacional de Pesquisas
Academia Brasileira de Ciencias
Governo do Estado do Bahia
Prefeitura da Cidade do Salvador
U.S. Atomic Energy Commission
The Ford Foundation (through the
  U.S. National Academy of Sciences)
The World Health Organization
Cornell University

The Organization of American
  States
The Population Council
Laboratorios Merck do Brasil
Governos da Suicia, Dinamarca,
  Italia, Austria, e Franca
Ciba-Geigy Quimica, S.A.
Oak Ridge National Laboratory
The University of Tennessee

U.S. National Academy of Sciences

Preface

These volumes contain the reports presented at the International Symposium on Physiological and Genetic Aspects of Reproduction, held in Salvador, Bahia, Brazil, December 3–7, 1973. The timely subject was chosen by a committee headed by Prof. Alexander Hollaender, scientist, scholar, and promoter of science in Latin America, whose energy and determination made this symposium—as the others in this series—a very successful scientific event.

The importance of research in the area of reproductive physiology has increased in proportion with the problem of world population growth, which is probably the most important problem faced by humanity today. In most developing countries, rapid population growth frustrates the efforts of governments to improve the living conditions of their people and aggravates social inequalities. Official measures to reduce population growth are usually slow and inefficient, and although there is not very much a working scientist can do to influence the government's actions, contributing to the understanding of man's reproductive processes is undoubtedly one of the ways in which he can help deal with the population crisis.

Because work in reproductive physiology and genetics may lead to radical changes not only in the number of beings in the world but also in the quality of human life, scientific meetings on these subjects are always watched—sometimes suspiciously—by the press and the public. This symposium was no exception and it attracted coverage by both the local and the international press, bringing to public attention the subjects discussed on the program. Some of the sessions were even attended by members of the lay public.

The symposium dealt very little with conception control itself. The topics were selected to cover the most important areas of reproductive genetics and physiology, from sex chromosomes to gametogenesis, from fertilization to gestation and parturition. The outstanding quality of the presentations reflected the outstanding ability of the participants, who were encouraged to discuss not only their recent work, but also the direction of their future research.

The symposium began with a thought-provoking lecture by R. Short on the possible influence of man's reproductive physiology on evolutionary patterns. Short's lecture—a perfect introduction—was followed by a series of basic reports on spermatogenesis and spermatology, ovogenesis and ovulation, hormones and receptors, chromosomes and genes, and fertilization. These were followed by another series of reports on the role of the reproductive tract's smooth muscle in reproduction, which included studies on the ovaries, epididymus, the fallopian tube, and the uterus. Sessions on embryogenesis, gestation, and parturition completed the second half of the symposium.

An effort has been made by the Editors to include in this book all the data presented by the participants in their formal papers. Because of technical difficulties, however, the many spirited discussions and short communications could not be included. The Editors are indebted to Ms. Katerine Giercik Chamberlain, who acted as editorial assistant and to Ms. Eliza Amoroso Lima and Ms. Dianne Davis for their help in the organization of the Symposium.

Salvador da Bahia   Elsimar M. Coutinho
New York   Fritz Fuchs

Contents

I. Reproduction and Genetics

II. Chromosomes and Genes

III. Hormones and Receptors

IV. Spermatogenesis and Spermatology

V. Ovum Development and Ovulation

Contents
of Part B

VI. Fertilization

VII. Smooth Muscle Function in Reproduction

VIII. Implantation and Embryogenesis

IX. Gestation and Parturition

Reproduction and Genetics

Reproduction and Genetics

1

Man, The Changing Animal

R. V. Short
M.R.C. Unit of Reproductive Biology
Edinburgh, Scotland

On December 27, 1831, Charles Darwin, a 22-year-old graduate fresh down from Cambridge, set sail aboard the Admiralty survey ship, *H.M.S. Beagle,* on a voyage around the world. Darwin was employed as a naturalist, and his observations were to revolutionize man's concept of himself. Sixty-three days out of Plymouth, the *Beagle* reached Bahia, the first port of call on the South American continent, and Darwin was immediately entranced: "Delight is a weak term to express the feelings of a naturalist who for the first time has wandered by himself in a Brazilian forest . . . such a day brings a deeper pleasure than he can ever hope to experience again" (Darwin, 1890).

Darwin's views on the origin of species (1859) were destined to bring him into head-on conflict with the preformationist views of the Church of that time, and his doctrine of evolution through natural selection was not immediately accepted, even by biologists. Common sense ultimately prevailed, and Darwinian concepts came to be the rock on which modern biology is founded. It is therefore time to take a fresh look at the situation, because theories, like species, may evolve with the passage of time.

The Jesuit priest Teilhard de Chardin (1959) was fascinated by man's origins and his destiny, and although his writings have been bitterly attacked by biologists of the caliber of Sir Peter Medawar (1967), a few important points remain. Teilhard de Chardin was one of the first to draw attention to the fact that man has been able to circumvent the blind, groping trial-and-error of natural selection by his ability to transmit experiences from one generation to another. Language and learning have, in effect, uniquely permitted man to indulge in a type of Lamarckian evolution, with the "inheritance" of acquired characteristics. Teilhard de Chardin saw this as supplanting the Darwinian type of evolution that has molded our physical development over the ages, but few can share his optimistic belief that this new phase of social evolution will unite the whole of mankind and lead us all to a focal Omega point of complete communion with God.

The idea that as a species we may have escaped the shackles of natural selection and embarked on a new phase in our evolution is a fascinating concept to explore further. Certainly, man has gained an extraordinary degree of control over his environment, thus eliminating many of the selection pressures that have made us what we are. At this point in our history, we may even question whether natural selection is likely to be of any significance in molding our future. The penalties exacted today are often totally unrelated to biological fitness: in what sense were the citizens of Hiroshima and Nagasaki ill suited to their environment; of what benefit to the future of mankind is a car crash? Group selection may have been important in the evolutionary process, but it is difficult to perceive any present-day advantages. For natural selection to operate at all, it is necessary to maintain a high and sustained level of selection for the character in question over many, many generations, and the very instability of our new phase of social evolution is sufficient to insure that this will never happen in the will-o'-the-wisp cultures of today. We often forget that it is impossible to select genetically for or against any character that makes its appearance after the end of the reproductive years. Thus the diseases of middle and later life, such as arteriosclerosis, coronary heart disease, and cancer, are conditions that have never been subjected to natural selection. Somebody who is not capable of reproducing can have no memorial, is perished as though he had never been.

But if the vehicle that brought us here is no longer suitable for our voyage into the future, at least we can learn much about our innate weaknesses by reflection on our origins.

It is axiomatic that man has been able to succeed in the struggle for survival because he has been reproductively efficient, and the most intense selection pressure has always been directed toward this end. Many factors go to make up reproductive efficiency, including age at puberty, birth interval, survival of the newborn, and duration of reproductive life span (Fig. 1). The burgeoning population of the present-day world is an unpleasant reminder of the grim twist of fate that has transformed our reproductive success into a reproductive excess that could lead us into a series of unimaginable ecological and cultural disasters. We must analyze why it is that this change has so suddenly come upon us, and we must take a glimpse into the future to see whether our existing biological mechanisms are compatible with the reproductive restraints that we shall be increasingly forced to impose on ourselves.

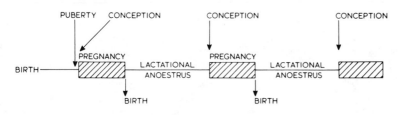

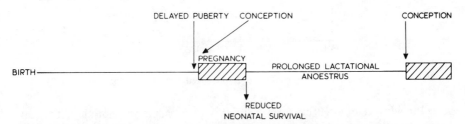

FIG. 1. Natural regulation of animal populations. Age at puberty, birth interval, and neonatal survival rate are the three principal density-dependent regulatory mechanisms. Under conditions of overcrowding, when food becomes scarce, puberty is delayed, neonatal survival rate is reduced, and lactational anestrus or amenorrhea is prolonged.

THE AGE AT PUBERTY

There is little information about the age at puberty in primitive human communities, but Tanner (1955) has documented a spectacular decline in the age at menarche in Europe and North America over the last hundred years (Fig. 2). Recent evidence (Dann and Roberts, 1973) suggests that this downward trend has now come to a halt, to give a mean age at menarche of just over 13 yr. The reasons for this downward trend are almost certainly related to nutrition, since Frisch (1974) has demonstrated that menarche is associated with a critical body weight of 47 kg (Table I). It seems that improved nutrition in childhood and adolescence has enabled individuals to attain this critical body weight at a much younger age.

Although the biological facts are undeniable, nobody has commented on the sociological consequences of this change (Fig. 3). A century ago, girls (and boys) were reaching reproductive maturity at the age of 17–18, which was about the time they were also becoming intellectually mature. In other words, they had the intellectual ability to cope with their newly acquired sexuality. Today, the two events are completely dissociated. Sexuality or physical maturity is attained

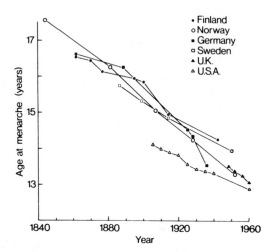

FIG. 2. The declining age at menarche. Reproduced from Austin and Short (1972).

well in advance of intellectual maturity. It is a reasonable assumption that sexual maturity is associated with the onset of sexual desires, but society has made no provision for this in its moral, legal, and ethical codes of behavior. We have yet to face up to the question of whether teenage sex is a sin to be suppressed and sublimated into a more socially acceptable direction, or whether we should take advantage of the situation, and exploit "sex for recreation" as a prelude to the socially responsible act of "sex for procreation" that comes with intellectual maturity.

When dealing with problems of this nature, which are entirely new to our experience, we can only find the correct solution by trial and error. In Darwinian selection, the mistakes were eliminated; in social selection, society has to pay the price and carry the burden of the experiments that fail.

The age at puberty has considerable implications for our system of sexual education. Traditionally, sexual behavior tends to be a self-taught exercise within the peer group, and we flatter ourselves as adults if we imagine that the young would remain innocent and ignorant if we did not teach them the facts of

TABLE I. Body Weights at Puberty[a]

Event	Body weight (kg)	
	Boys	Girls
Adolescent growth spurt	36	30
Maximum rate of weight gain	47	39
First menstruation (menarche)		47

[a]Data from Frisch (1974).

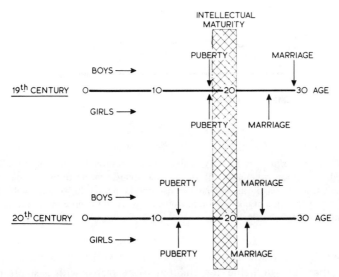

FIG. 3. Man, the changing animal. Comparative data for the population of Britain in the mid-nineteenth century and at present. There is no indication from the school and university curricula of a change in the age at intellectual maturity, but physical maturity now occurs much earlier. This poses the social problem of how to control sexuality in the years before the attainment of intellectual maturity.

life. The prolificacy of our species and our precocious maturity have introduced a new factor into the argument. Man has no innate knowledge of contraceptive technology, so this does need to be taught, and the lesson needs to be given before the practical class is likely to take place. There is still much resistance to be overcome before this obvious conclusion is accepted by even the most enlightened communities.

The time of puberty in most mammals marks the onset of an interesting sex difference in reproductive behavior (Fig. 4). The female invariably conceives at the first available opportunity, whereas territorial or hierarchical mechanisms usually prevent the young male from indulging in sexual activity for weeks, months, or years, depending on the life span of the species. Human societies have distorted this natural pattern by imposing cultural restraints on the time of conception in the female; in Britain it is a crime to have sexual intercourse with a girl under the age of 16, and marriage without parental consent is not allowed in England and Wales before the age of 18. Postponement of marriage until age 24 is being strongly advocated in Communist China. On the male side, we have tended to remove restraints. By opting for a monogamous rather than a polygamous sexual relationship, we have negated the "harem effect" and have given the male the opportunity to seek sexual satisfaction from his female peers as and when he wishes. It is perhaps not surprising that societies find such difficulty in

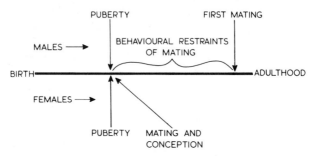

FIG. 4. The animal situation. Puberty in the female is invariably followed immediately by mating and conception, whereas territorial and hierarchical mechanisms operate to prevent young males from mating in the immediate postpubertal period. In Western civilizations, we have postponed the time of conception in women and are in the process of eroding many of the cultural restraints on men.

reimposing cultural restraints to control promiscuity. We have adequate evidence to show that it is desirable for children to be reared with a stable parental relationship, but experimentation rather than pontification will have to tell us what dangers, if any, promiscuity holds for the subsequent establishment of the pair bond.

THE BIRTH INTERVAL

Maximum reproductive efficiency presupposes a minimum birth interval; a female wild animal spends most of her life pregnant—since conception occurs at puberty, and she usually becomes pregnant again at the first postpartum ovulation. Thus the estrous cycle, which we have come to regard as the norm in our laboratory animals, seldom occurs in the wild state.

Lactation is frequently used as a device to regulate the birth interval, since it can postpone the time of the first postpartum ovulation, and in some animals it can also induce a state of arrested embryonic development. Under adverse environmental conditions and when food is scarce, the duration of lactational anestrus can become excessively prolonged.

In primates, menarche in the female is followed by a period of relative infertility when the animal may undergo a number of anovulatory cycles (Corner, 1923). In free-living wild chimpanzees, a period of 1–2½ yr may elapse between menarche and pregnancy (McGinnis, 1973), during which time the animals will have a number of menstrual cycles. This is probably the only time in their lives when they will menstruate repeatedly. In adults, lactational amenorrhea tends to merge into the ensuing pregnancy, and menstruation is a comparatively rare event (Van Lawick-Goodall, 1968).

Unfortunately, there appears to be no information available on the frequency of menstruation in primitive human communities, so we must rely on guesswork and analogy with the situation in our primate cousins. Certainly, we know that menarche is followed by a period of infertility associated with anovulatory cycles (Halewijn and De Waard, 1968; Döring, 1969). We also know that lactational amenorrhea can provide an effective means of spacing births under suboptimal nutritional conditions (Saxton and Serwadda, 1969), and this may be reinforced by cultural taboos that forbid intercourse while a woman is still breast-feeding (Malcolm, 1970). One of the immediate impacts of civilization has been to improve food supplies and so eliminate this important regulatory mechanism (Bonte and van Balen, 1969).

It seems highly probable that menstruation during the reproductive years would have been a relatively infrequent event. However, a number of menstrual cycles might separate the end of one period of lactational amenorrhea from the beginning of the next pregnancy, since women are not likely to be as fertile as chimpanzees. Not only do women fail to advertise the fact that they are about to ovulate, but they also fail to surround themselves with suitors and indulge in excessive sexual activity at this time. However, the fact remains that the reproductive years of primitive woman would have been mainly occupied by pregnancies and periods of lactational amenorrhea, rather than by menstrual cycles.

The contrast between what we must suppose was the "primitive" situation and the present-day state could hardly be more striking (Fig. 5). The immediate consequence of self-imposed infertility through contraception has been to bring about a dramatic increase in the frequency of menstrual cycles, and this has been reinforced by the declining age at menarche, a reduction in the period of lactational amenorrhea, and maybe even a postponement of the menopause. A woman's reproductive life span today may extend from menarche at 13 yr to menopause at 50 yr, and if she has only two children, she can expect about a 2 yr respite from menstrual cycles. Thus she would probably experience about 400 menstrual cycles during her life.

People have been surprisingly slow to appreciate the fact that an endless succession of menstrual cycles is something quite new in our evolutionary experience, which could represent a considerable health hazard. For example, careful studies of disease incidence in nuns, as compared to a control group of the general population, most of whom were married and presumably parous, established that nuns run 1.4–1.5 times the risk of getting cancer of the breast, and they also run a much higher risk of developing cancer of the ovary (Taylor et al., 1959). Recent evidence (MacMahon et al., 1973) points strongly to the fact that the risk of breast cancer increases sharply with the age at which a woman bears her first, full-term child (see Fig. 6). Women first parous before the age of 18 run about one-third of the breast cancer risk of women whose first child is born after the age of 35. MacMahon et al. commented on the fact that

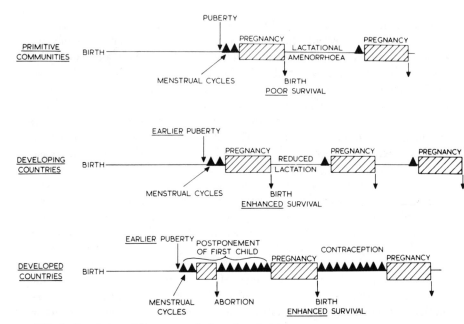

FIG. 5. Regulation of human populations. In primitive communities, puberty was delayed because of poor nutrition in infancy and childhood, there was a high neonatal mortality, and a long period of lactational amenorrhea was associated with breast-feeding. Relatively few menstrual cycles occurred because a woman was always either prepubertal, pregnant, or in lactational amenorrhea. In developing countries, improved food supplies and medical care hastened the onset of puberty, improved the neonatal survival rate, and reduced the period of lactational amenorrhea, thus leading to a spectacular increase in the rate of population growth. In developed countries, these same trends have continued, but economic factors have intervened to persuade couples to restrict family size by postponement of marriage, contraception, and abortion. The result has been a spectacular increase in the number of menstrual cycles experienced, particularly in the period between menarche and first pregnancy.

women with cancer of the breast also have a higher incidence of cancer of the body of the uterus, endometrial cancer, and probably cancer of the ovary, suggesting a common etiological cause. Other, less detailed studies have also shown that endometrial carcinoma is much more common in nulliparous women (Garrett, 1966), and it is a generally held belief among gynecologists that endometriosis and fibroids are much more frequently encountered among nulliparous women (Novak and Woodruff, 1967). The conclusion to be drawn from all this epidemiological evidence is that nulliparity, or late parity, carries a very significant health risk.

Unfortunately, no studies seem to have been carried out to determine whether the increased incidence of these conditions is directly dependent on the number of menstrual cycles a woman has experienced, or whether there is a direct beneficial effect of parity. On theoretical grounds it seems likely that the menstrual cycle itself is likely to be the culprit, since neither the breast, the brain, the ovary, nor the uterus was designed to withstand a monthly turmoil of hormonal changes for years on end. A convincing case for eliminating menstruation can be made solely on the grounds of the adverse consequence of repeated blood loss in women who are already on a marginal plane of nutrition, and the high cost of menstrual hygiene procedures in civilized communities. To this could be added the personal inconvenience and the undesirable changes in mood and performance that occur during the cycle (McCance *et al.*, 1937). These may become of increasing importance as women begin to assume a greater role in affairs outside the home.

It would be wrong to leave the subject of uterine pathology and the possible harmful effects of the menstrual cycle without some mention of cancer of the cervix. It has been long recognized that the incidence of cervical carcinoma is related to intercourse; the disease is almost unknown in nuns (Taylor *et al.*,

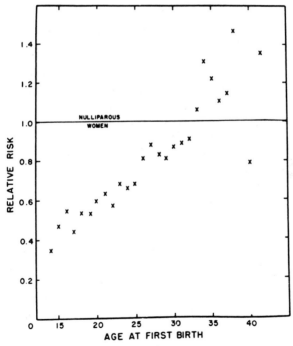

FIG. 6. *The relative risk of breast cancer in relation to the mother's age at the birth of her first child.* The risk of breast cancer in nulliparous women is taken as 1. The younger the maternal age at first pregnancy, the lower the risk. The cricial period seems to be the time elapsed from menarche to first birth, and this, in turn, may be related to the number of menstrual cycles experienced during this period. Reproduced from MacMahon *et al.* (1973).

1959) and is uncommon in unmarried women, although frequent in prostitutes. Boyd and Doll (1964) concluded that its incidence was clearly related to some factor associated with coitus, and that frequency of intercourse and penile hygiene were likely contributory factors. Perhaps this is the price we have had to pay for exploiting our sexuality. Certainly, man has earned himself the reputation of being the sexiest of the primates. The male has developed the largest genitalia (Morris, 1967), while the female has not only suppressed all outward and visible signs of ovulation, so that she remains perpetually attractive, but she has also succeeded in emancipating her sexual behavior from hormonal control, so that she will permit intercourse throughout most of the menstrual cycle, pregnancy, and even old age.

IMPLICATIONS FOR CONTRACEPTIVE RESEARCH AND DEVELOPMENT

It is a curious fact that all forms of contraception perpetuate the menstrual cycle, either indirectly, as in the case of the condom, coitus interruptus, vasectomy, tubal ligation, the intrauterine device, and the rhythm method, or by specific design, as in the case of the "pill." Much more attention needs to be devoted to the development of reversible forms of contraception that would induce long-lasting periods of amenorrhea. If it could be shown by epidemiological studies that the harmful effects of nulliparity are indeed due to the increased frequency of menstrual cycles, then it would immediately become of the utmost importance to suppress the menstrual cycle from menarche until the woman wants to conceive—since it is during this time, and this time alone, that the breast's susceptibility to cancer is determined. Although there are major racial differences in the age-specific incidence of breast cancer (Fig. 7), these are environmentally rather than genetically determined (MacMahon et al., 1973) and could be due to racial differences in the average time elapsed from menarche to first birth.

Suppression of menstrual cycles before first conception could easily be achieved by injections, implants, or oral administration of progestogens or even of estrogen–progesterone mixtures. In the future, it might be possible to make a more discreet intervention by using a biologically inert synthetic analogue of LHRH (luteinizing hormone releasing hormone), which would compete at the pituitary level with the natural hormone and so depress gonadotrophin secretion and hence ovarian endocrine activity. It might even be possible to use a combination of hormones (estrogen, progesterone, and prolactin) to develop the breast to the point of lactation soon after menarche, so that it would be protected against the deleterious effect of subsequent cycles.

At the end of her reproductive life span, when a woman has achieved her desired family size, it would again become desirable to suppress menstrual

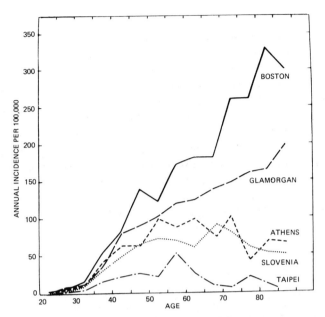

FIG. 7. Age-specific incidence rates of breast cancer in five different areas of the world. These differences can be shown to be due to environmental rather than genetic factors. Perhaps the lower rate in the poorer countries is due to a trend toward later menarche and earlier conception in these areas. Reproduced from MacMahon *et al.* (1973).

cycles. Ovariectomy at any age reduces the subsequent risk of mammary carcinoma (MacMahon *et al.*, 1973), so it would be sensible to keep the ovary in an inactive state to take advantage of this fact. Similar methods could be used to those adopted before the first pregnancy. It might even be possible to produce ovarian inactivity by active immunization against LHRH. Should the woman subsequently change her mind and desire another pregnancy, it should not be too difficult to induce ovulation with gonadotrophins, or with biologically active synthetic analogues of LHRH.

In ways such as these, contraception in the future may develop as a by-product of a general maternal health program designed to lower the incidence of breast cancer and diseases of the reproductive organs. In the United States at the present time, one woman in four undergoes a surgical menopause, and there are 30,000 deaths annually from breast cancer. Such statistics put the minimal health hazards of steroidal contraceptives in true perspective. Properly used, they might become lifesavers. In developing countries with little national or individual motivation to adopt family planning procedures, improved maternal health would be a far more acceptable objective.

We cannot blame our overpopulation problem on sexual overindulgence; it is a direct consequence of man's conquest of disease, resulting in improved fertility and enhanced neonatal survival. The emancipation of human sexual behavior from hormonal control, making sex perpetually available, may have been a most important factor in our social evolution. It is likely to have encouraged the pair bond and to have favored group cohesion, since competition between males would cease to be a continual divisive force.

Contraception is essentially a negative attitude, denying something that has hitherto been regarded as desirable—a large family. However, it could so easily become a positive step toward improved maternal health and well-being. Our penalty for having outstripped natural selection is that we can never achieve a steady state, and our legacy of natural density-dependent regulatory mechanisms that were designed to keep us in equilibrium with our environment can no longer operate effectively. Man is committed to being the changing animal, for as he was in the beginning, he is not now, nor ever shall be.

REFERENCES

Austin, C. R., and Short, R. V., eds. (1972), *Reproduction in Mammals,* Book 5: *Artificial Control of Reproduction,* Cambridge University Press, Cambridge.

Bonte, M., and van Balen, H. (1969), Prolonged lactation and family shoeing in Rwanda, *J. biosoc. Sci. 1:*97–100.

Boyd, J. T., and Doll, R. (1964), A study of the aetiology of carcinoma of the cervix uteri, *Br. J. Cancer 18:*419–434.

Corner, G. W. (1923), Ovulation and menstruation in *Macacus rhesus, Contr. Embryol. Carneg. Inst. 15:*73–102.

Dann, T. C., and Roberts, D. F. (1973), End of the trend? A 12-year study of age at menarche, *Br. Med. J. 2:*265–267.

Darwin, C. (1859), *Abstract of an Essay on the Origin of Species and Varieties Through Natural Selection,* John Murray, London.

Darwin, C. (1890), *Journal of Researches into the Natural History and Geology of the Countries Visited During the Voyage of HMS Beagle Round the World.*

Döring, G. K. (1969), The incidence of anovular cyles in women, *J. Reprod. Fertil., (suppl)6:*77–81.

Frisch, R. E. (1974), The critical weight at menarche and the initiation of the adolescent growth spurt, and the control of puberty, in: *The Control of the Onset of Puberty* (M. M. Grumbach, G. Grave, and F. Mayer, eds.), Wiley, New York.

Garrett, J. D. (1966), Constitutional factors in endometrial cancer, in: *New Concepts in Gynecological Oncology,* pp. 195–203 (G. C. Lewis, W. B. Wentz, and R. M. Jaffe, eds.), Davis, Philadelphia.

Halewijn, E. A. B.-V., and De Waard, F. (1968), Menstrual cycles shortly after menarche in European and Bantu girls, *Hum. Biol. 40:*314–330.

MacMahon, B., Cole, P., and Brown, J. (1973), Etiology of human breast cancer: A review, *J. Natl. Cancer Inst. 50:*21–42.

Malcolm, L. A. (1970), *Growth and Development in New Guinea—A Study of the Bundi People of the Madang District,* Monograph Series No. 1, Institute of Human Biology, Madang.

McCance, R. A., Luff, M. C., and Widdowson, E. E. (1937), Physical and emotional periodicity in women, *J. Hyg. 37:*571–611.

McGinnis, P. R. (1973), *Patterns of Sexual Behaviour in a Community of Free-Living Chimpanzees,* Ph.D. dissertation, University of Cambridge.

Medawar, P. B. (1967), *The Art of the Soluble,* Methuen, London.

Morris, D. (1967) The Naked Ape, Jonathan Cape, London, p. 52.

Novak, E. R., and Woodruff, J. D. (1967), *Novak's Gynecologic and Obstetric Pathology,* 6th ed., Saunders, Philadelphia.

Saxton, G. A., and Serwadda, D. M. (1969), Human birth interval in East Africa, *J. Reprod. Fertil. (suppl.)6:*83–88.

Tanner, J. M. (1955), *Growth at Adolescence,* 1st ed., Blackwell, Oxford.

Taylor, R. S., Carroll, B. E., and Lloyd, J. W. (1959), Mortality among women in 3 Catholic religious orders with special reference to cancer, *Cancer 12:*1207–1223.

Teilhard de Chardin, P. 1959), *The Phenomenon of Man,* William Collins Sons, London.

Van Lawick-Goodall, J. (1968), *The Behavior of Free-Living Chimpanzees in the Gombe Stream Reserve,* Animal Behaviour Monographs, Vol. I, Part 3, Ballière, Tindall and Cassell, London.

Section II

Chromosomes and Genes

2

Structure of Mammalian Chromosomes

David E. Comings
Department of Medical Genetics
City of Hope National Medical Center
Duarte, California

For many years one of the most controversial aspects of chromsome structure was the question of whether the chromatids were single- or multistranded. Despite hopeful expectations, the increased resolution offered by whole-mount electron microscopy did not provide an answer. What became apparent was that the chromatin was composed of a confusing, tangled array of chromatin fibers (DuPraw, 1966; Wolfe, 1965; Abuelo and Moore, 1969; Comings and Okada, 1970a,b, 1972; Lampert, 1971). Even utilizing tiny chromosomes, such as the microchromosomes of the chicken (Okada and Comings, 1970), it was impossible to determine whether one or two DNA molecules were present. The one exception came with studies of lampbrush chromosomes. Here the fine preparations by Miller (1969) showing transcription, down to the presence of attached RNA polymerase molecules, proved that at least the lampbrush loops were single-stranded.

Recently biochemical and biophysical studies of DNA renaturation kinetics (Laird, 1971; Britten and Kohne, 1968), DNA ultracentrifugation (Petes and Fangman, 1972), and viscioelastic retardation (Kavenoff and Zimm, 1973) have provided strong evidence in favor of uninemy. These findings, in conjunction with many past observations on DNA replication, recombination, mutation, and chromatid structure, provide impressive evidence that, except for some special situations (Gay *et al.,* 1970), chromatids are single-stranded. These and other details of chromosome structure have recently been reviewed (Comings, 1972c, 1973a) and will not be further discussed.

This work was supported by NIH Grant GM #15886 and The Norman V. Wechsler Research Fund.

CENTROMERIC AND INTERCALARY HETEROCHROMATIN

It has been appreciated for many years that the chromatin of interphase cells tends to occur in two states, heterochromatin and euchromatin. Heterochromatin is condensed throughout interphase, is genetically inactive, and is late replicating. Most heterochromatin is constitutive in type, occurring on homologous portions of homologous chromosomes.

Interest in the subject of heterochromatin has picked up considerably with the development of chromosome-banding techniques. These techniques have delineated the existence of two distinct types of constitutive heterochromatin: (1) centromeric and (2) intercalary.

In mammals, centromeric heterochromatin is detected by the C-banding technique. It is usually, but not always, localized around the centromeres. *In situ* hybridization (Pardue and Gall, 1970) and nuclear subfractionation studies (Yasmineh and Yunis, 1970, 1971; Comings and Mattoccia, 1972; Hatch and Mazrimas, 1970) indicate that when an organism possesses highly repetitious satellite DNA, this DNA is localized on the centromeric heterochromatin. It is important to point out, however, that organisms with very little repetitious satellite DNA, such as the Chinese hamster (Comings and Mattoccia, 1972), nevertheless still can have large amounts of C-band heterochromatin. This indicates that some C-band heterochromatin may contain DNA that is not highly repetitious. In the Chinese hamster this conclusion has been confirmed by *in situ* hybridization studies which show that some C-band heterochromatin shows no hybridization to highly repetitious DNA (Hsu, 1972).

The intercalary heterochromatin is not detected by C-banding but is seen by Q- or G-banding. It occurs in the chromosome arms. Autoradiographic studies indicate that the DNA of Q- and G-bands is late replicating (Ganner and Evans, 1971; Pathak *et al.,* 1973). Even better evidence of this is obtained by bromodeoxyuridine (BUdR) banding. If late-replicating DNA is labeled with BUdR, it fails to fully condense during mitosis. This produces a banding pattern that is the exact opposite of G-banding, which indicates to a high degree of resolution that G-bands contain late-replicating DNA (Zakharov and Egolina, 1972).

Evidence that intercalary heterochromatin is condensed onto the nuclear membrane during interphase comes from electron microscope autoradiography studies of *Microtus agrestis* (Comings and Okada, 1973). In this species almost all of the C-band heterochromatin is localized on the large masses on the sex chromosomes (Arrighi *et al.,* 1970). When these cells are labeled with tritiated thymidine, some nuclei can be seen in which the masses of C-band heterochromatin are unlabeled but in which a large amount of heterochromatin condensed onto the inner surface of the nuclear membrane is highly labeled (Comings and Okada, 1973). This is not the pattern of replicating euchromatin and is not at the location of the C-band heterochromatin, indicating that it represents the rather large amount of intercalary heterochromatin in the arms. Electron microscope autoradiography of cells labeled with tritiated uridine indicates that the condensed chromatin is genetically inactive. Thus, like centromeric heterochromatin, intercalary heterochromatin is condensed during interphase, genetically inactive, and is late replicating.

The DNA of intercalary heterochromatin is not highly repetitious. This has been demonstrated by examination of the renaturation kinetics of late-replicating Chinese hamster DNA (Comings and Mattoccia, 1970) and DNA of isolated heterochromatin and euchromatin (Comings and Mattoccia, 1972).

One of the most consistent characteristics of the DNA of intercalary heterochromatin is that it is slightly AT-rich. This has been demonstrated in a number of animals by DNA ultracentrifugation (Tobia et al., 1971; Flamm et al., 1971; Bostock and Prescott, 1971a,b; Comings, 1972a). Other independent evidence based on antinucleoside antibodies (Dev et al., 1972; Schreck et al., 1973), reaction to quinacrine mustard (Weisblum and deHaseth, 1972; Pachmann and Rigler, 1973), and acridine orange banding (Bobrow and Madan, 1973; Comings 1973b, de la Chapelle et al., 1973) is also consistent with the G-band heterochromatin being slightly AT-rich, but the DNA ultracentrifugation studies provide the most unambiguous demonstration of this fact.

The final characteristic of DNA of intercalary heterochromatin is that it is slightly undermethylated. This has been demonstrated by centriguation studies of DNA labeled with tritiated methylmethionine (Comings, 1972) and by indirect chromatographic analysis of the absolute content of methylcytosine (Burkholder and Comings, 1973). These two characteristics, slight AT-richness and undermethylation, are probably interrelated in that the deamination of methylcytosine results in thymidine. This reaction would result in a shift of a GC base pair to an AT base pair.

EVOLUTION OF INTERCALARY HETEROCHROMATIN

A case can be made for the proposition that in mammals and possibly other species the essential genes are relatively GC-rich and well methylated. For example, the euchromatic DNA is GC-rich, and if one examines the amino acid sequence of a number of proteins and extrapolates back to the base composition of the genes, a base composition of 44–48% is indicated, while the base composition of the DNA as a whole is only 40% (Comings, 1972b). During evolution, as gene duplication takes place, if the duplicated material adopts no new function it is released from selective pressure. As such, it may undergo mutations in the form of deamination of methylcytosine to thymidine bases, thus leading to relative AT-richness of the DNA between the essential genes. In addition, if longer stretches are genetically inactivated, the same mutation process could lead to a shift to AT-richness, loss of methylatable sites, and deficiency in methylcytosine. Further forces may then exist which lead to the nonrandom accumulation of this slightly AT-rich DNA. For example, it has been demonstrated in chromosome-breakage experiments that the interband regions are much more susceptible to breakage than the intercalary heterochromatin (Seabright, 1972). Such a differential susceptibility to breakage would mean that if a breakage and reunion occurred that brought two pices of heterochromatin together, they would be unlikely to be subsequently separated. However, if a breakage and reunion brought two pieces of euchromatin together, they could be separated. This would lead to a sink resulting in the tendency for clustering of the heterochromatin and, by default, clustering of the euchromatin. This may be the mechanism by which the intercalary heterochromatin becomes accumulated in sufficient degree to produce the banding in the chromosome arms (Comings, 1973c).

Thus one can visualize the following chain of events: gene duplication → release from selective pressures → methylcytosine to thymidine mutations → a shift to moderate AT-richness → association with specific chromosomal proteins → relative resistance to chromosome breakage → nonrandom accumulation of relatively AT-rich DNA → detectable bands in chromosome arms.

PROTEINS AND CHROMOSOME BANDING

Following the initial studies of chromosome banding, the prevailing opinion was that variations in the type of DNA along the chromosome were the most important factor in banding. Evidence is now beginning to swing to the opposite conclusion, that variations in proteins bound to DNA are the most important.

C-banding was based on the rationale that the DNA is first denatured by alkali and then renatured in the presence of salts. Since this worked, it seemed logical to conclude that this was a denaturation/renaturation procedure. However, studies with acridine orange have indicated that C-banding can be produced regardless of the state of denaturation or renaturation of the DNA (Comings *et al.*, 1973; Stockert and Lisanti, 1972). Further studies indicated that the C-band procedure generally results in an extraction of large amounts of non-C-band heterochromatin and that this also plays a significant role in C-banding (Comings *et al.*, 1973). Finally, examination of C-banded chromosomes by electron microscopy further demonstrates that the DNA in this region is highly resistant to the treatments involved in producing C-banding, while the rest of the DNA is readily extracted or destroyed. This then indicates that some type of protein intimately associated with C-band DNA is primarily responsible for C-banding.

In relation to G-banding, the important role of chromosomal proteins was more generally appreciated, especially since many of the techniques involved the use of proteolytic enzymes. It is not unlikely that the mechanism for producing G-banding is similar to that for C-banding, but of a less extreme degree.

This is verified by the observation that brief treatment of chromosomes with trypsin results in G-banding, while more prolonged treatment results in destruction of the G-bands such that only C-bands remain (Comings et al., 1973; Merrick et al., 1973). This conclusion is complicated somewhat by the existence of R-banding. Here certain types of treatment result in a banding pattern which is almost exactly opposite that of G-banding (Dutrillaux and Lejeune, 1971). It will take a significant amount of detailed biochemical investigation to determine the precise mechanism by which this occurs.

The banding which most clearly seemed to be dependent on the type of DNA present was Q-banding. Caspersson et al. (1969) originally felt that quinacrine mustard was specifically interacting with guanine bases, but in vitro studies of fluorescence of quinacrine in the presence of different types of DNA demonstrated that GC-rich DNA tends to quench quinacrine fluorescence, while DNA containing stretches of four or more adjacent AT pairs tends to markedly enhance fluorescence (Weisblum and deHaseth, 1972; Pachmann and Rigler, 1972). The observation that AT-rich satellites fluoresced intensely (Ellison and Barr, 1972) further indicated the dependence of this technique on base composition. However, some other observations indicated that proteins are very much involved. For example, mouse AT-rich satellite, which contains five adjacent AT base pairs (Southern, 1970) and is located around the centromeres, fluoresces poorly with quinacrine (Rowley and Bodmer, 1971). In the muntjac, the centromeric heterochromatin contains satellite DNA which has the same base composition as main-band DNA, but here again it stains very poorly by quinacrine fluorescence (Comings, 1971). Proteins are probably involved in modifying the staining reaction. In addition, Gottesfeld et al. (1974) have recently shown that condensed heterochromatin, isolated from Drosophila and rat nuclei, quenches quinacrine fluorescence much less than isolated euchromatic fractions. However, when the DNA is isolated from both of these fractions, the quinacrine is quenched as much as it is with purified whole DNA. This then proves that the proteins are playing an important role in modifying the quinacrine fluorescence. Because of these observations, we have done a number of studies on the effect of polylysine, polyarginine, and salts on quinacrine fluorescence and have shown that calf-thymus DNA complexed with polylysine can markedly alter the ability of the DNA to quench quinacrine fluorescence. These studies suggest that a major factor in Q-banding may be protein-induced variations in the ability of quinacrine to bind with chromatin (Comings et al., 1974). In conclusion, when regions of very AT-rich satellite DNA are present on the chromosomes, they fluoresce very brightly because of the tendency for AT-rich DNA to enhance fluorescence. However, the more subtle Q-bands out in the chromosome arms are probably due to DNA–protein interactions rather than to the relatively minor variations in base composition.

The proteins involved in chromosome banding are most likely nonhistone proteins. This conclusion is based on the fact that chromosomes can be treated for 4 h with 0.2 N HCl, and yet good C-, G-, and Q-banding is still produced (Comings and Avelino, 1974). When the acid-treated cells are subjected to SDS gel electrophoresis, it is apparent that the histones have been completely removed.

PROTEINS IN CHROMOSOME PAIRING

In addition to chromosome banding, proteins are probably extremely important in the mechanism of chromosome pairing. During the process of homologous chromosome pairing–during pachytene–a unique structure known as the synaptonemal complex is present. It has often been suggested that this is somehow responsible for the intimate base-specific process of homologous pairing. However, when the synaptonemal complex is examined by whole-mount electron microscopy and the DNA is dissolved away by DNase, it is apparent that this complex is predominantly composed of proteins and that the central element is not the site of homologous pairing of DNA duplexes (Comings and Okada, 1970c, 1972a). Studies of haploid organisms and other situations also suggest that the synaptonemal complex is a relatively nonspecific structure which will pull together nonhomologous chromosomal material. These observations suggest that the important part of specific chromosome pairing takes place prior to the laying down of the synaptonemal complex. It has been pointed out that DNA-binding proteins specific for certain base sequences, similar to the lac-repressor protein, have all of the capabilities of acting as chromosomal-pairing proteins (Comings and Riggs, 1971). A search for such proteins is in progress.

REFERENCES

Abuelo, J. G., and Moore, D. E. (1969), The human chromosome: Electronic microscopic observations on chromatin fiber organization, *J. Cell Biol. 41*:73–90.
Arrighi, F. E., Hsu, T. C., Saunders, P., and Saunders, G. F. (1970), Localization of repetitive DNA in the chromosomes of *Microtus agrestis* by means of *in situ* hybridization, *Chromosoma (Berl.) 32*:224–236.
Bobrow, M., and Madan, K. (1973), The effects of various banding procedures on human chromosomes, studies with acridine orange, *Cytogenet. Cell Genet. 12*:145–156.
Bostock, C. J., and Prescott, D. M. (1971a), Buoyant density of DNA synthesized at different stages of the S phase of mouse L cells, *Exp. Cell Res. 64*:267–274.
Bostock, C. J., and Prescott, D. M. (1971b), Buoyant density of DNA synthesized at different stages of S phase in Chinese hamster cells, *Exp. Cell Res. 64*:481–484.

Britten, R. J., and Kohne, D. E. (1968), Repeated sequences in DNA, *Science 161*:529–540.

Burkholder, G. D., and Comings, D. E. (1973), Unpublished observations.

Caspersson, T., Zech, L., Modest, E. J., Foley, G. E., Wagh, U., and Simonsson, E. (1969), Chemical differentiation with fluorescent alkylating agents in *Vicia faba* metaphase chromosomes, *Exp. Cell Res. 58*:128–140.

Comings, D. E. (1971), Heterochromatin of the Indian muntjac: Replication, condensation, DNA ultracentrifugation, fluorescent and heterochromatin staining, *Exp. Cell Res. 67*:441–460.

Comings, D. E. (1972a), The replicative heterogeneity of mammalian DNA, *Exp. Cell Res. 71*:106–112.

Comings, D. E. (1972b), Methylation of euchromatic and heterochromatic DNA, *Exp. Cell Res. 74*:383–390.

Comings, D. E. (1972c), The structure and function of chromatin, in: *Advances in Human Genetics,* pp. 237–431 (H. Harris and K. Hirschhorn, eds.), Plenum Press, New York.

Comings, D. E. (1973a), Biochemical mechanisms of chromosome banding and color banding with acridine-orange, *Nobel Symp. 23*:293–299.

Comings, D. E. (1973b), Model for the evolutionary origin of chromosome bands, *Nature (Lond.) 244*:576–577.

Comings, D. E. (1974), The structure of human chromosomes, in: *The Cell Nucleus,* (H. Busch, ed.), Academic Press, New York, pp. 537–563.

Comings, D. E., and Avelino, E. (1974), Mechanisms of chromosome banding. II. Evidence that histones are not involved. *Exp. Cell Res. 86*:202–206.

Comings, D. E., and Kovacs, B., Avelino, E., and Harris, D., Mechanisms of chromosome banding, IV, Quinacrine banding, submitted for publication.

Comings, D. E., and Mattoccia, E. (1970), Replication of repetitious DNA and the S period, *Proc. Natl. Acad. Sci. (U.S.A.) 67*:448–455.

Comings, D. E., and Mattoccia, E. (1972), DNA of mammalian and avian heterochromatin, *Exp. Cell Res. 71*:113–131.

Comings, D. E., and Okada, T. A. (1970a), Do half-chromatids exist? *Cytogenetics (Basel) 9*:450–459.

Comings, D. E., and Okada, T. A. (1970b), Whole mount electron microscopy of the centromere region of metacentric and telocentric mammalian chromosomes, *Cytogenetics 9*:436–449.

Comings, D. E., and Okada, T. A. (1970c), Whole mount electron microscopy of meiotic chromosomes and the synaptonemal complex, *Chromosoma (Berl.) 30*:269–286.

Comings, D. E., and Okada, T. A. (1972a), The architecture of meiotic cells and mechanisms of chromosome pairing, in: *Advances in Cell and Molecular Biology,* Vol. II, pp. 309–384 (E. J. DuPraw, ed.), Academic Press, New York.

Comings, D. E., and Okada, T. A. (1972b), Electron microscopy of chromosomes, in: *Perspectives in Cytogenetics,* pp. 223–250 (S. W. Wright, B. F. Crandall, and L. Boyer, eds.), Charles C Thomas, Springfield, Ill.

Comings, D. E., and Okada, T. A. (1973), DNA replication and the nuclear membrane, *J. Mol. Biol. 75*:609–618.

Comings, D. E., and Riggs, A. D. (1971). Molecular mechanisms of chromosome pairing, folding and function, *Nature (Lond.) 233*:48–50.

Comings, D. E., Avelino, E., Okada, T. A., and Wyandt, H. E. (1973), The mechanism of C- and G-banding of chromosomes, *Exp. Cell Res. 77*:469–493.

de la Chapelle, A., Schroder, J., Selander, R.-K., and Stenstrand, K. (1973), Differences in DNA composition along mammalian chromosomes, *Chromosoma (Berl.) 42*:365–382.

Dev, V. G., Warburton, D., Miller, O. J., Miller, D. A., Erlanger, B. F., and Beiser, S. M.

(1972), Consistent patterns of binding of antinucleoside antibodies to human metaphase chromosomes, *Exp. Cell Res. 74:*288–293.

DuPraw, E. J. (1966), Evidence for a "folded-fibre" organization in human chromosomes, *Nature (Lond.) 209:*577–581.

Dutrillaux, B., and Lejeune, J. (1971), Sur une nouvelle technique d'analyse du caryotype humain, *C. R. Acad. Sci. (Paris) 272:*2638–2640.

Ellison, J. R., and Barr, H. J. (1972), Quinacrine fluorescence of specific chromosome regions: Late replication and high AT content in *Samoaia leonensis, Chromosoma (Berl.) 36:*375–390.

Flamm, W. G., Bernheim, N. J., and Brubaker, P. E. (1971), Density gradient analysis of newly replicated DNA from synchronized mouse lymphoma cells, *Exp. Cell Res. 64:*97–104.

Ganner, E., and Evans, H. J. (1971), The relationship between patterns of DNA replication and of quinacrine fluorescence in the human chromosome complement, *Chromosoma (Berl.) 35:*326–341.

Gay, H., Das, C. C., Forward, K., and Kaufman, B. P. (1970), DNA content of mitotically active condensed chromosomes of *Drosophila melanogaster, Chromosoma (Berl.) 32:*213–223.

Gottesfeld, J. M., Bonner, J., Radda, G. K., and Walker, I. O. (1974), Biophysical studies on the mechanism of quinacrine staining of chromosomes, submitted.

Hatch, F. T., and Mazrimas, J. A. (1970), Satellite DNA's in the kangaroo rat, *Biochim. Biophys. Acta 224:*291–294.

Hsu, T. C. (1972), Personal communication.

Kavenoff, R., and Zimm, B. H. (1973), Chromosome-sized DNA molecules from *Drosophila, Chromosoma (Berl.) 41:*1–27.

Laird, C. D. (1971), Chromatid structure: Relationship between DNA content and nucleotide sequence diversity, *Chromosoma (Berl.) 32:*378–406.

Lampert, F. (1971), Attachment of human chromatin fibers to the nuclear membrane, as seen by electron microscopy, *Humangenetik 13:*285–295.

Merrick, S., Ledley, R. S., and Lubs, H. A. (1973), Production of G and C banding with progressive trypsin treatment, *Pediat. Res. 7:*39–44.

Miller, O. L. (1969), Portrait of a gene, *J. Cell. Physiol. (suppl. 1) 74:*225.

Okada, T. A., and Comings, D. E. (1970), Whole-mount electron microscopy of chicken microchromosomes, in: *28th Annual Proceedings of the Electron Microscopy Society of America,* (C. J. Arceneaux, ed.), Claitors Pub. Div., Baton Rouge, pp. 256–257.

Pachmann, U., and Rigler, R. (1972), Quantum yield of acridines interacting with DNA of defined base sequence, *Exp. Cell Res. 72:*602–608.

Pardue, M. L., and Gall, J. G. (1970), Chromosomal localization of mouse satellite DNA, *Science 168:*1356–1358.

Pathak, S., Hsu, T. C., and Utakoji, T. (1973), Relationships between patterns of chromosome banding and DNA synthetic sequences: A study of the chromosomes of the Seba's fruit bat, *Carollia perspicillata, Cytogenet. Cell Genet., 12:*157–163.

Petes, T. D., and Fangman, W. L. (1972), Sedimentation properties of yeast chromosomal DNA, *Proc. Natl. Acad. Sci. (U.S.A.) 69:*1188–1191.

Rowley, J. D., and Bodmer, W. F. (1971), Relationship of centromeric heterochromatin to fluorescent banding patterns of metaphase chromosomes in the mouse, *Nature (Lond.) 231:*503–506.

Schreck, R. R., Warburton, D., Miller, O. J., Beiser, S. M., and Erlanger, B. F. (1973), Chromosome structure as revealed by a combined chemical and immunological procedure, *Proc. Natl. Acad. Sci. (U.S.A.) 70:*804–807.

Seabright, M. (1972), The use of proteolytic enzymes for the mapping of structural rearrangements in the chromosomes of man, *Chromosoma (Berl.) 36:*204–210.

Southern, E. M. (1970), Base sequence and evolution of guinea pig α-satellite DNA, *Nature (Lond.) 227:*794–798.

Stockert, J. C., and Lisanti, J. A. (1972). Acridine-orange differential fluorescence of fast- and slow-reassociating chromosomal DNA after *in situ* DNA denaturation and reassociation, *Chromosoma (Berl.) 37:*117–130.

Tobia, A., Schildkraut, C. L., and Maio, J. J. (1971), DNA replication in synchronized cultured mammalian cells. I. Time of synthesis of molecules of different average guanine + cytosine content, *J. Mol. Biol. 54:*499–515.

Weisblum, B., and deHaseth, P. L. (1972), Quinacrine, a chromosome stain specific for deoxyadenylate-rich regions in DNA, *Proc. Natl. Acad. Sci. (U.S.A.) 69:*629–632.

Wolfe, S. L. (1965), The fine structure of isolated chromosomes, *J. Ultrastruct. Res. 12:*104–112.

Yasmineh, W. G., and Yunis, J. J. (1970), Localization of mouse satellite DNA in constitutive heterochromatin, *Exp. Cell Res. 59:*69–75.

Yasmineh, W. G., and Yunis, J. J. (1971), Satellite DNA in calf heterochromatin, *Exp. Cell Res. 64:*41–48.

Zakharov, A. F., and Egolina, N. A. (1972), Differential spiralization along mammalian chromosomes. I. BUdR-revealed differentiation in Chinese hamster chromosomes, *Chromosoma (Berl.) 38:*341–365.

3

Quantitation of Heterogeneous Human Heterochromatin: Microdensitometric Analysis of C- and G-Bands

M. E. Drets

Laboratory of Human Cytogenetics
Instituto de Investigación de Ciencias Biológicas
Montevideo, Uruguay

and

H. Seuanez

Department of Genetics
Facultad de Humanidades y Ciencias
Montevideo, Uruguay

Ever since Lejeune *et al.* (1959) reported the first chromosome aberration in humans, an impressive number of investigations have been carried out showing the great complexity of the human karyotype. These investigations were based on classical chromosome morphology and on autoradiographic data. Despite the large amount of data gathered on the human karyotype, the definite identification of many chromosomes of the human complement remained the main topic of controversy. Over the last 5 years, several investigations have aimed at the solution of this problem. Caspersson *et al.* (1968) reported a remarkable discovery: the chemical differentiation along the chromosomes by quinacrine mustard, a fluorescent dye. This finding proved to be extremely useful in the fields of basic and clinical research.

The development of a new staining technique by Arrighi and Hsu (1971) for heterochromatin, later called C-banding, was another important step toward chromosome identification. Their method revealed pericentromeric segments in most of the human chromosomes, but only a terminal segment in the Y chromosome.

The modification introduced by Drets and Shaw (1971), which revealed G-banding patterns along the chromosome arms, was derived from this procedure. It involved a very brief treatment with sodium hydroxide and incubation in highly concentrated sodium chloride–trisodium citrate for 60–72 h.

Throughout the period in question, and thereafter, several other procedures were published which have had far reaching significance in the area of cytology. As a result, it became evident that banding patterns could be produced in various experimental conditions (Bartalos and Rainer, 1971; Dutrillaux and Lejeune, 1971; Dutrillaux, 1973; Chernay et al., 1971; Lomholt and Mohr, 1971; Patil et al., 1971; Schnedl, 1971b; Shiraishi and Yoshida, 1971; Sumner et al., 1971; Utakoji, 1972).

Another significant advance was the development of a method for revealing banding patterns by enzymatic digestion (Dutrillaux et al., 1971; Seabright, 1971; Wang and Fedoroff, 1972; Chiarelli and Chiarelli, 1971) or by use of chemical agents before fixation (Hsu et al., 1973). Reviews on these discoveries have been published by Miller et al., (1973), Pearson (1972), and Schnedl (1973b).

The enzymatic procedures and the denaturation–reannealing techniques, as well as other methods for producing banding patterns, demonstrate the existence of different chromosome organizations along the chromatid.

Several researchers (Bahr et al., 1973; Comings et al., 1973; Lubs et al., 1973; Kato and Moriwaki, 1972; Schnedl, 1973a) have investigated this problem from different angles and with different experimental procedures. The molecular basis underlying banding patterns, as rendered manifest by available techniques, is still far from being thoroughly understood.

Enzymatic production of banded chromosomes has shown that proteins play an important role in chromosome organization. However, studies with anti-A (Dev et al., 1972) and anti-G (Schreck et al., 1973) immunoglobulin have defined not only the location of different bases in human chromosomes, but have also obtained Q-, G-, and R-banding patterns, as revealed by other procedures. Hence the DNA-bound proteins, the purine or pyrimidine bases distributed along the chromosome, and the specific differential binding capacity of the stains or fluorochromes used must all be interacting in the production of a banding pattern.

Identification of human chromosome landmarks and mapping of major bands obtained with different methods were proposed during the Paris Conference (1972). Each chromosome arm was divided into regions according to band distribution, each band being sequentially numbered. The suggested diagrammatic representation of Q-, G-, and R-bands resulted from comparing the information reported by several laboratories. This system of mapping had already been used for R-bands (Prieur et al., 1973). The proposed chromosome landmarks are easily recognized, but no quantitative data have been supplied to localize precisely any given band or point between two chromosome regions.

The results of comparative studies of banding patterns with fluorescence, proteolytic, and denaturation methods (Dutrillaux *et al.*, 1972), quinacrine fluorescence and acetic–saline–Giemsa techniques (Evans *et al.*, 1971), and immunofluorescence, quinacrine, and Giemsa G-banding techniques (Schreck *et al.*, 1973) have been reported, but they are mainly based on direct morphological analysis at the microscope. Hence it would appear that a new topological method for describing banding patterns, designed to permit standardization of collected data, is needed. Consequently, a new method is suggested in the second part of this report, aimed at a more accurate definition of the mapping parameters proposed at the Paris Conference.

The purposes of the present investigation were (1) to precisely locate G-bands along the chromosome arms and (2) to quantitate the size and structure of C-heterochromatic segments through relative measurements on curves obtained with a high-resolution microdensitometric system.

Microdensitometry on photographs has already been used by Caspersson *et al.* (1971a, and b) and Caspersson (1973). Densitometry of slides or negatives (Lubs and Ledley, 1973), direct exploration of some banded Leishman-stained human chromosomes (Lundsteen *et al.*, 1973), and analysis on television systems (Caspersson *et al.*, 1970) have also been used to study banding patterns. Unfortunately, no quantitative data on the relative positions of C- and G-bands have been published, which are necessary in order to develop a more accurate map of human chromosomes.

In this work, C- (human Y chromosome) and G- (chromosome No. 1) banded chromosomes were used for a pilot densitometric analysis. The method we followed combines the advantage of the contrast enhancement of photomicrographs by simple photographic procedures with the high amplification power of a photomultiplier. Moreover, the incomparable high contrast obtained with C- and G-banding procedures affords a better opportunity to obtain more informative tracings, thus permitting far more accurate band localization.

MATERIALS AND METHODS

Leukocytes from normal, unrelated, randomly selected Caucasian individuals were cultured following a modified method described by Edwards (1962). Colchicine (0.004 mg/ml; Merck, Darmstadt) was added 4 h before harvesting. Cells were resuspended in sodium citrate (1%) for 10 min, pelleted gently, and fixed in ice-cold 1:3 glacial acetic acid–methanol. The fix was changed three times each 10 min and was flame-dried in 70% methanol.

C-bands were obtained by a modification (Craig-Holmes *et al.*, 1973) of the original procedure of Arrighi and Hsu (1971). G-bands were obtained by the technique of Drets and Shaw (1971), with minor modifications. Slides were incubated at 63°C for approximately 60 h after treatment with NaOH for 30 s, followed by staining for 5 min in a buffered Giemsa stain solution. The Giemsa solution was prepared as follows: 1.5 ml Giemsa stock solution (Merck, Darmstadt), 1.5 ml absolute methanol, 1.5 ml of 0.1 M citric acid, and 30 ml of distilled water were adjusted to pH 6.7 with 0.2 M Na_2HPO_4 and taken to a final volume of 50 ml with distilled water.

About ten karyotypes per individual were established as a control. Nonbent chromosomes showing lack of distortion and high-resolution banding were selected.

Selected banded metaphases were photographed in a Photomicroscope II from Zeiss (Oberkochen) with a Neofluar immersion lens (100X) and phase

FIG. 1. Equipment presently used for automated chromosome densitometry at the Instituto de Investigación de Ciencias Biológicas, Montevideo. (1) Chopper and rectifier system, (2) centromere marker, (3) microscope, (4) photomultiplier, (5) H.T. power supply, (6) monitoring oscilloscope, (7) recorder, (8) control panel, (9) AC amplifier.

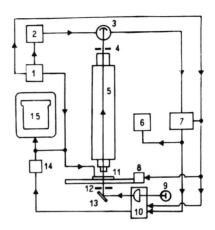

FIG. 2. *Diagram of distribution of components of the densitometer apparatus.* (1) Control panel, (2) H.T. power supply, (3) photomultiplier, (4) photomultiplier slit, (5) microscope, (6) oscilloscope, (7) AC amplifier, (8) microscope stage servomotor, (9) light source, (10) chopper and rectifier system, (11) centromere marker, (12) field diaphragm, (13) deflecting mirror, (14) low-frequency filter, (15) recorder.

contrast. Nomarski-interference phase contrast was also used with a Planapochromat immersion lens (100X). High Contrast copy film (Kodak, Rochester) was adjusted to a low-speed setting (DIN: 5) and developed in a Microdol developer (Kodak, Rochester) at 20°C for 9 min. Photomicrographs were enlarged 5000X for C-banded Y chromosomes and 4000X for G-banded chromosomes. Selected chromosomes were enlarged on Fine Grain positive film (Kodak, Rochester), developed for 2 min in diluted D-8 developer (1:1), fixed in acid fixer for 10 min, washed, dried, and mounted on a slide. The Y chromosome was placed so that its terminal heterochromatic segment would be recorded first in every instance. Chromosome No. 1 was oriented so that recording would start on its long arm first, identified by the presence of a characteristic heterochromatic segment at the paracentric region.

Straight G-banded chromosomes or those bent only at the centromere region were used. In the latter case, chromosomes were cut at the centromere and both arms were recorded separately.

The instrument used to analyze banded chromosomes microdensitometrically is a modification of the cytophotometer currently used in our laboratory (Drets, 1961) (Fig. 1). Its conventional distribution of parts is shown in Fig. 2. A Summar lens (f = 25 mm; 1:2.8) (Leitz, Wetzlar) and a Periplan eyepiece (10X) were used to obtain a final magnification of 100X on the photomultiplier (Fig. 1,4). Modulated (13 cycle/s) light beams (Field rectangular diaphragm, aperture 100 μm) (Fig. 2,12) were detected with a 1P28 (Fig. 2,3) diaphragmed photomultiplier (aperture 100 μm) (Fig. 2,4). The slit size corresponded to an actual chromosome area of 0.01 by 0.00025 μm. Chromosomes were run at a speed of 60 μm/s for recording with a servomotor activating the microscope stage (Fig. 2,8). The recordings were carried out in a Leeds and Northrup Speedomax recorder at a chart speed of 52.5 mm/min, which resulted in a final magnification 65,000X the actual chromosome size for the Y chromosome and 50,000X for chromosome No. 1. Since the area of the enlarged chromosome analyzed was approximately 400 μm^2, it was possible to record separately the chromatids of the same chromosome and to compare both of the curves obtained.

Since our staining procedure for G-banding reveals not only bands but also pericentromeric heterochromatin in many chromosomes, and since it is necessary to have a permanent localization of the centromere region in curves, an electromechanical device (Fig. 3) was developed that permanently marks the centromere position while densitometric curves are being recorded. With the aid of this adjunct, which we called the "centromere marker," the densitometer becomes programmed to "see" the centromere regardless of the presence or absence of heterochromatic segments on either side of this structure. Therefore, any measurement or calculation of band localization, referred to the centromere position, was greatly facilitated.

The functioning of the centromere marker is based on the charging of a condenser, C1 (Fig. 3), through a resistor, R5, and spring electrode (a). The translation of the centromere marker, accompanying the movement of the microscope stage, causes C1 discharge through resistors R2 and R1, producing a spike in the tracing. The main advantage of this device is that it is possible to change the position of the centromere pointer (Fig. 3b), which carries the electrodes in both directions along the specimen (±1.25 cm) from its central position. This allows precise localization of the centromere, which is identified

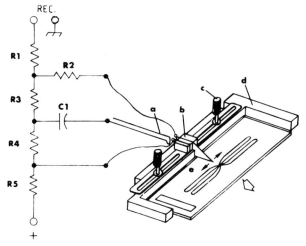

FIG. 3. *Centromere marker.* The apparatus diagram shows actual connections with the electronic circuit. The direction of translation of the system is indicated by an open arrow. (a) Spring electrode, (b) pointer with electrical contacts, (c) setting screws, (d) supporting frame, (e) slide with specimen.

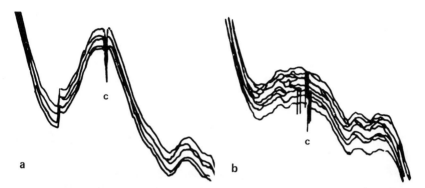

FIG. 4. *Tests of reproducibility of the centromere marker.* (a) Five scannings of the same centromere region of the human Y chromosome. Only one initial adjustment of the apparatus was done. (b) The same, but ten scannings with ten individual centromere adjustments. The amplitude was slightly modified in both cases in order to enhance the effect.

visually. The performance and accuracy (±0.5%) of this device were tested repeatedly by measuring the centromere index of favorable nonbent chromosomes. Examples of centromere-marking reproducibility tests are presented in Fig. 4 for several recordings of the same centromere region. These tests and the information gathered from about 3000 recordings of different normal chromosomes indicated that the instrument affords good reproducibility marking irrespective of chromosome size. The deviation found (±0.5%) is negligible since it represents about 0.0000125 μm of the actual Y chromosome size at the final curve magnification. Obviously, this is beyond the physical limits of the microscope system.

The procedure and sequence of adjustments were as follows: (1) identification of the centromere and centromere-marker (CM) adjustment, (2) trial scanning to judge the CM performance, (3) selection of the chromatid to be recorded, and (4) modulation of light beams and blank adjustment for 95–97% of transmittance (galvanometer reading).

All the recordings were carried out with a linear amplifier, as we also found that logarithmic recordings were not useful (Caspersson *et al.*, 1971b).

Complete length curves of both Y and No. 1 chromosomes were measured in millimeters. Both arms were measured from the centromere, and the parameters used for estimating q and p lengths for Y chromosomes are presented in Fig. 5.

Ten percent of the galvanometer deflection was neglected at both ends of the densitometric curves used for length measurements, as indicated in Fig. 5, in order to eliminate possible uncertainties in chromosome delimitation resulting from the diffraction fringe in each chromosome arm (Patau, 1960). A similar method was followed for chromosome No. 1.

Although curves represent "complete" chromosomes in a sense, it is evident that they supply only limited, linear information. Hence we considered it important to delimit and define chromosome structures in terms of chromosome densitometer tracings. These parameters were empirically established for chromosome quantitative measurements, after a number of preliminary recordings of banded chromosomes from different individuals. Figure 5 represents diagrammatically the recording for the Y chromosome.

For the purpose of this investigation, a "band" was defined as any clearly detectable densitometric peak which appeared as a galvanometer deflection of more than 5% (the background electronic noise of the whole system was less than 0.01%; the background noise determined by the emulsion grain was approximately 0.5%) in the same relative position in different individuals.

Because the terminal C-segment of the Y chromosome (H in Fig. 5) stains more intensely than the centromere region, its absorbance is correspondingly higher. This permitted us to define H as the part of the curve which exceeds the centromere peak, as shown in Fig. 5. However, it was necessary to introduce a correction factor (±10%) in curves from those individuals carrying a Y chromosome with a densely stained C-centromeric segment (Figs. 7e and 8d) or from those chromosomes with poorly stained heterochromatic segments but otherwise

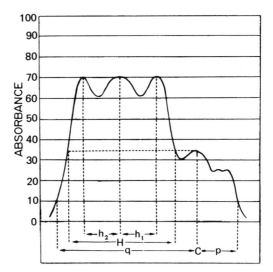

FIG. 5. Criteria used to estimate the heterochromatic segment (H) of the Y chromosome (see text). p, Short arm; c, centromere; q, long arm; h_1 and h_2, distances between densitometer peaks. Absorbance is represented in galvanometer arbitrary units. The diagram represents an actual three-banded Y chromosome, slightly modified.

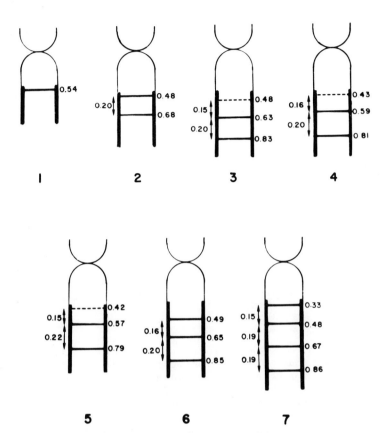

FIG. 6. Diagrammatic representation of the relative size of the hetero-chromatic segment and relative band position along the long arm of the Y chromosome. 1–7, Individual Nos. Interband distances are indicated by arrows and values. Dotted lines denote those peaks detected only in a small number of chromosomes in persons classified as two-band carriers (see also Table III and text). Note the increase of interband distance and the similarity of interband values in different persons.

suited for recordings. Finally, it was also possible to distinguish the short arm in curves which showed a lower absorbance than H or C (Fig. 8).

RESULTS AND DISCUSSION

Densitometric Measurements of the Y Chromosome and Statistical Approach

Different types of Y chromosomes observed in eight unrelated, randomly selected, normal individuals are shown in Fig. 7.

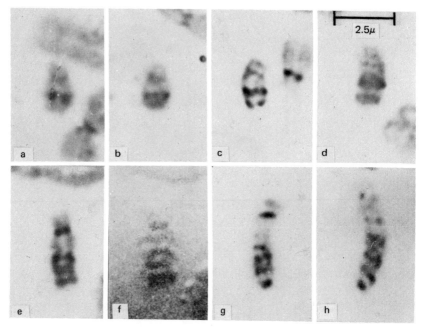

2.5μ

FIG. 7. C-banded Y chromosomes observed in different individuals. (a,b) Chromosomes showing one band, (c,d) two-banded chromosomes, (e) three-banded chromosomes, and (g,h) four-banded chromosomes, (f) three-banded chromosome as observed with the Zeiss Nomarski phase interference system. Note the relationship between the number of bands and the size of the terminal heterochromatic segment.

Table I shows mean values of the relative size of the G-terminal segment (H) measured in recordings of 280 chromosomes (Fig. 8). Relative size of heterochromatic segment values were obtained as the ratio H/q, measured in millimeters.

Regression was estimated by relating the two variables (H-length and q-length) by a linear equation. $Y = a_0 + a_1 \cdot X$ was used to estimate the length of the heterochromatic segment as a function of long-arm length:

$$a_0 = \frac{(\Sigma Y)(\Sigma X^2) - (\Sigma X)(\Sigma XY)}{N\Sigma X^2 - (\Sigma X)^2} = -0.929$$

$$a_1 = \frac{N\Sigma XY - (\Sigma X)(\Sigma Y)}{N\Sigma X^2 - (\Sigma X)^2} = 0.631$$

$$Y = -0.929 + 0.631 \cdot X$$

$X = b_0 + b_1 \cdot Y$ was used to estimate long-arm length as a function of the length of the heterochromatic segment:

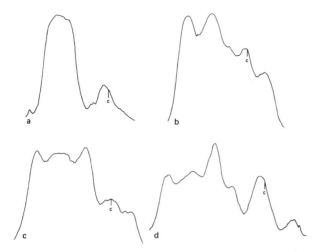

FIG. 8. Densitometric tracings of C-banded Y chromosomes.
(a) One band, (b) two bands, (c) three bands, (d) four bands.
Centromere region denoted by c. The short arm is also seen.

$$b_0 = \frac{(\Sigma X)(\Sigma Y^2) - (\Sigma Y)(\Sigma XY)}{N\Sigma Y^2 - (\Sigma Y)^2} = 30.82$$

$$b_1 = \frac{N\Sigma XY - (\Sigma X)(\Sigma Y)}{N\Sigma Y^2 - (\Sigma Y)^2} = 1.327$$

$$X = 30.82 + 1.327 \cdot Y \qquad Y = -23.22 + 0.753 \cdot X$$

TABLE I. Length Mean Values of
Terminal Heterochromatic Segment of
the Y Chromosome Estimated for
Eight Unrelated Individuals

Individual No.	n	$\bar{X}$	σ	$\sigma \bar{X}$
1	35	0.532	0.056	0.009
2	35	0.558	0.046	0.008
3	35	0.601	0.032	0.006
4	35	0.614	0.039	0.007
5	35	0.625	0.048	0.008
6	35	0.644	0.026	0.004
7	35	0.686	0.048	0.008
8	35	0.720	0.052	0.009

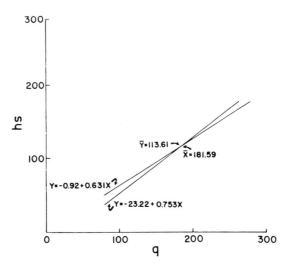

FIG. 9. Test of correlation between the long arm (q) and the heterochromatic segment (hs) of the Y chromosome.

Figure 9 shows the straight lines given by both equations. The point of intersection corresponds to $\bar{X}$ = 181.59, $\bar{Y}$ = 113.61.

The correlation coefficient $r = \Sigma xy / [(\Sigma x^2)(\Sigma y^2)]^{1/2} = (a_1 \cdot b_1)^{1/2} = 0.915$ was estimated. Assuming a null hypothesis for correlation, $t = r (N-2)^{1/2}/(1-r^2)^{1/2}$ for $\rho = 0$; $t = 37.88$; df = ∞; $P < 0.01$.

Since regression lines are coincident, showing a highly significant correlation for the sample $n = 280$, we assumed that values of both variables are normally distributed. If this is true, H/q will also be normally distributed.

Values of H/q were estimated for eight unrelated, randomly selected individuals. Preliminary estimations were made to find the minimally adequate sample size per individual, for significance at a 0.05 level. Assuming $t = \bar{D}/[S_1/n^{1/2})^2 + (S_2/n^{1/2})^2]^{1/2}$ for $\bar{D} = 0.017$, $\sigma_1 = 0.0358$, $\sigma_2 = 0.0310$, we have $n = 32$ chromosomes. This is similar to the number estimated by Neurath et al. (1972) for quantitative karyotyping in twins. Therefore, we used samples of $n = 35$ for our investigation.

Mean values (Table I) are presented in increasing order. The significance of differences found between the mean value of a given individual and the mean value of the individual next to him in the table was estimated by means of a t test:

$$t = \frac{(X_1 - X_2)[N_1 N_2/(N_1 + N_2)]^{1/2}}{[(N_1 - 1)S_1^2 + (N_2 - 1)S_2^2/N_1 + (N_2 - 2)]^{1/2}}$$

The test was also used for individuals who, although not next, showed similar banding patterns as shown in Fig. 6. Table II shows the values of t for the estimations and also those which appeared significant at a 0.05 and a 0.01 level. All these statistics were calculated with an Olivetti Programma 101 computer.

These t values confirm the existence of polymorphism of the heterochromatic segment of the long arm of the human Y chromosome.

Polymorphism of the Y chromosome had been observed early in cytogenetic studies. The first indication of the existence of a long Y in the general normal population was reported by Bender and Gooch (1961), while Muldal and Ockey (1961) detected a short one. Other reports (Bishop et al., 1962; de la Chapelle et al., 1963; Court-Brown et al., 1966; Makino et al., 1963) have confirmed these variations in length of the Y chromosome. Cohen et al. (1966) also observed size differences in ethnic groups. Finally, McKenzie et al. (1972) showed that the Y chromosome length is heritable from father to son, but variable from family to family, the variability being attributable to long-arm variations. These length variations have been associated with variations of the terminal fluorescent region (Borgaonkar and Hollander, 1971; Knuutila and Gripenberg, 1972; Labergé and Gagné, 1971; Lewin and Conen, 1971; Robinson and Buckton, 1971; Tishler et al., 1972; Wahlström, 1971). Schnedl (1971a) and Bobrow et al. (1971) have quantitatively shown the variation of the length of the fluorescent segment. However, the proximal part of the long arm also seems to be of variable size (Schnedl, 1971a).

In this series, we detected Y chromosomes carrying one- to five-banded C-terminal heterochromatic segments in addition to the pericentromeric band (Figs. 7a–h,10b). These findings were also confirmed by densitometric analysis

TABLE II. Significance of Differences Between Means (t Values) of Y-Terminal Heterochromatic Segments

Individual No.	Individual No.							
	1	2	3	4	5	6	7	8
1		2.08^a						
2			4.51^b					
3				1.46	2.53^a	6.15^b		
4					1.13	3.80^a		
5						1.98		
6							4.55^b	
7								2.88^b
8								

[a] Denotes significance at 0.05 level; df = 68.
[b] At 0.01 level; df = 68.

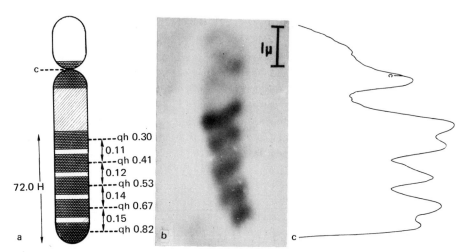

FIG. 10. Example of a five-banded Y chromosome. (a) Chromosome diagram and estimated values of band position and interband distances and relative size (%) of heterochromatic segment. (b) Photomicrograph of a five-banded Y chromosome observed in individual No. 8. Note that the proximal band is darker than the others. (c) Microdensitometric recording of chromosome shown in (b). Note the resolution of terminal and centromeric bands.

(Figs 8a–d, 10c). The complex nature of the fluorescent terminal segment (Zech, 1969) was pointed out by Manolov et al. (1971), who detected two fluorescent bands in this chromosome region. Kim et al. (1971) and Sperling and Lackmann (1971) also reported individuals carrying two fluorescent bands. A father and son both with very long Y chromosomes having four intensely fluorescent bands were reported as well (Wahlström, 1971). Our observations with the C-method confirm the existence of a variable number of C-terminal bands in the Y and add a case of a five-banded long Y chromosome.

An interesting problem is presented by individuals No. 3, 4, and 5. Although cytologically they were regarded as carriers of two-banded Y chromosomes, a few chromosomes presented an extra "third band," indicated by dotted lines in Fig. 6. Therefore, these individuals present a detectable variation in the number of densitometric peaks appearing as band "mosaics" for the terminal Y heterochromatic segment.

Mean relative band positions, as estimated from densitometric tracings, are presented in Table III and diagrammatically in Fig. 6. It is interesting to note that the differences between relative positions of bands seem to follow a definite pattern from individual to individual. Individual No. 2, who is a carrier of a two-banded Y chromosome, showed an interband difference of 0.20. This value appears to be practically identical for bands qh2–qh3 in individuals No. 3, 4, and 5 and for bands qh2–qh3 and qh3–qh4 in individual No. 7 (Fig. 6). However, the first (or proximal) interband region is slightly reduced, ranging from 0.15 to 0.16 in individuals No. 3–7.

TABLE III. Relative Band Positions as Estimated from Microdensitometric Recordings

Individual No.	Band No.	n^a	$\bar{X}$	σ	$\sigma_{\bar{X}}$	Individual No.	Band No.	n^a	$\bar{X}$	σ	$\sigma_{\bar{X}}$
1	qh1	34	0.540	0.069	0.012	5	qh1	17	0.421	0.049	0.012
							qh2	28	0.570	0.057	0.011
							qh3	34	0.788	0.050	0.009
2	qh1	34	0.481	0.061	0.010	6	qh1	22	0.487	0.044	0.009
	qh2	29	0.681	0.059	0.011		qh2	28	0.644	0.051	0.010
							qh3	29	0.853	0.037	0.007
3	qh1	23	0.479	0.035	0.007	7	qh1	21	0.328	0.054	0.012
	qh2	28	0.631	0.070	0.013		qh2	28	0.482	0.061	0.012
	qh3	33	0.825	0.046	0.008		qh3	31	0.674	0.064	0.012
							qh4	30	0.855	0.039	0.007
4	qh1	18	0.434	0.045	0.011	8	qh1	27	0.302	0.046	0.009
	qh2	26	0.585	0.064	0.012		qh2	24	0.414	0.037	0.008
	qh3	33	0.807	0.049	0.009		qh3	24	0.529	0.038	0.008
							qh4	22	0.665	0.044	0.009
							qh5	35	0.823	0.041	0.007

^{a}The symbol n stands for the number of chromosomes where given bands were detected.

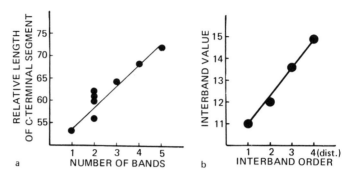

FIG. 11. *Plots of band data.* (a) Number of bands vs. relative size of C-terminal segment observed in the Y chromosomes of different individuals. (b) Interband order vs. interband distance value, as estimated for a five-banded Y carrier. 1, Proximal band; 4, distal band.

The increase of interband distance is much more remarkable in individual No. 8. This person carries a long Y chromosome with a prominent heterochromatic segment (H = 0.72) (Table I and Fig. 10b,c). If interband length is plotted vs. the position order of interband (ordered from centromere to telomere), the result is a straight line for interband distances of individual No. 8. These results may suggest that the separation of densitometric C-band peaks follows a linear increase in the direction of the telomere (Fig. 11b).

Another interesting aspect of the problem is that a relationship exists between the relative size of the C-terminal segment and the number of bands (Fig. 11a).

The Arrighi and Hsu procedure is derived from experiments developed by Pardue and Gall (1970) on *in situ* hybridization with mouse satellite DNA, and, reportedly, the heterochromatic segments revealed are composed mainly by highly repetitious DNA (Yunis *et al.,* 1971). Therefore, the variable number of densitometric peaks or bands we detected in the Y chromosome would represent repeated segments of chromosome material. These findings may suggest that tandem duplications are present in this chromosome segment. Moreover, the regularity of the increase in band separation observed in different individuals would indicate that the process of heterochromatin duplication does not involve equal chromosome segments but that new material is incorporated in each duplication. Moreover, the finding of a number of three-banded chromosomes in persons classified as two-band carriers raises the possibility that a variable DNA amplification process is operating in this chromosome segment.

Although the number of individuals and chromosomes studied is limited, and we do not wish to generalize our conclusions, we think this is the most natural explanation for our observations and measurements.

Band Mapping of Chromosome No. 1 and Nomenclature

Densitometric tracings of G-banded chromosomes of the whole human complement currently obtained in our laboratory are presented in Fig. 12. These curves were picked from over 1500 recordings from 20 unrelated, randomly selected individuals (ten males and ten females). We believe they represent characteristic patterns which can be taken as a reliable reference of the G-banding patterns obtained with our method (Drets and Shaw, 1971). Moreover, these patterns can be used for comparison with the ones published for fluorescence techniques (Caspersson, 1973).

In this part of our investigation, we used the densitometer on photographs of G-banded chromosomes to develop a new mapping methodology based on relative band position values. These measurements were carried out as described in Materials and Methods. Relative position values are practical for mapping banded chromosomes because they are independent of the usual variables present in chromosomes such as a cell division stage, colchicine or hypotonic artifacts, and intensity of staining of G-bands. We selected chromosome No. 1 as

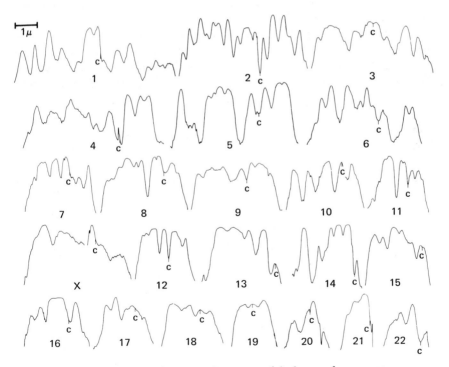

FIG. 12. G-banding densitometric patterns of the human chromosomes.

the largest one in the complement for examination of the constancy of G-banding in developing the new nomenclature.

No. 1 chromosomes from ten unrelated normal individuals (five males and five females) were used for this study. Different banded, nonbent chromosomes (Fig. 13) were selected, photographed, enlarged, and recorded as indicated previously.

Table IV shows pooled mean values estimated for each band in both chromatids. The table also shows the number of chromosomes from the sample where given bands were detected. Centromere indices were calculated using p and q lengths ($CI = p/q + p$) measured in complete chromosome curves in order to check the quality of the chromosome. Centromere indices (0.48 ± 0.01) obtained agreed closely with those published for intact chromosomes (Paris Conference, 1972).

G-band mean values are represented diagrammatically in Fig. 14. This diagram combines mean values found with the nomenclature and mapping proposed at the Paris Conference (1972). The precise localization of individual bands and chromosome landmarks (Fig. 14; landmark is denoted by a star) through relative band position estimations provides a greater map accuracy than a simple subjective evaluation of them.

In the present series of chromosomes, pericentromeric heterochromatin bands are denoted by 1p 0.06; 1p 0.09; 1q 0.09; 1q 0.15, and 1q 0.21, while other values indicate relative position of the G-bands in both chromosome arms. We found that the G-pattern of chromosome No. 1 is constant from person to

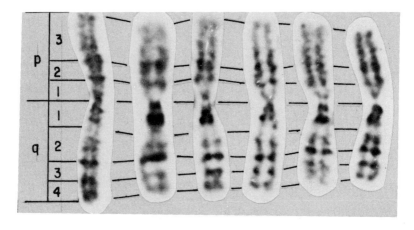

FIG. 13. *Different types of G-banded No. 1 chromosomes used for mapping.* p, short arm; q, long arm. The chromosomes are divided into regions and numbered according to the map suggested in Paris. Homologues of these chromosomes failed to show detectable polymorphism at the pericentromeric area.

TABLE IV. Relative G-Band Positions
Estimated for 100 No. 1
Chromosomes from Ten Unrelated Individuals

	n^a	$\bar{X}$	σ	$\sigma_{\bar{X}}$
	80	0.923	0.019	0.002
	55	0.842	0.018	0.003
	40	0.744	0.037	0.006
	60	0.621	0.017	0.002
p	48	0.557	0.024	0.003
	70	0.466	0.020	0.002
	71	0.401	0.023	0.003
	64	0.210	0.020	0.002
	52	0.085	0.000	0.000
C				
	67	0.020	0.001	0.000
	58	0.091	0.016	0.002
	63	0.149	0.015	0.001
	67	0.208	0.020	0.002
	57	0.283	0.018	0.002
q	42	0.337	0.019	0.003
	55	0.415	0.013	0.002
	64	0.457	0.014	0.002
	86	0.597	0.033	0.004
	95	0.769	0.025	0.003
	89	0.922	0.019	0.002

[a]The symbol n stands for the number of chromosomes where given bands were detected; p, short arm; C, centromere; q, long arm.

person. The same fact was observed for fluorescent patterns (Caspersson, 1973). Relative values have a fairly low dispersion (ranging from $\sigma = 0.013$, $\sigma_{\bar{X}} = 0.002$ to $\sigma = 0.037$, $\sigma_{\bar{X}} = 0.006$). We have some indications that these values are better adjusted if they were considered intrapersonally, but this view must be confirmed in a significative number of individuals. On the other hand, since the long arm has shown polymorphism at the centromeric area (Craig-Holmes and Shaw, 1971; Kim, 1973), we think that values estimated for G-bands along this arm will be somewhat changed in C-polymorphic chromosomes. Hence for those cases where chromosome C-polymorphism is found, a constant for correction should be introduced. We are studying polymorphic No. 1 chromosomes in order to estimate the magnitude of this correction constant.

The method for locating G-bands along the chromosome arm proved to be simple, informative, and quite adaptable for routine analysis, since it involves unsophisticated instrumentation. In addition, the new nomenclature suggested will enable better information exchange among laboratories, since it describes

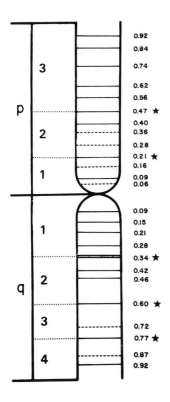

FIG. 14. Diagram of G-banded chromosome No. 1. Left: Nomenclature according to Paris proposals. Middle: Bands in their relative position. Solid lines indicate those bands computerized and statistically analyzed in this study; dotted lines indicate variable bands observed in curves. No quantitative data are yet available for these bands. Landmark separating region No. 1 from region No. 2 is indicated by a double line and is tentatively located at q1 0.34. Right: Simplified relative values as estimated from 1283 calculations. Stars denote Paris chromosome landmarks.

bands in their precise relative position—independently of the observer's ability to detect them.

Moreover, this nomenclature can be extended to other chromosomes of the human complement, permitting the investigator a comparison of banding patterns obtained with the different available techniques. It is also possible that band polymorphisms—for instance, the ones found for C-bands (Craig-Holmes and Shaw, 1971; Craig-Holmes *et al.,* 1973)—or even minor morphological variations related to human disease could be detected and mapped in terms of change of their relative position in the chromosomes.

SUMMARY

Denaturation methods have shown that it is possible to reveal pericentromeric heterochromatin and specific banding patterns in human chromosomes.

The size and structure of C-bands of the human Y chromosome, as well as the distribution of G-bands along the chromosome arms, were investigated by high-resolution microdensitometry in order to detect their precise relative localization. A simple densitometer and a device capable of automatically marking the centromere position during densitometric tracings are described. Estimations of the relative size of the C-terminal segment of 280 Y chromosomes from different, unrelated individuals showed that this chromosome region is polymorphic. A series of eight individuals carrying one to five C-banded terminal segments in the long arm of the Y were studied, and a relationship between the number of bands and the relative size of the C-segment was detected. Similar values of the relative interband distance of C-terminal bands and a gradual increase in it from centromere to telomere were also found. Individuals classified as two-banded Y carriers also had a number of chromosomes with three bands. These findings suggest that a variable duplication mechanism is present in the distal heterochromatic segment of this chromosome.

Relative G-band position values for both arms of 100 No. 1 chromosomes from ten unrelated persons were estimated. The constancy of these values showed that it is feasible to map G-bands very accurately in terms of relative position. A new nomenclature based on these findings which can be combined with the mapping proposed at the Paris Conference is suggested. Application of this new methodology to band localization is briefly discussed.

ACKNOWLEDGMENTS

The authors with to express their gratitude to Professor K. Lewis, Botany School, Oxford, for stimulating and productive discussions and to Dr. M. Shaw, Medical Genetics Center, Houston, for her critical remarks and advice on the manuscript. The assistance of Dr. A. Martins Costa, Institute of Biology, Campinas, and I. Pereira Filha, Institute of Biosciences, Recife, is greatly appreciated. We are indebted to Mrs. B. R. de Olivera for the expert technical assistance she rendered. We also wish to thank the Blood Bank of the University Hospital of the Faculty of Medicine, Montevideo, for providing blood samples, and Olivetti de Uruguay, S.A., and the Faculty of Sciences, Montevideo, for computer facilities. We are grateful to Dr. R. Kolski, Faculty of Sciences, Montevideo, who made it possible for one of us to take part in this investigation. This work was supported in part by OEA/AID/FORGE/SUDAMTEX grants.

REFERENCES

Arrighi, F. E., and Hsu, T. C. (1971), Localization of heterochromatin in human chromosomes, *Cytogenetics (Basel) 10:*81–86.

Bahr, G. F., Mikel, U., and Engler, W. F. (1973), Correlates of chromosomal banding at the level of ultrastructure, *Nobel Chromosome Identification 23:*280–289.

Bartalos, M., and Rainer, J. D. (1971), Human chromosome mapping with an ammoniacal silver staining procedure, *Acta Genet. Med. Gemellol. 21:*139–142.

Bender, M. A., and Gooch, P. C. (1961), An unusually long human Y chromosome, *Lancet 2:*463–464.

Bishop, A., Blank, C. E., and Hunter, H. (1962), Heritable variation in length of the Y chromosome, *Lancet 2:*18–20.

Bobrow, M., Pearson, P. L., Pike, M. C., and El-Alfi, O. S. (1971), Length variation in the quinacrine-binding segment of human Y chromosomes of different sizes, *Cytogenetics (Basel) 10:*190–198.

Borgaonkar, D. S., and Hollander, D. H. (1971), Quinacrine fluorescence of the human Y chromosome, *Nature (Lond.) 230:*52.

Caspersson, T. (1973), Procedures for the study of the reproducibility of normal mammalian banding patterns and for analysis of aberrant chromosome patterns, *Nobel Chromosome Identification 23:*50–55.

Caspersson, T., Farber, S., Foley, G. E., Kudynowski, J., Modest, E. J., Simonsson, E., Wagh, U., and Zech, L. (1968), Chemical differentiation along metaphase chromosomes, *Exp. Cell Res. 49:*219–222.

Caspersson, T., Lindsten, J., Lomakka, G., Wallman, H., and Zech, L. (1970), Rapid identification of human chromosomes by TV-techniques, *Exp. Cell Res. 63:*477–479.

Caspersson, T., Castleman, K. R., Lomakka, G., Modest, E. J., Møller, A., Nathan, R., Wall, R. J., and Zech, L. (1971a), Automatic karyotyping of quinacrine mustard stained human chromosomes, *Exp. Cell Res. 67:*233–235.

Caspersson, T., Lomakka, G., and Zech, L. (1971b), The 24 fluorescence patterns of the human metaphase chromosomes–Distinguishing characters and variability, *Hereditas (Lund) 67:*89–102.

Chernay, P. R., Hsu, L. Y. F., Stheicher, H., and Hirschhorn, K. (1971), Human chromosome identification by differential staining: G group (21-22-Y), *Cytogenetics (Basel) 10:*219–224.

Chiarelli, B., and Chiarelli, M. S. (1971), Bandeggiamenti dei cromosomi con tripsina, *Rev. Antropol. 57:*269–271.

Cohen, M. M., Shaw, M. W., and MacCluer, J. W. (1966), Racial differences in the length of the human Y chromosome, *Cytogenetics (Basel) 5:*34–52.

Comings, D. E., Avelino, E., Okada, T. A., and Wyandt, H. E. (1973), The mechanism of C- and G-banding of chromosomes, *Exp. Cell Res. 77:*469–493.

Court-Brown, W. M., Jacobs, P. A., Buckton, K. E., Tough, I. M., Kuenssberg, E. V., and Knox, J. D. E. (1966), *Chromosome Studies on Adults,* pp. 1–91, Cambridge University Press, Cambridge.

Craig-Holmes, A. P., and Shaw, M. W. (1971), Polymorphism of human constitutive heterochromatin, *Science 174:*702–704.

Craig-Holmes, A. P., Moore, F. B., and Shaw, M. W. (1973), Polymorphism of human C-band heterochromatin. I. Frequency of variants, *Am. J. Hum. Genet. 25:*181–192.

de la Chapelle, A., Hortling, E., Edgren, J., and Kaariainen, R. (1963), Evidence for the existence of heritable large human Y chromosomes unassociated with developmental disorder: A cytogenetical and clinical study of four males with hypogonadism one with mongolism and their relatives, *Hereditas 50:*351–360.

Dev, V. G., Warburton, D., Miller, O. J., Miller, D. A., Erlanger, B. F., and Beiser, S. M. (1972), Consistent pattern of binding of antiadenosine antibodies to human metaphase chromosomes, *Exp. Cell Res. 74:*288–293.

Drets, M. E. (1961), Ratio recorder for cytophotometry based on an image discriminator apparatus, *Mikroskopie 16:*341–348.

Drets, M. E., and Shaw, M. W. (1971), Specific banding patterns of human chromosomes, *Proc. Natl. Acad. Sci. U.S.A. 68:*2073–2077.

Dutrillaux, B. (1973), Nouveau système de marquage chromosomique les bandes T, *Chromosoma (Berl.) 41:*395–402.

Dutrillaux, B., and Lejeune, J. (1971), Sur une nouvelle technique d'analyse du caryotype humain, *C.R. Acad. Sci. (Paris) 272:*2638–2640.

Dutrillaux, B., De Grouchyde, J., Finaz, C., and Lejeune, J. (1971), Mise en évidence de la structure fine des chromosomes humaines par digestion enzymatique (Pronase en particulier), *C.R. Acad. Sci. (Paris)*, *273*:587–588.

Dutrillaux, B., Finaz, C., De Grouchy, J., and Lejeune, J. (1972), Comparison of banding patterns of human chromosomes obtained with heating, fluorescence, and proteolytic digestion, *Cytogenetics (Basel)* *11*:113–116.

Edwards, J. H. (1962), Chromosome analysis from capillary blood, *Cytogenetics (Basel)* *1*:90–96.

Evans, H. J., Buckton, K. E., and Sumner, A. T. (1971), Cytological mapping of human chromosomes: Results obtained with quinacrine fluorescence and the acetic–saline–Giemsa techniques, *Chromosoma (Berl.)* *35*:310–325.

Hsu, T. C., Pathak, S., and Shafe, D. A. (1973), Induction of chromosome cross banding by treating cells with chemical agents before fixation, *Exp. Cell Res. 79*:484–487.

Kato, H., and Moriwaki, K. (1972), Factors involved in the production of banded structures in mammalian chromosomes, *Chromosoma (Berl.) 38*:105–120.

Kim, M. A. (1973), Polymorphismus des konstitutiven Heterochromatins bein menschlichen A1-Metaphasechromosomen, *Humangenetik 18*:213–217.

Kim, M. A., Bier, L., Pawlowizki, I. H., and Pfeiffer, R. A. (1971), Human Y chromosomes with two fluorescing bands after staining with quinacrine derivatives, *Humangenetik 13*:238–240.

Knuutila, S., and Gripenberg, U. (1972), The fluorescence pattern of   human Yq+ chromosome, *Hereditas (Lund) 70*:307–308.

Labergé, C., and Gagné, R. (1971), Quinacrine mustard staining solves the length variations of the human Y chromosome, *Johns Hopkins Med. J. 128*:79–83.

Lejeune, J., Gautier, M., and Turpin, R. (1959), Étude des chromosomes somatiques de neuf enfants mongoliens, *C.R. Acad. Sci. (Paris) 248*:1721–1722.

Lewin, P. K., and Conen, P. E. (1971), Fluorescent Y screening of hospitalized newborns, *Nature (Lond.) 233*:334–335.

Lomholt, B., and Mohr, J. (1971), Human karyotyping by heat–Giemsa staining and comparison with fluorochrome techniques, *Nature New Biol. 234*:109–110.

Lubs, H. A., and Ledley, R. S. (1973), Automated analysis of differentially stained human chromosomes, *Nobel Chromosome Identification 23*:61–76.

Lubs, H. A., McKenzie, W. H., and Merrick, S. (1973), Comparative methodology and mechanisms of banding, *Nobel Chromosome Identification 23*:315–322.

Lundsteen, C., Ernst, P., and Philip, J. (1973), Microspectrophotometry of trypsin Leishman-stained human chromosomes, *Nature (Lond.) 242*:613–615.

Makino, S., Sasaki, M. S., and Yamada, K. (1963), A long Y chromosome in human chromosomes, *Chromosoma (Berl.) 14*:154–161.

Manolov, G., Manolova, Y., Fiskesjö, G., and Levan, A. (1971), The complexity of the fluorescent pattern of the human Y chromosome, *Hereditas (Lund) 68*:328–331.

McKenzie, W. H., Hostetter, T. L., and Lubs, H. A. (1972), Y family study: Heritable variation in the length of the human Y chromosome, *Am. J. Hum. Genet. 24*:686–693.

Miller, O. J., Miller, D. A., and Warburton, D. (1973), Application of new staining technique to the study of human chromosomes, in: *Progress in Medical Genetics,* Vol. IX, pp. 1–47 (A. G. Steinberg and A. G. Bearn, eds.) Grune and Stratton, New York.

Muldal, S., and Ockey, C. H. (1961), Muscular dystrophy and deletion of Y chromosome, *Lancet 2*:601.

Neurath, P. W., Lin, P. S., and Low, D. A. (1972), Quantitative karyotyping: A model twin study, *Cytogenetics (Basel) 11*:457–474.

Pardue, M. L., and Gall, J. G. (1970), Chromosomal localization of mouse satellite DNA, *Science 168:*1356–1358.

Paris Conference (1971): Standardization in Human Genetics (1972), in: *Birth Defects,* Vol. VIII, No. 7, pp. 1–43, Original Article Series, The National Foundation, New York.

Patau, K. (1960), The identification of individual chromosomes, especially in man, *Am. J. Hum. Genet. 12:*250–276.

Patil, S. R., Merrick, S., and Lubs, H. A. (1971), Identification of each human chromosome with a modified Giemsa stain, *Science 173:*821–822.

Pearson, P. (1972), The use of new staining techniques for human chromosome identification, *J. Med. Genet. 9:*264–275.

Prieur, M., Dutrillaux, B., and Lejeune, J. (1973), Planches descriptives des chromosomes humains (Analyse en bandes R et nomenclature selon la Conférence de Paris, 1971), *Ann. Génét. 16:*39–46.

Robinson, J. A., and Buckton, K. E. (1971), Quinacrine fluorescence of variant and abnormal Y chromosomes, *Chromosoma (Berl.) 35:*342–352.

Schnedl, W. (1971a), Fluoreszenzuntersuchungen über die Längenvariabilität des Y-Chromosoms beim Menschen, *Humangenetik 12:*188–194.

Schnedl, W. (1971b), Analysis of the human karyotype using a reassociation technique, *Chromosoma (Berl.) 34:*448–454.

Schnedl, W. (1973a), Observations on the mechanisms of Giemsa staining methods, *Nobel Chromosome Identification 23:*342–345.

Schnedl, W. (1973b), Banding patterns in chromosomes, *Int. Rev. Cytol.* in press.

Schreck, R. R., Warburton, D., Miller, O. J., Beiser, S. M., and Erlanger, B. F. (1973), Chromosome structure as revealed by a combined chemical and immunochemical procedure, *Proc. Natl. Acad. Sci. (U.S.A.) 70:*804–807.

Seabright, M. (1971), Rapid banding technique for human chromosomes, *Lancet 2:*971–972.

Shiraishi, Y., and Yoshida, T. H. (1971), Differential staining of human chromosomes by treatment with urea, *Proc. Jap. Acad. 47:*729–731.

Sperling, K., and Lackmann, I. (1971), Large human Y chromosome with two fluorescent bands, *Clin. Genet. 2:*352–355.

Sumner, A. T., Evans, H. J., and Buckland, R. A. (1971), A new technique for distinguishing between human chromosomes, *Nature New Biol. 232:*31–32.

Tishler, P. V., Lamborot-Manzur, M., and Atkins, L. (1972), Polymorphism of the human Y chromosome: Fluorescent microscope studies on the sites of morphologic variation, *Clin. Genet. 3:*116–122.

Utakoji, T. (1972), Differential staining patterns of human chromosomes treated with potassium permanganate, *Nature (Lond.) 239:*168–169.

Wahlström, J. (1971), Are variations in length of Y chromosome due to structure changes? *Hereditas 69:*125–128.

Wang, H. C., and Fedoroff, S. (1972), Banding in human chromosomes treated with trypsin, *Nature New Biol. 235:*52–53.

Yunis, J. J., Rolda, L., Yasmineh, W. G., and Lee, J. C. (1971), Staining of satellite DNA in metaphase chromosomes, *Nature (Lond.) 231:*532–533.

Zech, L. (1969), Investigation of metaphase chromosomes with DNA-binding fluorochromes, *Exp. Cell Res. 58:*463.

This manuscript is dedicated to Drs. T. C. Hsu and F. Arrighi, pioneers in studies of human heterochromatin.

4

Ultrastructure of Genetic Activity in Eukaryotic Cells

O. L. Miller, Jr.

Department of Biology, University of Virginia
Charlottesville, Virginia

Aimée H. Bakken

Department of Zoology, University of Washington
Seattle, Washington

and

Barbara A. Hamkalo

Departments of Molecular Biology and Biochemistry
and
Cell and Developmental Biology
University of California, Irvine, California

In this chapter, we review our observations of ultrastructural aspects of genetic activity within nuclei of three types of eukaryotic cells: (1) a highly specialized cell, the amphibian oocyte; (2) a nondifferentiating cell system, cultured HeLa cells; and (3) a differentiating cell system, the blastoderm stage of *Drosophila melanogaster* embryogenesis. These results are discussed at greater length in Hamkalo *et al.* (1973a,b), Hamkalo and Miller (1973), and Miller and Bakken (1972).

The methods used to prepare material for electron microscopy are described in detail in the papers just cited. The key steps are (1) rapid isolation of nuclear contents under conditions that minimize chances of shocks which would disrupt the normal amount of transcriptive activity occurring within the living cell, and dispersal of the nuclear material under conditions that minimize enzymatic or shear degradation; (2) mild fixation with buffered formalin, followed by centrifugal attachment of specimen to grids coated with thin carbon films made hydrophilic by glow-discharging; (3) drying of the grid after rinsing in a solution containing a surface tension–reducing agent to minimize specimen distortion during drying; and (4) staining with heavy metal ions to increase electron contrast of the specimen.

AMPHIBIAN OOCYTES

During middle to late oogenesis, oocytes of most amphibia contain nuclei ranging from near 0.5 mm to near 1.0 mm in diameter. Such nuclei are easily isolated into isotonic saline using jewelers forceps and a simple dissecting microscope. The nuclei are then cleaned of yolk with a pipette. The nuclear envelopes are removed with jewelers forceps, and the nuclear contents are transferred by pipette to the experimental medium of choice. Although we have examined species of several amphibian genera with essentially similar results, the observations described here are based primarily on studies with the spotted newt, *Triturus viridescens.*

Ribosomal RNA Genes

In amphibian oocytes, ribosomal RNA (rRNA) genes are amplified during early oogenesis to produce many hundredfold the haploid number of these genes (Bird *et al.,* 1973; Hourcade *et al.,* 1973). Following pachytene, the amplified genes are present in hundreds of extrachromosomal nucleoli active in the synthesis of 40S rRNA precursor molecules (rpRNA) that are processed to form the 18S rRNA and 28S rRNA of cytoplasmic ribosomes. *In situ* and in isotonic saline, these nucleoli typically are dense spheres, some 5–15 μm in diameter, and various lines of evidence show that the rRNA genes are localized within the central cores of the nucleoli. When transferred from isotonic saline to distilled water, the nucleoli rapidly come apart. If such dispersed nucleoi are centrifuged onto grids and prepared for electron microscopy, the unwound rRNA genes can be visualized because of the high degree of RNA polymerase activity on each gene (Fig. 1). Between 80 and 100 polymerases simultaneously transcribe each gene to form a gradient of rpRNA molecules in successive stages of maturation. Proteins complex with the nascent RNA molecules at the transcription points, coiling up the RNA to form ribonucleoprotein (RNP) fibrils that are only one-tenth or so the length of the RNA molecules within them. Small, dense granules appear on the free ends of the RNP fibrils near the initiation end of each gene.

The rRNA genes, as delimited by the gradients of attached RNP fibrils, are about 2.3 μm long when unstretched. This length is close to the 2.6–2.7 μm of B-conformation DNA required to code for the 40S rpRNA molecule of amphibia (Loening *et al.,* 1969; Perry *et al.,* 1970). The shorter length of the active genes probably is due to some denaturation of the DNA within each of the closely spaced transcription sites. The rRNA genes repeat with the same transcriptional

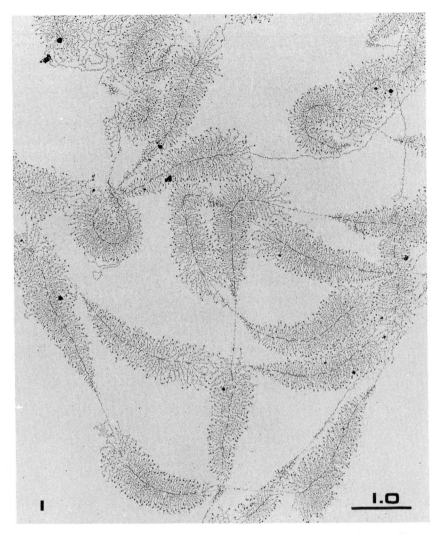

FIG. 1. Ribosomal RNA genes isolated from an oocyte of the spotted newt, Triturus viridescens. The genes are localized by the gradients of ribonucleoprotein fibrils containing ribosomal RNA precursor molecules in successive stages of maturation. The genes show similar transcriptional polarity and are separated by transcriptionally inactive DNA segments. Magnification line equals 1 μm.

polarity along a single, duplex DNA molecule. They are not immediately adjacent, however, but are separated by "spacer" segments of DNA that do not appear to be transcribed. In oocytes of *T. viridescens,* the large majority of these segments are about one-fourth the length of an rRNA gene, although considerably longer ones are found.

RNA Synthesis on Lampbrush Chromosomes

During the pachytene stage of amphibian oogenesis, RNA synthesis is essentially stopped in the coiled, tightly paired chromosomes. During the ensuing diplotene stage, the chromosomes uncoil into the "lampbrush" condition and enter an extended period of RNA synthesis. This synthesis occurs on thousands of pairs of lateral loops, each pair of loops extending from one of the thousands of chromomeres forming the long main axes of the oocyte chromosomes at this stage. Each loop typically shows one thin and one thick end at the point of insertion into its chromomere. There is evidence that the axis of each loop is a duplex DNA molecule and that the bulk of each loop is RNP.

When lampbrush chromosomes are dispersed in distilled water and prepared for electron microscopy by our techniques, the sites of RNA synthesis can be visualized as thin RNP fibrils attached to RNA polymerase molecules closely spaced on the DNA axes of lateral loops, with the fibrils forming gradients of increasing fibril length from the thin toward the thick insertion end of each loop (Fig. 2). Thus, similar to nucleolar genes, polymerase molecules are found closely packed together on active sites within the chromosome complement of the oocyte. On the lateral loops, however, the RNA molecules synthesized appear to be one to two orders of magnitude larger than the mature rpRNA molecules made on nucleolar genes. Unfortunately, no functional role can yet be assigned to the RNA produced on any specific pair of lateral loops during amphibian oogenesis.

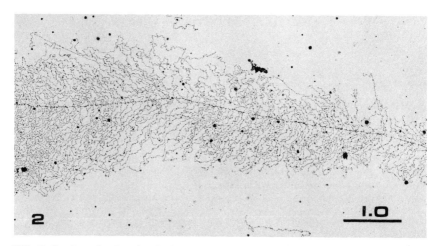

FIG. 2. Portion of a lampbrush chromosome loop at the thin, chromomere insertion end where RNA synthesis is initiated. Thin ribonucleoprotein fibrils are attached to RNA polymerase molecules closely spaced on the DNA axis of the loop. Isolated from an oocyte of *Triturus viridescens.* Magnification line equals 1 μm.

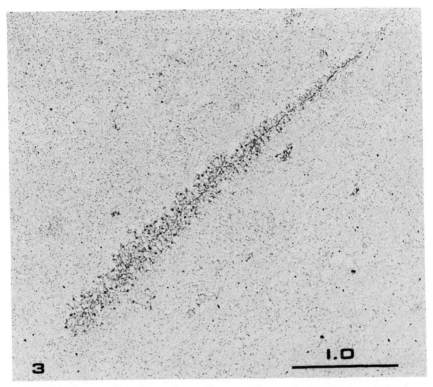

FIG. 3. A putative rRNA gene isolated from a log phase HeLa cell culture. Some 100–150 RNA polymerases are present on such active segments of the genome. Magnification line equals 1 μm.

HELA CELLS

For study of HeLa cells, aliquots of log-phase cultures in spinner flasks were diluted 1:9 with cold Joy detergent (Procter & Gamble) solution to give a final detergent concentration of 0.33% at pH 8.7. After 30 s or so, the material was fixed and prepared for electron microscopy by our usual methods. Control observations with phase contrast microscopy demonstrated that HeLa cell nucleoli disperse during this isolation.

Ribosomal RNA Genes

Clusters of genome segments exhibiting the structural configurations shown in Fig. 3 were observed in our HeLa cell preparations. Such loci are similar to amphibian rRNA genes in that the segments are loaded with RNA polymerases, granules appear on the ends of the attached RNP fibrils, adjacent loci are separated by inactive portions of the chromosome, and neighboring loci have the same transcriptive polarity. The active segments are longer, about 3.5 μm, and contain more RNA polymerases, some 100–150, than do the amphibian rRNA genes. The longer length of these loci, as well as their structural similarity to amphibian rRNA genes, strongly suggests that these segments are rRNA genes. The rpRNA molecule of mammals would require about 4.5 μm of B-conformation DNA for synthesis (Loening, 1970). If we assume that each locus is foreshortened somewhat by the high degree of transcriptive activity occurring within a single locus—as appears to be the case with the amphibian rRNA genes—then the observed length of these segments seems reasonable for an active mammalian rRNA gene.

Chromosomal RNA Synthesis

On portions of the HeLa genome other than that containing putative rRNA genes, RNP fibrils are relatively widely spaced, and no well-defined gradients of fibrils have been observed so far. It is probable that almost all of this RNA synthesis is the production of large heterogeneous nuclear RNA molecules, many or all of which contain messenger RNA portions (Jelinek *et al.*, 1973). Our observations indicate that initiations by RNA polymerases for synthesis of this type of RNA occur at a low rate per locus in this nondifferentiating cell.

DROSOPHILA MELANOGASTER EMBRYOS

After eggs had been cleared from fertilized *Drosophila melanogaster* females, newly laid eggs were collected for 2 h and used 4 h later. During the 4- to 6-h period at 25°C, embryos are in the blastoderm stage, and definitive nucleoli are found during the interphase stage of the differentiating embryonic cells (Sonnenblick, 1965). Embryos were plunged into cold 0.1% Joy at pH 8–9, the chorions were removed, and contents were pressed from the vitelline membranes. After several minutes of dispersal, specimens were prepared by our usual techniques.

Ribosomal RNA Genes

As with the HeLa cell cultures, we found structural configurations within the *Drosophila* genome amazingly similar to the rRNA genes of amphibia, i.e., closely spaced polymerases, granules appearing on the ends of the nascent RNP fibrils, similar polarity, and spacer segments separating neighboring loci (Fig. 4). In *Drosophila,* the typical spacer is slightly shorter relative to gene length than in *T. viridescens,* but longer spacers have also been observed. Again, the length of these loci (2.6–2.7 μm) is close to the length of B-conformation DNA (about 2.85 μm) necessary to code for the rpRNA molecule of the cell type (Perry *et al.,* 1970).

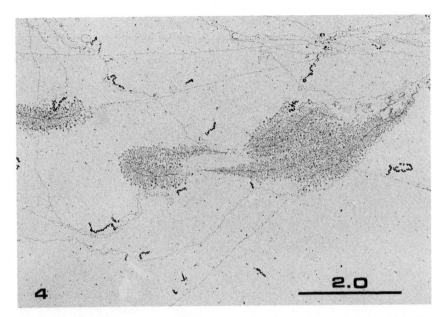

FIG. 4. *Putative rRNA genes isolated from a blastoderm-stage embryo of Drosophila melanogaster.* Magnification line equals 2 μm.

Chromosomal RNA Synthesis

When nonnucleolar regions of genomes isolated from 4–6 h embryos are examined, considerably more activity, as measured by attached RNP fibrils, is found than in HeLa cells. The spacing of RNA polymerases on individual loci is certainly not as close as that on lateral loops of lampbrush chromosomes of amphibian oocytes, but well-defined gradients of RNP fibrils are present (Fig. 5). This pattern of activity may be the result of an increase in the synthesis of messenger RNAs specific for the differentiation events occurring at this stage.

SUMMARY

Observations on the ultrastructural patterns of genetic activity are reviewed for three very different eukaryotic cell types. The number of transcribing RNA polymerases per unit length of active loci within nonnucleolar portions of the genome differs in the three cell types—being very high in amphibian oocytes, intermediate in differentiating *Drosophila* embryo cells, and low in rapidly growing HeLa cells. Although strict proof is not yet available, the very close structural similarities of clustered loci from a human cell and an insect cell to the known rRNA genes of amphibian oocytes, as well as the relationship of loci lengths to the size of the rpRNA molecules synthesized in the respective cell

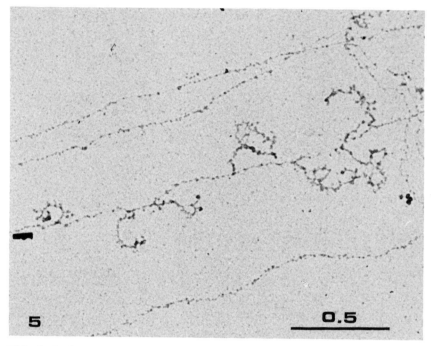

FIG. 5. Gradient of ribonucleoprotein fibrils present on a nonnucleolar portion of a genome isolated from a blastoderm embryo of Drosophila melanogaster. Magnification line equals 0.5 μm.

types, strongly suggest that such loci are indeed rRNA genes. It therefore seems likely that very active rRNA genes of all eukaryotic cells will prove to resemble one another closely. No functional role can yet be assigned, in any of the three cell types, either to the terminal granules on the RNP fibrils attached to rRNA genes or to the spacers separating such genes.

To conclude, we hope that the type of probe discussed in this chapter can be used to gain unique information regarding patterns of gene action in many other cells, including reproductive cells of humans and other mammals.

REFERENCES

Bird, A., Rochaix, J., and Bakken, A. (1973), The mechanism of gene amplification in *Xenopus laevis* oocytes, in: *Molecular Cytogenetics,* pp. 49–58 (B. A. Hamkalo and J. Papaconstantinou, eds.), Plenum Press, New York.

Hamkalo, B. A., and Miller, O. L., Jr. (1973), Electron microscopy of genetic activity, *Ann. Rev. Biochem. 42:*379–396.

Hamkalo, B. A., Miller, O. L., Jr., and Bakken, A. H. (1973a), Ultrastructural aspects of genetic activity, in: *Molecular Cytogenetics,* pp. 315–323 (B. A. Hamkalo and J. Papaconstantinou, eds.), Plenum Press, New York.

Hamkalo, B. A., Miller, O. L., Jr., and Bakken, A. H. (1973b). Ultrastructure of active eukaryotic genomes, *Cold Spring Harbor Symp. Quant. Biol. 38:*915–919.

Hourcade, D., Dressler, D., and Wolfson, J. (1973), The nucleolus and the rolling circle, *Cold Spring Harbor Symp. Quant. Biol. 38:*537–550.

Jelinek, W., Molloy, G., Salditt, M., Wall, R., and Darnell, J. E. (1973), Origin of mRNA in HeLa Cells and the Implications for Chromosome Structure, *Cold Spring Harbor Symp. Quant. Biol. 38:*891–898.

Leoning, U. E. (1970), The mechanism of synthesis of ribosomal RNA, *Symp. Soc. Gen. Microbiol. 20:*77–106.

Leoning, U. E., Jones, K. W., and Birnstiel, M. L. (1969), Properties of the ribosomal RNA precursor in *Xenopus laevis;* comparison to the precursor in mammals and plants, *J. Mol. Biol. 45:*353–366.

Miller, O. L., Jr., and Bakken, A. H. (1972), Morphological studies of transcription, *Acta Endocrinol. (suppl.) 168:*155–177.

Perry, R. P., Cheng, T.-Y., Freed, J. J., Greenberg, J. R., Kelly, D. E., and Tartof, K. D. (1970), Evolution of the transcriptional unit of ribosomal RNA, *Proc. Natl. Acad. Sci. (U.S.A.) 65:*609–616.

Sonnenblick, B. P. (1965), The early embryology of *Drosophila melanogaster,* in: *Biology of Drosophila,* pp. 62–167 (M. Demerec, ed.), Hafner, New York.

5

Sex Chromosome Activity in Germ Cells

Mary F. Lyon

MRC Radiobiology Unit
Harwell, Oxon, England

Although the XX–XY sex determination system of mammals has been well known for a long time, the exact function of the X and Y chromosomes is much less clear, particularly in the germ cells. The Y chromosome is known to play a paramount role in sex determination (Welshons and Russell, 1959). In the presence of the Y, the gonad develops as a testis and the animal becomes male. The developing testis secretes testosterone, and this in turn induces male differentiation of the Wolffian ducts, external genitalia, etc. (Jost, 1970; Price, 1970). The function of the X chromosome in sex differentiation has recently become clearer. The X chromosome of the mouse carries a gene which is concerned with the response of target organs to androgen in such a way that the combined action of its gene product and testosterone results in the activation or derepression of genes required in male differentiation. The existence of the gene was discovered through a mutation in which the altered gene product caused a lack of response to testosterone and hence the syndrome of testicular feminization, from which the gene takes its name (symbol *Tfm*) (Lyon and Hawkes, 1970; Ohno and Lyon, 1970). Affected animals chromosomally XY (*Tfm*/Y) appear externally female but have testes and no other reproductive organs, whereas *Tfm*/+ heterozygotes are normal females, except that some of their somatic cells are unresponsive to androgen (Tettenborn *et al.*, 1971). If Ohno (1967, 1973) is correct that genes X-linked in one mammalian species are X-linked in all, then the X chromosomes of all mammals carry a gene corresponding to the *Tfm* locus in mice.

Thus functions for both the X and Y chromosomes in embryonic sex determination and differentiation are known, but it is to be expected that these chromosomes will also have roles in the differentiation of the germ cells

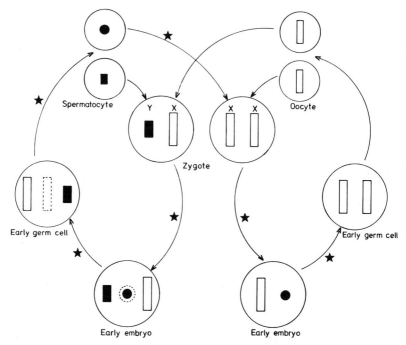

FIG. 1. X-chromosome activity states at different stages of the life cycle. Active chromosomes are white, inactive ones are black. Activity states in the male can be inferred from animals with supernumerary X chromosomes (XXY, etc.), here shown with dotted outline. Asterisks denote a change of activity.

themselves, and here the exact details of the picture are much less clear. A striking feature of the mammalian X chromosome is its variable activity state. In somatic cells only a single X chromosome is active (Fig. 1), but in female germ cells at least two and probably all X chromosomes present are active (Epstein 1969, 1972; Gartler et al., 1972). The same is thought to be true of early male germ cells, whereas in later stages of spermatogenesis both the X and the Y chromosome appear inactive (Lyon 1970, 1972). Incorrect X chromosome dosage leads either to death of germ cells or to their impaired performance. This chapter considers whether there is any evidence that response to androgen (i.e., the *Tfm* locus) is involved in this effect.

FEMALE GERM CELLS

The importance of correct X chromosome dosage in female germ cells can be seen in human X0 females, who are sterile with absence of germ cells. Oocytes can be observed in the ovaries of X0 fetuses (Singh and Carr, 1966), but all disappear before puberty. By contrast, X0 female mice are fertile and may have numerous litters. It is now clear, however, that their germ cells are impaired, since their reproductive life ends earlier than that of comparable XX mice through earlier loss of oocytes from the ovary (Lyon and Hawker, 1973). Although the ovaries of young X0 mice appear histologically normal, those of 9- to 10-month-old animals have very few oocytes remaining, and the bulk of the ovary consists mainly of persistent corpora lutea. It is theoretically possible that this earlier loss of oocytes could be the result of wrong dosage of the *Tfm* locus and hence a reduced response to androgen. Androgens are produced in the ovary, but their function is not known (Parkes and Deanesly, 1966). It is conceivable that a response to them might be required for normal survival of oocytes. If this is so, then oocytes of females with the genotype *Tfm*/0, which have no response to androgen, should be more severely affected than those of +/0 females, with a single gene dose of responsiveness to androgen (Table I). At Harwell, two *Tfm*/0 females were found, both of which were fertile. They were killed at 6 and 9 months of age, respectively, and their ovaries were no more severely affected than those of +/0 mice of comparable age (Lyon and Glenister, 1974). However, these results differ from those of Ohno *et al.* (1973), who found six *Tfm*/0 females which did show very rapid ovarian degeneration, so that very few oocytes remained at an age of only 12–16 weeks. The discrepancy between these two sets of results is at present unexplained, and so there remains some doubt as to whether a response to androgen is involved in survival of female germ cells.

TABLE I. Effective Gene Dosage for Response to Androgen

Genotype	Soma	Germ cells		
		Female	Early male	Late male
XX	1	2	2	–
$X^{Tfm}X$	$\frac{1}{2}$	1	1	–
X0	1	1	1	0
$X^{Tfm}0$	0	0	–	–
$X^{Tfm}Y$	0	–	0	0
XY	1	–	1	0

MALE GERM CELLS

It is perhaps somewhat more likely that a response to androgen should be involved in the survival or differentiation of male germ cells. Some information on this response comes from observations on the testes of male mice with testicular feminization, genetically *Tfm*/Y. In these animals, spermatogenesis proceeds to the primary spermatocyte stage, and normal first meiotic diakinesis stages are observed (Lyon and Hawkes, 1970) (Figs. 2 and 6). This suggests that a response to androgen is not required for normal spermatogenesis up to this stage. On the other hand, it is not possible to say whether the arrest of spermatogenesis at meiosis is due to a lack of response to androgen or whether some more indirect effect of the *Tfm* gene, such as cryptorchidism, is implicated.

Another effect of X-chromosome dosage is seen in chromosomally XXY or XX males, which are known in various mammalian species. In all cases they are sterile, with death of germ cells. This suggests that all X chromsomes present in early male germ cells are active, as in the female, but that the activity of more than one X chromosome is fatal to the male germ cell. Supporting evidence was obtained by Cattanach *et al.* (1971) using an autosomal gene, *Sxr*, which

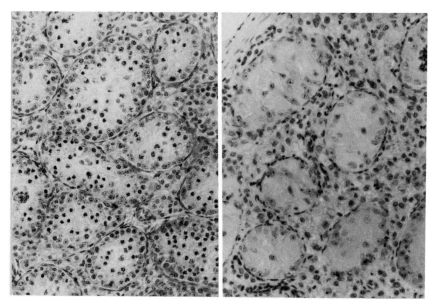

FIG. 2. Testis of Tfm/Y male mouse with testicular feminization. Spermatogenesis proceeds in all tubules to the spermatocyte stage.

FIG. 3. Testis of sex-reversed X⁺X⁺ Sxr/+ male mouse. There is no spermatogenesis, and tubules are lined only with Sertoli cells.

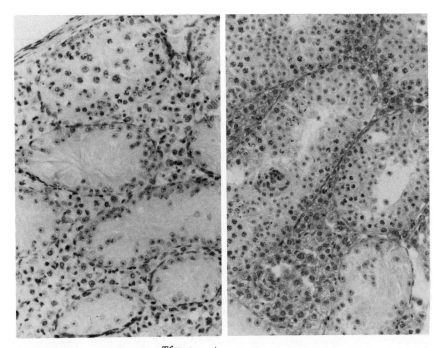

FIG. 4. Testis of sex-reversed $X^{Tfm}X^+$ *Sxr/+ male mouse.* In this animal, spermatogenesis was observed in some tubules and appeared to be arrested at the spermatocyte stage.

FIG. 5. Testis of chromosomally XXY male mouse, showing tubules with spermatogenesis. Numerous spermatids are present, in contrast to Fig. 4. Most of this testis was devoid of spermatogenesis, as in the tubule sections at lower edge.

sex-reverses genetic female mice to males. If the sex-reversed animals were chromosomally XX, the testes lacked germ cells, whereas in sex-reversed XO males spermatogenesis was present and proceeded until the late spermatid or spermatozoal stage.

If this effect of X-chromosome dosage were mediated through a response to androgen, then sex-reversed mice which carried the mutant *Tfm* allele on one of their X chromosomes should have in effect only a single gene dose of androgen responsiveness in their germ cells and so have less severely affected testes than non-*Tfm* XX males (Table I). A number of these animals were bred by crossing *Tfm++/++Blo* ♀ X *+Ta +/Y Sxr/+* ♂ (or for a few preliminary animals *TfmTa/++* ♀ X *++/Y Sxr/+* ♂). The XX offspring sex-reversed by the *Sxr* gene were diagnosed as such by the presence of variegation for the X-linked marker genes, tabby (*Ta*) and/or blotchy (*Blo*), in phenotypic males (or by small testes in phenotypic males in the preliminary crosses). The presence of the *Tfm* gene was diagnosed, again, by making use of the variegation for closely linked markers and

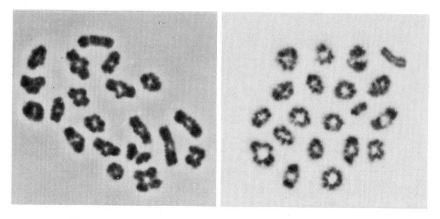

FIG. 6. *Normal first meiotic division in Tfm/Y male mouse.* Note XY bivalent. From Lyon and Hawkes (1970).

FIG. 7. *First meiotic division in a* $X^{Tfm}X^+$ *Sxr/+ sex-reversed male mouse.* Note univalent of size comparable to the X chromosome.

also, in most animals, by somewhat impaired development of male accessory glands, or an intersexual phenotype. Serial sections of testes were compared from X^{Tfm}/X^+ $Sxr/+$ and X^+/X^+ $Sxr/+$ sibs, and in addition chromosome preparations were made from the testes of a number of animals by Meredith's (1969) method.

Histological studies of seven testes from five $Sxr/+$ males and 11 testes from nine $Tfm/+$ $Sxr/+$ males revealed that, in all animals, the majority of the testis tubules were devoid of spermatogenic elements and were lined solely with Sertoli cells (Fig. 3). No difference between $Tfm/+$ $Sxr/+$ and $+/+$ $Sxr/+$ was noted. Thus there is no evidence that a response to androgen is involved in the death of germ cells in XX male mice.

However, in a few tubules of some testes of both groups of mice, spermatogenesis was proceeding (Fig. 4). This phenomenon was seen in eight out of 11 testes of $Tfm/+$ $Sxr/+$ and four out of seven testes of $+/+$ $Sxr/+$. In all except two cases (both $Tfm/+$), only a single tubule of a testis was affected, but the greater part of this tubule was filled with spermatogenic cells. In one of the two exceptions, two tubules were affected, and in the other, four were affected. In the $+/+$ $Sxr/+$ animals, spermatogenesis appeared to be proceeding at least to the late spermatid stage, whereas in at least three of the 12 patches in $Tfm/+$ $Sxr/+$ no stages later than spermatocytes were observed.

The chromosome preparations also revealed meiosis in one out of six $+/+$ $Sxr/+$ testes and four out of 17 $Tfm/+$ $Sxr/+$ testes. In all cases, only 39 chromosomes were present in these meioses, comprising 19 bivalents and a univalent of size appropriate for a single X chromosome (Fig. 7). In those testes in which meioses were found there were also numerous mitoses, assumed to be spermatogonial mitoses, and these had a modal chromosome number of 39 in all animals. Altogether, 95 meioses and 62 mitoses—all with 39 chromosomes—were found in the five animals. The same phenomenon has also been found by Cattanach (1974) in *Sxr/+* animals. The interpretation was that these cells were chromosomally X0. They were assumed to have arisen by spontaneous chromosome loss. Random spontaneous chromosome loss probably occurs in normal animals, with subsequent death of the deficient cells. In these XX males, by contrast, the X chromosome loss had enabled germ cells to survive in the testis, whereas all cells with the full complement of chromosomes had died. It should be emphasized that the soma of the animals was known to be chromosomally XX from the presence of variegation for X-linked genes and/or because, where done, somatic chromosome counts gave a modal number of 40 chromosomes.

Spermatogenesis in some testis tubules, or even complete testes, has been reported in XX or XXY human males (Ferguson-Smith, 1966) and goat males (Basrur and Coubrough, 1964; Basrur and Kanagawa, 1969). In addition, it has been observed in two out of four XXY mice studied at Harwell (Fig. 5). It is suggested that the same phenomenon of spontaneous X-chromosome loss accounts for the survival of spermatogenic cells in these cases. Thus this finding helps to strengthen the evidence that it is incorrect X-chromosome dosage which leads to death of male germ cells in these genotypes. However, since there was no observed difference between *Tfm/+ Sxr/+* and *+/+ Sxr/+* animals, there is no reason to think that a response to androgen is involved.

A point of interest concerns the stage of spermatogenesis reached in the individual tubules of the various types of males. As far as could be observed, at least some late spermatids were present in each active tubule in the four *+/+ Sxr/+* males and the two XXY males in which spermatogenesis was seen. However, in at least three out of the 12 tubules in *Tfm/+ Sxr/+*, spermatogenesis appeared to be arrested at the spermatocyte stage, and two others appeared to have very few spermatids. Random X-chromosome loss in these last animals should in some cases leave a *Tfm/0* germ cell and in others a *+/0* germ cell. As already mentioned, in *Tfm/Y* male mice spermatogenesis is similarly arrested at meiosis. It therefore seems possible that in those tubules of *Tfm/+Sxr/+* where spermatogenesis was arrested at meiosis the germ cells were genetically *Tfm/0* and in those where spermatogenesis proceeded beyond meiosis the germ cells were *+/0*. However, it is also possible that the observed differences were the result of random X-chromosome inactivation in Sertoli cells or other somatic cells of these XX males, leading to unresponsiveness to androgen in some tubules.

CONCLUSION

To summarize, the evidence indicates that the activity of two X chromosomes is required for normal survival of female germ cells, but there is doubt whether a response to androgen, and hence the *Tfm* locus, is involved. The activity of more than one X chromosome appears to be fatal to male germ cells, and here there is no evidence that the *Tfm* locus is involved. It therefore seems highly probable that there remain another gene or genes on the X chromosome which are concerned in the survival and differentiation of germ cells and which remain to be discovered.

SUMMARY

The X chromosome of mammals shows monoallelic activity in somatic cells, but in germ cells the activity state appears to be different. In female germ cells, all X chromosomes present are thought to be active, and such activity is necessary for normal survival of the oocytes. Lack of an X chromosome (i.e., the XO condition) leads in some species to sterility through death of oocytes, and in the mouse to shortened reproductive life. In early stages of male germ cells, again all X chromosomes present are active and in this case the presence of more than one X (as in XXY) leads to cell death. The X chromosome of the mouse, and presumably all mammals, carries the *Tfm* locus, concerned with response of target organs to androgen. Attempts have been made to test whether this locus is concerned in the effect of X-chromosome dosage on survival of germ cells, but there is no clear evidence that it is.

ACKNOWLEDGMENTS

I am very grateful to Mr. P. H. Glenister for assistance with chromosome preparations, histology, and photography.

REFERENCES

Basrur, P. K., and Coubrough, R. I. (1964), Anatomical and cytological sex of a Saanen goat, *Cytogenetics (Basel)* 3:414.
Basrur, P. K., and Kanagawa, H. (1969), Anatomic and cytogenetic studies on 19 hornless goats with sexual disorders, *Ann. Genet. Select. Anim.* 1:349.
Cattanach, B. M. (1974), Genetic disorders of sex determination in mice and other mammals, p. 129, in: *Proceedings of the Fourth International Congress on Congenital Malformations,* International Congress Series No. 310, Excerpta Medica, Amsterdam.
Cattanach, B. M., Pollard, C. E., and Hawkes, S. G. (1971), Sex-reversed mice: XX and XO males, *Cytogenetics (Basel)* 10:318.
Epstein, C. J. (1969), Mammalian oocytes: X chromosome activity, *Science* 163:1078.
Epstein, C. J. (1972), Expression of the mammalian X chromosome before and after fertilization, *Science* 175:1467.

Ferguson-Smith, M. A. (1966), Sex chromatin, Klinefelter's syndrome and mental deficiency, in: *The Sex Chromatin*, p. 277 (K. L. Moore, ed.), Saunders, Philadelphia.

Gartler, S. M., Liskay, R. M., Campbell, B. K., Sparkes, R., and Gant, N. (1972), Evidence for two functional X chromosomes in human oocytes, *Cell Diff. 1:*215.

Jost, A. (1970), Hormonal factors in sex differentiation of the mammalian foetus, *Phil. Trans. Roy. Soc. Lond. Ser. B 259:*119.

Lyon, M. F. (1970), Genetic activity of sex chromosomes in somatic cells of mammals, *Phil. Trans. Roy. Soc. Lond. Ser. B 259:*41.

Lyon, M. F. (1972), X-chromosome inactivation and developmental patterns in mammals, *Biol. Rev. 47:*1.

Lyon, M. F., and Glenister, P. H. (1974), Evidence from *Tfm/O* that androgen is inessential for reproduction in female mice, *Nature (Lond.), 247:*366.

Lyon, M. F., and Hawkes, S. G. (1970), X-linked gene for testicular feminization in the mouse, *Nature (Lond.) 227:*1217.

Lyon, M. F., and Hawker, S. G. (1973), Reproductive lifespan in irradiated and unirradiated chromosomally X0 mice, *Genet. Res. 21:*185.

Meredith, R. (1969), A simple method for preparing meiotic chromosomes from mammalian testis, *Chromosoma (Berl.) 26:*254.

Ohno, S. (1967), *Sex Chromosomes and Sex-Linked Genes,* Springer, Berlin.

Ohno, S. (1973), Ancient linkage groups and frozen accidents, *Nature (Lond.) 244:*259.

Ohno, S., and Lyon, M. F. (1970), X-linked testicular feminization in the mouse as a noninducible regulatory mutation of the Jacob Monod type, *Clin. Genet. 1:*121.

Ohno, S., Christian, L., and Attardi, B. (1973), Role of testosterone in normal female function, *Nature New Biol. 243:*119.

Parkes, A. S., and Deanesly, R. (1966), The ovarian hormones, in: *Marshall's Physiology of Reproduction,* Vol. III., p. 570 (A. S. Parkes, ed.), Third edition, Longmans, London.

Price, D. (1970), *In vitro* studies on differentiation of the reproductive tract, *Phil. Trans. Roy Soc. Lond. Ser. B 259:*133.

Singh, R. P., and Carr, D. H. (1966), The anatomy and histology of X0 human embryos and fetuses, *Anat. Rec. 155:*369.

Tettenborn, U., Dofuku, R., and Ohno, S. (1971), Noninducible phenotype exhibited by a proportion of female mice heterozygous for the X-linked testicular feminization mutation, *Nature New Biol. 234:*37.

Welshons, W. J., and Russell, L. B. (1959), The Y-chromosome as the bearer of male determining factors in the mouse, *Proc. Natl. Acad. Sci. (U.S.A.) 45:*560.

6

Chromosomal Errors
and Reproductive Failure

Kurt Benirschke

Department of Reproductive Medicine
University of California, San Diego
La Jolla, California

Chromosomal errors are now known to be important causes of some human congenital anomalies, of most spontaneous abortions, and also of infertility, but not until the last few years have reliable estimates of their frequency been available. Jacobs (1972a) has summarized the data on gross chromosomal errors ascertained in five surveys of newborn populations, totaling 24,468 births. In 15,012 male and 9456 female newborns, 126 chromosomal errors were recognized, representing 0.5% of this population. This is a minimal estimate, because presumably many mosaic individuals escaped recognition in the two to ten cells counted per individual lymphocyte culture and because most of these surveys were done before the development of fluorescence and banding techniques. Only about 40 of these chromosomally abnormal newborns had abnormal phenotypes at birth; 86 had sex chromosomal errors or balanced translocations not likely to become clinically manifest until later life, usually during the reproductive years, if at all. Prospective studies of their development and the consequences of these errors will ultimately be of importance in improving our ability to provide proper genetic counseling.

From these figures the mutation rate was calculated. In 28 newborns with chromosomal rearrangements whose parents were studied cytogenetically, 21 errors were found to be inherited and seven were new events. If these figures are representative of the whole group, the overall mutational frequency would be at least 1.85×10^{-3} per gamete per generation or 0.2×10^{-3} per gamete per generation for new structural aberrations. Searle (personal communication) has commented that this is not too unlike the frequency of spontaneous translocations in the mouse, estimated to be 1×10^{-3} per gamete.

Evidence for the assumption that the figures just cited for man are underestimates of the frequency of chromosomal errors of zygotes comes from at least two sources. It is now known that a majority of early spontaneous abortions are the result of chromosomal errors. Trisomies, X monosomy, and polyploidies are the most important abnormalities found, and one must surmise that the corresponding nullisomic gametes lead to zygotic loss prior to recognition of pregnancy. These aspects are detailed by Boué and Boué (this book Vol. II, Chap. 48). Further, fluorescent microscopic analysis of quina- crine-stained spermatozoa reveals that at least Y nondisjunction occurs more frequently than the 0.25% maximal error rate calculated from the newborn figures just cited. Two Y-fluorescent spots are detectable in some 1–2% of ejaculated sperm (Sumner et al., 1971), although neither their fertilizing capacity nor that of other aneuploid sperm is yet known for mammals.

In conclusion to these introductory remarks it can be said that chromosomal nondisjunction at meiosis and some translocations appear to be common events in man, resulting in numerous spontaneous abortions, a few severely defective newborns, and a relatively large number of sex chromosomally unbalanced survivors. Of translocations ascertained in newborns, two-thirds are inherited and one-third are new mutations.

One may ask whether these sex chromosomally abnormal genotypes and balanced rearrangements are of importance with respect to reproductive failure. Court-Brown (1967), who estimates the frequency of balanced rearrangements in the general population to be at least 0.5%, provides some data that suggest that the reproductive fitness of such individuals is reduced. Prospective studies are very meager as yet, and final judgment of reproductive potential in all the individuals identified in the surveys cited must await their maturation. At present, data are available principally from three sources: (1) case reports and family studies of individuals with sex chromosomal errors and mosaicism or with translocations, (2) surveys of infertile couples, and (3) surveys of women with habitual abortion. This chapter reviews these three categories of reports that attempt to define what role chromosomal errors play in reproductive failure.

SEX CHROMOSOMAL ERRORS

Klinefelter's syndrome is almost invariably associated with azoospermia, and the few cases in which meiotic activity or fertility was found have been summarized by Luciani et al. (1970). These authors describe normal meiosis in an XY/XXY individual with oligospermia and surmise that the patients with this syndrome reported to be fertile are likely mosaics. Borgaonkar et al. (1970) reviewed the 53 XXYY cases reported and found that postpubertal patients invariably have atrophic testes without spermatogenesis. The situation is less clear in the XYY anomaly. The first patient with this anomaly reported by Sandberg *et al.* (1961) had fathered seven offspring; others have had severe hypogonadism (Skakkebaek *et al.*, 1970).

The offspring of men with 47,XYY have had a remarkable deficiency of extra Y chromosomes. Meiotic studies on XYY males partially account for this deficiency. In most cases reported, only XY primary spermatocytes are found, although Hultén and Pearson (1971) found YY bivalents and a 2.95% frequency of YY spermatozoa. Diasio and Glass (1970) also found an excess of YY spermatozoa in an XYY man. For counseling purposes, fluorescence analysis of sperm might be useful, as the latter patients may constitute those XYY men whose offspring are more likely to be XYY than those of the remainder, in whom spermatogonial XY selection, possibly through mitotic Y loss, has operated.

Only few cases of Y/autosome translocation with an additional normal Y have been reported, and so far fluorescence analysis has been reported for only four (Lundsteen and Philip, 1973). In some, congenital anomalies were found (Develing *et al.*, 1973); others were apparently normal and fertile. For still others no clinical data are available. The identification of the additional Y rests on brilliant fluorescence in the translocation chromosome and has yet to be confirmed by meiotic study. The difficulty in interpretation is exemplified by the findings in a patient with presumptive X/Y translocation recently reported from our laboratory (Khudr *et al.*, 1973a). This 31-year-old woman was identified in a fluorescence study of habitual aborters. She had had one normal girl and then four spontaneous abortions. All cells had one abnormal X, a presumptive X/Y translocation (Fig. 1). This was confirmed by all techniques currently available; unfortunately, meiosis studies failed. Her father and one brother had, in addition to a normal Y chromosome, a brilliantly fluorescent enlarged short arm of one No. 15 chromosome (Fig. 2); the mother was normal. The fluorescence seen in chromosome No. 15 of the father and brother is rare; it may be interpreted either as a Y/15 translocation or as a structural variant. Also, we can only infer from measurements and from the other banding techniques employed that the Y of the t(X;Y) of the proband did not represent the short arm of her father's abnormal chromosome No. 15. Thus extreme caution must be employed in the interpretation of such rearrangements until they can be proved by meiotic analysis. Moreover, although our patient was identified in a group of habitual aborters, there is no evidence that her X anomaly led to the miscarriages. Indeed, her last abortus lacked a fluorescent spot and is thus presumed not to have received the abnormal X.

At least eight presumably balanced X/autosome translocations have been reported in man (Sarto *et al.*, 1973). These patients were remarkable in that, in contrast to the t(X;Y) patient just described, seven had late replication of the normal X and five of seven had amenorrhea. Two were familial cases or had

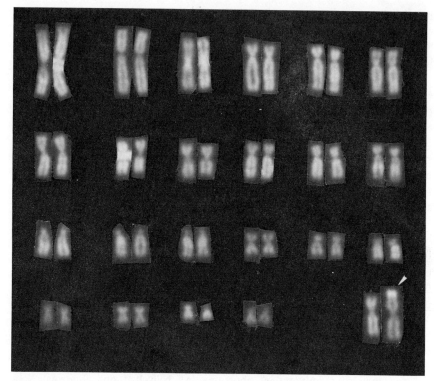

FIG. 1. *Karyotype of presumptive Y to X translocation (arrow) in a woman with one daughter and four consecutive abortions.* The fluorescent end of the abnormal X represents the long arms of Y.

abnormalities in offspring. The authors make a strong point that a causal relationship between the t(X;A) and amenorrhea exists, not only because five of seven had this symptom but also because two were ascertained in surveys of primary amenorrhea (19 of 50 with primary amenorrhea had chromosomal errors, two of 50 controls did).

Equally difficult to understand is the reproductive performance of XXX women. Of the 33 children reported to be born to such women, all had normal sex chromosomes, although two had trisomy 21 (Kadotani *et al.*, 1970a). In order to explain the absence of the expected 50% X-aneuploid zygotes, it must be concluded that some selective force is involved, presumably segregating the additional X into polar bodies. Alternatively, mitotic nondisjunction in germ cells could eliminate one X in embryonic stages. Direct meiotic study on ova from XXX women would be desirable. It is unknown whether the trisomy G of two children in this group was related to the XXX condition in the mother. The frequency of similar occurrences in XXX and other parental errors (Zergollern *et al.*, (1964) suggest such a possibility.

Patients with Turner's syndrome are characterized by the presence of infertility and primary amenorrhea, among other stigmata. Of those adjudged to be nonmosaic 45,X, only three have had normal offspring (Grace *et al.,* 1973). The variability of phenotypes in gonadal dysgenesis is only partially related to the chromosome findings (Eberle *et al.,* 1973), and a relatively large number of mosaics exist, at times complex. They are frequently identified among patients seen for primary amenorrhea and oligomenorrhea. In our ongoing study of such patients, the first 11 confirm the findings in the literature (Table I). Six were mosaics, three were classical X0, and two were XX. No good phenotype/genotype correlation existed, and there had been no pregnancies. In some other patients reported, mosaicism was the apparent cause of repeat abortions. Hsu *et al.* (1972) reported repeat abortions or reproductive difficulty in two women with X/XX/XXX mosaicism and reviewed the cases of two patients with X/XX and one with XX/XXX mosaicism having similar histories. In one family, mosaicism of sex chromosomes has been found in three generations, one woman having repeat abortions (Siegelman, 1972).

Mosaics are rarely vigorously separated from chimeras. Eleven true chimeras have been identified in man (Benirschke *et al.,* 1972); nine were XX/XY. They are usually ascertained because of ambiguous genitalia or ovotestes. The degree of sexual ambiguity differs, parallel to some extent with the clonal distribution of the cell lines. When the heterosexual gonad is removed, fertility should be possible but has not been reported.

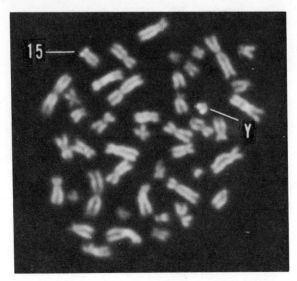

FIG. 2. Metaphase of father of patient in Fig. 1. The normal Y is indicated, as is the No. 15 chromosome with unusual fluorescence of the short arms.

TABLE I.   Clinical and Cytogenetic Data on 11 Consecutive Patients

Patient	Age (yr)	Height/weight (cm/kg)	Menses	Webbing of neck	Shield chest	Breast development	External genitalia
1. S.L.	19	133/47.5	1° Am	− (short) neck)	+	None	Large clitoris
2. C.D.	12	115/27.5	1° Am	−	+	None (wide-spaced nipples)	?
3. K.A.	15	117/28.4	1° Am	+	+	None	?
4. B.J.	18	139/40.9	−	−	+	Minimal	Normal
5. E.W.	16	155/45	−	−	−	None	Normal
6. L.T.	28	163/50	2° Am	−	−	Normal	Normal
7. M.K.	15	131/51.8	1° Am	+	+	None (wide-spaced nipples)	Normal
8. C.A.	22	140/45	1° Am	−	−	Minimal	Normal
9. L.G.	36	144/56.8	−	− (short neck)	−	Small	Normal
10. P.G.	20	146/56	−	−	−	Minimal	Normal
11. C.C.	22	168/645	2° Am	−	−	Small	Normal

[a]Six are mosaics, three have classical monosomy X, two have presumably normal chromosomes.

ith Amenorrhea/Oligomenorrhea Studied by the Author[a]

Uterus	Gonads	Karyotype	Lymphocytes	Gonad or skin	FSH/LH (mIU/ml)
nfantile	Streak (left) Testis	45,X/46,XYq–	94% 45,X	80% 45,X (testis)	80/41
?	?	45,X/46,XYr	10% 45,X		
?	?	45,X	100% 45,X		
nfantile	Streaks	45,X	100% 45,X	90% 45,X (ovary) 100% 45,X (skin)	202/73
Rudimentary uterine horns	Streaks	45,X/46,XX	15% 45,X		187/65
nfantile	Streaks	45,X/46,XX	10% 45,X		223/99
Rudimentary uterine horns	Streak (left) No gonad (right)	45,X/46,XY	99% 45,X		137/22
Infantile	Streaks	45,X	100% 45,X		105/55
nfantile	Streaks	45,X/46,XX	95% 45,X		
Normal	Streaks	46,XX	100% 46,XX		48/52
Infantile	Streaks	46,XX	100% 46,XX (1–2% Barr bodies only)		222/81

TRANSLOCATIONS

There is now a good deal of information available about individuals with various types of translocations. Nevertheless, it is as yet difficult to arrive at a unifying predictive thesis of their meiotic behavior and its reproductive consequences. Usually the anomalies are ascertained through chromosomal surveys or from analysis of a defective child. While sophisticated analysis describes break points, meiotic behavior, and segregation patterns in some cases, it is still not clear why seemingly identical anomalies differ in their consequences. Moreover, few studies are as yet available that determine the risk of such chromosomal errors when they are ascertained in population surveys. For convenience, translocations are here divided into insertions, inversions, reciprocal translocations, and Robertsonian "fusion-translocations."

While insertions can superficially appear to be reciprocal translocations involving a two-point break and rearrangement, three-point rearrangements in one or more chromosomes can be envisaged. Indeed, the consequences of rearrangements seen as normal and abnormal (aneusomic) genotypes often suggest insertions. By detailed banding technique analysis, at least two familial cases of presumed insertions have been discovered. One involved chromosomes No. 3 and 7 (Grace *et al.*, 1972), the other chromosome No. 2 (Therkelsen *et al.*, 1973). The aneusomics were congenitally malformed individuals; abortions have not been described.

Inversions were equally difficult to identify prior to the development of banding techniques, unless grossly different arm ratios were produced in the affected chromosome. Presumably for these reasons only about 25 had been reported when Wahrman *et al.* (1972) described three children with anomalies and pericentric inversions of chromosome No. 9. In one kindred, the inversion was present for at least four generations, in the other it must have been present for five generations. Moreover, two heterozygotes produced a normal homozygote. The authors produce some evidence that little disadvantage is conferred by the inversion and that the anomalies found in the sibships are not causally related to the inversion. Banding studies now permit greater precision in ascertaining the size of the inverted piece, and thus correlations with possible meiotic abnormalities such as unequal exchange in loops may become feasible. Although inversion loops have not yet been demonstrated unequivocally in human meiosis, they must be inferred to have occurred in at least two reported families. The first was ascertained because of a child with cri-du-chat syndrome (Faed *et al.*, 1972). The large inversion of chromosome No. 5 was traced in four generations by the G-banding technique; repeat abortions and neonatal deaths were common in the family. The second was an example of inversion of chromosome No. 13 (Taysi *et al.*, 1973). Partial features of the D_1-trisomy syndrome led to ascertainment, and quinacrine fluorescence study clearly identified the duplicated piece in the proposita. Although the inverted D_1 of the mother had superficially similar features to that in the preceding case, it differed in the banding study, being much smaller. Therefore, predictions of crossing over within loops and a possible relation to the size of inversion as well as effects on reproductive losses have to be empirical for the moment. The need for complete exploration of families with repeat wastage has been stressed by Hsu *et al.* (1970), who found an inversion of chromosome No. 2 in the mother and increased chromosome breakage frequency in the father of a family with multiple abortions and one stillbirth with anomalies.

Reciprocal translocations are often ascertained when congenital anomalies develop in the progeny produced by unbalanced gametes. A large number of such cases are on record, and family study often shows numerous balanced carriers of such translocation without known increase in reproductive losses. At other times, repeat abortions, anomalies, and even sterility result from translocations. No general statement relating these events to one type of rearrangement but not to another can be made as yet. In virtually none of the families studied has the abortus been analyzed and shown to be aneusomic. Kadotani and Ohama (1968) found five spontaneous abortions to be followed by a normal child in a family where the husband had an apparently balanced C/D translocation. In another family with repeat abortions studied by Kadotani *et al.* (1970c), the father had a D/G translocation, the mother one between B and C elements. Knight *et al.* (1971) describe five abortions, one child with multiple anomalies, and one normal child for a mother who had a balanced B/D translocation (?5/14). The unusual distribution of chromosomes in this kindred suggested to the authors that irregular events at meiosis are presently unpredictable. In any event, the calculated frequency of abnormal gametes is not found in the zygotes resulting from such translocations, and more precise studies are needed before proper genetic counseling can be offered. Figure 3 shows the pedigree of a family in which the high frequency of spontaneous abortions was thought to be related to a reciprocal translocation, which by G-banding could be determined as t(8q−; 13q+). Both male and female balanced carriers had this reproductive wastage, but, as in other cases, the abortuses themselves could not be studied (Khudr *et al.*, 1973b). On the other hand, a man ascertained in the same study of sterile couples to have a translocation t(10p+; 15q−) had severe oligospermia, presumably because of the rearrangement. One can only hope that detailed banding studies and cytogenetic examination of the abortuses will clarify the reasons for sterility, aneuploid offspring, and normal segregation in these various situations.

Translocations among the acrocentric chromosomes are the most frequent rearrangement, and our understanding of D/D, D/G, and G/G translocations is currently under intense study with the newer techniques. This rearrangement, often referred to as Robertsonian fusion, occurs spontaneously in perhaps one to

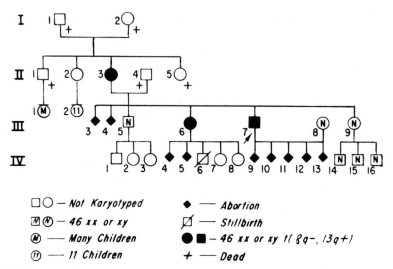

FIG. 3. Pedigree of family identified because of habitual abortion of III/7. Three members had a reciprocal translocation t(8q–;13q+).

three individuals per 1000, is not inducible by mutagens or irradiation, is nonrandom with t13/14 and 14/21 being much more common, and may be the result of exchange at meiotic pairing rather than of breakage and fusion (Hecht and Kimberling, 1971). This is further supported by the very frequent dicentric nature of the fusion product (Niebuhr, 1972). These anomalies are ascertained by (1) surveys, (2) presence of congenital anomaly (trisomy 21, 13, other), and (3) repeat abortions or sterility (Cohen, 1971). When homologous chromosomes are involved, as in t(22;22) (Schwinger, 1973), there is a simple explanation for the repeated abortions; however, the reviews show this to be an uncommon event, and it is usually supported only by autoradiography and not by banding studies. What is difficult to understand as yet is why seemingly identical rearrangements lead to different pedigrees. Thus in a study of five kindreds deGrouchy *et al.* (1970) found that numerous abortions had occurred in one with t(13;15) and one with t(13;14), while the others—t(13;14) and t(14;15)— did not have this sequel. Fraccaro *et al.* (1973) found that of 92 men attending an infertility clinic four had t(13;14), but other investigators have not found such a direct relationship, according to Palmer *et al.* (1973). In their study of two large kindreds with this translocation, the carrier females of one had 60% abortions, while 30% of conceptions from male carriers were aborted; the figures for the other family were 19 and 6.7%. The reasons for these discrepancies are currently not understood; all that can be said is that reproductive failure is somehow correlated with these translocations. How complex the study of repeat pregnancy wastage can be is exemplified by the report of Knörr *et al.* (1969).

These authors studied a woman with D_2/G translocation who had eight abortions, the last of which showed an apparently normal, balanced translocation. The patient also had a bicornuate uterus, which may well have been the cause of the abortions rather than the translocation. Twelve other patients with uterine anomalies studied by these authors had normal karyotypes.

INFERTILE COUPLES

Several surveys of infertile couples have been made, but in most the chromosome analysis has focused on or been limited to the male. In the report by Dutrillaux (1973), over 50% of 271 subfertile men were studied by banding analysis and the value of these techniques is clearly indicated. Unlike in previous studies (see Ferguson-Smith, 1972), where some 11% of oligospermic males attending infertility clinics were found to have Klinefelter's syndrome, Dutrillaux (1973) found only four cases in his 81 azoospermic patients, three of whom had some meiotic activity. Altogether he reported 3% major chromosomal structural anomalies, a substantial increase over that in the general population. There were three D/D and one D/G Robertsonian translocations in oligospermic or azoospermic men, one t(5;8), one t(11q+;22q−), and one t(1;X) reciprocal

TABLE II. Five Surveys of Infertile Men
(593 men with 33 anomalies = 5.5%)[a]

XXY	6
XY/XXY;X/XY etc.	7
Inv. Y	2
t(D;D)	8
t(D;G)	1
Recipr. t	3 (? + 2)
Inv. 7	1
Gr	1
Mar +	2
Total	33

[a]Distribution of abnormal chromosome findings in five surveys of infertile men (Chandley, 1970; Dutrillaux, 1973; Fraccaro et al., 1973; Kjessler, 1966; McIlree et al., 1966). These figures do not include patients with abnormal length of Y, large satellites, etc. Some studies include only chromatin-negative men, others give no data on sperm counts or testis study. Two studies were done with chromosome banding.

translocations, as well as one pericentric inversion in seven men in whom the presumptive loop was again not demonstrable. In addition, four men with metacentric Y and 38 with various irregularities of heterochromatic segments were identified, although the contribution of these to sterility is presently unclear. The case of reciprocal translocation t(11q+;22q−) is of great interest. The deletion of a long arm on a G chromosome could be shown to be the result of translocation of this piece to chromosome No. 11, yet meiotic study showed no evidence of a reciprocal translocation. Moreover, classical staining failed to reveal the translocation.

On the other hand, Chandley *et al.* (1972) found a quadrivalent at diakinesis in an azoospermic man adjudged to have normal mitotic chromosomes. Despite banding study, the exact nature of the reciprocal translocation (presumed to be (Cp−;Eq+) could not be defined. These two cases appear to have great importance in the interpretation of studies on infertile men. They indicate that men with tiny translocations, difficult or impossible to detect by regular chromosome study, may have meiotic problems; conversely, multivalents may be absent in patients with demonstrated translocations. Perhaps reciprocal translocations are a more important cause of oligospermia, but most have escaped our detection to date. Luciani (1970) found no meiotic errors in 20 infertile men.

Of 131 subfertile men who were sex chromatin negative, Kjessler (1966) found six with abnormal karyotypes, one D/D translocation, four mosaics (XY/XXY; X/XY), and one with additional marker chromosome. Two other men had variations of the size of Y, but Kadotani *et al.* (1971) found in a study of 219 males that the length of Y follows a normal distribution and does not correlate with infertility.

In chromatin-negative patients with sperm counts of less than 20 million/ml, McIlree *et al.* (1966) found three errors, and Fraccaro *et al.* (1973) identified four t(13;14) in 92 infertile men and referred to a few similar studies. In other studies, a few cases of additional marker chromosomes of undefined origin have been correlated with azoospermia in otherwise normal men (Chandley, 1970), but their frequency or significance is not yet known. Some of the patients had inherited the element from their mothers, whose reproductive efficiency was apparently not affected.

In aggregate, it appears from these studies that chromosomal errors are exceedingly rare in infertile couples in which the male partner has a normal sperm count. An appreciable number of oligospermic patients, 10 million/ml or less, have Robertsonian and reciprocal translocations; other defects such as inversions, so far all pericentric, and additional marker chromosomes are also found.

Kadotani *et al.* (1970b) investigated the chromosomal status of both partners of 88 couples with primary sterility. They had all been married for 3 years or more, and no apparent cause for the infertility had been detected clinically. Six errors were found, three in men and three in women. One man was 47,XXY, and two had unusually long Y (significance not known); one woman had an apparent deletion of both arms of chromosome No. 1, and two had similar defects in No. 3. Since banding studies were not possible then, reciprocal translocations cannot be excluded.

It is of parenthetical interest that spermatogenesis of three male individuals with trisomy 21 was adjudged to be approximately normal, albeit trivalents and univalent G chromosomes were identified (Schröder et al., 1971). Finally, it has recently been suggested that the cause of undescended testes may be chromosomal errors in this tissue (Mininberg and Bingol, 1973). Five of seven patients with unilateral and four of six with bilateral undescended testes had abnormal mitotic chromosomes (after tissue culture) in the testes, but they had normal lymphocyte karyotypes. The abnormalities were usually designated as C+ or C−, and their significance, or whether they arose in culture, is currently not known.

At the moment, it is impossible to make accurate predictions from chromosomal studies which rearrangements will lead to sterility and/or to aneuploid gametes. In XXY men, sterility is usually the case but its chromosomal reason is uncertain. Why maturation arrest occurs in some but not all XYY men is similarly unexplained. Jacobs (1972b) has suggested that reproduction in individuals ascertained without bias (in surveys) is unimpeded and segregation of rearranged chromosomes occurs as expected. In males ascertained by abnormal phenotype (biased), reproduction may be impeded; at least a few aneuploid zygotes are produced. On the other hand, a much increased frequency of aneuploid offspring is found in families where the mother has a rearrangement. Jacobs estimates the risk at as five to ten times that of males, and, as others have, she infers the possibility of greater haploid selection of aneuploid male gametes. There are no hypotheses currently testable in man that might provide an answer to the question of why trivalents or quadrivalents identified at diakinesis in the individuals with translocations should present a barrier to meiosis in some but not in others.

HABITUAL ABORTION

Chromosomal errors play some role in recurrent abortion, but the incidence is difficult to ascertain for numerous reasons. Habitual abortion is rare (0.4% of pregnancies), and various criteria have been used for its delineation; usually it is defined as three or more consecutive spontaneous miscarriages. In many surveys only the female has been studied, although a rearranged genome in the male has sometimes been shown to be the probable cause of the abortions. Frequently nothing is known of endocrine anomalies, infections, or structural aberrations of the uterus, and overlaps with the other categories here reported also exist. Most

TABLE III. 819 Members of Families with Repeat
Abortions (83 errors)

	Females	Males	Total
Robertsonian translocations			
D/D	19		
D/G	2	1	
G/G		1	23
Reciprocal translocations	6	4	
Possible translocations			
(added, deleted material)	9	8	27
Pericentric inversions	2	1	3
Isochromosome 18	1		1
Sex chromosome mosaics	6	1	
Autosomal mosaics	1	2	10
Total	46	18	64

[a]Composite of studies of families with repeat/habitual
abortions (Bhasin *et al.*, 1973; Käosaar and Mikelsaar,
1973; Khudr, 1974; Rott *et al.*, 1972).

regrettably, of all the reports here summarized, the abortus has been studied in
only seven and only once was it found to be aneuploid. Finally, some series
include malformed infants, with or without chromosomal errors, as indicative of
repeat failure, at times this being the index case. No prospective study with rigid
criteria has as yet been done that can give a delineation of the probable
frequency of chromosomal abnormalities in habitual abortion.

Despite these shortcomings, some interesting case material has accumulated.
Khudr (1974) has summarized all studies to date, including our own 14 couples.
To this list three additional studies should be added (Table III). In consecutive
published series, 819 individuals have been studied, more women than their
husbands, and 83 presumptive chromosomal errors have been identified, or 11%
of these, 54 were in women and 29 in men, but these figures are not very
meaningful, since far fewer men have been studied in these infertile couples.
Moreover, the validity of some of the errors is dubious because banding studies
of most of the presumed deletions were not conducted and because the nine
abnormal Y chromosomes found were probably of no importance (Kadotani *et
al.*, 1971). If these nine "abnormal Y" cases were excluded and also those whose
contribution to the abortions was very doubtful—i.e., t(X;Y), enlarged satellites,
frequent endoreduplication, various types of aberrations in culture—then there
remain 64 errors, or 7.9% of all studied partners in habitual abortions had

identifiable chromosomal errors. Robertsonian fusions (No. 23) were most numerous, followed by reciprocal exchanges among various elements (No. 10). Seven sex chromosomal mosaics were found, three pericentric inversions, three autosomal mosaics, 13 cases of extra chromosomal material, four with material deleted from various elements, and one isochromosome 18 (Table III).

This frequency of errors found in couples with habitual abortions is not impressive, even though it considerably exceeds that in the general population. Presumably the 7.9% represents an underestimate, considering that rigid exclusion of structural uterine anomalies, infections, etc. was not practiced for this case material and only very few banding studies were done. Of great importance in future studies will be the inclusion of cytogenetic analysis of the abortus itself. Of the seven so far studied, only one had aneuploid (D+) complement; the others were either balanced carriers (five) or normal (one). Looking at this problem from another direction, Boué and Boué (1973) found no correlations in the karyotype abnormality of the abortus in a study of 43 women with two consecutive abortions.

CONCLUSION

Chromosomal errors play an important role in human reproductive failure; however, present knowledge permits few generalizations. Numerically speaking, sex chromosomal errors and translocations of various types are the most important.

In males, the possession of additional X chromosomes nearly always results in completely azoospermia, the few fertile patients with Klinefelter's syndrome presumably being mosaics. Although some individuals with XYY sex chromosomes are fertile, others are oligospermic and infertile. The reason for this difference in these populations and the mechanism of the apparently frequent loss of one Y from their germ cells are not yet understood.

Most 45,X women are sterile and amenorrheic, and those with various mosaic populations may have recurrent abortions. The mechanism of germ cell loss in embryonic 45,X individuals, eventuating in streak ovaries, is not understood. Women with 47,XXX chromosomes have apparently normal reproductive function, although some have offspring with other aneuploidies.

Investigations of infertile men show that at least 5.5% have chromosome errors, nearly one-half of which involve sex chromosomes. The remainder have translocations, more often Robertsonian than reciprocal. The frequency of the latter is presumably underestimated. Recent studies combining banding analysis and meiotic investigations clearly indicate the necessity for employing both methodologies to ascertain errors completely. Almost all infertile men with chromosome errors have sperm counts below 10 million/ml. No current hypothesis adequately explains faulty spermatogenesis in Robertsonian or reciprocal translocations; female meiosis is virtually unaffected by these rearrangements.

In habitual abortion, approximately 8% of female or male partners have chromosomal errors, much more commonly studied and ascertained in the female. Approximately equal numbers of Robertsonian and reciprocal translocations account for the majority of errors, the remainder being inversions, mosaics, etc. As with infertile men, the most prevalent error is D/D translocation, usually t(13;14). Why these identical rearrangements are associated with infertility and abortions in some families but not in others is totally unexplained at present, numerous theories notwithstanding. It must be pointed out that the abortus of such pedigrees has rarely been investigated, an important deficiency in our knowledge.

ACKNOWLEDGMENTS

Dr. G. Khudr participated in the study of many families; his help and the support of a grant from the Rockefeller Foundation (RF 70029) are gratefully acknowledged.

REFERENCES

Benirschke, K., Naftolin, F., Gittes, R., Khudr, G., Yen, S. S. C., and Allen, F. H. (1972), True hermaphroditism and chimerism, *Am. J. Obstet. Gynecol. 113:*449.

Bhasin, M. K., Foerster, W., and Fuhrmann, W. (1973), A cytogenetic study of recurrent abortion, *Humangenetik 18:*139.

Borgaonkar, D. S., Mules, E., and Char, F. (1970), Do the 48,XXYY males have a characteristic phenotype? *Clin. Genet. 1:*272.

Boué, J., and Boué, A. (1973), Chromosomal analysis of two consecutive abortuses in each of 43 women, *Humangenetik 19:*275.

Chandley, A. C. (1970), Chromosome studies on testicular cells of subfertile men, in: *The Human Testis,* p. 151 (E. Rosemberg and C. A. Paulsen, eds.), Plenum Press, New York.

Chandley, A. C., Christie, S., Fletcher, J., Frackiewiez, A., and Jacobs, P. A. (1972), Translocation heterozygosity and associated subfertility in man, *Cytogenetics (Basel) 11:*516.

Cohen, M. M. (1971), The chromosomal constitution of 165 human translocations involving D group chromosomes identified by autoradiography, *Ann. Génét. 14:*87.

Court-Brown, W. M. (1967), *Human Population Cytogenetics,* North-Holland, Amsterdam.

deGrouchy, J., Crippa, L., and German, J. (1970), Études autoradiographiques des chromosomes humains, VII. Cinq observations de t(DqDq) familiales, *Ann. Génét. 13:*19.

Develing, A. J., Conte, F. A., and Epstein, C. J. (1973), A Y-autosome translocation 46,X, t/Yq−:7q+) associated with multiple congenital anomalies, *J. Pediat. 82:*495.

Diasio, R. B., and Glass, R. H. (1970), The Y chromosome in sperm of an XYY male, *Lancet 2:*1318.

Dutrillaux, B. (1973), *Nobel Symp. Chromosome Identification 23:*205.

Eberle, P., Ammermann, M., and Wolf, H. (1973), Zur Variabilität des weiblichen Turner-syndroms: Chromosomenanalysen und klinische Befunde bei 17 typischen und atypischen Fällen, *Arch. Gynäkol. 213:*202.

Faed, M. J. W., Marrian, V. J., Robertson, J., Robson, E. B., and Cook, P. J. L. (1972), Inherited pericentric inversion of chromosome 5: A family with history of neonatal death and a case of the "cri du chat" syndrome, *Cytogenetics (Basel) 11:*400.

Ferguson-Smith, M. A. (1972), in: *Human Genetics* (Proceedings of the Fourth International Congress of Human Genetics), p. 195 (J. deGrouchy, F. J. G. Ebling, and I. W. Henderson, eds), Exerpta Medica, Amsterdam.

Fraccaro, M., Maraschio, P., Pasquali, F., Tiepolo, L., Zuffardi, O., and Giarola, A. (1973), Male infertility and 13/15 translocation, *Lancet 1:*488.

Grace, E., Sutherland, G. R., and Bain, A. D. (1972), Familial insertional translocation, *Lancet 2:*231.

Grace, H. J., Quinlan, D. K., and Edge, W. E. B. (1973), 45,X lymphocyte karyotype in a fertile woman, *Am. J. Obstet. Gynecol. 115:*279.

Hecht, F., and Kimberling, W. J. (1971), Patterns of D chromosome involvement in hunan (DqDq) and (DqGq) Robersonian rearrangements, *Am. J. Hum. Genet. 23:*361.

Hsu, L. Y. F., Barcinski, M., Shapiro, L. R., Valderrama, E., Gertner, M., and Hirschhorn, K. (1970), Parental chromosomal aberrations associated with multiple abortions and an abnormal infant, *Obstet. Gynecol. 36:*723.

Hsu, L. Y. F., Garcia, F. P., Grossmann, D., Kutinsky, E., and Hirschhorn, K. (1972), Fetal wastage and maternal mosaicism, *Obstet. Gynecol. 40:*98.

Hultén, M., and Pearson, P. S. (1971), Fluorescent evidence for spermatocytes with two Y chromosomes in an XYY male, *Ann. Hum. Genet. 34:*273.

Jacobs, P. A. (1972a), Chromosome mutations: Frequency at birth in humans, *Humangenetik 16:*137.

Jacobs, P. A. (1972b), in: *The Genetics of the Spermatozoon*, p. 346 (R. A. Beatty and S. Gluecksohn-Waelsch, eds.), Bogtrykkeriet Forum, Copenhagen.

Kadotani, T., and Ohama, K. (1968), A preliminary note on a partial C/D translocation related to repeated abortions, *Proc. Jap. Acad. 44:*397.

Kadotani, T., Ohama, K., and Makino, S. (1970a), A case of 21-trisomic Down's syndrome from the triplo-X mother, *Proc. Jap. Acad. 46:*709.

Kadotani, T., Ohama, K., Nakayama, T., and Tabuchi, A. (1970b), Chromosome studies in primary sterility, *Am. J. Obstet. Gynecol. 106:*489.

Kadotani, T., Ohama, K., Sofuni, T., and Hamilton, H. B. (1970c), Aberrant karyotypes and spontaneous abortion in a Japanese family, *Nature (Lond.) 225:*735.

Kadotani, T., Ohama, K., Takahara, H., and Makino, S. (1971), Studies on the Y chromosome in human males from fertile and infertile couples, *Jap. J. Hum. Genet. 16:*35.

Käosaar, M. E., and Mikelsaar, A. V. N. (1973), Chromosome investigation in married couples with repeated spontaneous abortions, *Humangenetik 17:*277.

Khudr, G. (1974), Cytogenetics of habitual abortion, a review, *Obstet. Gynecol. Surv., 29:*299.

Khudr, G., Benirschke, K., Judd, H. L., and Strauss, J. (1973a), Y to X translocation in a woman with reproductive failure, a new rearrangement, *JAMA 226:*542.

Khudr, G., Naftolin, F., Benirschke, K., Zarate, A., and Guzman-Toledano, R. (1973b), Unusual translocations and reproductive failure, *Obstet. Gynecol. 41:*542.

Kjessler, B. (1966), Karyotype meiosis and spermatogenesis in a sample of men attending in infertility clinic, in: *Monographs in Human Genetics,* Vol. 2, Karger, Basel.

Knight, L. A., Sakaguchi, S., and Luzzatti, L. (1971), Unusual mechanism of transmission of a maternal chromosome translocation, *Am. J. Dis. Child. 121:*162.

Knörr, K., Knörr-Gärtner, H., and Uebele-Kallhardt, B. (1969), Beispiel für die Bedeutung zytogenetischer Untersuchungen bei habituellen Aborten, *Geburtsh. Frauenh. 29:*792.

Luciani, J. M. (1970), Les chromosomes méiotiques de l'homme, II. Le nucleole. Les chiasmas, III. La stérilité masculine, *Ann. Génét. 13:*169.

Luciani, J. M., Mattei, A., Devictor-Vuillet, M., Rubin, P., Stahl, A., and Vague, J. (1970), Étude des chromosomes meiotiques dans un cas de maladie de Klinefelter avec spermatogenése et caryotype 46,XY/47,XXY, *Ann. Génét. 13:*249.

Lundsteen, C., and Philip, J. (1973), Y/22 translocation in a YY male, *Cytogenet. Cell Genet. 12:*53.

McIlree, M. E., Price, W. H., Court-Brown, W. M., Tulloch, W. S., Newsam, J. E., and Maclean, N. (1966), Chromosome studies on testicular cells on fifty sub-fertile men, *Lancet 2:*69.

Mininberg, D. T., and Bingol, N. (1973), Chromosomal abnormalities in undescended testes, *Urology 1:*98.

Niebuhr, E. (1972), Dicentric and monocentric Robertsonian translocations in man, *Humangenetik 16:*217.

Palmer, C. G., Morris, J. L., Thompson, B. H., and Nance, W. E. (1973), Fertility and 13/14 translocation, *Lancet 1:*728.

Rott, H. D., Richter, E., Rummel, W. D., and Schwanitz, G. (1972), Chromosomenbefunde bei Ehepaaren mit gehäuften Aborten, *Arch. Gynäkol. 213:*110.

Sandberg, A. A., Koepf, G. F., Ishihara, T., and Hauschka, T. S. (1961), An XYY human male, *Lancet 2:*488.

Sarto, G. E., Therman, E., and Patau, K. (1973), X inactivation in man: A woman with t(Xq−; 12q+), *Am. J. Hum. Genet. 25:*262.

Schröder, J., Lydecken, K., and de la Chapelle, A. (1971), Meiosis and spermatogenesis in G-trisomic males, *Humangenetik 13:*15.

Schwinger, E. (1973), Translocation 22/22? *Lancet 2:*854.

Skakkebaek, N. E., Philip, J., Mikkelsen, M., Hammen, R., Nielsen, J., Perbøll, O., and Yde, H. (1970), Studies on spermatogenesis, meiotic chromosomes, and sperm morphology in two males with a 47,XYY chromosome complement, *Fertil. Steril. 21:*645.

Siegelman, M. (1972), X0/XX and X0/XY mosiacism: A study of a family, *Obstet. Gynecol. 39:*510.

Sumner, A. T., Robinson, J. A., and Evans, H. J. (1971), Distinguishing between X, Y and YY-bearing human spermatozoa by fluorescence and DNA content, *Nature New Biol. 229:*231.

Taysi, K., Bobrow, M., Balci, S., Madan, K., Atasu, M., and Say, B. (1973), Duplication/ deficiency product of a pericentric inversion in man: A cause of D_1 trisomy syndrome, *J. Pediat. 82:*263.

Therkelsen, A. J., Hultén, M., Jonasson, J., Lindsten, J., Christensen, N. C., and Iversen, T. (1973), Presumptive direct insertion within chromosome 2 in man, *Ann. Hum. Genet. 36:*367.

Wahrman, J., Atidia, J., Goitein, R., and Cohen, T. (1972), Pericentric inversions of chromosome 9 in two families, *Cytogenetics (Basel) 11:*132.

Zergollern, L., Hoefnagel, D., Benirschke, K., and Corcoran, P. A. (1964), A patient with trisomy 21 and a reciprocal translocation in the 13–15 group, *Cytogenetics 3:*148.

7

Agonadism XY with Familial Recurrence

Cora de M. Pedreira, Kleyde Mendes Lopes Ramos, and
Lucy I. S. Peixoto

Laboratory of Human
Genetics, Department of Biology,
Institute of Biology, Federal University of Bahia
Bahia, Brazil

and

Benedito Barreto de Oliveira

Medical and Public Health School
Catholic University of Bahia
Bahia, Brazil

Agonadism is one of the abnormalities of sexual development. Among such abnormalities are gonadal dysgenesis, as in Turner's syndrome and its variations; true hermaphroditism; pseudohermaphroditism; and testicular feminization. Anomalies of structure and function exist to varying degrees in all these forms. Streak gonad is the histological stigma of pure XX or XY or mixed gonadal dysgenesis. Possession of ovotestis (both a testis and an ovary), malformations, or infantilism of the external genitalia are usual somatic traits, whereas amenorrhea and delay of puberty are the functional expressions of such deviations.

We are reporting a case of familial agonadism that conforms to the concept of "true agonadism" as proposed by Overzier and Linden (1956).

CASE HISTORIES

Case No. 1

E. L. B. J. (St. Izabel Hospital No. 218867) was a 15-yr-old male who had been brought to the hospital for consultation by his father on November 22,

1972, because he had undescended testes. Physical examination showed height 165 cm, weight 54 kg, and mental and physical development normal. All clinical data were within normal limits by careful physical exploration, except for bilateral absence of testes in the scrotal sac. The length and proportion of the phallus were normal for the chronological age. Pubic hairs were scanty, as is usual in this ethnic group, mulatto, but the pattern of distribution was definitely masculine (Figs. 1 and 2). Diagnosis of bilateral cryptorchism was established.

An exploratory laparotomy was performed for orthopexy and testicular biopsy on December 6, 1972. It was undertaken by three expert surgeons. An extensive inguinal and abdominal exploration was performed, but no gonads or mass of cells resembling a gonadal structure were found. Ducts, vasa deferens, epididymes, or remnants of Müllerian or Wolffian elements were not found. The surgeons first explored the right inguinal canal and peritoneal cavity. Thereafter the left side was examined with similar results. No structure of the reproductive apparatus was found in the pelvis or abdominal cavity.

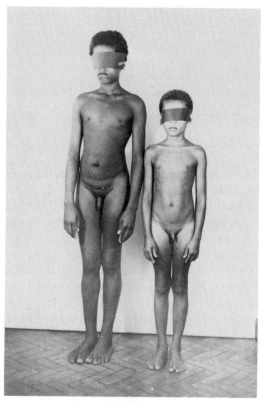

FIG. 1. *Case No. 1, age 15 yr, and Case No. 2, his brother, age 10 yr.*

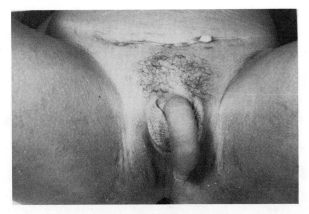

FIG. 2. External genitalia, Case No. 1.

Therefore, our group undertook a study of this case from the genetic point of view. The patient was the second living child of a large sibship, as seen in Fig. 3. His only brother was 10 yr old and had the same congenital anorchia syndrome. His parents, simple rural agricultural workers, were apparently normal both physically and mentally and had normal karyotypes. The mother had been pregnant 14 times and was expecting her fourteenth child at the time of our first interview. Two sons and five daughters were alive. Five pregnancies had ended in abortion, and one male child had died at the age of 7 months. The fourteenth child, born after our first interview, was a full-term female. All of the girls were normal. Besides the two sons, the parents did not know of any similar occurrence in their families.

The buccal smear of the propositus was chromatin negative, and his karyotype was normal 46,XY (Fig. 4). The urinary gonadotropins (6 UR/24 h) and 17-ketosteroids (9.6 mg/24 h; Jayle) were both within the normal limits for men.

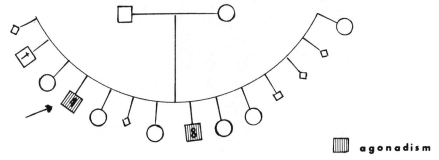

IIIIII **agonadism**

FIG. 3. Pedigree of the sibship. No. 4 is the propositus and No. 8 is his younger brother.

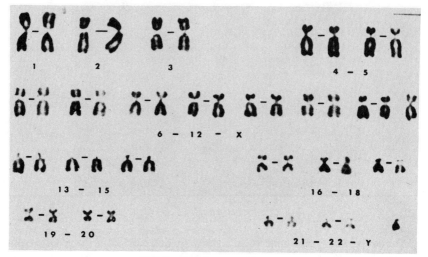

FIG. 4. Karyotype, Case No. 1.

His psychological behavior and preferences were completely in accordance with his male status.

Case No. 2

J. G. B. J. (St. Izabel Hospital No. 227236) was the 10-yr-old brother. Mental and physical development appeared normal (Fig. 1).

The external genitalia showed a phallus with the normal proportions, but his testes had never been felt (Fig. 5). This boy was the result of the eighth pregnancy. His father did not agree to a surgical approach. Buccal smear was chromatin negative, and his karyotype revealed a normal chromosomal comple-

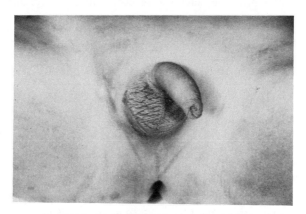

FIG. 5. External genitalia, Case No. 2.

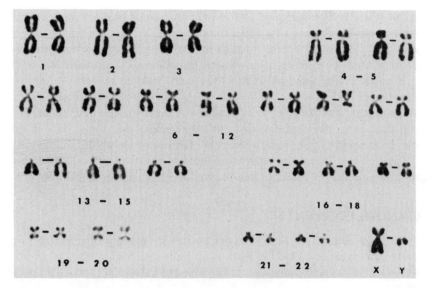

FIG. 6. Karyotype, Case No. 2.

ment 46,XY (Fig. 6). Urinary gonadotropin levels were below 6 UR/24 h, and 17-ketosteroids were 5.2 mg/24 h.

DISCUSSION

The case reported here seems to be one of an extreme form of agonadism with complete gonadal agenesis and absence of any internal genital structure. No similar case appears in the literature available to us.

Some hypotheses were raised to explain these interesting and exceptional cases. The familial recurrence suggests a genetic etiology, and cryptorchism and many other errors of sexual development are frequently identified as chromosomal disorders. However, karyotype studies failed to support this theory since no morphological, numerical, or structural aberration could be detected by the usual methods of karyotypology. The propositus and his brother were normal 46,XY. The possible action of a genetic inducer in the earliest stages of morphogenesis cannot be excluded. The presence of male gonads in the first weeks of embryonic life with early resorption after induction of proper development of external genitalia, as suggested by Federman (1967), may be admitted. Transient presence of a testis is a plausible hypothesis, if Jost's experimental results also apply in man. In the absence of testes, the female phenotype would predominate (Jost, 1947). The occurrence of testes which vanished about 10–15 weeks after having produced hormonal substances capable of inducing external masculinization (e.g., Witschi, 1951) is conceivable, although difficult to explain.

On the other hand, explanation of this syndrome would be much more difficult in the complete absence of a testis during embryogenesis; we would have to hypothesize that other organs, such as adrenal glands, can produce hormones able to enhance the differentiation of some masculine sex characteristics.

It might also be suggested that gonadal cells could be scattered throughout other tissues and thus not be recognized by the surgical approach. We can dismiss as highly unlikely the possible action of some teratogenic environmental agent such as viruses or drugs, since this abnormality was found only in two males born several years apart, whereas the females in the sibship were normal.

Cases such as those here reported indicate that further experimental investigations are needed to elucidate the mechanisms involved in such malformations.

ACKNOWLEDGMENTS

We thank Dr. Dirceu A. M. Ferreira for urinary gonadotropin and 17-ketosteroid determinations, Drs. Iris Ferrari and Edilson G. Vieira Brito for chromosome microphotographs, and Drs. A. Pedreira and Pamela Moriearty for English revision.

REFERENCES

Allan, C. B. (1970), *Desarrollo intra Uterino,* Trad. Salvat Editores, S. A. Barcelona.

Bergada, C., Cleveland, W. W., Jones, H. W., Jr., and Wilkins, L. (1962), Variants of embryonic testicular dysgenesis: Bilateral anorchia and the syndrome of rudimentary testes, *Acta Endocrinol. 40:*521–536.

Emson, H. E., and Buckwold, A. E. (1965), Agonadism, *Can. Med. Ass. J. 93:*1080.

Federman, D. D. (1967), *Abnormal Sexual Development,* pp. 84–88, Saunders, Philadelphia.

Ferguson-Smith, M. A., and Johnston, A. W. (1960), Chromosome abnormalities in certain diseases of man, *Ann. Int. Med. 53:*359.

Jost, A. (1947), Sur le role des gonades foetales dans la differenciation sexuelle somatique de l'embryon de Lapin, *C. R. Ass. Anat. 34:*255.

Overzier, C., and Linden, H. (1956), Echter Agonadismus (Anorchismus) bei Geschwistern, *Gynaecologia (Basel) 142:*215.

Sohval, A. R. (1964), Hermaphroditism with "atypical" or "mixed" gonadal dysgenesis, *Am. J. Med. 36:*281.

Stempfell, R. S., Jr. (1970), Abnormalities of the sexual differentiation, in: *Endocrine and Genetic Diseases of Childhood* (L. I. Gardner, ed.), Saunders, Philadelphia.

Witschi, E. (1951), Embryogenesis of the adrenal and the reproductive glands, *Rec. Progr. Hormone Res. 6:*1.

Section III

Hormones and Receptors

8

Molecular Basis of Hormonal Action

Sheldon J. Segal, Rufus Ige, and Mario Burgos
The Population Council
Rockefeller University
New York, New York

There is considerable interest in the mechanism by which steroid hormones elicit characteristic responses in specific target cells. Through the years, various theories have been proposed to explain the basis for the activity of this class of hormones. For example, it has been proposed that steroid hormones may influence membrane permeability of target cells (Segal and Scher, 1967), the transport of metabolites (Segal, 1967), or the formation of cyclic AMP (Szego and Davis, 1967). Other theories invoke a stimulatory effect on specific enzyme systems (Mueller, 1965), an allosteric effect of steroid–protein macromolecules (Talwar *et al.*, 1964), or the activation of gene function (Talwar and Segal, 1971). Evidence supporting the concept that steroid hormones influence gene function has come from several experimental systems, including studies of the effects of estradiol on the rat uterus (Jensen and Jacobson, 1962) and those of progesterone on the chick oviduct (O'Malley *et al.*, 1969). In each case, a primary event after hormone stimulation is rapid increase in the rate of synthesis of messenger RNA. The qualitative nature of the RNA produced differs in the hormone-stimulated and the nonstimulated cell (Trachewsky and Segal, 1967). The effects of these hormones on their respective target cells can be prevented by the inhibition of DNA-dependent RNA synthesis, through the administration of actinomycin D (Talwar and Segal, 1963).

In recent years, a new line of experimentation has evolved, providing direct evidence for the role of hormone-stimulated RNA in the conversion of steroid-dependent cells from the quiescent to the active state. Biologically active RNA can be extracted from the uteri of estrogen-stimulated rats, and this extract is capable of producing in nonstimulated rat uterine epithelium the morphological appearance characteristic of the stimulated state (Segal *et al.,* 1965). The possibility that such an extract contains a residue of contaminating estradiol molecules cannot be ruled out completely (Tuohimaa *et al.,* 1972a). This explanation, however, would not account for the inactivity of RNA preparations derived from other organs of estrogen-treated rats or for the loss of biological activity when RNA from the uteri of estrogen-stimulated rats is preincubated with pancreatic RNase. The latter observations suggest that after the hormone initiates biosynthesis of RNA it is not necessarily involved in subsequent steps leading to the morphological changes.

Similar observations pertaining to the action of progesterone have been made. Treatment of estrogen-primed chicks with progesterone increases the rate of synthesis of nuclear RNA by the oviduct, induces the appearance of new species of RNA (O'Malley *et al.,* 1960), and consequently evokes oviduct synthesis of the hormone-dependent protein avidin (Hertz *et al.,* 1943). The concept that the effect of progesterone is mediated through RNA is supported by the observation that total RNA extracted from progesterone-stimulated chick oviducts can induce avidin synthesis in chicks treated with stilbestrol (Tuohimaa *et al.,* 1972b). Neither RNA from other organs nor oviductal RNA hydrolyzed enzymatically is capable of eliciting this biological response. The shell gland, a specialized region of the chick's Müllerian duct system, does not synthesize avidin in response to progesterone, but does produce avidin when treated with RNA extracted from the oviduct of progesterone-stimulated chicks (Tuohimaa *et al.,* 1972b). Tissue minces of chick oviduct synthesize avidin when progesterone is added *in vitro* to the incubation medium; a total RNA extract of progesterone-stimulated oviducts can duplicate this *in vitro* effect of the hormone (Tuohimaa *et al.,* 1972b). Considerable purification of RNA can be achieved by nitrocellulose trapping (Brawerman *et al.,* 1972). This poly(A)RNA from the oviduct of hormone-treated chicks codes for the synthesis of avidin in a rabbit reticulocyte lysate system (Rosenfeld *et al.,* 1972).

Thus these are examples of homologous *in vivo* transfer of the message for avidin synthesis coded in response to progesterone, as well as of both homologous and heterologous *in vitro* systems in which RNA coded for avidin induces the synthesis of this progesterone-dependent protein, even though the hormone is absent. Furthermore, a highly purified poly(A)RNA synthesized in the oviduct of one avian species under progesterone stimulation can initiate avidin synthesis in another avian species.

METHODS

Preparation of RNA

Female chicks were received in the laboratory from a commercial hatchery on the first day after hatching. They were treated with stilbestrol by subcutaneous injection of 0.5 mg/0.05 ml sesame oil daily for 5 days (days 2–6 after hatching). On day 7, the chicks were administered 5 mg progesterone in 0.25 ml propylene glycol by subcutaneous injection. Chicks thus treated, usually in batches of 100, were sacrificed 12 h after the single injection of progesterone, since this is the approximate time of maximum RNA synthesis in the estrogen-primed, progesterone-treated chick (O'Malley et al., 1969). The oviducts were dissected out, separated from the larger, muscular shell gland, and frozen in glass vessels over dry ice. Extraction of poly(A)RNA was based on the method of Brawerman et al. (1972). Chick or pigeon oviducts were homogenized in 10–15 ml of buffer per gram of tissue. The buffer was 100 mM tris-HCl (pH 7.6), 0.5% sodium dodecylsulfate (SDS), 3 mM $MgCl_2$, 0.32 M sucrose. The homogenate was filtered through cheesecloth and centrifuged at 15,000g for 20 min. One volume of water-saturated phenol was added to the supernatant. After being stirred at 4°C for 30 min, the mixture was centrifuged at 4000g for 30 min. One volume of buffer (100 mM tris-HCl, pH 9.0; 0.5% SDS) was added to the nonaqueous residue, and stirring and centrifuging were repeated. The aqueous phases were combined, and the RNA was precipitated by addition of 0.1 vol of 1 M NaCl and 2.5 vol of ethanol. The alcoholic solution was stored at −20°C overnight. Following centrifugation, the precipitate was washed three times with 0.1 M NaCl–66% ethanol solution. The RNA was dissolved in distilled water and washed five or six times with equal volumes of cold ether. The final ether traces were removed with an air stream. The total RNA fraction, diluted twentyfold, was passed through a nitrocellulose column 40 mm long and 15 mm in diameter equilibrated with the diluent buffer (500 mM KCl; 1 mM $MgCl_2$; 10 mM tris-HCl, pH 7.6). The nitrocellulose was transferred into a centrifuge tube and the RNA eluted with high pH buffer (100 mM tris-HCl, pH 9.0; 0.5% SDS). The RNA solution was repeatedly chilled to 4°C and centrifuged to remove traces of SDS.

The same procedure was used to prepare purified RNA from the oviducts of stilbestrol-primed, progesterone-treated pigeons that were 6 wk old when hormone treatment was begun.

In Vivo Studies

The nitrocellulose-trapped RNA, dissolved in saline solution, was placed in the oviducts of ether-anesthetized chicks or pigeons by means of a 27-gauge needle and a Hamilton syringe. The volume used was 100 μl. The recipient birds were of the same age and had the same schedule of stilbestrol priming as described above. The birds were sacrificed 24 h later, and the avidin content of each treated oviduct, as well as of various controls, was determined by means of a sensitive and specific assay based on binding of avidin to ^{14}C-carbonyl-labeled biotin. A similar procedure was used to test chick RNA in Xenopus laevis. Adult females were anesthetized with Finquel (tricaine methanesulfonate) and a segment of the oviduct was isolated by silk surgical sutures. Into this segment was placed the preparation of RNA in a volume of 100 μl, and the avidin content was determined 24 h later. The *Xenopus* females had intact ovaries which were preovulatory, so that pretreatment with estrogen was not required.

Avidin Assay

Avidin assay was based on the method of Korenman and O'Malley (1967). Tissue was homogenized in 6 ml of 0.02 M phosphate buffer, pH 7.1, containing 0.07 M KCl, 0.004 M $MgCl_2$, and 0.07 M NaCl, and centrifuged at 5000g for 30 min. To 2 ml of supernatant was added 0.5 ml of ^{14}C-biotin (0.01 μCi) in 0.02 M ammonium carbonate solution. The ^{14}C-biotin (20 mCi/mmol) was obtained from The Radiochemical Centre, Amersham, England. The mixture was stirred and left at room temperature for 15 min. One milliliter of bentonite solution (10 mg of bentonite per milliliter of 0.2 M ammonium carbonate) was added. The mixture was centrifuged at 2000g for 10 min. The precipitate was dissolved in 2 ml of 0.2 M ammonium carbonate, and the centrifugation and purification procedure was repeated until the supernatant gave no significant count above the background when dissolved in aquasol. The precipitate was then dissolved in 10 ml of aquasol and counted. Computation of micrograms of avidin per gram of oviduct was based on a standard curve using avidin obtained from Sigma Chemical Company.

Electron Microscopy

The 7-day-old chicks were anesthetized with a mixture of ether and 5% CO_2 in O_2. The heart was exposed, and after the inferior cava vein had been opened at the heart level, the left ventricle was punctured with an 18-gauge needle and 10 ml of diluted Ringer with 15% distilled water was perfused to clear the blood from the circulatory system. The aorta was exposed and cannulated. Five percent glutaraldehyde in 0.1 M s-collidine buffer, pH 7.4, was perfused at room temperature. The perfusion lasted approximately 30 min. The oviduct was removed and the magnum portion sectioned into small strips. Fixation was continued by immersion in fresh fixative to complete 1 h, followed by a 1-h wash in s-collidine buffer, 0.1 M pH 7.4, with $CaCl_2$ and sucrose (Burgos *et al.*, 1967). The subsequent steps were refixing during 1 h in 1% OsO_4, 0.1 M s-collidine buffer, pH 7.4, with $CaCl_2$ and sucrose, treating for 20 min in 1% uranyl acetate in water, dehydrating through ethyl alcohols and propylene oxide, and embedding in epon aralidite mixture. Thick and thin sections were cut in a Porter Blum ultramicrotome and stained with toluidine blue borax and lead-uranyl salts, respectively. Observations and micrographs were made in a Phillips 300 microscope.

Portions of the magnum of perfused oviducts were opened, and the inner surface was exposed and sectioned in small squares of approximately 5 mm. They were left in 1% OsO_4, 1 M s-collidine buffer, pH 7.4, with $CaCl_2$ and sucrose in the cold for 4 h, then dehydrated through acetones from 70% to 100% and dehydrated and dried in the critical-point drying apparatus (Denton) with liquid CO_2. The blocks were mounted in colloidal graphite and covered with carbon and gold in a Denton vacuum evaporator. The specimens were studied in an Autoscan (ETEC Corporation) at 20 kV at a magnification of 1500–20,000X.

RESULTS

Morphology

The 7-day chick oviduct is characterized by a single, low columnar epithelium. There are occasional invaginations, but no distinct glandular development. The fine structure reveals an absence of secretory activity. More details of the fine structure are described in the caption of Fig. 2. At the level of the scanning electron microscope, it is evident that some hormonally independent differentiation of the epithelium occurs. Occasionally, single cilia are observed across the entire surface of the oviduct, and scattered clusters of cilia from either a single cell or groups of contiguous cells can be observed (Fig. 1).

Stilbestrol treatment causes an increase in cell height (Fig. 4), but the most characteristic feature of the estrogen-treated oviduct is the development of secretory glands, opening into the lumen of the oviduct. The development of cilia is evident, but large areas of the surface do not have cilia (Fig. 3). At the opening of glands, some of the columnar lining epithelial cells have dense or clear secretory granules in abundance. There is no evidence of secretory activity along most of the free border of the oviductal lumen.

Exposure to progesterone, after treatment with stilbestrol, causes an enhancement of secretory activity and more extensive ciliogenesis. The latter process is striking when viewed on the surface (Fig. 5) or in the ultrathin sections (Fig. 6). The cell height is increased; the cytoplasm has an abundance of membrane organelles and polysomes. The nucleus is rich in particulate matter and the nucleoli are complex and elaborate.

RNA-treated animals have oviducts that are almost indistinguishable from those resulting from progesterone treatment. Cilia formation is extensive and there is evident secretory activity (Fig. 7). Basal bodies are seen at the free border and in deeper portions of the cells as well. It is evident that ciliary processes are being organized even in many cells that do not have cilia protruding into the lumen (Fig. 8).

These observations can be summarized as follows. The undifferentiated

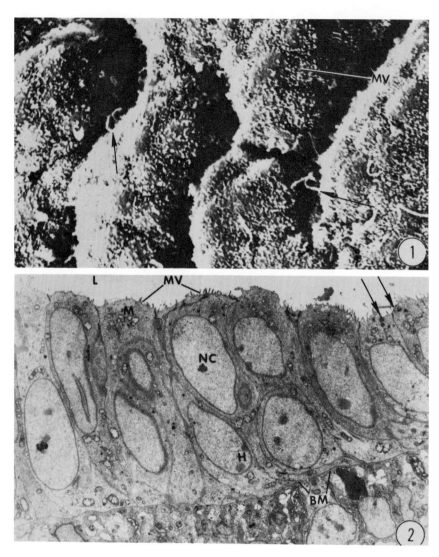

FIGS. 1 and *2. A portion of the magnum zone of the oviduct of untreated 7-day-old-chicks.*
Figure 1 is a scanning electron micrograph (SEM), and Fig. 2 is a transmission electron
micrograph (TEM), both magnified 2700X. Figure 1 shows a few ciliated processes (arrows)
emerging from the oviduct inner surface, which is partially covered with short microvilli
(MV). Figure 2 shows a portion of the epithelial surface. Visible features are scattered short
microvilli (MV), a basal body and a portion of cilia (arrows), the pale nuclei with
heterochromatin clumps (H), and a few small and dense nucleoli (NC); mitochondria (M) are
pale and globular and have few cristae. Lumen (L) and basement membrane (BM) are
indicated.

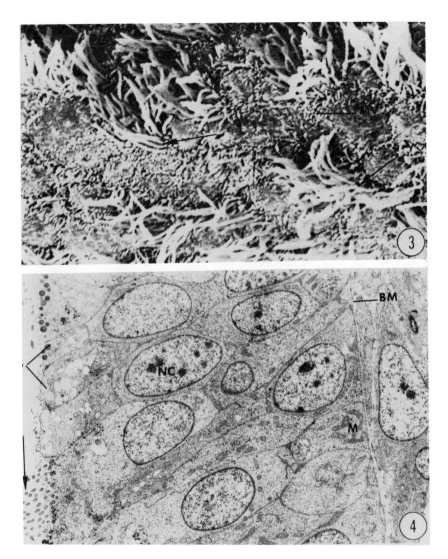

FIGS. 3 and *4. The magnum portion of the oviduct of 7-day-old chicks treated with stilbestrol and saline.* Figure 3 is a SEM micrograph and Fig. 4 a TEM micrograph, both at 2700×. Figure 3 shows the oviduct surface partially covered by clusters of cilia (arrows) and short microvilli. Figure 4 shows a portion of the epithelial surface, lumen (at left), and basement membrane (BM); the cells have ciliated processes (arrow) and some secretory activity. Nuclei are denser and with more prominent nucleoli (NC); mitochondria (M) are elongated, dense, and more numerous than those in Fig. 2.

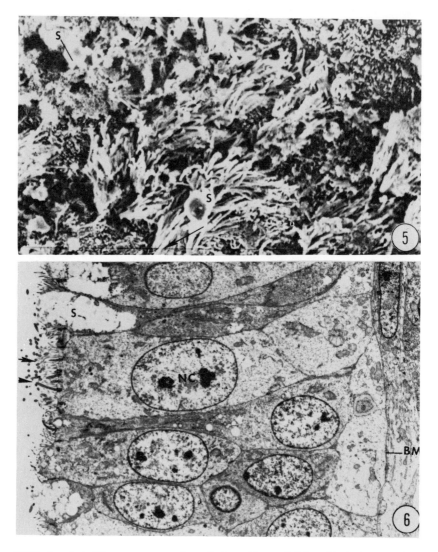

FIGS. 5 and 6. *The magnum portion of the oviduct of 7-day-old chicks treated with stilbestrol and progesterone.* Figure 5 is a SEM micrograph and Fig. 6 a TEM micrograph, both at 2700X. Figure 5 is a surface view of the numerous clusters of ciliated processes (arrow) coated by the secretory product of the glandular cells. Numerous tightly packed microvilli are shown in areas full of cilia. Figure 6 shows a portion of the surface epithelium with ciliated cells (arrow) and glandular cells (S). The nuclei are larger and denser with prominent nucleoli (NC), and the cells are taller than those in Figs. 2 and 4. Lumen is to the left and basement membrane (BM) to the right.

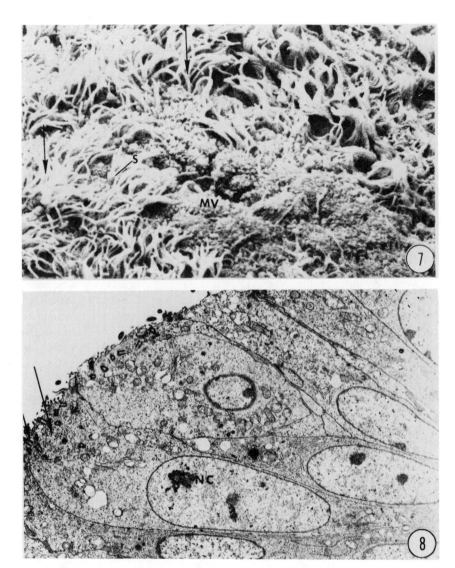

FIGS. 7 and *8. The magnum portion of the oviduct of 7-day-old chicks treated with stilbestrol and RNA.* Figure 7 is a SEM micrograph and Fig. 8 a TEM micrograph, both at 2700×. Figure 7 shows the luminal surface with numerous ciliated processes (arrows) emerging from an irregular surface with microvilli (MV) and secretory material (S). Figure 8 shows a portion of the surface epithelium; the cells contain numerous basal bodies and dense particles related to ciliogenesis (arrows). The nuclei are large and have well-developed nucleoli (NC). The secretory activity is less marked than that shown in Fig. 6.

oviductal cells can undergo a spontaneous specialization of ciliated cells in the absence of hormone stimulation. This results in isolated cilia across the surface of the oviduct, but there is no evidence of secretory function. With stilbestrol treatment, waves of ciliogenesis are initiated, glandular development occurs, and an abundance of dense secretory granules appear in the glandular epithelial cells and occasionally in the bordering oviductal lining. Subsequent treatment with progesterone increases the amount of secretory activity. The secretory granules found within the glandular epithelium are frequently polymorphic, and secretory material is present in the glands and in the oviductal lumen. The luminal secretion tends to cause a matting of cilia when portions of the oviduct are prepared for scanning electron microscopy. The addition of progesterone has a pronounced effect on cilia formation as well. Within 24 h, almost the entire oviductal surface becomes ciliated.

Avidin Synthesis

Avidin synthesis by the chick oviduct is shown in Table I. It should be noted that earlier results revealed that an intraoviductal dose of 500 μg of total RNA from stilbestrol/progesterone-treated chick oviducts was required to stimulate avidin synthesis in estrogen-primed chicks (Szego and Davis, 1967). Nitrocellulose trapping effects a purification of approximately fiftyfold. The RNA recovered after nitrocellulose chromatography stimulates avidin synthesis at a dose of 10 μg. This activity is lost when the poly(A) RNA is pretreated with pancreatic RNase. The oviduct of the stilbestrol-primed chick responds to

TABLE I. Avidin Synthesis by the Chick Oviduct in Response to Homologous and Heterologous RNA

| Number of cases | Final 24-h treatment[a] | | | Avidin (μg/g) |
	Material	Amount (μg)	Route	
6	None	–	–	0
6	Saline	–	i.o.	0
6	Progesterone	5000	s.c.	1.86 ± 0.76
7	Chick RNA	10	i.o.	0.83 ± 0.42
6	Chick RNA, RNase-incubated	10	i.o.	0
10	Pigeon RNA	10	i.o.	0.5 ± 0.2

[a]All chicks were pretreated with 0.5 mg stilbestrol daily for 5 days. s.c., Subcutaneous; i.o., intraoviductal. Bovine pancreatic RNase was used. Treatment of RNA was for 10 min at 37°C, followed by inactivation of the enzyme by heat (65°C). The chicks used were Rhode Island Reds, obtained from Hall Brothers Hatchery, Wallingford, Connecticut.

TABLE II. Avidin Synthesis by the Pigeon Oviduct in Response
to Homologous and Heterologous RNA

| Number of cases | Final 24-h treatment[a] | | | Avidin (μg/g) |
	Material	Amount (μg)	Route	
10	None	–	–	0
12	Progesterone	5000	s.c.	0.9 ± 0.4
6	Pigeon mRNA	10	i.o.	0.12 ± 0.03
10	Chick mRNA	50	i.o.	0.53 ± 0.25
6	Chick mRNA, RNase-incubated	50	i.o.	0

[a]All pigeons were pretreated with 0.5 mg stilbestrol daily for 5 days. s.c.,
Subcutaneous; i.o., intraoviductal. Bovine pancreatic RNase was used.
Treatment of RNA was for 10 min at 37°C, followed by inactivation of the
enzyme by heat (65°C). The pigeons used were White Carneaux, obtained
from Palmetto Pigeon Plant, Sumter, South Carolina.

poly(A) RNA extracted from the oviducts of pigeons treated with stilbestrol and
progesterone. There is no avidin present in the oviducts of stilbestrol-primed
chicks serving as controls (intraoviductal instillation of saline).

Like the chick oviduct, and that of several other species reported previously
(Hertz and Sebrell, 1943), the oviduct of the estrogen-primed pigeon synthesizes
avidin in response to progesterone. At approximately 24 h after the administration of progesterone, the highest levels of avidin in the pigeon oviduct are
achieved. This response is also brought about by intraoviductal administration of
homologous oviductal RNA prepared from hormone-treated pigeons (Table II).

A dose of 10 μg of poly(A) RNA elicits a significant level of avidin synthesis.
The pigeon oviduct also responds to poly(A) RNA recovered from hormone-
treated chicks. Pretreatment of the RNA preparation with pancreatic RNase
eliminates the activity.

Avidin is found in the egg jelly of amphibians (Hertz and Sebrell, 1942).
Presumably, it is synthesized in some portion of the oviduct, although this has
not been demonstrated. The administration of progesterone in high dosage,
either in the dorsal lymph sac or intraoviductally, fails to cause measurable
avidin synthesis by the oviduct of Xenopus laevis females. Avidin is produced,
however, after the instillation of 50 μg of mRNA isolated from the oviduct of
progesterone-treated chicks (Table III).

DISCUSSION

The heterospecific transfer of hormonal stimulation, through the mediation
of hormone-induced RNA in vivo, is of interest with respect to the specificity of

TABLE III. Avidin Synthesis by *Xenopus* Oviduct in Response to Heterologous RNA

Number of cases	24-h treatment[a]			Avidin (μg/g)
	Material	Amount	Route	
4	None	–	–	0
4	Progesterone	5 mg	i.o.	0
4	Progesterone	5 mg	d.l.	0
4	Chick RNA	50 μg	i.o.	0.13

[a]*Xenopus* specimens were mature females with preovulatory ovaries intact (*Xenopus laevis* Daudin). i.o., Intraoviductal; d.l., dorsal lymph sac.

RNA coding in the vertebrate classes, as well as in relation to the evolution of hormonal control mechanisms. Evidently the progesterone–receptor complex (O'Malley and Toft, 1971) interacts with highly similar or identical chromatin acceptor sites in the nuclei of the chick, the pigeon, and *Xenopus,* and does not discriminate among them. Thus once the hormone stimulates the production of RNA coded for avidin synthesis in the oviductal nuclei of any of the species tested, the hormone molecule itself is no longer required and the newly synthesized RNA can complete the steps leading to avidin synthesis, interchangeably among the oviductal cells of the several species. This may be the physiological basis for the interspecies cross-reaction of many hormones. The activity of chick RNA in *Xenopus* is of particular interest. Progesterone itself, at least under the conditions used, is unable to cause avidin synthesis in *Xenopus* oviduct. Possibly the dose, mode of administration, or timing of exposure and sacrifice was not optimal for the demonstration of the role of progesterone in the control of avidin synthesis by the amphibian oviduct. Nevertheless, the response to chick RNA suggests that the synthetic pathways for avidin synthesis have evolved in the *Xenopus* oviduct and that this evolutionary development occurred prior to the evolution of the control mechanism by progesterone found to exist in avian species. It will be of interest to determine whether progesterone itself, or a related progestin, is normally produced by the *Xenopus* ovary.

The morphological observations reveal that a small degree of spontaneous differentiation of ciliated cells occurs in the epithelium of the chick oviduct prior to gonadal development and sex-hormone stimulation. There is no secretory gland development without estrogen influence. With the onset of estrogenic stimulation, ciliogenesis and glandular development proceed and secretory activity begins. The addition of progesterone markedly increases the secretory activity and causes new types of secretory granules to appear. The oviductal surface becomes abundantly ciliated within 24 h after the initiation of progesterone stimulation. All of the morphological effects of progesterone can be achieved by RNA extracted from hormone-stimulated oviducts. Thus both the morphological and the physiological effects of progesterone can be brought about by the homologous or heterologous transfer of RNA (Segal *et al.,* 1973).

Most likely, the active component is a form of messenger RNA, since it is highly purified by nitrocellulose trapping (Brawerman *et al.,* 1972). It is clear that a contaminating residue of progesterone cannot account for the avidin synthesis noted after RNA administration (Tuohimaa, *et al.,* 1972b). This conclusion is confirmed by the present observation of avidin induction with the purified RNA preparation that is active at a dose as low as 10 μg. As in earlier experiments with either progesterone-induced RNA or estrogen-induced RNA, enzymatic degradation with pancreatic RNase eliminates the activity.

These experiments do not reveal whether the exogenous RNA is translated directly or acts in some manner at the nuclear level to influence transcription of avidin-coded RNA. A lack of absolute antigenic identity among the avidin molecules produced by different species, if found to exist, would provide an excellent experimental basis for resolution of this question.

SUMMARY

The action of progesterone in mediating the synthesis of avidin by the chick oviduct can be stimulated by the intraoviductal instillation of nitrocellulose-trapped RNA from hormonally prepared chick or pigeon oviduct. Similarly, the pigeon oviduct synthesizes avidin in response to chick oviduct RNA. Thus a heterospecific transfer of hormonal stimulation, through the transfer of progesterone-induced RNA, is demonstrated. This can also be achieved between vertebrate classes. The oviduct of *Xenopus laevis* synthesizes avidin in response to mRNA extracted from the progesterone-stimulated chick, even though progesterone itself does not cause avidin synthesis at the doses employed. The morphological effects of progesterone, including the stimulation of cilia formation and secretory activity, can also be achieved by the intraoviductal administration of nitrocellulose-trapped RNA. The biological activity is lost following pancreatic RNase digestion. The fiftyfold purification achieved by nitrocellulose chromatography of the total RNA preparation suggests that the activity resides in a messenger RNA fraction.

ACKNOWLEDGMENTS

The authors are grateful to Mr. Andrew Gonzalez, Mr. Delbert Layne, and Mr. Edward Tovar for their technical assistance. This work was supported by USPHS Grant No. HD 05671.

REFERENCES

Brawerman, G., Medecki, J., and Lee, S. Y. (1972), A procedure for the isolation of mammalian messenger ribonucleic acid, *Biochemistry 11:*637–641.

Burgos, M. H., Vitale-Calpe, R., and Tellez de Iñón, M. T. (1967), Studies on paraformaldehyde fixation for electron microscopy, *J. Microscop. 6:*457–468.

Hertz, R., and Sebrell, W. E. (1942), Occurrence of avidin in the oviduct and secretions of the genital tract of several species, *Science 96:*257.

Hertz, R., Fraps, R. M., and Sebrell, W. E. (1943), Induction of avidin formation in the avian oviduct by stilbestrol plus progesterone, *Proc. Soc. Exp. Biol. Med. 52:*142–144.

Jensen, E. V., and Jacobson, H. T. (1962), Basic guides to the mechanism of estrogen action, *Rec. Progr. Hormone Res. 18:*387–414.

Korenman, S. G., and O'Malley, B. W. (1967), Avidin assay: A new procedure suitable for tissue fraction, *Biochim. Biophys. Acta 140:*174–176.

Mueller, G. C. (1965), The role of RNA and protein synthesis in estrogen action, in: *Mechanisms of Hormone Action,* pp. 228–245 (P. Karlson, ed.), Academic Press, New York.

O'Malley, B. W., and Toft, D. O. (1971), Progesterone-binding components of chick oviduct, *J. Biol. Chem. 246:*1117–1122. O'Malley, B. W., McGuire, W. L., Kohler, P. O., and Korenman, S. G. (1969), Studies on the mechanism of steroid hormone regulation of synthesis of specific proteins, *Rec. Progr. Hormone Res. 25:*105–160.

Rosenfeld, G. C., Comstock, J. P., Means, A. R., and O'Malley, B. W. (1972), A rapid method for the isolation and partial purification of specific eucaryotic messenger RNA's, *Biochem. Biophys. Res. Commun. 47:*387–392.

Segal, S. J. (1967), Regulatory action of estrogenic hormones, in: *Control Mechanisms in Developmental Processes,* pp. 264–280 (M. Locke, ed.), Academic Press, New York.

Segal, S. J., and Scher, W. (1967), Estrogens, nucleic acids, and protein synthesis in uterine metabolism, in: *Cellular Biology of the Uterus,* pp. 114–150. (R. M. Wynn, ed.), Appleton-Century-Crofts, New York.

Segal, S. J., Davidson, O. W., and Wada, K. (1965), The role of RNA in the regulatory action of estrogen, *Proc. Natl. Acad. Sci. (U.S.A.) 54:*782–787.

Segal, S. J., Ige, R., Tuohimaa, P., and Burgos, M. (1973), Progesterone-dependent mRNA: Heterospecific activity in vivo, *Science,* in press.

Szego, C. M., and Davis, J. S. (1967), Adenosine 3',5'-monophosphate in rat uterus: Acute elevation by estrogen, *Proc. Natl. Acad. Sci. (U.S.A.) 58:*1711–1718.

Talwar, G. P., and Segal, S. J. (1963), Prevention of hormone action by local application of actinomycin-D, *Proc. Natl. Acad. Sci. (U.S.A.) 50:*226–230.

Talwar, G. P., and Segal, S. J. (1971), Studies on mechanism of action of estrogens, in: *The Sex Steroids,* pp. 241–272 (K. W. McKerns, ed.), Appleton-Century-Crofts, New York.

Talwar, G. P., Segal, S. J., Evans, A., and Davison, O. W. (1964), The binding of estradiol in the uterus: A mechanism for depression of RNA synthesis, *Proc. Natl. Acad. Sci. (U.S.A.) 52:*1059–1066.

Trachewsky, D., and Segal, S. J. (1967), Selective stimulation of ribonucleic acid synthesis in uterine nuclei by estradiol-17-beta, *Biochem. Biophys. Res. Commun. 27:*588–594.

Tuohimaa, P., Segal, S. J., and Koide, S. S. (1972a), Study on uterine ribonucleic acid with estrogenic activity, *J. Steroid Biochem. 3:*503–513.

Tuohimaa, P., Segal, S. J., and Koide, S. S. (1972b), Induction of avidin synthesis by RNA obtained from chick oviduct, *Proc. Natl. Acad. Sci. (U.S.A.) 69:*2814–2817.

9

The Mode of Action of Steroid Hormones: Some Recent Findings

Etienne-Emile Baulieu

Laboratoire de Chimie Biologique
Faculté de Médicine
Unité de Recherches sur le Métabolisme Moléculaire
et la Physio-Pathologie des Stéroides de
l'Institut National de la Santé et de la Recherche Médicale
Paris, France

Hormones are chemical signals which connect different parts of the organism. Steroids are small (molecular weight on the order of 300), rather rigid, lipophilic molecules. In mammals, the main steroid hormones are the gluco- and the mineralocorticosteroids, which are vital for the survival of the individual, and the sex steroids, the main subject of the present discussion, which are essential to the reproductive processes and thus to the maintenance of the species.

There is evidence that, beyond the remarkable diversity of effects of hormones, the major features of both the primary interaction of steroids with the target cells and the onset of the response may be similar, and the concepts discussed here receive much support from the data of many investigators studying a variety of systems. Only the very early steps in hormone action are considered here, since once the response has been triggered the hormone itself plays no more role and can leave the cell. Further changes proceed according to the state of differentiation, aging, nutrition, etc. of the target cell and follow different patterns which are not discussed in this chapter. Steroid hormones may be involved in irreversible changes of the state of differentiation, and this is clearly the case with estrogens (e.g., in immature chick oviduct) and androgens (e.g., in differentiating male secondary sex organs in mammals). Only reversible systems are dealt with here. The growth-promoting effect, as in the responses of the immature or castrated adult rat uterus to estradiol or ventral prostate to testosterone, will be more particularly examined.

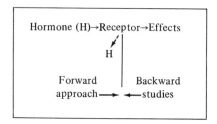

FIG. 1. Strategy for studying hormone action. After the hormone–receptor interaction which switches on the response, H leaves (dashed arrow).

Although they often stimulate sizable macroscopic events, hormones are themselves in very low concentration when on the way to or at the site of action. One nanomole can be taken as a sort of general mean concentration that is observed in many hormonal systems. It corresponds approximately to 0.3 ng/ml of steroid (i.e., 20 μg for a 60-kg human body taken as a homogeneous container) and approximately to 1000 molecules per cell arbitrarily assuming an even cellular distribution. Therefore, it was logical that a *forward approach* to study of the mechanism of hormone action, following the steroid on its way to the "receptor," where the last and most fundamental interaction with the cell takes place (Fig. 1) (Baulieu *et al.*, 1971), could be developed only by use of highly labeled tritiated compounds. Important advances have been made recently, especially in the methods for purifying the estradiol receptor. The phenomenon of receptor "activation," which may be the earliest effect of a hormone in the cell, and the control of receptor availability in target cells are hopefully related to cellular "receptivity."

The effects of hormones can also be analyzed in *backward studies*, looking for the earliest molecular events which follow the exposure to a hormone. These investigations are limited not only because of present technical difficulties, but also because they must be based on an arbitrary decision as to which of the cellular constituents to measure, inspired for the best—or the worst—by current theories in cell biology.

STEROID HORMONES AND PROTEINS

General

The steroid hormones are constantly interacting with different specific proteins during the processes involved in their biosynthesis, distribution, transfer, and final fate in target cells. Specificity means that the steroid structure is "understood," and only proteins can provide the necessary spatial configuration and reactivity. This "qualitative" specificity cannot be dissociated from a quantitative parameter, high affinity, since the interacting sites have to deal with low concentrations of hormone molecules.

There are catalytic proteins, enzymes, at the level of which the hormone is transformed into other products. These "metabolites" are either inactive, as in classical degradative metabolism, or active, and indeed there exists an activating metabolism, which has been recently recognized.

There are also noncatalyzing specific binding proteins, which have also been studied recently. Their concentration is of the same order of magnitude as that of the hormonal ligand, in contrast to enzymes, which are present in much lower amounts than their substrates and products. Their analysis has necessitated some methodological developments. The binding proteins essentially found in the plasma are called "transport" proteins. The others, present in target cells, are called "receptors."

It may be more useful to classify proteins according to their function than according to their localization. For instance, there are receptors in hormone-secreting cells of the corpus luteum and of the testis (interstitial cells) which bind estradiol, and receptors in hepatocytes which metabolize hormones and respond to estrogens and glucocorticosteroids. Conversely, there are enzymes metabolizing steroids in most target cells.

The intracellular location of receptor proteins implies that steroid hormones penetrate into their target cells. This fundamental difference from other hormones, which most likely stop at the membrane level, is naturally of the greatest importance. Another important consideration is that the steroid–protein interactions are noncovalent binding.

Binding Determinations

The various techniques for binding determinations have been reviewed in terms of their practicality, precision, and also adherence to the physical principles for meaningful determination of the parameters (Baulieu *et al.*, 1970).

Calculations of binding equilibrium may be very simple if there is a single binding system, and for all the steroid-binding proteins so far tested the law of mass action is followed. The Scatchard plot is the most convenient since it linearizes the data. However, as indicated on the second row of Fig. 2, if there is not just one "specific" binding system (S) of relatively high affinity and low capacity (saturable) but rather, as in most biological samples, an S system plus a "nonspecific" system (NS) characterized by low afffinity and/or nonsaturability (infinite or practically infinite capacity), the Scatchard plot is difficult to use and almost impossible when the situation is more complex.

To overcome this difficulty, we have proposed the "proportion graph" methodology, a log-log plot which makes it possible to cover several orders of magnitude of total hormone concentration and to expand the scale of representation of the bound ligand (because it is expressed as the log of a proportion). By use of such a representation, a complex binding mixture can be studied (Fig. 2); the affinity and concentration of sites are determined with the help of a computer program.

Based on the fact that in most cases a slow dissociation of the hormone–protein complex corresponds to a high affinity, we often use a method called "differential dissociation." The technique simplifies the binding situation before calculation: the unbound ligand is constantly removed (e.g., by charcoal adsorption), whether it is originally free or released from complex(es), and this leads to the elimination, over a given period of time, of the rapidly dissociating components. As indicated in Fig. 3, it is thus possible to see the first-order dissociation of the higher-affinity complex, and then by extrapolating back to the ordinate axis to readily determine the concentration of its binding sites in the original mixture (Baulieu *et al.*, 1970).

Kinetic measurements of the association and dissociation rate constants are also of great interest, and can be successfully obtained (Truong and Baulieu, 1971).

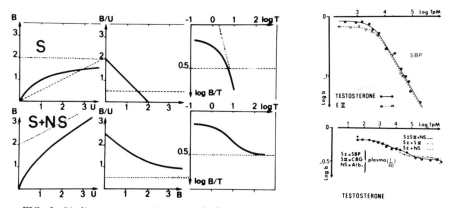

FIG. 2. *Binding representation and calculation.* Two binding systems are represented, S ("specific"), of high affinity and limited capacity, and NS ("nonspecific"), of weaker affinity and not saturable under the usual experimental conditions. The two systems follow the law of mass action and are independent. The graphs on the left deal with a theoretical example. On the upper row, the two systems S and NS are represented separately. The Scatchard plot linearizes S, the parameters of which are easy to obtain. On the lower row, the S + NS sum is drawn. The direct plotting and the Scatchard plot do not allow complete representation of binding, and the proportion graph is very useful. The two graphs on the right show actual experiments with purified SBP binding testosterone (T) and estradiol (E_{II}) (upper) and human plasma (1/40 diluted) (lower) where T binds to two specific proteins, SBP and transcortin (CBG), and to nonspecific protein, mostly albumin (ALB). In the latter case, black dots are experimental points and the three curves are obtained by computing on the basis of three different programs: only the model with two S and one NS fits the data. B, U, and T, are bound, unbound, and total ligand concentration, respectively, and b is B/T.

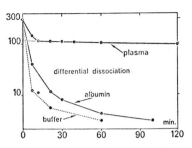

FIG. 3. *"Differential dissociation."* The radio-active mixture is agitated in the presence of an adsorbant which takes up the unbound ligand (dextran-coated charcoal). Hormone (radioactive cortisol) is removed rapidly in the presence of a buffer solution or of fast-dissociating hormone–albumin complexes. When unbound or rapidly released hormone has been adsorbed, the high-affinity hormone–CBG complex of the plasma dissociates slowly (ordinate in 10^3 cpm).

TRANSPORT PLASMA PROTEINS

In general, steroid hormones are distributed to organs after a relatively long voyage in the blood plasma.* Plasma proteins bind approximately 90% of the steroids, although their hydrosolubility would be enough to insure solubilization.

Albumin, because of its very high concentration, is a reasonable candidate for hormone binding and can bind most steroid hormones with a K_D on the order of 10–100 μM. However, it does not show specificity, and for most hormones there appears to be another plasma protein(s) of higher affinity and of relatively narrow specificity which takes in charge by far the most of each one. Westphal (1971) has reviewed this topic. Table I is a summary of the main well-characterized proteins, in fact all glucoproteins. These include transcortin or *corticosteroid binding globulin* (CBG) (see Westphal, 1971), human *sex steroid binding plasma protein* (SBP) (Mercier-Bodard *et al.*, 1970), rat estradiol binding plasma protein (EBP) (Raynaud *et al.*, 1971), rabbit testosterone binding globulin (R-TeBG) (Mahoudeau and Corvol, 1973), and guinea pig progesterone binding plasma protein (PBP) (Milgrom *et al.*, 1973d). Their hormonal specificity and their concentration indicate that they are not necessary for hormone action (even if some subtle regulation may be involved). For example, there is no estradiol and/or testosterone high-affinity binding protein in adult rat plasma,† and neither the SBP of the human nor the EBP of the rat binds diethylstilbestrol, an active nonsteroidal estrogen. The physicological determinant of guinea pig PBP concentration is also quite puzzling, since it is found in the maternal blood but not in the fetus, whereas the rat EBP is a fetoprotein. Another aspect is the simultaneous presence of several high-affinity binding proteins for a given hormone. For example, testosterone is bound by both SBP and CBG; Fig. 2 shows testosterone binding to the complex mixture of human

---

*There are a few exceptions of regional distribution, such as testosterone, which is secreted by interstitial cells and partially passes directly into the seminiferous tubules.

†In the rat there is no testosterone binding globulin, but in both the rabbit and the rat an androgen binding protein (ABP) (French and Ritzen, 1973) has been isolated from the vas difirens which may be involved in the delivery of testosterone to the epididymis.

TABLE I. Extracellular Steroid Binding Proteins[a]

	Binding						Concentration	
	F,B	P	T	E_II	DES		μM	Regulation
Corticosteroid binding globulin (CBG) human, rat, guinea pig plasma	+++	+++	+	±	0	Human adult Pregnant human Pregnant Guinea pig	0.7 2.0 50	Estrogens ↑ Thyroxin↑
Sex steroid binding plasma protein (SBP) human	–	–	+++ 5α++++	+++ Estrone ±	0	Human adult Pregnant human	0.07 0.02	Estrogens ↑
Estradiol binding plasma protein (EBP) rat	–	–	–	+++ Estrone++++	0	Rat fetus Rat adult	75 0	Fetoprotein
Progesterone binding plasma protein (PBP) pregnant guinea pig	–	+++	+	0		Pregnant guinea pig Fetus	20 0	Estrogens →
Testosterone binding globulin (R - TeBG) rabbit plasma	0	0	+++ 5α++++	± Estrone ±	0		0.18	
Androgen binding protein (ABP) rat efferent duct fluid	–	–	+++ 5α++++	–	–		0.085	

[a] F, Cortisol; B, corticosterone; P, progesterone; T, testosterone; 5α, testosterone 5α-metabolites; E_II, estradiol; DES, diethylstilbestrol; + and 0, relative affinity (++++ and +++ in the 1–10 nM range for K_D at 4°C).

plasma proteins and to purified SBP, incidentally demonstrating that the proportion graph can directly give both the concentration and the affinity of SBP in a mixture also containing CBG and albumin, as well as the proportion of testosterone binding to the different proteins.

Conversely, rather different ligands may be bound by the same protein with high affinity $(K_A \sim 10^{8-9} \ M^{-1})$, most likely to the same site, e.g., glucocorticoids and progesterone to CBG and estradiol and testosterone to SBP, a finding which has not been satisfactorily explained in physiological terms.

Finally, the role of specific steroid binding plasma proteins is still unknown. It has been suggested that they intervene in the secretion of hormone from the glandular cells or that they protect hormones against red cell and liver metabolizing enzymes. There is also the possibility that they cross the vascular wall and recognize some target cell membrane element, or even enter the cell; indeed, CBG has been found in uterine cells (Milgrom and Baulieu, 1970). However, it is generally accepted at present that they do not serve for directed transport but only as a sort of reservoir and/or buffer system, facilitating delivery if there is more tissue demand or protecting target cells in case of a hormone excess; this function appears quite possible because it is now known that the pattern of steroid hormone secretion can be discontinuous (Hellman et al., 1970).

ENTRY INTO TARGET CELLS

Since steroid hormones enter target cells, the modalities involved in the penetration process must be discussed. It has generally been assumed that there is a nonspecific simple diffusion permitting virtually unlimited numbers of these nonionic lipidic and small molecules to pass easily through lipoprotein membranes.* Therefore, there should also be diffusion into nontarget cells, from which the hormones could reflux immediately, in contrast to their fate in target cells where they encounter enzymes and/or intracellular binding proteins.

There is some evidence (Milgrom et al., 1973a) that there may be a protein-mediated step controlling the entry of estradiol into rat uterus target cells. Experimentally, the stability of the estrogen–receptor complex in the uterus permits measurement of the intracellular hormone once it has entered the cell, since it dissociates very slowly and can be conveniently determined. Conversely, the features pertinent to the entry of the hormone must be distinguished from those related to the receptor characteristics, possible metabolism, exit, etc. In other words, entry is only one step in a series of events.

Three sets of data have been obtained. First, calculations of the rate of entry vs. concentration indicate saturability (Fig. 4a), with an apparent affinity corre-

---

*The charged steroid sulfates and glucuronides do not enter cells except in the placenta and the liver.

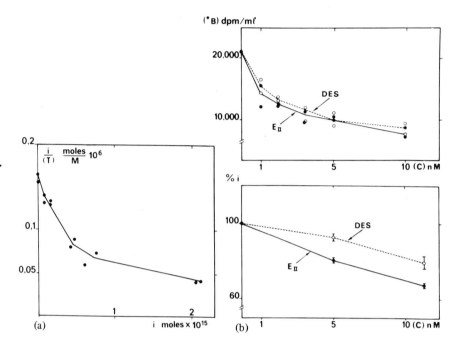

FIG. 4. Entry of estradiol into immature rat uterus target cell. (a) Saturability. The graph (Scatchard-like plot) correlates i, the incorporation of estradiol per uterine horn per minute, and T, the total concentration of steroid obtained at 37°C in 5-min experiments over a concentration range of 0.1–50 nM of ^{3}H-estradiol. (b) Specificity. Competition with radioactive estradiol for entry by nonradioactive estradiol (E_{II}) and diethylstilbestrol (DES) at 37°C. The upper graph shows binding (B) of ^{3}H-estradiol, 0.5 nM, to the cytosol receptor in the presence of various concentrations of nonlabeled estrogens. The lower graph shows incorporation (i) measured in 5-min experiments with various concentrations of competitor (C) and ^{3}H-estradiol, 1 nM. i 100% is obtained in the absence of competitor.

sponding to a $K_D \sim 5$ nM (whereas the K_D of the intracellular receptor under the same experimental conditions is ~ 0.5 nM). Second, there is hormone specificity for the entry step, since estrone and estriol behave similarly to estradiol but nonestrogenic hormones do not. Moreover, the competition of estradiol and diethylstilbestrol with radioactive estradiol for entry is differential, whereas they have the same competitive binding activity for the intracellular receptor, a finding which clearly makes it possible to distinguish between the two interactions (Fig. 4b). Third, experiments where uterine tissue is exposed to SH blocking agents such as α-iodoacetamide, dithiobisnitrobenzoic acid (DTNB), and parachloromercurophenyl sulfonate (PCMPS), which is reputed not to enter cells, indicate an inhibition of entry not explained by the inhibition of the intracellular binding protein. This favors involvement of a protein in the entry step. No energy source seems necessary for the entry phenomenon, which is not affected by various active transport inhibitors. This apparent protein-facilitated diffusion remains to be proven autonomously and not indirectly due to another of the sequential events of the hormone's fate. Its molecular basis is still unkown, and it is not even excluded that the intracellular receptor in a membrane position could have different properties from the solubilized form.

METABOLISM IN TARGET CELLS AND THEIR ACTION

Once the circulating steroid has entered the target cell, there are two possibilities.

First, only this steroid is found at all times in the tissue, and therefore its direct involvement in action is probable; in other words, there is no metabolic chemical transformation into another steroid, and the interaction of the hormone with the cellular constituent(s) is only "physical." This is the case in the immature and adult castrated rat uterus exposed to estrogen, in which unchanged estradiol is recovered (Jensen and Jacobson, 1962). Indeed, this is not only an interesting result *per se* but also an argument against the possibility that the hormone acts as a cosubstrate (coenzyme). An example is the enzymatic step directing a steroidal hydrogen atom into a privileged pool of pyridine nucleotide and then changing the metabolism equilibrium (Talalay and Williams-Ashman, 1960).

In fact, in many (most) cases both the original steroid and its metabolites are in the target tissue. This is true even for estradiol in the uterus of the adult (intact) rat and many other animals, in which estrone is very often found, too. In the androgen-responsive tissues, where several testosterone metabolites and the corresponding enzymes (review in Ofner, 1968) are found, the question of a direct relationship between local steroid metabolism and action is raised.

There may indeed be some "ancillary" metabolism at the target cell level, decreasing the availability of the hormone to the receptor or contributing to its exit after interaction with the receptor. These are obviously interesting possibilities for modulation of hormone action, even if the regulatory mechanism is then indirect.

In 1967, following the description of the so-called 17β-hydroxy metabolic pathway of testosterone (Baulieu and Mauvais-Jarvis, 1964), we began to evaluate the role of androgen metabolism at the target level.

Simultaneously and independently, the elegant *in vivo* studies of J. Wilson demonstrated that androstanolone (or 5α-dihydrotestosterone; DHT) is retained in the nuclei of target tissues (Bruchovsky and Wilson, 1968; Wilson and Gloyna, 1970), a finding also independently obtained in *in vitro* experiments by S. Liao

(Anderson and Liao, 1968). However, the link between metabolic formation and hormone action does not follow automatically. For example, the nuclear localization of androstanolone may be the result of its formation after testosterone action has taken place. The Lasnitzkis' technique of ventral prostate explant culture for 6 days offers a rather unique possibility of correlating metabolism and action, since metabolites are necessarily produced in the cultivated responsive tissue, and a collaborative work was undertaken with Cambridge (Baulieu *et al.*, 1968). Testosterone can maintain the young adult rat prostatic epithelial cell structure and keep it apparently functional; this is obtained with the same 10 nM concentration as found in normal rat plasma, using a continuous perfusion of the culture chamber (Robel and Baulieu, 1972), which might remove metabolic and/or steroidal inhibitors. Cultivated cells are identical to those obtained directly from the living animal.

While it acts, testosterone is metabolized in prostate explants (Fig. 5). No 5β-metabolites are formed. All metabolites are 5α-reduced, and the 5α-reductase enzyme, located in the endoplasmic reticulum, is obtained after cell fractionation in the microsomal fraction and in the nuclear fraction, where it probably is part of the external nuclear membrane (Moore and Wilson, 1972). Incidentally, the relatively low affinity (K_M on the order of 10 μM) and the small number of molecules of 5α-reductase per cell (100?; Roy, 1971) are interesting but rather puzzling findings. Androstanolone (dihydrotestosterone), the most important metabolite, has been introduced into the prostate culture instead of testosterone, and it displays a very great efficiency, eventually leading to more cell division than testosterone induces—in other words, to hyperplasia. It has been known for a long time that androstanolone is an active compound, but the activity of a tetrahydro metabolite, 3β-androstanediol, was discovered from *in vitro* work, since following systemic administration to the rat it has no effect on

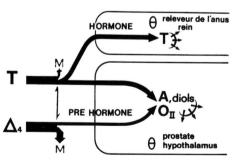

FIG. 5. Testosterone: a hormone and a prehormone. In rat target organs such as the levator ani muscle, testosterone (T) is directly active, as a hormone should be. In other target organs such as the ventral prostate and hypothalamus, the activity is at least in part mediated through the formation of metabolite(s) (androstanolone A or dihydrotestosterone, androstanediols, estradiol E_{II}), and testosterone is a prehormone. Androstenedione (Δ^4) is always a prehormone. Testosterone and androstenedione have a peripheral detoxification metabolism into metabolites (M) and are partly interconvertible.

androgen-sensitive structures. In the culture system, 3β-androstanediol preserves cell size and maintains protein synthesis, but even with a relatively high dose (10 μg/ml) no cell division has been observed.

The metabolism of androgens in cultivated explants parallels the effects on epithelial cells (Robel *et al.*, 1971). For example, 3α-androstanediol is interconvertible with androstanolone and has about the same effect (slightly less); epiandrosterone gives only 3 β-androstanediol and has only a very weak action.

Second, it is hypothesized that at the target level, testosterone may be transformed to metabolites of different complementary activities, which together can explain the overall testosterone action. It should, however, be pointed out that it has not been definitively proven that testosterone is without an activity of its own, or that the metabolism and the action take place in the same cells. Indeed in the prostate, the situation is complex, and, besides the epithelial growth, there is regression of the connective tissue.

The concept that testosterone action is mediated by active metabolites* leads to some ultimate regulatory possibilities for the cells in regard to the steroid input from the plasma; consequently, such a final regulatory system may be altered in pathological disorders.

It has been suggested that the lack of response to testosterone of insensitive tissues in the testicular feminization syndrome could be explained as a defect in androstanolone formation. Actually, androstanolone is inactive in affected individuals, and this observation rules out the hypothesis, although it is possible that insensiviity to hormone may primarily involve a defect in receptor synthesis (Bullock *et al.*, 1971).

To see whether testosterone undergoes the same metabolic transformation in all androgen-sensitive tissues as in the prostate, testosterone and androstanolone concentrations were determined in various organs of normal adult rats. A relatively high concentration of androstanolone was found in the ventral pros-

---

*Usually, the steroids produced by the adrenals, the testes, and the ovaries (and eventually the placenta) are called *hormones*. They are released into the venous blood from the gland and are distributed to various organs. This does not correspond really to the meaning of *hormone* (Greek ωρμεω = *to excite*). Even though dehydroepiandrosterone sulfate is secreted by the adrenals (Baulieu *et al.*, 1965; Vande Wiele *et al.*, 1963), it is probably not active *per se*. *Inter alia*, it goes to the placenta, where it is transformed into estrogens. This was the first *prehormone* described, which we initially called a "privileged substrate," since its significance is due to its distribution and access to certain enzymes (Baulieu *et al.*, 1965). The placental sulfatase is very active and releases dehydroepiandrosterone, which is subsequently oxidized and "aromatized." In the liver, the sulfatase is less active and there is further hydroxylation at the 16α-position, giving 16α-hydroxy-dehydroepiandrosterone sulfate, which secondarily goes to the placenta where it gives estriol. The concept of prehormones has been enlarged by the observation of transformation of steroids into active compounds at the target level.

TABLE II. Testosterone and Androstanolone in Rat Plasma and Tissues[a]

	Testosterone	Androstanolone
Plasma	2.5 ± 0.3	≤ 0.2
Seminal vesicles	2.2 ± 0.3	2.0 ± 0.6
Ventral prostate	2.0 ± 0.4	2.8 ± 0.5
Levator ani muscle	7.9 ± 0.5	≤ 0.2
Thigh muscles	2.9 ± 0.5	≤ 0.4
Hypothalamus	13.7 ± 2.0	2.0 ± 0.4
Pituitary gland	60.5 ± 5.5	≤ 6
Brain parietal cortex	1.3 ± 0.1	≤ 0.4
Kidney	12.5 ± 0.5	3.0 ± 1.1
Small intestine	≤ 0.2	≤ 0.2

[a] ng/g (organs) or ml (plasma), mean ± SEM. ≤, Values too low to be measured accurately; their upper limit is given.

tate and seminal vesicles, whereas it was absent in the plasma. In the levator ani, a muscle dependent on testosterone for its growth (although the androgen does not provoke cell division), there was more hormone than in the blood, and no metabolite. The concentration found in peripheral muscles and kidney was also compatible with a concentration mechanism itself (for comparison, see the brain cortex level, shown in Table II).

Other findings contribute to the idea that testosterone is a molecule which connects different parts of the organism through different patterns of transformation into various steroids in target organs. Several activities of "aromatizable" androgens can be reproduced with estrogens, such as control of pituitary hormone secretion, regulation of sexual behavior, and nuclear uptake of steroidal radioactivity by hypothalamus neurons. Therefore, the possibility arises that testosterone (or Δ^4-androstenedione) action at the brain level could be mediated through transformation into estrogen. A series of elegant papers have substantiated this possibility, showing that the necessary enzymes are present in the hypothalamus (Naftolin et al., 1971). The situation may be more complex, since there is a fair amount of androstanolone in the hypothalamus and pituitary gland (Table II), and androstanediols are more active than testosterone in reducing LH secretion in the castrated rat (Zanizi et al., 1973). The fact that circulating testosterone is a source of different active steroids (Fig. 5) offers pharmacologists the possibility of intervening more specifically at the target level.

At the present time, it is not known whether such concepts can be generalized to other hormones, progesterone in particular. It is also interesting that the recent findings concerning the D vitamins have similarly led to linking of sterol metabolism and action.

RECEPTORS

Cytosol and Nuclear Receptors

In target cells, the active steroid, whether it comes as such from the blood or is an active metabolite, interacts with an intracellular specific binding protein called, for convenience, the "cytosol" receptor,* since it is easily obtained in the soluble fraction of the tissue homogenate after high-speed centrifugation of all particles, and is therefore probably originally located in the cytoplasm.

Indeed, the presence of such a high-affinity protein could have been foreseen from Jensen's and Glascock's experiments on uptake and retention of highly labeled steroid by the atrophic uterus. The curves obtained by Jensen and Jacobson (1962) give a sort of physiological visualization of the slow dissociation rate of hormone–receptor complexes (see uterus vs. plasma concentration over time). The first biochemical approaches to the problem were those of Talwar *et al.* (1964), using Sephadex chromatography, and then those of Toft and Gorski (1966), who used gradient ultracentrifugation. There followed a series of findings with all steroid hormones, for most target tissues, essentially showing great similarities (Raspé, 1971).

In a hypotonic tris extract, the cytosol receptor appears as an entity with a sedimentation coefficient of about 8S (Fig. 6), showing relatively lesser density than expected from Sephadex chromatography analysis; the molecular weight may be provisionally fixed at about 250,000. Dissociation by high ionic strength solutions (0.5 M KCl) gives a structure(s) with a sedimentation coefficient of

Receptor at this stage means intracellular specific binding protein.

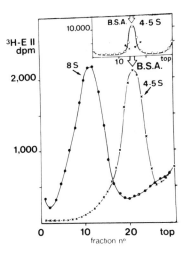

FIG. 6. *Ultracentrifugation in low salt (tris) or high salt (0.5 M KCl) sucrose gradient of rat uterus cytosol receptor.* Castrated rat uterus cytosol incubated 90 min with ^{3}H-estradiol, 1 nM, at 0°C is first centrifuged in KCl-containing sucrose gradient. The 4–5S region (○) is collected, dialyzed appropriately, and rerun in sucrose gradient with (X) or without (●) salt. This indicates the reversible transformation of the receptor (Rochefort and Baulieu, 1971). BSA, Bovine serum albumin (sedimentation coefficient 4.6S).

4–5S exhibiting the same binding characteristics as the 8S entity. The question of whether there is one or several binding sites per 8S entity and per 4–5S "subunit" and whether the 8S is composed of one or several type(s) of binding or nonbinding subunits will be resolved only after purification of the material. This is very difficult because there is not much material (approximately 10^3 sites per cell), necessitating a purification of $\geqslant 10^5$ from the soluble protein extract. Moreover, the molecule tends to aggregate, probably because of its hydrophobic properties. Major progress has been obtained by two groups using affinity chromatography for purifying a calcium-treated form of the calf uterus estradiol receptor which does not give much aggregates (Sica *et al.*, 1973; Truong *et al.*, 1973) (Fig. 7 and Table IV); however, problems are still pending because the "native" form is yet to be purified. There is no evidence that the cytosol receptor contains either lipid or glucid. Whatever the steroid is, the affinity measured at equilibrium corresponds to a K_D of 1–0.1 nM; preliminary observations indicate that the kinetic components of this affinity may not be identical in all cases. For example, the estrogen–uterus receptor complex has a particularly slow dissociation rate. This explains in part some of the difficulties encountered in the elution of the receptor from affinity chromatography columns (Truong *et al.*, 1973).

There is very strict hormone specificity, which can be quantified, and in the estrogen series, for instance, the more powerful the hormone the greater its affinity; this holds for both the steroidal and nonsteroidal compounds. Conversely and complementarily, nonestrogenic steroids (such as androgens) do not compete for estrogen binding sites even if different receptors are present in the

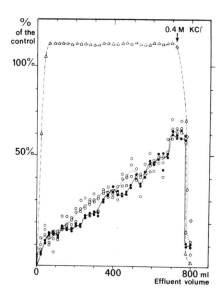

FIG. 7. Affinity chromatography of estradiol receptor (calf uterus): A representative experiment. Estradiol binding activity and proteins in the effluents of a 2-ml agarose-7α column during the application of the sample (720 ml of cytosol) and the initial washing. Free binding sites (•) and total binding sites (○) were measured. Total proteins were estimated (△). The arrow indicates the beginning of the washing.

TABLE IV. Affinity Chromatography Purification of
Calf Uterus Receptor

	Crude cytosol	7α-Agarose eluate[a]
Volume (ml)	720	25
Protein (mg/ml)	12	0.06
Receptor Activity (bound E_{II})		
dpm/ml	315,500	637,500
pmol/ml	2.84	5.74
total pmol	2,025	143
Specific activity		
dpm/mg protein	26,000	10,600,000
pmol/mg protein	0.23	94.40
Purification		408
Recovery (%)		
From cytosol[a]		7
From column[a]		12
From column + rinsing buffer[b]		15

[a]The agarose 7α-column included a 7α-undecanoic acid di-
propylamino derivative (Truong et al., 1973).

[b]After elution exchange at 30°C.

[c]After elution exchange at 30°C and additional rinsing at
30°C. In this experiment, 60% of the receptor was bound to
the column (1215 pmol).

same tissue extract, as in the case with uterus, where androgen binding is also observed. There is also organ specificity, since one does not find binding in organs not targets for the hormone in question. One can even wonder whether the receptor is an "all or nothing" constituent of the tissue or whether there is a gradient of receptor concentration among various tissues (then only technical limitations would prevent the demonstration of rare specific binding in certain cells). Another example of hormone and organ specificity is the mirror image of androstanolone binding in ventral prostate and testosterone binding in levator ani muscle, which fits well with the endogenous steroid pattern.

Evaluation of the receptor content of target cells has indicated that it varies with the ontogenic stage and various physiological parameters. For example, in the guinea pig uterus, using an assay which accounts for the binding sites occupied by endogenous hormone, Milgrom et al. (1973c) demonstrated variations of the progesterone (cytosol) receptor content which did not follow the plasma progesterone values over the estrus cycle (Fig. 8). This result may indicate that preovulatory progesterone which encounters many receptor molecules is important for implantation, corroborating the work of Deanesly, who obtained the implantation even when castration had been performed 3 days after ovulation. The induction of progesterone receptors by estrogen and the remark-

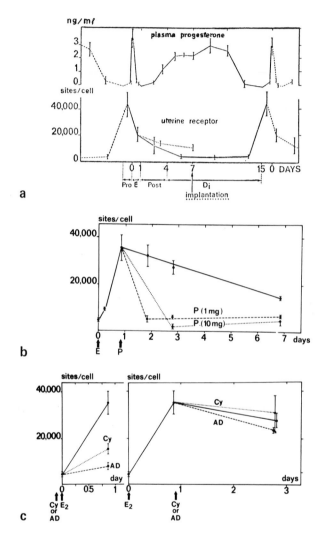

FIG. 8. Guinea pig uterus progesterone receptor: estral variations and hormonal control.
(a) Estrus cycle. While progesterone evolves in the plasma with a periovulatory peak and a
luteal increase (during post- and diestrus periods), there is a cycle of progesterone receptor
in the uterus with a peak at proestrus (Pro E). Whether or not implantation takes place, the
level on the seventh day does not change very much. (b) Induction of receptor by estrogen
(E) is shown on the left, and is reduced by cycloheximide (Cy) or actinomycin (AD). After
the peak at 20 h, the decay is slow in the absence of hormone, whether or not Cy or AD is
injected at 20 h (approximate half-life 5.5 days). (c) "Inactivation" of receptor by progesterone (P). After induction of the receptor by estrogen, mimicking the proestrus period,
the progesterone administered at the twentieth hour leads to an accelerated decay of the
receptor compatible with the decrease found in the estrus cycle.

able rapid regression caused by progesterone itself, which may explain the cyclic variations during the cycle, are a clear demonstration of the environmental dependence of hormone receptor content. More recent observations of Mester *et al.* (1974) show that effects of estradiol and progesterone on the level of estrogen receptor are different in endometrium and myometrium of the castrated rat uterus, and this may explain the changes observed in early pregnancy (before and at the time of implantation). Knowledge of the hormonal control of steroid receptors and therefore of target cell "receptivity" should lead to new methods of fertility control using hormone analogues, agonists, and/or antagonists (Baulieu, 1974).

Most binding studies are based on equilibrium experiments. Kinetic studies (Geynet *et al.*, 1972) led to the very surprising observation that in the estrogen series, based on binding to calf uterus receptor, the difference in affinity between estradiol (more tightly bound) and estrone and estriol (weaker estrogens) can be ascribed to the higher rate constant of association of the former, and not to a faster dissociation of complexes formed by the latter, as was generally postulated. Such studies are of great importance in order to understand hormone and antihormone activities and eventually devise new compounds. However, at the theoretical level, it is not known whether or not the binding to receptor proteins is important in terms of rate or occupation.

A most important feature of the so-called cytosol receptor is its affinity for the nucleus. When target cells *in vivo* or *in vitro* are exposed to a physiological concentration of radioactive hormone, there is a rapid preferential localization of radioactivity in the nucleus. This has been discovered autoradiographically using aldosterone and a toad bladder preparation (Fanestil and Edelman, 1966). Thanks to the Stumpf dry-mount freezing technique, this observation has been generalized to sex steroid hormones. A series of important independent biochemical reports (Brecher *et al.*, 1967; Jensen *et al.*, 1968; Gorski *et al.*, 1968) confirm the "neonuclear" location of hormone in target cells after exposure to steroid and show that it is protein bound. In other words, the high-affinity binding protein is not found in the nuclear extracts obtained with a 0.5 M KCl extract of cells not exposed to hormone; rather, a hormone–receptor complex is found associated with the nuclei a few minutes after exposure of the cells to the hormone. The data apparently show that it derives from the steroid–cytosol receptor complex. Such a hormone-dependent association of the cytosol receptor with the corresponding nuclei has been observed with practically all steroid hormones using their target cell cytosol receptor and nuclei in *in vitro* recombination experiments. It seems that the hormone gives the cytosol receptor the new property, which necessarily implicates a conformational change, to attach to some nuclear element, a so-called acceptor. This "activation" of the receptor results in an apparent translocation of the steroid–protein complex from cytoplasm to nucleus. A clear demonstration of the obligatory role of the steroid has

TABLE III. Basic Features of the "Activation" of Steroid Receptors (acellular experiments)[a]

H	Incubation	R	Incubation	Nuclei or DNA	H bound to nuclei or DNA
+	37°C	0	37°C	+	No
+	37°C	+	37°C	+	Yes
+	37°C	+	0°C	+	Yes
+	0°C	+	0°C	+	No
+	0°C, salt	+	0°C	+	Yes
0	37°C or 0°C, salt or not	+	37°C or 0°C	+	No

[a]The steroid hormone H is incubated with the cytosol receptor R under conditions which are either 0°C low salt, or 37°C low salt, or 0°C high salt. Details are found in Milgrom *et al.* (1973b) and Alberga *et al.* (1974). The incubation of the receptor–hormone complex with either nuclei or DNA is performed in low salt, either at 0°C or at 37°C. The hormone bound to nuclei or DNA is measured. Only typical and most important results are reported, in a very schematic way. From the first horizontal line, it may be seen that there is no binding of hormone to nuclei in the absence of receptor. The second line indicates that the incubation of the hormone–receptor complex at 37°C followed by incubation at 37°C with the nuclear element(s) gives binding. Indeed, if the hormone–receptor complex has been activated at 37°C, the incubation with the nuclear elements can take place in the cold (third line). However, as the fourth line shows, the 37°C step is necessary to give the hormone–receptor complex the ability to bind nuclei or DNA. The fifth line indicates that the increase of temperature can be replaced by salt activation of the receptor. Finally, the last line shows that, whatever the incubation conditions, hormone is necessary for the transformation of the receptor which makes it bind to nuclei or DNA. The possibility of replacing nuclei or DNA by various polyanions has justified the designation of the phenomenon as "acidophilic" activation accelerated by temperature and high ionic strength.

been obtained in acellular systems, cytosol receptor–nucleus and cytosol receptor–DNA (Milgrom *et al.,* 1973b; Higgins *et al.,* 1973). The receptor transformation which takes place at low ionic strength is very much temperature accelerated (Table III). Elevated ionic strength can also speed up the activation of the hormone–receptor complex, even in the cold. It seems that the two conditions, temperature and ionic strength, do not have additive effects. The transformed complex is "acidophilic" and binds not only to purified nuclei and various DNAs but also to several polyanions including Sephadex derivatives (carboxymethyl, sulfopropyl). Conversely, binding of the activated hormone–receptor complex to nuclei or DNA can take place rapidly in the cold and is dissociated by high ionic strength. The nuclear acceptor specificity is not clearly defined, even though in the cytosol–nucleus reconstituted system some specificity has been observed. The experiments of many groups, including our own, implicate DNA in nuclear acceptor activity, whereas O'Malley's group holds the opinion that a nonhistone chromatin acidic protein fraction ("AP 3") is an important and organ-specific factor for increasing the binding (O'Malley *et al.,* 1972).

Finally, one is dealing with a hormone–receptor complex inserted at the nuclear level, such that it can be extracted only with a relatively high salt concentration, as are chromatin proteins. Indeed, this localization is of great interest and has led us to test if the cytosol receptor was an obligatory vector in the hormone-induced changes of gene expression. C. Raynaud-Jammet has used an immature rat or calf uterus nuclear preparation and measured the incorporation of radioactive triphosphonucleoside into RNA (Raynaud-Jammet and Baulieu, 1969) after the exposure to either estradiol 1 nM buffer solution, cytosol alone, or the cystosol–hormone 1 nM complex. Only preincubation with the last increases incorporation into RNA. Control experiments include alteration of the cytosol fraction by preheating. These experiments have been repeated and developed (Arnaud et al., 1971; Mohla et al., 1972) and indicate that there is some heat-sensitive cytosol component necessary for the response, presumably the cytosol receptor protein. These results still suffer from many limitations, including the lack of analytical work concerning RNA and RNA polymerase activities, the difficulty of reproducibility, and contradiction between the high augmentation observed in these *in vitro* conditions (150–300%) and the relatively modest very early RNA increase observed *in vivo* after injection of estradiol (see later). It is likely that although all the pieces of the cellular machinery are not present and/or disposed as they are physiologically, some fundamental molecular interaction takes place under these experimental conditions, and paradoxically it may be stated that they have given evidence for some fundamental molecular characteristics even though they may not fully reproduce the physiological situation.

Nonhistone Chromatin (NHC) Binding Protein of Very High Affinity

There is no evidence that the cytosol receptor is the last intracellular binding protein to which the active steroid attaches before action is initiated. Therefore, the possibility remains that hormone brought into the nucleus may be ultimately transferred onto another binding entity, presumably present in the chromatin before exposing to hormone. Fractionation of purified nuclear proteins from calf endometrium (Alberga et al., 1971) and more recently from rat DMBA-induced mammary tumor, followed by binding experiments using estradiol in the 1 pM range, have indicated that only the nonhistone chromatin fraction demonstrates hormone-specific binding. The affinity is extraordinarily high ($K_A \gtrsim 10^{14}$ M^{-1}), to the point that one cannot ascertain whether or not it is covalent. This high affinity makes the NHC protein a suitable candidate for picking up steroid released by the cytosol neonuclear transfer system (Baulieu et al., 1971) (this binding NHC is naturally different from the "AP 3" acceptor discussed before). Obviously, such a protein may play a role in hormone action if there is no unbound estradiol in the nucleus (NHC would be immediately saturated) but only the hormone imported by and dissociating from the neonuclear receptor.

Moreover, the hormone–NHC complex should have a short half-life in order to be operational as a regulator, and then either the protein itself should turn over rapidly or the complex should dissociate very rapidly (as soon as it has interacted with the cellular responsive constituent).

"Insoluble" Nuclear Receptor

Indeed, the story of intracellular steroid binding proteins is not ended. In our own group, there are controversies among my colleagues as to the cellular localization of the cytosol receptor, the respective role and meaning of the neonuclear receptor and the NHC binding protein, etc. Moreover, there is another type of binding protein to which Lebeau is particularly devoted (Lebeau et al., 1973). In chick liver nuclei (as well as in uterine nuclei), she has found specific binding sites not salt extractable and not dependent on the cytosol receptor. They have a high affinity for estrogens ($K_D \sim 0.1$ nM) and they are solubilized using trypsin under mild conditions (Lebeau et al., 1974).

Finally, the receptor is an entity with which the hormone interacts at a "receptive" site similar to those of all the binding proteins observed in the plasma and the tissues. A coupling mechanism (transducer) "informs" the "executive" site via a single or a multiple protein system. The site may be catalytic if the receptor is an enzyme, or it may be a binding site for another protein (e.g., nucleic acid polymerase) or a polynucleotide sequence (e.g., DNA) if the receptor is a repressor, a protein for positive control or for unwinding the nucleic structure.

In terms of control systems at the gene level, it follows that if the cytosol–neonuclear receptor is "the" receptor, a "positive" control at the DNA level is probable, provided that the efficient interaction is direct (and not via another protein already bound to DNA). If the receptor is a protein like NHC already present in the chromatin, the control may or may not be of the "negative" type. Future experiments with the purified components of the steroid-controlled regulatory mechanism(s) may shed light on some fundamental problems that exist today in the biology of higher organisms.

THE FIRST HOUR AFTER HORMONE EXPOSURE—KEY INTERMEDIARY PROTEINS?

In spite of the increasing knowledge about the physicochemical characteristics and the cellular localization of binding proteins, until now "the" receptor has not been definitively identified, and its executive ability remains unknown for all steroid hormones. It is therefore necessary to continue to study the effects of hormones "backward" toward zero time, when the hormone–receptor interaction and the onset of the first response occur.

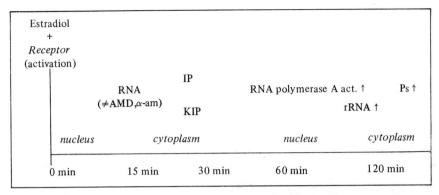

FIG. 9. Early responses to estradiol in the rat uterus: "KIP" and a cascade sequence of events. The formation of the activated estradiol–receptor complex takes place at time 0. There is an indication that synthesis of the physically defined induced protein (IP) and of the phenomenologically defined key intermediary protein (KIP) occurs within 30 min. Are they the same? They share in any case the same timing and dependency on a sensitive actinomycin D (AMD) and α-amanitin (α-am) step, presumably mRNA synthesis, taking place in the 15 first min. Secondarily, there is more RNA polymerase A activity (blockable by inhibition of protein synthesis) and rRNA, and finally proteins (Ps) increase.

Again we shall consider the rat atrophic uterus, for which estradiol is a reversible growth-promoting agent. There is an increase of all types of cells, primarily in size and secondarily in number (Mueller *et al.*, 1972). Indeed, there is an increase in protein 2–3 hr after estradiol exposure (and also an augmentation in water inhibition, phospholipid, etc., part of it, if not all, dependent on protein and RNA synthesis). Whereas all classes of RNA have increased by 3–5 h, ribosomal RNA synthesis is mainly if not exclusively augmented already at 1–3 h. There is a parallel increase of the low-salt RNA polymerase activity of isolated nuclei (Gorski, 1964), and considering the multiplicity of enzymes in eukaryotic cells and the effects of α-amanitin, it can be attributed to an increase of RNA polymerase A (or I, insensitive to α-amanitin) activity, implicating the nucleolar enzyme(s) responsible for (pre) rRNA synthesis.

There remains a "lag period" of about 1 h, and what occurs during these first 60 min at the transcriptional and/or the post-transcriptional level probably determines the subsequent polymerase, RNA, and protein increases.

G. Mueller and J. Gorski have pointed out the possibility of an early increase in protein synthesis, promoted by estradiol at the translational level; such a hypothesis is derived from the effects of protein synthesis inhibitors such as puromycin and cycloheximide injected at the same time as estradiol, which suppress the secondary augmentation of RNA polymerase activity and RNA synthesis (Gorski *et al.*, 1965). We reinterpret these interesting results in referring basically to transcription control (Baulieu *et al.*, 1972) (Fig. 9). We favor a "cascade" of events, centered on the early synthesis of a (or a very limited number of) key intermediary proteins (KIP). Such an estrogen-induced synthesis would be critical for the subsequent increase of RNA polymerase A activity and rRNA synthesis. The latter would be secondarily implicated in a post-transcriptional increase of protein synthesis, this effect being fundamentally different from Tomkin's hypothesis (Tomkins et al., 1969). Later, a general increase of mRNAs for most proteins would occur.

The blocking effect of actinomycin D given at the time of estrogen, the nuclear location of the estradiol–receptor complex, the in vitro experiments of Raynaud-Jammet (1969), and some new results reported in the next two paragaphs indicate localization of the estrogen–receptor complex effect at the transcriptional level. Admittedly, however, the case is not definitive, and other theoretical possibilities cannot be excluded formally.

The increase of α-amanitin-resistant RNA polymerase A observed 1–3 h after estradiol injection can be partially maintained for a period of time in surviving uterine slices incubated at 37°C. In control slices from noninjected animals, RNA polymerase remains constant. If cycloheximide is introduced into the incubation medium, there is no effect on the control polymerase level, but there is a very rapid decrease of the estrogen-induced polymerase activity (Nicolette and Mueller, 1966; Raynaud-Jammet et al., 1972; Mueller et al., 1972). The same result is found with α-amanitin (Raynaud-Jammet et al., 1972). These results support the concept that KIP sustains the maintenance of the increased polymerase activity and continues to be synthesized in the surviving slices under the control of RNA synthetized by α-amanitin-sensitive RNA polymerase B, probably mRNA.

The preceding results draw a phenomenological profile of KIP. It is then necessary to see whether or not physically observed protein(s) induced by estrogen has some of the properties postulated for KIP. An induced protein ("IP") was described by Notides and Gorski (1966), visible in the uterine-soluble protein EDTA extract approximately 1 h after estrogen injection in the immature rat and identifiable by a double-labeling technique and gel electrophoresis. Wira obtained the IP induction in vitro (Wira and Baulieu, 1971), as did Katzenelenbogen and Gorski (1972), making it possible to test metabolic inhibitors (Fig. 10). Cycloheximide abolishes all protein synthesis, but actinomycin D and α-amanitin introduced at the same time as estradiol suppress only IP synthesis. However, when either of the RNA synthesis inhibitors is added to the medium 15 min after estradiol, IP synthesis is still obtained, as if enough mRNA has accumulated (these results remain essentially qualitative; quantiative studies were not too successful in our hands). IP cannot be detected, however, in uterine nuclei (Pennequin et al., 1974).

The early RNA requirement of both synthesis of IP and increase of polymerase A led to a labeling experiment with radioactive uridine after exposure of uterus to estradiol for 15 min in vivo or in vitro. A cytoplasmic 15S RNA peak was detected (and sometimes another 8S peak) (Wira and Baulieu, 1972). Since

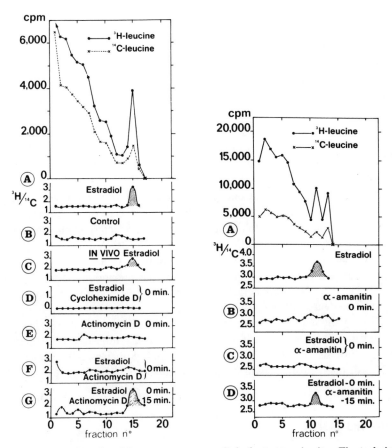

FIG. 10. Protein (IP) induced by exposure to estradiol of rat uterus in vitro. The technique involves double-labeling of the protein by leucine incorporation (estrogen-treated and controlled uteri) and fractionation of soluble protein by polyacrylamide gel electrophoresis. The increase of the isotopic ratio indicates the induced protein. Antimetabolites are introduced at zero time or 15 min after estradiol. An *in vitro* experiment (injection of estradiol and secondarily *in vitro* incubation of uterus with radioactive leucine) is reported to show the similarity with the *in vitro* phenomenon.

this very early discrete RNA species is neither of the ribosomal nor of the 5S or 4S type, it is not impossible that it represents a mRNA entity for (K)IP. This limited RNA synthesis seems somewhat inconsistent with results indicating an increase at 30 min of nuclear polymerase B activity, early increase of nuclear RNA, augmentation of radioactive actinomycin D binding 15 min after estradiol, and even our already mentioned *in vitro* studies. Do all nuclear events lead to only a few cytoplasmic RNA species? An enzymatic estimation of solubilized polymerase(s) A and B and a determination of the α-amanitin binding polymerase(s) B have indicated no change of the nucleoplasmic B enzyme(s) up to 6 h, while the enzyme A activity is increased at 1.5 h (Courvalin, unpublished).

Finally, all these results can be ordered as a cascade of events including an initial nuclear event at the transcriptional level followed by the migration into the cytoplasm of mRNA for a specific protein IP. It is clear that none of the properties of IP is incompatible with those defining KIP, which, in order to activate nucleolar RNA polymerase activity, must act at some nuclear level. Another interesting aspect is the coincidence of the very low number of high-affinity estradiol-binding protein NHC molecules, which, if it is the receptor, could correspond nicely to the activation of a single gene, of KIP for example.

Naturally, we realize that our presentation of these series of events may be arbitrary, and it should be pointed out that (1) the mechanism of transcription, if the first effects are to be found at that level, is completely unknown; (2) there is no demonstrated direct relationship between 15S RNA and IP; (3) IP may or may not be KIP; (4) the eventual mechanism by which KIP initiates RNA polymerase A activity is not understood; (5) the precise mechanism by which the increase of RNA polymerase activity and of rRNA synthesis could lead to amplified protein synthesis is also unknown.

Most of these questions can eventually be tested experimentally. However, it will be difficult to determine if, besides the induced synthesis of a KIP-activating rRNA synthesis, there is a concomitant primary increased synthesis of the mRNAs of many proteins (which become visible only relatively late).

CONCLUSIONS

Systematic interaction with proteins leads to more specificity for the small low-information-containing molecules that are steroids. In the course of its natural history, a given steroid molecule may interact successively with transport proteins, entry protein, intra-target-cell cytoplasmic protein, and nuclear proteins.

Steroid hormones are inducers of protein synthesis* in higher organisms, where substrate induction seems rare (if there is any). In microorganisms, substrates present in the medium may modify metabolism through change of the corresponding enzyme synthesis, and it has been demonstrated that the regulatory protein sensitive to the information given by the substrate (say, the repressor protein) is distinct from the induced protein (say, the metabolic enzyme which naturally also recognizes the substrate). In higher organisms, the interconnection between organs involves specialized chemical signals, the hormones, circulating in the cellular environment, i.e., *le milieu intérieur,* and eventually bringing the order for protein synthesis. Indeed, the cause–effect relationship between the signal and the metabolic effect is less direct than in bacteria; this may be called freedom, luxury, or complications in higher organisms.

In the last few years, many hormones have been shown to act through a cAMP increment in their target cells, the cyclic nucleotide acting as a second messenger, as proposed by Sutherland. However, the mechanism of action of cAMP is still largely unknown. It has been established that most features of steroid action cannot be ascribed to cAMP, and steroids penetrating into target cells may themselves play the overall role of both the primary polypeptide hormone and the cAMP. That cAMP, cGMP, as well as prostaglandins, neurotransmitters, and other hormones such as insulin and growth hormones may interfere with steroid hormone action and modulate it secondarily is possible, however.

Another problem, related to the previous comments, is to decide whether or not a given steroid hormone encounters one or several different receptors in one target cell.† For instance, specific interactions occur with the membrane and with the cytosol and nuclear receptors. At each level, some "execution" could follow, the sum of the effects constituting the overall hormone response. There is no definitive solution to this problem at the present time, even though the author would be in favor of a decisive receptor effect at the gene level.

Whether or not the basic initial mechanism is similar in various systems on which steroid hormones are active is another question. Up to now, intracellular receptor proteins have been found in all steroid target cells. In thymocytes regressing after exposure to corticosteroid (Munck, 1971), there is indication of an early actinomycin D sensitive step, which makes the lytic effect surprisingly similar to the growth of uterine cells exposed to estrogen. Nor it is known whether the synthesis of a few specific proteins (e.g., in hepatic cells induced by glucocorticosteroids or in estrogen-treated liver or oviduct in the chick) is also secondary to the synthesis of an intermediary product like KIP. The alternative may be that, in these cases, there is direct synthesis of the corresponding mRNAs (Lee *et al.*, 1970). It still remains most probable that in all cases the initial switch consists of the conformational change ("allosteric") of a receptor protein. The activated executive site, catalytic or not, induces some change at the gene transcription level which secondarily modifies the enzyme content and

*Theories that the cellular changes are provoked by the direct interaction of the steroid with enzyme(s) of general metabolism—for instance, glutamodehydrogenase (Tomkins and Maxwell, 1963)—have not been proven correct. As discussed previously, however, we cannot exclude that the executive site of the receptor is enzymatic, but in such case it is likely pertaining to the RNA-synthesizing machinery.

†*Note added in proof:* Some evidence has been obtained in this matter: I Jung-Testas and E. E. Baulieu, 1974, Plusieurs récepteurs par cellule pour la même et pour différentes hormones stéroides: Conséquences pharmacologiques possibles, *Comptes Rendus des séances de l'Académie des Sciences*, in press.

therefore the activity of the cell. If this is so, detailed chemical knowledge of the steroid receptors will be decisive for a better understanding of gene control in embryonic cells. Moreover, measurements of steroid receptors, including by immunological techniques, will open in practical terms the new field of hormone receptivity and therefore new possibilities for controlling hormone-dependent processes, especially those implicated in reproductive events.

ACKNOWLEDGMENTS

I am indebted to my colleagues and to the technical and secretarial members of our group for creative, competent, and friendly collaboration in the past and present years. Laboratory expenses have been partially met by grants from the Délégation Générale à la Recherche Scientifique et Technique, the Centre National de la Recherche Scientifique, the Foundation pour la Recherche Médicale Française, la Ligue Nationale Française contre le Cancer, the Population Council, and the Ford Foundation.

REFERENCES

Alberga, A., Massol, N., Raynaud, J. P., and Baulieu, E. E. (1971), Estradiol binding of exceptionally high affinity by a non histone chromatin protein fraction, *Biochemistry* *10:*3835–3843.

Alberga, A., Ferrez, M. and Baulieu, E. E. (1974), Estradiol receptor-DNA interactions: Binding studies by liquid polymer phase partition, in preparation.

Anderson, K. M., and Liao, S. (1968), Selective retention of dihydrotestosterone by prostatic nuclei, *Nature 219:*277–279.

Arnaud, M., Beziat, Y., Guilleux, J. C., Hough, A., and Mousseron-Canet, M. (1971), Les récepteurs de l'oestradiol dans l'utérus de génisse: Stimulation de la biosynthèse de RNA *in vitro, Biochim. Biophys. Acta 232:*117–131.

Baulieu, E. E. (1974), Antiprogesterone effect and mid-cycle (perivulatory) contraception, in preparation.

Baulieu, E. E., and Mauvais-Jarvis, P. (1964), Studies on testosterone metabolism. I. Conversion of testosterone-17α-^{3}H to 5α- and 5β-androstane-3α,17β-diol-17α-^{3}H: A new "17β-hydroxyl pathway," *J. Biol. Chem. 239:*1569–1577.

Baulieu, E. E., Corpéchot, C., Dray, F., Emiliozzi, R., Lebeau, M. C., Mauvais-Jarvis, P., and Robel, P. (1965), An adrenal-secreted "androgen": Dehydroisoandrosterone sulfate. Its metabolism and a tentative generalization on the metabolism of other steroid conjugates in man, *Rec. Progr. Hormone Res. 21:*411–500.

Baulieu, E. E., Lasnitzki, I., and Robel, P. (1968), Metabolism of testosterone and action of metabolites on prostate glands grown in organ culture, *Nature (Lond.) 219:*1155–1156.

Baulieu, E. E., Raynaud, J. P., and Milgrom, E. (1970), Measurement of steroid binding proteins, *Acta Endocrinol. (suppl. 147) 64:*104–121.

Baulieu, E. E., Alberga, A., Jung, I., Lebeau, M. C., Mercier-Bodard, C., Milgrom, E., Raynaud, J. P., Raynaud-Jamet, C., Rochefort, H., Truong, H., and Robel, P. (1971), Metabolism and protein binding of sex steroids in target organs: An approach to the mechanism of hormone action, *Rec. Progr. Hormone Res. 27:*351–419.

Baulieu, E. E., Alberga, A., Raynaud-Jammet, C., and Wira, C. (1972), New look at the very early steps of oestrogen in uterus. *Nature (Lond.) 236:*236–239.

Brecher, P. I., Vigersky, R., Wotiz, H. S., and Wotiz, H. H. (1967), An *in vitro* system for the binding of oestradiol to rat uterine nuclei, *Steroids 10:*635–651.

Bruchovski, N., and Wilson, J. D. (1968), The conversion of testosterone to 5α-androstan-17β-ol-3-one by rat prostate *in vivo* and *in vitro, J. Biol. Chem. 243:*2012–2021.

Bullock, L. P., Bardin, C. W., and Ohno, S. (1971), The androgen insensitive mouse: Absence of intramolecular androgen retention in the kidney, *Biochem. Biophys. Res. Commun. 44:*1537–1543.

Fanestil, D. D., and Edelman, I. S. (1966), Characteristics of the renal nuclear receptors for aldosterone, *Proc. Natl. Acad. Sci. (U.S.A.) 56:*872–879.

French, F. S., and Ritzen, E. M. (1973), A high-affinity-androgen-binding protein (ABP) in rat testis: Evidence for secretion into efferent duct fluid and absorption by epididymis, *Endocrinology 93:*88–95.

Geynet, C., Millet, C., Truong, H., and Baulieu, E. E. (1972), Estrogens and antiestrogens, *Gynecol. Invest. 3:*2–29.

Gorski, J. (1964), Early estrogen effects on the activity of uterine ribonucleic acid polymerase, *J. Biol. Chem. 239:*889–892.

Gorski, J., Noteboom, W. D., and Nicolette, J. A. (1965), Estrogen control of the synthesis of RNA and protein in the uterus *J. Cell. Comp. Physiol. (suppl. 1) 66:*91–98.

Gorski, J., Toft, D., Syamala, G., Smith, D., and Notides, A. (1968), Hormone receptors: Studies on the interaction of estrogen with the uterus, *Rec. Progr. Hormone Res. 24:*45–80.

Hellman, L., Nakada, F. M., Curti, J., Weitzman, E. D., Kream, J., Roffwarg, H., Ellman, S., Fukushima, D. K., and Gallagher, T. F. (1970), Cortisol is secreted episodically by normal man, *J. Clin. Endocrinol. Metab. 30:*411–422.

Higgins, S. J., Rousseau, G. G., Baxter, J., and Tomkins, G. M. (1973), Early events in glucocorticoid action, *J. Biol. Chem. 248:*5866–5872.

Jensen, E. V., and Jacobson, H. I. (1962), Basic guides to the mechanism of estrogen action, *Rec. Progr. Hormone Res. 18:*387–414.

Jensen, E. V., Suzuki, T., Kawashima, T., Stumpf, W. E., Jungblut, P. W., and DeSombre, E. E. (1968), A two-step mechanism for the interaction of estradiol with rat uterus, *Proc. Natl. Acad. Sci. (U.S.A.) 59:*632–638.

Katzenellenbogen, B. S., and Gorski, J. (1972), Estrogen action *in vitro, J. Biol. Chem. 247:*1299–1305.

Lebeau, M. C., Massol, N., and Baulieu, E. E. (1973), An insoluble receptor for oestrogens in the "residual" nuclear proteins of chick liver, *Eur. J. Biochem. 36:*294–300.

Lebeau, M. C., Massol, N., and Baulieu, E. E. (1974), Extraction, partial purification and characterization of the "insoluble estrogen receptor" from chick liver nuclei, *FEBS Letters 43:*107–111.

Lee, K. L., Reel, J. R., and Kenney, F. T. (1970), Regulation of tyrosine α-ketoglutarate transaminase in rat liver, *J. Biol. Chem. 245:*5806–5812.

Mahoudeau, J. A., and Corvol, P. (1973), Rabbit testosterone-binding globulin. I. Physico-chemical properties, *Endocrinology 92:*1113–1119.

Mercier-Bodard, C., Alfsen, A., and Baulieu, E. E. (1970), Sex steroid binding plasma protein (SBP), *Acta Endocrinol. (suppl. 147) 64:*204–224.

Mester, I., Martel, D., Psychoyos, A., and Baulieu, E. E. (1974), Hormonal control of oestrogen receptor in the uterus and receptivity for ovoimplantation in the rat. *Nature (Lond.),* in press.

Milgrom, E., and Baulieu, E. E. (1970), Progesterone in uterus and plasma. I. Binding in rat uterus 105,000g supernatant, *Endocrinology 87:*276–287.

Milgrom, E., Atger, M., and Baulieu, E. E. (1937a), Studies on estrogen entry into uterine cells and on estradiol–receptor complex attachment to the nucleus: Is the entry of estrogen into uterine cells a protein-mediated process. *Biochim. Biophys. Acta 320:* 267–283.

Milgrom, E., Atger, M., and Baulieu, E. E. (1973b), Acidophilic activation of steroid hormone receptors, *Biochemistry 12:*5198–5205.

Milgrom, E., Luu Thi, M., and Baulieu, E. E. (1973c), Control mechanisms of steroid hormone *receptors* in the reproductive tract, *Acta Endocrinol. 74 (suppl. 180):*380–403.

Milgrom, E., Allouch, P., Atger, M., and Baulieu, E. E. (1973d), Progesterone-binding *248:*1106–1114.

Mohla, S., De Sombre, E. R., and Jensen, E. V. (1972), Tissue specific stimulation of RNA synthesis by transformed estradiol–receptor complex, *Biochem. Biophys. Res. Commun. 42:*661–667.

Moore, R. J., and Wilson, J. D. (1972), Localization of the reduced-nicotinamide adenine dinucleotide phosphate: Δ4-3-Testosteroid 5α-oxydoreductase in the nuclear membrane of the rat ventral prostate, *J. Biol. Chem. 247:*958–967.

Mueller, G. C., Herranen, A. M., and Jervell, K. F. (1958), Studies on the mechanisms of action of estrogens. *Rec. Progr. Hormone Res. 14:*95–140.

Mueller, G. C., Vondehaar, B., Kim, U. H., and Le Mahieu, M. (1972), Estrogen action: An inroad to cell biology, *Rec. Progr. Hormone Res. 28:*1–49.

Munck, A. (1971), Glucocorticoid inhibition of glucose uptake by peripheral tissues: Old and new evidence, molecular and physiological significance, *Perspect. Biol. Med. 14:* 265–273.

Naftolin, F., Ryan, K. V., and Petro, Z. (1971), Aromatiziation of androstenedione by the diencephalon, *J. Clin. Endocrinol. 33:*368–370.

Nicolette, J. A., and Mueller, G. C. (1966), *In vitro* regulation of RNA polymerase in estrogen-treated uteri, *Biochem. Biophys. Res. Commun. 24:*851–857.

Notides, A., and Gorski, J. (1966), Estrogen-induced synthesis of a specific uterine protein, *Proc. Natl. Acad. Sci. (U.S.A.) 56:*230–235.

Ofner, P. (1968), Effects and metabolism of hormones in normal and neoplastic prostate tissue, *Vitamins Hormones 26:*237–291.

O'Malley, B. W., Spelsberg, T. C., Schrader, W. T., Chytil, F., and Steggles, A. W. (1972), Mechanism of interaction of a hormone receptor complex with the genome of an eukaryotic target cell, *Nature (Lond.) 235:*141–144.

Pennequin, P., Robel, P. and Baulieu, E. E. (1974), Steroid induced early protein synthesis in rat uterus and prostate, in preparation.

Raspé, G. (ed.) (1971), *Steroid Hormone Receptors,* Vol. 7 of *Advances in the Biosciences,* Pergamon Press, Vieweg, Oxford.

Raynaud, J. P., Mercier-Bodard, C., and Baulieu, E. E. (1971), Rat estradiol binding plasma protein (EBP), *Steroids 18:*767–788.

Raynaud-Jammet, C., and Baulieu, E. E. (1969), Action de l'oestradiol *in vitro* augmentation de la biosynthèse d'ARN dans les noyaux utérins, *C.R. Acad. Sci. (Paris) 268:* 3211–3214.

Raynaud-Jammet, C., Catelli, M. G., and Baulieu, E. E. (1972), Inhibition by α-amanitin of the estradiol-induced increase in α-amanitin insensitive RNA polymerase in immature rat uterus, *FEBS Letters 22:*93–96.

Robel, P., and Baulieu, E. E. (1972), Irrigation continue appliquée à la culture organo-typique, *C.R. Acad. Sci. (Paris)* 274:3295–3298.

Robel, P., Lasnitzki, I., and Baulieu, E. E. (1971), Hormone metabolism and action: Testosterone and metabolites in prostate organ culture, *Biochimie* 53:81–96.

Rochefort, H., and Baulieu, E. E. (1971), Effect of KCl, CaCl$_2$, temperature and oestradiol on the uterine cytosol *receptor* of oestradiol, *Biochimie* 53:893–907.

Rosenfeld, F. S., Hellman, L., Roffwarg, H., Weitzman, E. D., Fukushima, D. K., and Gallagher, T. F. (1971), Dehydroisoandrosterone is secreted episodically and synchronously with cortisol by normal man, *J. Clin. Endocrinol Metab.* 33:87–97.

Roy, A. B. (1971), The steroid 5α-reductase activity of rat liver and prostate, *Biochimie* 53:1031–1040.

Sica, V., Nola, E., Parikh, I., Puca, G. A., and Cuatrecasas P. (1973), Affinity chromatography and the purification of estrogen receptors, *J. Biol. Chem.* 248:6543–6558.

Talalay, P., and Williams-Ashman, H. G. (1960), I. Mechanisms of hormone action: Participation of steroid hormone in the enzymatic transfer of hydrogen, *Rec. Progr. Hormone Res.* 16:1–47.

Talwar, G. P., Segal, S. J., Evans, A., and Davidson, O. W. (1964), The binding of the estradiol in the uterus: A mechanism for derepression of RNA synthesis, *Proc. Natl. Acad. Sci. (U.S.A.)* 52:1059–1066.

Toft, D., and Gorski, J. (1966), A receptor molecule for oestrogen isolation from the rat uterus and preliminary characterization, *Proc. Natl. Acad. Sci. (U.S.A.)* 55:1574–1581.

Tomkins, G. M., and Maxwell, E. S. (1963), Some aspects of steroid hormone action, *Ann. Rev. Biochem.* 32:677–708.

Tomkins, G. M., Gelehrter, T. D., Granner, D., Martin, D., Jr., Samuels, H., and Thompson, E. B. (1969), Control of specific gene expression in higher organisms, *Science* 166:1474–1480.

Truong, H., Torelli, V., and Baulieu, E. E. (1973), Purification of oestradiol *receptor* by affinity chromatography: Representative experiments, *FEBS Letters* 35:289–294.

Truong, H., and Baulieu, E. E. (1971), Interaction of uterus cytosol receptor with estradiol: Equilibrium and kinetic studies, *Biochim, Biophys. Acta* 237:167–172.

Vande Wiele, R., MacDonald, P., Gurpide, E., and Lieberman, S. (1963), Studies on secretion and interconversion of the androgens, *Rec. Progr. Hormone Res.* 19:275–310.

Westphal, U. (1971), *Steroid Protein Interactions,* Vol. 4 of *Monographs on Endocrinology,* Springer Verlag, Berlin, Heidelberg, New York.

Wilson, J. D., and Gloyna, R. E. (1970), The intranuclear metabolism of testosterone in the accessory organs of reproduction, *Rec. Progr. Hormone Res.* 26:309–336.

Wira, C. R., and Baulieu, E. E. (1971), Synthèse protéique stimulée *in vitro* par l'oestradiol dans l'utérus de ratte, *C.R. Acad. Sci. (Paris)* 273:218–221.

Wira, C. R., and Baulieu, E. E. (1972), Réponse ribonucléique précoce de l'utérus à l'oestradiol, *in vivo* et *in vitro, C.R. Acad. Sci. (Paris)* 274:73–76.

Zanisi, M., Motta, M., and Martini, L. (1973), Inhibitory effects of 5α-reduced metabolites of testosterone on gonadotrophin secretion, *J. Endocrinol.* 56:315–316.

10

Progesterone-Progestin Receptors

J. P. Raynaud, D. Philibert, and G. Azadian-Boulanger

Centre de Recherches Roussel-Uclaf
Romainville, France

On the basis of exhaustive studies on several classes of hormonal steroids (e.g. estrogens, androgens, and corticosteroids), it is now widely accepted that a steroid–cytosol protein interaction is a prerequisite for the elicitation of a hormonal response and that a specific target tissue receptor corresponds to each class of steroids. Binding to this receptor controls cell response, high affinity giving rise to high activity. High activity, however, does not necessarily result from high affinity since factors such as plasma binding and metabolism intervene in modulating response. It is nevertheless likely that a highly potent compound, the activity of which is not due to metabolic transformation, is tightly bound by its corresponding specific receptor. This compound, when labeled with high specific activity, may be used to tag the receptor and thus affords a means of studying the parallelism between *in vitro* competition for the receptor and *in vivo* activity for series of structurally related compounds.

O'Malley *et al.* (1970) were the first to identify a progesterone-specific receptor in the chick oviduct. This elegant piece of work was later extended to the estrogen-exposed uterus of mammals such as the guinea pig (Milgrom *et al.*, 1970), rabbit (Wiest and Rao, 1971), mouse, and rat (McGuire and DeDella, 1971; Feil *et al.*, 1972). Recently a progestin-specific receptor has also been identified in the uterus of immature animals by the use of a highly potent progestin as a tag (Philibert and Raynaud, 1973, 1974).

The purpose of this chapter is to establish a correlation between binding to this progestin-specific uterine cytosol receptor and well-defined facets of progesterone action by comparing structurally similar derivatives of norprogesterone and nortestosterone. Binding was measured *in vitro* by determining their competitive effect on the progestin-tagged uterine cytosol receptor of the rabbit and mouse; activity was measured *in vivo* by determining their ability to induce endometrial proliferation in the rabbit (progestomimetic activity) and their inhibitory effect on the estradiol-induced uterine weight increase in the mouse (antiestrogenic activity).

MATERIALS AND METHODS

Steroids

[1,2-^{3}H] Cortisol (36 Ci/mmol) was supplied by the C.E.A., Saclay, France. [1-^{3}H] Progesterone (27 Ci/mmol) and [6,7-^{3}H] 17,21-dimethyl-19-norpregna-4,9-diene-3,20-dione (R5020*) (51 Ci/mmol) were synthesized by Roussel-Uclaf and tested for radiochemical purity (>98%) by thin-layer chromatography. The corresponding radioinert steroids, testosterone, nortestosterone (17β-hydroxy-estr-4-en-3-one), and the steroids shown in Fig. 1 were also synthesized by Roussel-Uclaf (Velluz *et al.*, 1961, 1963, 1965, 1966; Nominé *et al.*, 1965).

Animals

Immature female Normandy rabbits (600–900 g) and Hartley guinea pigs (18–20 days old) of our own breeding, immature female Swiss-SPF mice (17–19 days old) from IFFA Credo (France), and Sprague-Dawley SPF rats (17–21 days old) from Charles River (France) were used. They were fed a synthetic diet and water *ad libitum* and maintained in air-conditioned surroundings under controlled lighting conditions.

Progestomimetic Activity

Groups of five immature female rabbits were primed from day 1 to day 5 by daily subcutaneous administration of 5 μg estradiol (total dose 25 μg) in 0.5 ml of a 5% solution of benzyl alcohol in sesame oil. Progesterone or the test compound in the same solvent was then daily administered subcutaneously from day 6 to day 10. On day 11, the rabbits were sacrificed, the uterus was excised, and the endometrium fixed in Bouin's fluid for histological examination. The transformation of the uterine endometrium was graded according to McPhail's scale (1–4). The dose giving rise to a response of 2 McPhail units, indicative of definite progestomimetic activity, was taken as the active dose. The relative

*R5020: The relative binding and activity ratios. as defined in the text, are as follows: $[P/C]_R^B = 3$, $[P/C]_M^B = 7$, and $[P/C]_R^A = 83$, $[P/C]_M^A = 56$.

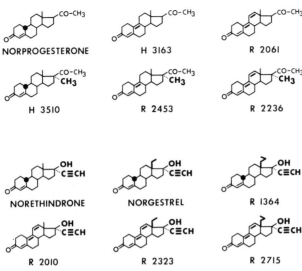

FIG. 1. *Test steroids.* Norprogesterone series: norprogesterone (19-nor-pregn-4-ene-3,20-dione; H3163 (19-nor-pregna-4,9-diene-3,20-dione); R2061 (19-nor-pregna-4,9,11-triene-3,20-dione); H3510 (17-methyl-19-nor-pregn-4-ene-3,20-dione); R2453 (17-methyl-19-nor-pregna-4,9-diene-3,20-dione); R2236 (17-methyl-19-nor-pregna-4,9,11-triene-3,20-dione). Nortestosterone series: norethindrone (17-hydroxy-19-nor-17α-pregn-4-en-20-yn-3-one); norgestrel (13-ethyl-17-hydroxy-18,19-dinor-17α-pregn-4-en-20-yn-3-one); R1364 (13-propyl-17-hydroxy-18,19-dinor-17α-pregn-4-en-20-yn-3-one); R2010-norgestrienone (17-hydroxy-19-nor-17α-pregna-4,9,11-trien-20-yn-3-one); R2323 (13-ethyl-17-hydroxy-18,19-dinor-17α-pregna-4,9,11-trien-20-yn-3-one); R2715 (13-propyl-17-hydroxy-18,19-dinor-17α-pregna-4,9,11-trien-20-yn-3-one).

potency of each steroid, as compared to progesterone, was expressed as a ratio of active dose of progesterone (P) to active dose of test compound (C) and denoted $[P/C]_R^A$ (A = activity, R = rabbit) (Clauberg, 1930).

Antiestrogenic Activity

Groups of four immature female mice received, daily for 3 days, simultaneous subcutaneous injections of 0.09 μg estradiol (total dose 0.27 μg) and various doses of progesterone and test compound each in 0.1 ml of a 5% solution of benzyl alcohol in sesame oil. The animals were sacrificed 24 h after the last administration, and the uterus was excised and weighed. Antiestrogenic activity is given by the inhibition of the estradiol-induced uterine weight increase. The active dose was taken as the dose which gave rise to 50% inhibition. The relative potency of each steroid was expressed as above and was denoted $[P/C]_M^A$ (M = mouse) (Dorfman *et al.*, 1961).

Sucrose Density Gradients

The uteri of untreated animals were excised, weighed, minced, pooled, homogenized in 3 vol of 0.01 M tris-HCl, 1 mM EDTA, 12 mM thioglycerol buffer (pH 7.4) containing glycerol (10%, v/v) in an ice-cooled Teflon–glass homogenizer, and centrifuged at 105,000g for 90 min at 4°C. The supernatant was incubated with 1 nM labeled steroid in the absence or presence of 100 nM radioinert competitor for 1 h at 4°C, then was layered (0.3 ml) on a 5–20% sucrose gradient prepared in homogenization buffer and centrifuged at 45,000 rpm for 16 h at 4°C in a Beckmann L$_3$50 centrifuge using an SW50.1 rotor. The radioactivity of 2-drop fractions collected from the bottom of the tubes was counted by liquid scintillation. Protein concentration was measured by the method of Lowry *et al.* (1951).

Equilibrium Dialysis

Total cytosol was prepared from the uteri of rabbits primed as described, or from the uteri of mice pretreated with daily subcutaneous injections of 0.09 μg estradiol for 3 days (total dose 0.27 μg). These conditions resemble those used for the determination of antiestrogenic activity. A Nojax dialysis bag containing either 1 ml of this cytosol or of diluted serum (1/100) was introduced into 15 ml of the abovementioned buffer containing 0.25 nM labeled R5020 and 1–250 nM radioinert steroid. After magnetic stirring at 4°C for 24 h, the radioactivity of two 0.2-ml samples from inside and outside the bag was determined.

The results obtained were represented in a proportion graph in which the log of the fraction of bound ($b = B/T$) and unbound ($u = U/T$) ligand is plotted against the log of the total ligand concentration (T). B and U are the concentrations of bound and unbound ligand, respectively ($T = B + U$). In this form of representation, a line parallel to the abscissa is characteristic of nonspecific binding only, a plateau giving way to a sloping curve of a single specific binding system, and an S-shaped curve of both specific and nonspecific binding. The advantage of this method is that, in the last case, the experimental curve may be decomposed into its constituent specific and nonspecific elements, thus enabling the determination of the true specific binding. Briefly, this is done as follows. The calculation of the limits of log b − log u as T approaches 0 or ∞ permits the determination of log $[K_{ns}N_{ns} + K_sN_s]$ and log $K_{ns}N_{ns}$ given, respectively, by e_2 and e_1 (see Fig. 3). K and N refer to the intrinsic association constant and number of binding sites of the specific (s) or nonspecific (ns) system. The curve, log b_s, is then drawn by carrying out a log $K_{ns}N_{ns}$ translation of log u and subtracting the nonspecific binding ($b_s = b - b_{ns}$). The extrapolation of the asymptote to this curve when $T \to \infty$ gives the value of log N_s at the intersection with the abcissa (e_3). The best solutions and limits of N_s, K_s, and $K_{ns}N_{ns}$ are calculated from these graphical approximations by series expansion and matricial analysis, using a computer program which also carries out a statistical significance test on the experimental and calculated functions. An analysis of the advantages of the proportion graph over the classic Lineweaver and Burk (1934) and Scatchard (1949) plots and more detailed explanations on the calculation of binding parameters have been published elsewhere (Baulieu *et al.*, 1970; Baulieu and Raynaud, 1970; Raynaud, 1973a).

In competition experiments, 1–250 nM radioinert competitor was added to a tracer concentration (0.25 nM) of labeled R5020. In this instance, a different form of representation was used. The log of the expression $(b-b_{min})/(b_{max}-b)$, denoted logit fraction bound, was plotted against the concentration of radioinert steroid added. The concentration required to reduce bound radioactive R5020 to the value $(b_{max}+b_{min})/2$ (logit fraction bound = 0) was calculated for each steroid tested. Relative binding potential $[P/C]^B$ was defined for each steroid and species ($[P/C]^B_R$ for the rabbit and $[P/C]^B_M$ for the mouse) as the ratio of the progesterone (P) concentration leading to a 50% decrease (logit fraction bound = 0) in bound labeled R5020 to the test compound (C) concentration giving rise to the same decrease.

RESULTS

Specificity and Physicochemical Binding Parameters of the Progestin Receptor

Figure 2 illustrates the progestin specificity of the "7–8S" receptor, as established in experiments carried out under strictly identical conditions on the unprimed animal. The weakest competitor is progesterone itself. The addition of the highly potent progestins R5020, H3510, and norgestrel results in either partial (rabbit and guinea pig) or virtually complete suppression (mouse and rat) of the R5020-labeled peak. Labeled cortisol binds in the "4S" region and constitutes an ideal marker.

The physicochemical parameters of the interaction between labeled R5020 and binding protein were measured from the proportion graphs illustrated in Fig. 3 for the estrogen-primed immature mouse and rabbit. Binding studies with 1/100 diluted serum (mouse) gave rise to a line parallel to the abscissa characteristic of nonspecific binding only. An S-shaped curve indicative of both specific and nonspecific binding was observed for the uterine cytosol of the mouse and rabbit. The graphical decomposition of this curve is shown in the top right-hand panel. Calculations are briefly explained in the Materials and Methods section. R5020 binds to rabbit and mouse uterine cytosol with an equilibrium-intrinsic dissociation constant of 0.5 ± 0.1 (nM) (Table I). The value for the rabbit confirmed previous results; that for the mouse, reproduced in three different

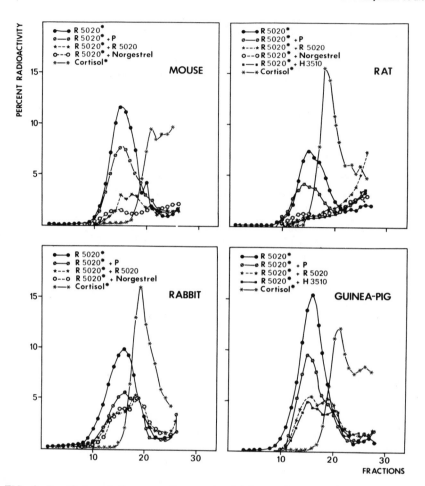

FIG. 2. *Specificity of the progestin receptor in the uterine cytosol of the unprimed immature animal.* *, Labeled compound; P, progesterone; R5020, 17-21-dimethyl-19-nor-pregna-4,9-diene-3,20-dione; H3510, 17-methyl-19-nor-pregn-4-ene-3,20-dione; norgestrel, 13-ethyl-17-hydroxy-18,19-dinor-17α-pregn-4-en-20-yn-3-one.

experiments, was lower than the previously published value (Philibert and Raynaud, 1973, 1974). A similar variability in results has already been noted by Feil *et al.* (1972) and may be due, in this instance, to differences in the condition of the animals (primed and unprimed) and in protein concentration, factors known to influence dissociation constant values (Faber *et al.*, 1972). The value of 0.5 ± 0.1, also recorded for the rabbit and guinea pig, is probably a more faithful record of R5020 binding in the mouse.

TABLE I. Binding of R5020 to Uterine Cytosol from Primed Animals[a]

	Protein (mg/ml)	$1/K_s$	N_s	K_{ns}/N_{ns}
Mouse	0.9	0.4 ± 0.1	1.0 ± 0.2	0.37 ± 0.08
	1.2	0.50 ± 0.02	2.0 ± 0.1	0.34 ± 0.02
	1.3	0.5 ± 0.1	1.5 ± 0.4	0.36 ± 0.09
Rabbit	1.1	0.5 ± 0.1	1.2 ± 0.3	0.61 ± 0.08

[a]Intrinsic dissociation constant ($1/K_s$) and number of specific binding sites (N_s) in nM as determined by equilibrium dialysis at $4°C$.

Competition studies (bottom panels of Fig. 3) have established that 19-nor derivatives, unlike cortisol and testosterone, compete for the progesterone receptor. Nortestosterone has a slight effect, while both R5020 and norgestrel are powerful competitors. Identical results were obtained for both species.

Correlations Between *In Vitro* Binding and *In Vivo* Biological Activity

Figures 4 and 5 illustrate the effect of structural modifications of the norprogesterone and nortestosterone molecules on *in vitro* binding to the uterine cytosol receptor of the estrogen-primed immature rabbit and mouse and on *in vivo* biological activity as given by endometrial proliferation in the rabbit and inhibition of the estradiol-induced uterine weight increase in the mouse. The results deduced from these graphs have been summarized in Tables II, III, and IV.

Norprogesterone Series

In Vitro Binding. In rabbit uterine cytosol, norprogesterone ($[P/C]^B_R = 2.5$) displaces bound radioactive R5020 to a greater extent than progesterone ($[P/C]^B_R = 1$ by definition). The introduction of one additional double bond (Δ^9) decreases the competitive effect with the result that the compound H3163 ($[P/C]^B_R = 1.0$) is only as effective as progesterone. The introduction of two additional double bonds (Δ^9, Δ^{11}) decreases competitiveness even further: a $[P/C]^B_R$ ratio of only 0.2 was obtained for R2061.

In the presence of a 17α-methyl substituent, the same decrease in competitive effect was observed with increasing number of double bonds ($[P/C]^B_R = 5.0 \rightarrow 2.0 \rightarrow 0.6$). However, this substituent led to a doubling in affinity, whether for the mono-, di-, or triene. Parallel results were recorded for mouse uterine cytosol.

In Vivo Biological Activity. All the compounds are more active than progesterone, both on the endometrial proliferation and on uterine weight inhibition tests.

The lack of a methyl in position 10 of the progesterone molecule considerably increases progestomimetic activity ($[P/C]_R^A = 12.5$), but the introduction of one (Δ^9) or two (Δ^9, Δ^{11}) double bonds into the 19-nor molecule decreases it, although the activity nevertheless remains superior to that of progesterone ($[P/C]_R^A$ for H3163 = 4.2, $[P/C]_R^A$ for R2061 = 3.1). The addition of a

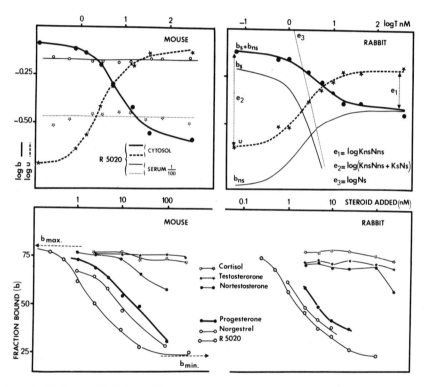

FIG. 3. Binding of labeled R5020 to the uterine cytosol progestin receptor from estrogen-primed immature mice and rabbits. Competition for the R5020-tagged progestin-receptor by radioinert steroid. Top panels: Proportion graphs illustrating binding of labeled R5020, as measured by equilibrium dialysis at 4°C. In the right-hand graph, the binding curve has been analyzed and decomposed into its constituent specific and nonspecific elements. Bottom panels: Graphs illustrating the decrease in bound labeled R5020 on addition of radioinert competitor. The values b_{max} and b_{min} are used as explained in the Materials and Methods section to derive the logit form of representation used in Figs. 4 and 5.

TABLE II. Active Doses[a] for *In Vitro* Binding[b] and *In Vivo* Activity[c]

	Norpro-gesterone	H3163	R2061	Proges-terone	H3510	R2453	R2236
Binding rabbit	2	5	25	5	1	2.5	9
Binding mouse	4	12	90	13	2	5	30
Activity rabbit	10	30	40	125	40	2.5	20
Activity mouse	10	70	40	250	2	70	10

[a] Active doses are expressed in nM for binding, in μg for activity.
[b] As given by a 50% competitive effect.
[c] As given by an endometrial response of 2 McPhail units in the rabbit and by 50% inhibition of the estradiol-induced uterine weight increase in the mouse.

17α-methyl substituent (H3510) to norprogesterone also decreases activity ($[P/C]_R^A = 3.1$). This activity is, however, considerably increased ($[P/C]_R^A = 50$) on addition of an extra double bond (Δ^9), giving rise to the most progesto-mimetic molecule of the series (R2453), and is only slightly increased ($[P/C]_R^A = 6.3$) on addition of two double bonds (Δ^9, Δ^{11}).

Results on antiestrogenic activity in the mouse reveal that norprogesterone is

TABLE III. Active Doses for *In Vitro* Binding[a] and *In Vivo* Activity[b]

	Noreth-indrone	Norges-trel	R1364	Proges-terone	R2010	R2323	R2715
Binding rabbit	7	2.5	15	5	25	25	100
Binding mouse	22	6	36	13	150	50	30
Activity rabbit	650	10	35	125	150	c	
Activity mouse	35	10	25	250	750	90	30

[a] As given by a 50% competitive effect.
[b] As given by an endometrial response of 2 McPhail units in the rabbit and by 50% inhibition of the estradiol-induced uterine weight increase in the mouse.
[c] No response attaining 2 McPhail units is obtained whatever the dose.

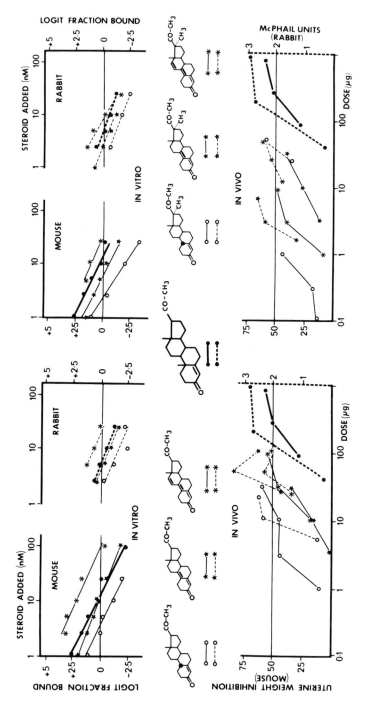

FIG. 4. Effect of structural modifications of the norprogesterone molecule on in vitro binding to the uterine cytosol progestin receptor of the estrogen-primed immature mouse and rabbit and on in vivo biological activity (antiestrogenic activity in the mouse and progestomimetic activity in the rabbit). Binding was measured by competition for the uterine cytosol progestin receptor tagged with radioactive R5020. Solid lines illustrate results for the mouse, dotted lines for the rabbit. The left-hand panel shows the effect of the introduction of double bonds, the right-hand panel shows the effect of the introduction of a 17α-methyl substituent.

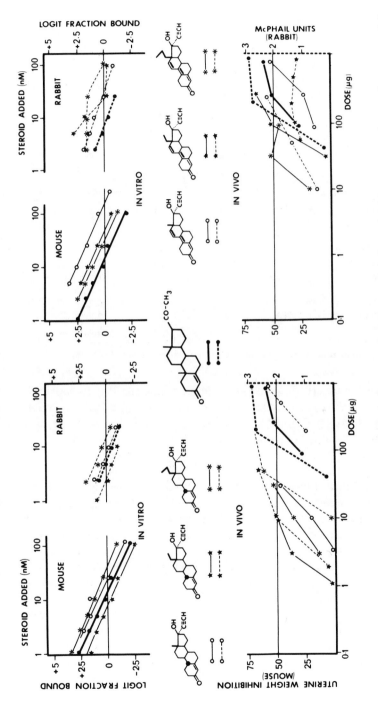

FIG. 5. Effect of structural modifications of the nortestosterone molecule on in vitro binding to the uterine cytosol progestin receptor of the estrogen-primed immature mouse and rabbit and on in vivo biological activity (antiestrogenic activity in the mouse and progestomimetic activity in the rabbit). Binding was measured by competition for the uterine cytosol receptor tagged with radioactive R5020. Solid lines illustrate results for the mouse, dotted lines for the rabbit. The left-hand panel shows the effect of the introduction of a 13β-substituent, the right-hand panel shows the effect of the simultaneous introduction of double bonds.

TABLE IV. Relative Binding and Activity[a] as Deduced from Tables II and III

	Rabbit		Mouse	
	Binding	Activity	Binding	Activity
Progesterone	$[P/C]_R^{B=1}$	$[P/C]_R^{A=1}$	$[P/C]_M^{B=1}$	$[P/C]_M^{A=1}$
Norprogesterone	2.5	12.5	3.3	25
H3163	1.0	4.2	1.1	3.6
R2061	0.2	3.1	0.15	6.3
H3510	5.0	3.1	6.5	125
R2453	2.0	50	2.6	3.6
R2236	0.55	6.3	0.45	25
Norethindrone	0.7	0.2	0.6	7.1
Norgestrel	2.0	12.5	2.2	25
R1364	0.35	3.6	0.35	10
R2010	0.2	0.8	0.1	0.3
R2323	0.2		0.25	2.8
R2715	0.05		0.4	8.3

[a]Progestomimetic activity in the rabbit, antiestrogenic activity in the mouse.

markedly more active ($[P/C]_M^A = 25$) than progesterone and that its activity is decreased on introduction of double bonds in Δ^9 and in Δ^9,Δ^{11} positions ($[P/C]_M^A$ for H3163 = 3.6, $[P/C]_M^A$ for R2061 = 6.3). The presence of a 17α-methyl substituent either does not affect activity ($[P/C]_M^A$ for R2453 = 3.6) or enhances activity, in particular in the case of the monoene ($[P/C]_M^A$ for H3510 = 125), the most potent antiestrogen.

Correlation Between Binding and Activity. From the above observations on the norprogesterone series, it is possible to deduce that binding in the mouse and rabbit is correlated and that compounds less competitive than progesterone may nevertheless be more active, possibly as a result of a decrease in metabolic clearance rate. Antiestrogenic activity and binding are correlated in the case of all the monoenes (norprogesterone and H3510) and dienes (H3163 and R2453). Progestomimetic activity and binding are correlated only for the non-17α-methyl-substituted monoene (norprogesterone) and diene (H3163). In the case of the 17α-methyl derivatives, a peculiar inversion in activity occurs: a decrease in binding on addition of a double bond leads to a decrease in antiestrogenic activity but to an increase in progestomimetic activity. As regards the trienes, marked dissociation between binding and activity occurs. These compounds are less competitive on the receptor, but nevertheless exhibit pronounced activity.

Nortestosterone Series

In Vitro Binding. All the ethynyl nortestosterone derivatives, except for norgestrel ($[P/C]_R^B$ = 2.0 and $[P/C]_M^B$ = 2.2), are less effective than progesterone in displacing bound radioactive R5020 from binding to rabbit and mouse uterine cytosol.

In Vivo Biological Activity. Progestomimetic potency decreases considerably, as compared to progesterone, in the case of norethindrone ($]P/C]_R^A$ = 0.2), but increases markedly on replacing the 13β-methyl with an ethyl ($[P/C]_R^A$ = 12.5) and less markedly on replacing with a propyl ($[P/C]_R^A$ = 3.6). The presence of three double bonds leads to a general decrease in activity. One compound, the 13β-ethyl triene (R2323), never gives rise to a significant response of 2 McPhail units: increasing doses result in a decrease in activity.

As regards antiestrogenic activity, norethindrone is more active than progesterone ($[P/C]_M^A$ = 7.1). The activity increases on replacing the 13β-methyl with an ethyl ($[P/C]_M^A$ = 25) or propyl ($[P/C]_M^A$ = 10), as in the case of progestomimetic activity. In the triene series, the replacement of a methyl with an ethyl or with a propyl leads to a progressive increase in activity ($[P/C]_M^A$ = 0.3→2.8→8.3).

Correlation Between Binding and Activity. From the above observations for the nortestosterone series, it appears that binding in the mouse and rabbit is correlated, except in the case of R2715, which competes very weakly for the progesterone receptor in the rabbit ($[P/C]_R^B$ = 0.05). Progestomimetic activity and binding are not perfectly correlated: the compound which competes most— norgestrel— is the most active, but although norethindrone is a more successful competitor than R1364, it is less progestomimetic. The same observation holds true for the correlation between antiestrogenic activity and binding: norgestrel competes most and is the most powerful antiestrogen, but whereas norethindrone competes more than R1364, it is less active. The trienes are all weak competitors, but R2715 exhibits some definite antiestrogenic activity.

Conclusions

The *in vitro* correlation between progesterone binding in the rabbit and mouse was obtained by plotting $[P/C]_R^B$ against $[P/C]_M^B$ for each compound, the value for progesterone being taken as unity. A near perfect correlation was obtained as shown in Fig. 6.

None of the compounds of the ethynyl nortestosterone series is as active as the most potent progestin (R2453) and antiestrogen (H3510) of the norprogesterone series. However, the 13β-ethyl-substituted ethynyl nortestosterone derivative (norgestrel) combines both marked progestomimetic and antiestrogenic activities.

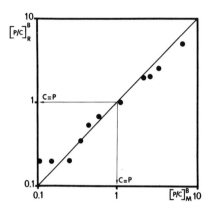

FIG. 6. Correlation between binding of the test steroids to the uterine cytosol progestin receptors from estrogen-primed immature mice and rabbits, as determined by displacement of labeled R5020 in equilibrium dialysis experiments. The correlation is obtained by plotting the activity ratio of the rabbit $[P/C]_R^B$ against that of the mouse $[P/C]_M^B$ for each steroid.

DISCUSSION

With the aid of two devices, namely, stabilization of steroid–receptor complexes with glycerol (Feil *et al.*, 1972) and use of a tag to identify a specific receptor, it has been possible to track down the elusive progestin receptor in the uterine cytosol of immature animals from four species (Philibert and Raynaud, 1973, 1974).

It has been established in previous studies that in a medium involving several specific binding systems, a compound with a high affinity for a single specific receptor may be used to tag this receptor and thus isolate it from the other receptors for further study. A tritium-labeled progestin, 100 times more potent than progesterone and with a high affinity for a "7–8S" receptor in uterine cytosol, has been used in this way to avoid interference by other specific receptors, such as the CBG-like progesterone binding which occurs in the rat and rabbit (Milgrom and Baulieu, 1970; McGuire and Bariso, 1972; Philibert and Raynaud, 1974) and which has so far impeded the study of the "7–8S" progesterone receptor. It has been demonstrated that this progestin binds to a "7–8S" receptor in uterine cytosol from immature mice, rats, rabbits, and guinea pigs and that this binding is progestin specific. Cross-competition studies have determined that this "7–8S" receptor cannot be mistaken for an "8–9S" estradiol or "4S" CBG-like progesterone receptor.

The present studies have established that a similar entity was being considered in these four species with different hormonal patterns, since in experiments carried out under strictly identical conditions for a comparison of sedimentation coefficients (Stancel *et al.*, 1973), the same coefficient and progestin specificity were recorded for each species. Moreover, a perfect correlation was observed between binding in the rabbit and mouse for the 12 test compounds.

Interaction with the uterine cytosol "7–8S" progestin receptor is a *sine qua non* condition for the induction of progestomimetic activity since testosterone and cortisol—compounds devoid of this activity—do not compete, whereas all compounds with a higher binding affinity than progesterone are much more progestomimetic than progesterone. Therefore, the search for highly potent progestins involves, as an initial step, the search for a compound which binds tightly to this "7–8S" receptor. Competition experiments may be used to determine the structural specifications for a good fit, while conformational analysis will map out the ideal molecule for high progestinicity. In the present experiments, it has been observed that the lack of a methyl group at position 10 of the progesterone molecule increases binding. Alkylation of the norsteroid in position 17α leads to an even further increase, as noted for estrogens (Raynaud *et al.*, 1973) and androgens (Liao *et al.*, 1973). The introduction of double bonds at Δ^9, Δ^{11}, as well as hydroxylation in position 17 (unpublished data), decreases binding.

In the case of compounds with only moderate affinity for the "7–8S" uterine cytosol receptor, extraneous factors such as plasma binding (Raynaud, 1973b), transport from the site of administration to the target tissue, and metabolic stability or transformation (Raynaud *et al.*, 1973), which always affect the form and availability of the unbound, *viz.* active, steroid at the receptor site, become critical in the determination of progestomimetic activity. Thus R1364, which is less tightly bound than ethynyl nortestosterone, is nevertheless more active. *In vivo*, R1364 persists longer in its active form than ethynyl nortestosterone, since lengthening of the chain in position 13 of the nortestosterone molecule has, in fact, reduced metabolic clearance rate (Raynaud, 1971).

Compounds with low affinity have also yielded most interesting results. The weak progestomimetic activity of R2323 is compatible with low affinity. However, exhaustive biological studies have, in fact, established that this compound is primarily an antiprogesterone agent (Sakiz and Azadian-Boulanger, 1971). It would appear that R2323 belongs to the class of antihormones which exert their action by competition for the corresponding hormonal receptor, as opposed to the class which impedes hormonal activity without interfering with binding to this receptor (Hubinont *et al.*, 1972). Progestins themselves fall into this latter class. They are classified as antiestrogens since they inhibit the estradiol-induced uterine weight increase in the mouse, but they do not compete for the uterine cytosol estrogen receptor (Sakiz *et al.*, 1974).

An attempted correlation between antiestrogenic activity and binding to the uterine cytosol progestin receptor in the mouse has established that strong competitors are very potent antiestrogens, but this is not sufficient evidence for concluding that the antiestrogenic activity is a corollary of the progestinicity of the molecule. The introduction of a double bond into the 17α-methyl norprogesterone molecule decreases binding in both the mouse and rabbit, but it decreases antiestrogenic activity and increases progestomimetic activity. Since binding in these two species is perfectly correlated, either antiestrogenic activity can be dissociated from progestinicity and is not related to binding to the progestin receptor or the observed dissociation is due to interspecies divergences in extraneous factors affecting activity. Only by measuring both activities in the same species can the existence or lack of a correlation be established. This point is fundamental to the further study of progestins and will decide whether progestins devoid of antiestrogenic activity can exist.

To conclude, binding to the "7–8S" receptor can be used as a basis for selecting highly active progestins, since binding to this receptor in several species has been definitely associated with progestinicity. By screening the compounds simultaneously on similar models based on *in vitro* binding to the estrogen-, androgen-, etc., specific receptors, it should be possible to evaluate their estrogenic, androgenic, etc., character. An analysis and general synthesis of these tests would go far in revealing which types of substitution affect which kinds of activity. Testing the compounds on isolated binding systems is, however, only a first step in elucidating hormone action. The intracellular location of, and the changes undergone by, receptors during the cycle (Milgrom *et al.*, 1972), under the control of a delicate hormonal balance, have to be taken into account. An experimental model which brings into play the actions of estradiol and progesterone in a definite time sequence has already been described for the rabbit (Sakiz *et al.*, 1974) and may constitute the basis of an investigation into the action of agonists and antagonists on a "dynamic" functional receptor control system at a biological and molecular level.

SUMMARY

The identification of a "7–8S" progesterone/progestin-specific receptor in the uterine cytosol of various species has enabled us to correlate some aspects of the biological activity of progesterone with binding to a target tissue protein. Improvements in technique and the use of a highly potent radioactive progestin as a tag led to the detection of a "7–8S" progestin-specific receptor in the immature animal. Sucrose gradient ultracentrifugation studies established its binding specificity, whereas equilibrium dialysis was used to determine physicochemical binding parameters. A marked parallelism was observed in several species with entirely different hormonal patterns (rat, mouse, rabbit, and guinea pig). In a correlation study, the *in vitro* competition of several nortestosterone and norprogesterone derivatives for this uterine receptor was related to their *in vivo* progestinicity. A possible relationship between antiestrogenic and progestomimetic activity via binding to the progestin receptor was investigated.

REFERENCES

Baulieu, E. E., and Raynaud, J. P. (1970), A "proportion graph" method for measuring binding systems, *Eur. J. Biochem. 13:*293–304.

Baulieu, E. E., Raynaud, J. P., and Milgrom, E. (1970), Measurement of steroid binding proteins, *Acta Endocrinol. (suppl.) 147:*104–121.

Clauberg, C. (1930), Zur Physiologie und Pathologie der Sexualhormone, im besonderen des Hormons des Corpus Luteum. 1. Mitt. Der biologische Test für das Luteohormon (das spezifische Hormon des Corpus Luteum) am infantilen Kaninchen, *Zentralbl. Gynaekol. 54:*2757–2770.

Dorfman, R. I., Kincl, F. A., and Ringold, H. J. (1961), Antiestrogen assay of neutral steroids administered by gavage, *Endocrinology 68:*43–49.

Faber, L. E., Sandmann, M. L., and Stavely, H. E. (1972), Progesterone binding in uterine cytosols of the guinea pig, *J. Biol. Chem. 247:*8000–8004.

Feil, P. D., Glasser, S. R., Toft, D. O., and O'Malley, B. W. (1972), Progesterone binding in the mouse and rat uterus, *Endocrinology 91:*738–746.

Hubinont, P. O., Hendeles, S. M., and Preumont, P. (eds.) (1972), *Hormones and Antagonists, Fourth International Seminar on Reproductive Physiology and Sexual Endocrinology, Brussels, Karger, Basel.*

Liao, S., Liang, T., Fang, S., Castañeda, E., and Shao, T. C. (1973), Steroid structure and androgenic activity, *J. Biol. Chem. 248:*6154–6162.

Lineweaver, H., and Burk, D. (1934), The determination of enzyme dissociation constants, *J. Am. Chem. Soc. 56:*658–666.

Lowry, O. H., Rosebrough, N. J., Farr, A. L., and Randall, R. J. (1951), Protein measurement with the folin phenol reagent, *J. Biol. Chem. 193:*265–275.

McGuire, J. L., and Bariso, C. D. (1972), Isolation and preliminary characterization of a progestogen-specific binding macromolecule from the 273,000*g* supernatant of rat and rabbit uteri, *Endocrinology 90:*496–506.

McGuire, J. L., and DeDella, C. (1971), *In vitro* evidence for a progestogen receptor in the rat and rabbit uterus, *Endocrinology 88:*1099–1103.

Milgrom, E., and Baulieu, E. E. (1970), Progesterone in uterus and plasma. I. Binding in rat uterus 105,000*g* supernatant, *Endocrinology 87:*276–287.

Milgrom, E., Atger, M., and Baulieu, E. E. (1970), Progesterone in uterus and plasma. IV. Progesterone receptor(s) in guinea pig uterus cytosol, *Steroids 16:*741–754.

Milgrom, E., Atger, M., Perrot, M., and Baulieu, E. E. (1972), Progesterone in uterus and plasma. VI. Uterine progesterone receptors during the estrus cycle and implantation in the guinea pig, *Endocrinology 90:*1071–1078.

Nominé, G., Bucourt, R., Tessier, J., Pierdet, A., Costerousse, G., and Mathieu, J. (1965), Agencements stéroïdes triéniques et activité progestative, *C.R. Acad. Sci. 260:*4545–4548.

O'Malley, B. W., Sherman, M. R., and Toft, D. O. (1970), Progesterone "receptors" in the cytoplasm and nucleus of chick oviduct target tissue, *Proc. Natl. Acad. Sci. (U.S.A.) 67:*501–508.

Philibert, D., and Raynaud, J. P. (1973), Progesterone binding in the immature mouse and rat uterus, *Steroids 22:*89–98.

Philibert, D., and Raynaud, J. P. (1974), Progesterone binding in the immature rabbit and guinea pig uterus, *Endocrinology 94:*627–632.

Raynaud, J. P. (1971), Metabolism of contraceptive steroids in man, in: *Proceedings III International Congress on Hormonal Steroids, Hamburg, 1970,* pp. 915–922 (V. H. T.

James and L. Martini, eds.), International Congress Series 219, Excerpta Medica, Amsterdam.

Raynaud, J. P. (1973a), A computer program for the analysis of binding experiments, *Computer Programs Biomed. 3:*63–78.

Raynaud, J. P. (1973b), Influence of rat estradiol binding plasma protein (EBP) on uterotrophic activity, *Steroids 21:*249–258.

Raynaud, J. P., Bouton, M. M., Gallet-Bourquin, D., Philibert, D., Tournemine, C., and Azadian-Boulanger, G. (1973), Comparative study of estrogen action, *Mol. Pharmacol. 9:*520–533.

Sakiz, E., and Azadian-Boulanger, G. (1971), R2323—An original contraceptive compound, in: *Proceedings III International Congress on Hormonal Steroids, Hamburg, 1970,* pp. 865–871 (V. H. T. James and L. Martini, eds.), International Congress Series 219, Excerpta Medica, Amsterdam.

Sakiz, E., Azadian-Boulanger, G., and Raynaud, J. P. (1974), Anti-estrogens, antiprogesterones, in: *Proceedings IV International Congress of Endocrinology, Washington, 1972,* pp. 988–994, International Congress Series 273, Excerpta Medica, Amsterdam.

Scatchard, G. (1949), The attraction of proteins for small molecules and ions, *Ann. N.Y. Acad. Sci. 51:*660–672.

Stancel, G. M., Leung, K. M. T., and Gorski, J. (1973), Estrogen receptors in the rat uterus. Multiple forms produced by concentration-dependent aggregation, *Biochemistry 12:*2130–2136.

Velluz, L., Nominé, G., Bucourt, R., Pierdet, A., and Tessier, J. (1961), L'extension de la synthèse totale dans le groupe des nortestostérones, *C.R. Acad. Sci. 252:*3903–3905.

Velluz, L., Nominé, G., Bucourt, R., and Mathieu, J. (1963), Un analogue triénique de la testostérone, *C.R. Acad. Sci. 257:*569–570.

Velluz, L., Valls, J., and Nominé, G. (1965), Fortschritte in der Totalsynthese von Steroiden, *Angew. Chem. Int. Ed. Eng. 77:*185–205.

Velluz, L., Matthieu, J., and Nominé, G. (1966), Contraceptive compounds and total synthesis of steroids, *Tetrahedron (suppl) 8 (part II):*495–505.

Wiest, W. G., and Rao, B. R. (1971), Progesterone binding proteins in rabbit uterus and human endometrium, in: *Advances in the Biosciences 7, Schering Workshop on Steroid Hormone "Receptors," Berlin, Dec. 7–9, 1970,* p. 251, Pergamon Press, Vieweg, New York.

Spermatogenesis and Spermatology

11

Endocrine Control of Spermatogenesis

E. Steinberger, A. Steinberger, and B. Sanborn
Program in Reproductive Biology and Endocrinology
University of Texas Medical School at Houston
Houston, Texas

In 1927 Smith demonstrated conclusively that the pituitary gland is essential for testicular development and for maintenance of spermatogenesis. The physiological role of gonadotropic hormones and testosterone in the spermatogenic process has been intensively investigated in the past 45 yr (for review, see E. Steinberger, 1971). E. Steinberger and Duckett (1967) proposed that various segments of spermatogenesis may require specific, but not necessarily the same, hormones—testosterone being primarily concerned with the completion of meiosis and FSH with the final steps of spermiogenesis. This hypothesis has been elaborated upon in the past (for review, see A. Steinberger and E. Steinberger, 1973), but recent information (E. Steinberger and A. Steinberger, 1972; E. Steinberger *et al.*, 1973; E. Steinberger, 1974) prompts its further modification, primarily with respect to the role of testosterone in the early segments of the spermatogenic process (Fig. 1). The role of FSH, beyond its possible effect on the maturation of spermatids during the initial wave of spermatogenesis, remains unclear (E. Steinberger and Duckett, 1967).

The experimental data on which this hypothesis was based were obtained from various physiological studies and different experimental designs involving ablation of the pituitary gland, its hormonal suppression, replacement therapy, and studies in tissue culture. All of these approaches suffer from drawbacks since a number of assumptions had to be made to permit interpretation of the data.

To investigate the hormonal requirements for the initiation of spermatogenesis and completion of the first spermatogenic wave, immature animals were utilized. This information was frequently utilized in analyzing the hormonal requirements for the maintenance of spermatogenesis in adults. Such extrapola-

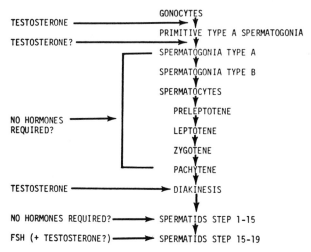

FIG. 1. Proposed scheme for the hormonal control of first wave of spermatogenesis.

tion from the immature animals to adults has been shown to be invalid. The initial wave of spermatogenesis appears to require a different hormonal milieu than that which can maintain the spermatogenic process after it has been established (E. Steinberger and A. Steinberger, 1969). Actually, the initiation of spermatogenesis in immature animals, its maintenance in adults, and its reinitiation in adult posthypophysectomy-regressed testes may differ in their precise hormonal requirements. Consequently, conclusions based on extrapolations from these three different experimental models may require reevaluation.

The experimental approach utilizing hormonal suppression of pituitary gonadotropins, for example, treatment with estrogens, appeared to be a good model for the study of the effect of pituitary hormone deprivation on spermatogenesis. Estrogens were chosen since no evidence was available to indicate that they might have a direct effect on the testes. This approach has, indeed, been utilized for this purpose, as well as for the investigation of negative-feedback mechanisms and the suppressive action of estrogens on pituitary gonadotropins. However, recently obtained evidence tends to throw considerable doubt on the interpretation of studies which utilized estrogen blockade of the pituitary gland. These studies will be discussed in greater detail below.

Tissue culture techniques offer a well-controlled experimental system, particularly as far as extraneous influences are concerned. However, recent information suggests that some conclusions drawn from tissue culture, regarding hormonal regulation of spermatogenesis, need to be modified.

Last, the role of testosterone in maintaining spermatogenesis, demonstrated as early as the 1930s, should be examined with greater scrutiny in light of sporadic reports in the older literature and more systematic studies conducted recently which suggest that steroids other than testosterone may also maintain spermatogenesis.

It appears that while the basic concepts concerned with the overall requirement of pituitary hormones and androgens for the development and maintenance of testicular function remain valid, many details related to the physiological action of these hormones, or their specific role in spermatogenesis, require reevaluation. In the past several years, information has begun to accumulate concerning the molecular mechanisms involved in hormonal regulation of spermatogenesis which allows us to formulate, although in a highly tentative fashion, a hypothesis for the molecular mechanisms of action of the trophic hormones in the seminiferous epithelium.

ESTROGEN BLOCKADE OF PITUITARY GONADOTROPINS

One of the techniques used to study the effects of gonadotropins on spermatogenesis has been histological evaluation of the seminiferous epithelium and measurement of various biochemical parameters in the testes of animals treated with estrogens. This experimental approach evolved from observations that administration of estrogens to male rats produces atrophy of the testes and sex accessory organs, and that this atrophy can be prevented by simultaneous administration of testosterone. Under these conditions, the pituitary gonadotropin levels show a gradual and progressive decrease, and 4–6 wk after initiation of the treatment are markedly depressed. These findings suggest that estrogens block the production of pituitary gonadotropins, resulting ultimately in cessation of androgen production by the testes. The absence of androgens, in turn, causes atrophy of secondary sex accessories, and the combined absence of androgens and gonadotropins results in arrest of spermatogenesis.

A recent study demonstrates that administration of estradiol benzoate to rats at dose levels of 50 or 200 μg/day, for a period of 7 days, fails to induce changes in circulating levels of LH, but produces a marked drop in plasma and testicular levels of testosterone as early as 24 h after the first injection of estradiol (Table I) (Chowdhury, 1973; Chowdhury et al., 1974). The pituitary concentration of LH shows a gradual decrease after prolonged (14–28 days) estrogen therapy associated with only a slight decline in the circulating levels (Steinberger, Chowdhury, and Tcholakian, unpublished). The drop in testicular testosterone is not entirely surprising, since Samuels et al. (1964) and Oshima et al. (1967) demonstrated that in vitro conversion of radiolabeled precursors to androgens is markedly reduced in incubates of testicular tissue obtained from animals treated with estradiol. These experiments clearly demonstrate that estradiol has a direct effect on the testes, producing rapid cessation of testosterone production. Consequently, in experiments utilizing "estrogen blockade"

TABLE I. Effect of Estradiol Benzoate (EB) on Luteinizing Hormone (LH) and Testosterone (T) Levels

Treatment[a]	Time	Plasma T (ng%)	Testes T ng/g	Testes T ng/testis	LH μg/pit	LH ng/ml serum
Normals (6)	–	95.2 ± 11.9[b]	84.6 ± 5.5	112.9 ± 6.5	10.9 ± 0.26	2.08 ± 0.12
50 μg EB (6)	24 h	33.0 ± 1.8	6.9 ± 0.4	9.5 ± 0.4	10.8 ± 0.41	1.80 ± 0.05
50 μg EB (6)	7 days	22.8 ± 0.8	4.3 ± 0.4	5.0 ± 0.7	8.5 ± 0.6	1.98 ± 0.16
500 μg EB (6)	24 h	40.6 ± 9.0	9.0 ± 0.2	11.8 ± 0.3	9.1 ± 1.1	2.1 ± 0.22
500 μg EB (6)	7 days	36.2 ± 7.0	6.9 ± 0.4	7.9 ± 0.5	4.8 ± 0.5	1.7 ± 0.09

[a] Adult male rats were injected daily with the indicated amount of EB and sacrificed 24 h or 7 days after initiation of the experiment.
[b] Mean ± SE.

of pituitary gonadotropins, a major effect on the gonads and sex accessories must have been due to cessation of testosterone production by the testes, caused directly by the estrogen treatment rather than by diminished gonadotropin levels.

STUDIES ON SPERMATOGENESIS IN TISSUE CULTURE

Attempts were made to study mammalian spermatogenesis *in vitro* utilizing tissue culture techniques. A number of early studies were conducted in organ culture of testes grown on plasma clots containing chick embryo extracts. This method was later refined to utilize chemically defined, liquid media which permit identification of factors essential for germ cell differentiation (for review, see A. Steinberger and E. Steinberger, 1970). By use of chemically defined media and stringently defined culture conditions, testes from animals of different species and ages were grown for periods of several months (A. Steinberger *et al.*, 1964; E. Steinberger *et al.*, 1964a; A. Steinberger *et al.*, 1970; A. Steinberger and E. Steinberger, 1967). However, only the Sertoli cells, peritubular cells, and primitive type A spermatogonia were maintained for the entire culture period, while spermatids survived only for several days and spermatocytes for 3–4 wk. Addition to the cultures of gonadotropins, testosterone, or other hormones had no effect on these events. However, differentiation of germ cells up to late pachytene stage of the meiotic division was promoted in hormone-free media by adding proper concentrations of vitamins A, B, and C (E. Steinberger *et al.*, 1964b) or glutamine (A. Steinberger and E. Steinberger, 1965, 1966).

It should be noted that under these conditions only a single wave of spermatogenic activity took place, with the newly formed spermatocytes inevitably degenerating at the late pachytene stage of differentiation. Thus far, culture conditions have not been defined which allow completion of the meiotic division or maturation of spermatids to occur *in vitro*.

When cultures were initiated with testes from newborn animals, the gonocytes (the only germ cells present in the testes of these animals) differentiated into pachytene spermatocytes, but not as efficiently as did spermatogonia in testes of older animals (Table II) (E. Steinberger *et al.*, 1970). Even though differentiation of the gonocytes proceeded without addition of hormones to the culture medium, it now appears likely that some hormones may have been carried over into the culture with the tissue. Testes of newborn animals contain a high concentration of testosterone, compared to adult testes (Tcholakian and Steinberger, unpublished), which may have stimulated the differentiation of gonocytes *in vitro*. Testes grown in organ culture for several days were also shown to convert progesterone to testosterone (A. Steinberger *et al.*, 1969; E. Steinberger *et al.*, 1970). Thus our earlier concept that initiation of spermatogenesis does not require hormones may need to be modified. That high local

TABLE II. Relationship between the Yield of Spermatocytes in Organ Culture and Age of the Donor Animal

Age of animal (days)	Most advanced germ cells present prior to cultivation	Age of culture (days)	Number of cultures	Percent of tubules containing spermatocytes[a]
Newborn	Gonocytes	19	32	1
1	Gonocytes	19	40	1
2	Gonocytes	18	48	1
3	Gonocytes	16	42	1–3
4	Primitive type A spermatogonia	15	10	28
5	Primitive type A spermatogonia	13	12	32
6	Type A spermatogonia	12	12	38
7	Type B spermatogonia	11	10	51
8	Type B spermatogonia	10	18	58

[a]Average values based on evaluation of over 200 cross-sections of seminiferous tubules per culture (E. Steinberger *et al.*, 1970).

concentration of testosterone can induce spermatogenesis is supported by an *in vivo* observation of gonocyte differentiation in testis bearing a testosterone-secreting tumor without concomitant differentiation in the contralateral testis of a 6-yr-old patient (Root *et al.*, 1972; E. Steinberger *et al.*, 1973).

THE ROLE OF ANDROGENS IN SPERMATOGENESIS

Walsh *et al.* (1934) and others demonstrated that treatment with testosterone commencing at the time of hypophysectomy will maintain spermatogenesis (for review, see E. Steinberger, 1971; A. Steinberger and E. Steinberger, 1973). Since testosterone has been considered to be the major male sex hormone, it has been generally accepted that testosterone *per se* is directly responsible for the observed effects on spermatogenesis. However, the discovery that dihydrotestosterone, rather than testosterone, is the active androgen in the prostate (Wilson and Loeb, 1965; Anderson and Liao, 1968) prompted investigation of the effect of a series of 5α-reduced androgens on the maintenance of spermatogenesis (Chowdhury and Steinberger, 1973). Table III summarizes the data obtained by these investigators. All androgens utilized in this study (5α-androstanediol, androsterone, dihydrotestosterone, and testosterone) were capable of maintaining spermatogenesis and sex accessory organs in hypophysecto-

TABLE III. Effect of Various Androgens on Testes and Sex Accessories in Adult Hypophysectomized Rats

Treatment[a]	Testes weight (mg)	Diameter of seminiferous tubules (μm)	Seminal vesicles (mg)		Prostate (mg)
			Full	Empty	
Testosterone	2671 ± 159[b]	247.7	1297.8 ± 123.0	489.0 ± 67.5	775.0 ± 80.9
Androstenedione	2275 ± 151	192.8	562.7 ± 107.0	251.0 ± 37.0	356.6 ± 44.8
Dehydroepiandrosterone	2191 ± 105	202.2	149.0 ± 31.6	93.6 ± 19.8	136.4 ± 27.3
Androstanediol	2896 ± 82	268.2	1249.8 ± 109.0	478.0 ± 25.6	805.6 ± 114.5
Dihydrotestosterone	2935 ± 45	250.6	1295.0 ± 92.8	552.0 ± 72.2	903.0 ± 74.3
Control (untreated hypophysectomized rats)	676 ± 65	119.3	42.8 ± 11.0	38.1 ± 9.9	nil

[a]Daily subcutaneous injections of 2 mg of steroid in 0.1 ml sesame oil commencing on the day of hypophysectomy and continuing for 30 days.
[b]Mean ± SE.

mized animals. Moreover, when several C-21 steroids were tested in the same system (E. Steinberger and Chowdhury, 1973), it was observed that they also maintained spermatogenesis but failed to prevent atrophy of the sex accessory organs (Table IV). These findings are not entirely surprising since reports have appeared sporadically in the past suggesting that some 5α-reduced androgens and C-21 steroids may have the capacity to maintain spermatogenesis in hypophysectomized rats. However, the data do raise questions concerning the molecular specificity of androgens in spermatogenesis. While it is possible to visualize that 5α-reduced androgens may share with testosterone the ability to support spermatogenesis, it is much more difficult to understand how C-21 steroids, particularly pregnenolone, a steroid which was considered to be hormonally inactive, could produce this effect.

To explain these observations, several possibilities can be considered. The C-21 steroids could have a direct effect on spermatogenesis or they could be metabolized to active androgens in the periphery or in the testes. It is unlikely that peripheral conversion would produce sufficiently high concentration of androgens in the testes to support spermatogenesis since the sex accessory organs in animals treated with the C-21 steroids become almost as atrophic as in the hypophysectomized controls, suggesting very low, if any, circulating levels of androgens. The possibility of significant intratesticular conversion to androgens also seems unlikely, since very little if any escapes into the peripheral circulation—as evidenced by the atrophy of sex accessories. Furthermore, recent study (E. Steinberger and Ficher, 1973) has shown that within 10–12 days after

TABLE IV. Effect of Various C-21 Steroids on Testicular and Sex Accessory Weights in Hypophysectomized Rats

Treatment[a]	testes (mg)	Seminal vesicles (mg)		Prostate (mg)
		Full	Empty	
Intact controls	2640 ± 141[b]	192.8 ± 28.2	94.7 ± 8.4	153.3 ± 12.7
Hypophysectomized controls	949 ± 61	42.4 ± 3.9	40.4 ± 4.3	10.0 ± 2.0
Hypox + progesterone	2519 ± 59	70.4 ± 10.4	58.2 ± 6.4	29.8 ± 5.7
Hypox + pregnenolone	2327 ± 135	53.0 ± 4.3	49.0 ± 4.0	22.6 ± 3.1
Hypox + 17-OH pregnenolone	2328 ± 17	80.7 ± 17.6	55.0 ± 3.8	24.0 ± 2.0
Hypox + 17-OH progesterone	2008 ± 66	54.7 ± 6.4	49.3 ± 5.1	20.1 ± 2.1

[a]Daily subcutaneous injections of 2 mg of steroid in 0.1 ml sesame oil commencing on the day of hypophysectomy and continuing for 30 days.
[b]Mean ± SE.

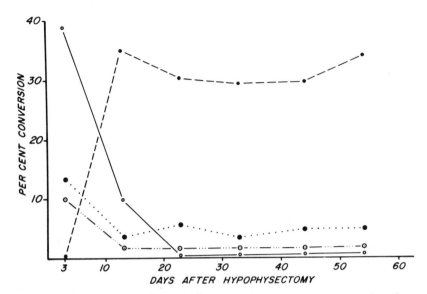

FIG. 2. *Metabolism of* ³H-*progesterone in incubates of testicular tissue from hypophysectomized rats.* --- ● ---, 20α-dihydroprogesterone; ——— o ———, testosterone; ··· ● ···, 5α-androstanedione; ··· —⊙— ···, androsterone.

hypophysectomy the testicular tissue loses the capacity to convert ³H-progesterone to ³H-androgens *in vitro* (Fig. 2). This speaks against the likelihood of intratesticular conversion of C-21 steroids to androgens. However, specific evidence for direct action of C-21 steroids on spermatogenesis is still lacking.

ROLE OF FSH IN SPERMATOGENESIS

The role of FSH in spermatogenesis remains unclear. However, recent studies (discussed below) appear to shift the emphasis from its direct effect on the late steps of spermatid development to a possible "permissive" role in the molecular mechanisms of steroid hormone action on spermatogenesis.

Greep and Fevold (1937) suggested that LH is responsible for stimulating the Leydig cells to produce androgens, while FSH is primarily concerned with stimulation of the seminiferous epithelium. This hypothesis quickly evolved into a controversy when the observation was made that testosterone will maintain spermatogenesis in hypophysectomized animals in the absence of FSH (e.g., Walsh *et al.*, 1934). Despite numerous efforts to define the role of FSH in spermatogenesis, except for data obtained by E. Steinberger and Duckett (1967) suggesting that FSH may be involved in the late steps of spermiogenesis, no clear evidence for the role of FSH in spermatogenesis has been provided. A number of studies provided evidence for possible indirect participation of FSH in the spermatogenic process and brought up the possibility that FSH may exert its effect via the Sertoli cells (Lacy and Lofts, 1965). E. Steinberger *et al.* (1964b) have shown that FSH added to organ cultures of immature testes induces maturation of Sertoli cells, as evidenced by morphological parameters. The morphological changes induced in organ culture were similar to changes occurring in the Sertoli cells *in vivo* during sexual maturation (Sapsford, 1963; Flickinger, 1967).

It has been implied by some investigators (Murphy, 1965; Courot, 1962, 1967) that FSH is capable of stimulating replication of the Sertoli cells. These studies were based on enumeration of Sertoli cell nuclei per tubule cross-section, a method which is open to many sources of error (e.g., changes in tubule diameter). Thus, the apparent increase in the number of Sertoli cell nuclei in FSH-treated animals may have been caused by factors other than stimulation of cell replication.

In a subsequent study (A. Steinberger, 1973), sexually immature or hypophysectomized adult rats treated with FSH revealed no change in the mitotic index of Sertoli cells compared to untreated intact or hypophysectomized animals. It appears therefore that FSH does not affect the normal proliferative pattern of the Sertoli cells and that this process may be genetically inscribed and regulated at the cellular level. This conclusion is also supported by studies in organ culture (A. Steinberger and E. Steinberger, 1971).

Numerous attempts have been made to define the cellular sites of action of FSH in the mammalian testes. In view of observations, although sparse, of FSH effects on the Sertoli cells, it is not surprising that the Sertoli cell has been increasingly considered to be the main (if not the only) target cell for FSH activity in the seminiferous tubule. There are at least two additional lines of evidence which indicate that this may be the case. Studies on localization of labeled gonadotropins conducted at the bright-light (Mancini *et al.*, 1967, 1968; Steinberger and Steinberger, unpublished) and electron microscope level (Castro *et al.*, 1970, 1972) showed that FSH enters into the seminiferous tubules, where it becomes localized primarily in Sertoli cell cytoplasm and occasionally in spermatogonia and spermatocytes. Labeled LH was not observed inside the seminiferous tubules and was localized mostly in the interstitial cells. The preferential localization of FSH in the Sertoli cells indicates either the primary site of its biological activity or possibly a site of temporary storage or modification before exerting its effect on another cell type in the seminiferous tubule.

Seminiferous tubules separated from interstitial tissue were shown to specifically bind radiolabeled FSH (Means and Vaitukaitis, 1972; A. Steinberger *et al.*, in press). FSH was also shown to increase the level of cAMP in incubates of seminiferous tubules (Dorrington *et al.*, 1972, A. Steinberger and Heindel, unpublished). Steinberger *et al.* (in press) attempted to identify which cells in the seminiferous tubules contain specific FSH receptors. Germinal cells, Sertoli cells, and peritubular cells, isolated by using tissue culture and other methods, were each tested for their ability to bind ^{125} I-FSH. Neither peritubular or germ cells bound the hormone to a significant degree, and the binding could not be diminished by excess amounts of unlabeled FSH. On the other hand, seminiferous tubules which were depleted of germinal elements showed no decrease in FSH binding compared to normal seminiferous tubules, which contained all germinal elements. Incubation in presence of excess amounts of unlabeled FSH reduced the binding of [125] I-FSH to the seminiferous tubules by over 70%, while LH had essentially no effect. The degree of inhibition observed with LH could be accounted for by FSH contamination of the LH preparation. These results provide additional evidence for the Sertoli cells being the primary target of FSH activity in the seminiferous tubules.

The binding experiments, together with experiments on the localization of FSH, seem to suggest that the biological activity of FSH on spermatogenesis may be either limited to the Sertoli cells or at least mediated by some events taking place in the Sertoli cells.

MOLECULAR MECHANISMS CONCERNED WITH HORMONAL CONTROL OF SPERMATOGENESIS

A number of experiments have suggested that FSH may affect certain biochemical parameters in the testis (Tables V and VI). Means and Hall (1968) have shown increased protein synthesis in the testes of immature animals treated with FSH. The stimulation of protein synthesis did not occur in intact mature rats but could be demonstrated in hypophysectomized animals treated with FSH. Similarly, an increase in RNA synthesis was observed in FSH-treated immature animals (Means, 1971). FSH increased the cAMP levels in seminiferous tubules *in vitro* (Dorrington *et al.*, 1972), and treatment of adult hypophysectomized rats with FSH apparently activated testicular cAMP-dependent protein kinase (Means, 1973).

These observations prompted us to investigate changes in some additional molecular parameters which may be involved in hormonal action in the testis. An androgen-binding protein has been observed in rat testis (Ritzen *et al.*, 1973; Hansson *et al.*, 1973). It is apparently transported with the testicular fluid into the epididymis (French and Ritzen, 1973). Hypophysectomy decreases testicular and epididymal levels of this protein, and FSH treatment apparently restores them (Hansson *et al.*, 1974; Vernon *et al.*, 1973).

We investigated the testicular androgen binding protein utilizing kinetic (Scatchard plots) and physical (polyacrylamide gel electrophoresis) methods. After hypophysectomy, little change in the concentration of the high-affinity sites (K_{assoc} = ~4 $\times$ 10^8 M^{-1}, n = 0.3 pmol/mg soluble protein) could be observed for the first 10 days (Fig. 3). By 30 days after hypophysectomy, the binding-protein levels were essentially undeterminable (i.e., all the observed binding was of low affinity). Daily FSH treatment, beginning immediately

TABLE V. Biological Effects of FSH on Immature Rat Testes

Age of rat (days)	Treatment	Adenylate cyclase[a] (pmol cAMP/mg P)	Activated protein kinase[a] (%)	Protein synthesis[b] (^{14}C-Lys, dpm/mg P)	RNA synthesis[c] (^{3}H-Cyt, cpm/μg RNA)
15–16	Control	9.5	23	900	—
	FSH	86.0	60	1300	—
20	Control	—	—	1600	2096
	FSH	—	—	2800	4186
28	Control	—	—	1900	—
	FSH	—	—	2100	—

[a]Means (1973).
[b]Means and Hall (1968).
[c]Means (1971).

TABLE VI. Biological Effects of FSH on Testes from Mature Hypophysectomized Rats

Interval after hypophysectomy	Treatment	cAMP content (pmol/mg P)		Protein synthesis (^{14}C-Lys, dpm/mg P)
Intact controls	Control	28[a]	12.4[b]	500[c]
	FSH	30	20.8	490
4 h	Control	–	–	425
	FSH	–	–	660
10 days	Control	33	–	250
	FSH	70	–	480
21–25 days	Control	25	–	220
	FSH	65	–	380
31–36 days	Control	30	24.8	–
	FSH	125	159.0	–

[a]Isolated seminiferous tubules; Dorrington *et al.* (1972).
[b]Isolated seminiferous tubules; Heindel and Steinberger (unpublished).
[c]Means and Hall (1968).

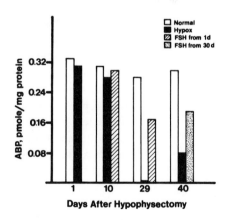

FIG. 3. Effect of hypophysectomy and FSH treatment on the androgen-binding protein in rat testis. Rats, 100 days old on day of surgery, were injected with NIH-FSH-P1 (75 μg in saline twice daily, subcutaneously) immediately following hypophysectomy (hatched bars) or after 30 days regression (dotted bars). The testes were perfused, decapsulated, minced, homogenized in 0.01 M tris (pH 7.4), and spun (100,000g). The cytosols (10% glycerol added) were extracted with 1 mg carbon/mg P for 16 h at 4°C, spun, and incubated with ³H-testosterone in 30% glycerol, 0.01 M tris (pH 7.4) for 16 h at 0°C. Unbound hormone was removed by addition of 0.7 ml of a carbon/dextran suspension (0.33%/0.033%) in buffer, shaking for 15 s, and spinning for 2 min, at 2000 rpm. The contribution of low-affinity binding components was assessed by addition of 400 ng unlabeled testosterone in the incubation mixture. Scatchard plots were used for analysis. From Sanborn, Elkington, and Steinberger (in press).

following hypophysectomy, maintained the level of binding protein above that of the hypophysectomized controls. FSH administration for 10 days, beginning 30 days after hypophysectomy, at a time when the high-affinity binding protein is not detectable (<0.08 pmol/mg protein), restored the level to half that observed in normal testis.

The cell or cells of origin and the functions of the androgen-binding protein are not yet known. We (Sanborn, Elkington, and Steinberger, in press), as well as others (Vernon *et al.*, 1973), have observed that the number of binding sites/mg soluble protein increases in cryptorchism, suggesting that Sertoli cells might be a source. It is possible that there is a testicular function for this androgen-binding protein, or at least for some component of its androgen-binding activity. This component would then be an androgen "receptor" protein, in the sense described for hormone-binding proteins in other hormone-dependent tissues (Williams-Ashman and Reddi, 1971; Jensen and DeSombre, 1972).

By looking at the newly acquired information in the light of the available physiologic data, it can be reasoned that spermatogenesis does, indeed, cease in animals deprived of the pituitary gland, and hence of gonadotropins and testosterone. Thus some or all of these hormones must be involved in the process of maintaining spermatogenesis. Since testosterone *alone* can maintain spermatogenesis, but is unable to reinitiate this process, one must assume that some permissive action required for the effect of testosterone is missing after testicular regression occurs. In light of this reasoning the following could be proposed (Figure 4):

1. FSH binds to the Sertoli cells and stimulates the production of cyclic AMP. Cyclic AMP effects activation of cyclic AMP–dependent protein kinase (RC). Cyclic AMP itself, the activated protein kinase (C), or another FSH "messenger" increases RNA and protein synthesis by a variety of mechanisms. One product of this increased synthetic activity is an androgen receptor protein.

2. Testosterone enters the Sertoli cell and binds (possibly after metabolic conversion) to the receptor protein, resulting in activation of the steroid– receptor complex. The complex itself may directly affect the germinal epithelium. Alternatively, via a series of events triggered by transport of the hormone–receptor complex to the Sertoli cell nucleus, a new messenger (m) may be produced which in turn influences events in the germinal epithelium. In addition, testosterone alone could have a direct effect on the germinal cells. This series of events could explain the initiation of spermatogenesis.

3. The maintenance of spermatogenesis with testosterone could be explained if it is assumed that one effect of the hormone–receptor complex is to signal regeneration of the receptor protein. This idea is supported

by the fact that in hypophysectomized animals, as testosterone slowly decreases, the androgen-binding activity decreases. Once it is depleted, it can be induced with FSH. Possibly the hormone—protein complex is self-renewing, but once the receptor is gone it cannot be induced with testosterone alone; that again requires the action of FSH. This would explain the role of FSH in spermatogenesis (E. Steinbeger and Duckett, 1965, 1967), the ability of testosterone to maintain spermatogenesis in the absence of FSH (Walsh *et al.*, 1934; E. Steinberger and Nelson, 1955), the failure of testosterone to reinitiate spermatogenesis (Nelson and Gallagher, 1936; Woods and Simpson, 1961), and the failure of FSH alone to maintain the spermatogeneic process (Woods and Simpson, 1961; Berswordt-Wallrabe and Newmann, 1966).

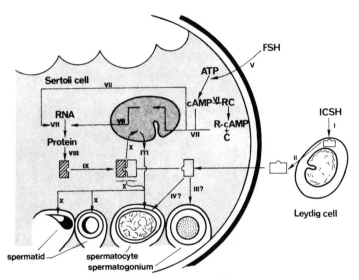

FIG. 4. Possible molecular effects of the gonadotropins and testosterone related to the control of spermatogenesis. I, Stimulation of testosterone production in the Leydig cell by ICSH. II, Transport of testosterone into the seminiferous tubules and into Sertoli cells—the "active" androgen from here on is given as testosterone, but it may well be a metabolite of testosterone. III, Possible direct interaction of testosterone with germinal cells to initiate a wave of spermatogenesis. IV, Possible direct action of testosterone on spermatocytes to promote meiotic division. V, Production of cyclic AMP (cAMP) in the seminiferous tubules as a result of FSH binding and stimulation of adenylate cyclase. VI, Activation of cAMP-dependent protein kinase (RC) by cAMP. VII, Increased RNA and protein synthesis effected by cAMP, a protein kinase component, or another FSH "messenger" by a variety of mechanisms. VIII, Increased androgen receptor protein as a result of the increased synthetic activity. IX, Complex formation between testosterone and the receptor protein. X, Direct interaction of the hormone—receptor complex with germinal cells resulting in the progression of spermatogenesis, or indirect interaction via a "message" (m) generated as a result of events in the Sertoli cell controlled by this complex.

SUMMARY

The hypothesis proposed is that testosterone is the primary spermatogenic hormone. It may directly affect the early stages of spermatogenesis, namely the spermatogonial development, and may possibly be capable of permitting the meiotic division to undergo completion. It alone, however, is insufficient for the maturation of spermatids. FSH is responsible for inducing testosterone receptor protein in the Sertoli cell, which then, in complex with testosterone, is capable of promoting full spermatogenesis.

REFERENCES

Anderson, K. M., and Liao, S. (1968), Selective retention of dihydrotestosterone by prostatic nuclei, *Nature (Lond.) 219:*277.

Berswordt–Wallrabe, R. v., and Neumann, F. (1966), Failure to induce effects in the testes of hypophysectomized rats concomitantly treated with a FSH preparation and the anti-androgen, cyproterone acetate, in: *Proceedings of the 5th World Congress on Fertility and Sterility,* pp. 581–584, International Congress Series Excerpta Medica, Amsterdam.

Castro, A. E., Seiguer, A. C., and Mancini, R. E. (1970), Electron microscopic study of the localization of labeled gonadotropins in the Sertoli and Leydig cells of the rat testis, *Proc. Soc. Exp. Biol. Med. 133:*582–586.

Castro, A. E., Alonso, A., and Mancini, R. E. (1972), Localization of follicle-stimulating hormone and luteinizing hormone in the rat testis during immunohistological tests, *J. Endocrinol. 52:*129–136.

Chowdhury, M. (1973), Direct effect of estradiol on testosterone production by rat testes, *Biol. Reprod. 9:*81–82.

Chowdhury, A. K., and Steinberger, E. (1973), Effect of 5α-reduced androgens on initiation and maintenance of spermatogenesis, *Biol. Reprod. 9:*62–63.

Chowdhury, M., Tcholakian, R., and Steinberger, E. (1974), An unexpected effect of 17β-oestradiol on luteinizing hormone and testosterone, *J. Endocrinol., 60:*375–376.

Courot, M. (1962), Action des hormones gonadotropes sur le testicule de l'agneau impubère: Résponse particuliere de la lignee sertolienne, *Ann. Biol. Anim. Biochim. Biophys. 2:*157–161.

Courot, M. (1967), Endocrine control of the supporting and germ cells of the impuberal testis, *J. Reprod. Fertil. (suppl.)2:*89–101.

Dorrington, J. H., Vernon, R. G., and Fritz, I. B. (1972), The effect of gonadotropins on the 3′,5′-AMP levels of seminiferous tubules, *Biochem. Biophys. Res. Commun. 46:*1523–1528.

Flickinger, C. J. (1967), The postnatal development of Sertoli cells of the mouse, *Z. Zellforsch. Mikrosk. Anat. 78:*92–113.

French, F. S., and Ritzen, E. M. (1973), A high-affinity androgen binding protein (ABP) in rat testis: Evidence for secretion into efferent duct fluid and absorption by epididymis, *Endocrinology 93:*88–95.

Greep, R., and Fevold, H. (1937), The spermatogenic and secretory function of the gonads of hypophysectomized adult rats treated with pituitary FSH and LH, *Endocrinology 21:*611–618.

Hansson, V., Djøseland, O., Reusch, E., Attramadal, A., and Torgerson, O. 1973), An androgen binding protein in the testis cytosol fraction of adult rats: Comparison with the androgen binding protein in the epididymis, *Steroids 21:*457–474.

Hansson, V., Djøseland, O., Reusch, E., Attramadal, A., and Torgersen, O. (1974), FSH stimulation of testicular androgen binding protein, *Nature New Biology 246:*56–58.

Jensen, E. V., and deSombre, E. R. (1972), Mechanism of action of the female sex hormones, *Ann. Rev. Biochem. 41:*203–230.

Lacy, D., and Lofts, B. (1965), Studies on the structure and function of the mammalian testis. I. Cytological and histochemical observations after continuous treatment with oestrogenic hormone and the effects of F.S.H. and L.H., *Proc. R. Soc. Lond. Ser. B 162:*188–197.

Mancini, R. E., Castro, A., and Seiguer, A. C. (1967), Histological localization of follicle-stimulating and luteinizing hormones in the rat testis, *J. Histochem. Cytochem. 15:*516–525.

Mancini, R. E., Seiguer, A. C., and Lloret, A. P. (1968), The effect of gonadotropins on the testis of hypophysectomized patients, in: *Gonadotropins,* pp. 503–512 (E. Rosemberg, ed.), Geron-X, Los Altos, Calif.

Means, A. R. (1971), Concerning the mechanism of FSH action: Rapid stimulation of testicular synthesis of nuclear RNA, *Endocrinology 89:*981–989.

Means, A. R. (1973), Specific interaction of ^{3}H-FSH with rat testis binding sites, in: *Receptors for Reproductive Hormones,* pp. 431–448 (B. W. O'Malley and A. R. Means, eds.), Plenum Press, New York.

Means, A. R., and Hall, P. F. (1968), Protein biosynthesis in the testis. I. Comparison between stimulation by FSH and glucose, *Endocrinology 82:*597–602.

Means, A. R., and Vaitukaitis, J. (1972), Peptide hormone "receptors"; specific binding of ^{3}H-FSH to testis, *Endocrinology 90:*39–46.

Murphy, H. D. (1965), Sertoli cell stimulation following intratesticular injections of FSH in the hypophysectomized rat, *Proc. Soc. Exp. Biol. Med. 118:*1202–1205.

Nelson, W. O., and Gallagher, T. F. (1936), Some effects of androgenic substances in rat, *Science 84:*230–232.

Oshima, H., Wakabayashi, K., and Tamaoki, B. (1967), The effect of synthetic estrogen upon the biosynthesis *in vitro* of androgen and luteinizing hormone in the rat, *Biochim. Biophys. Acta 137:*356–366.

Ritzen, E. M., Dobbins, M. C., Tindall, D. J., French, F. S., and Nayfeh, S. N. (1973), Characterization of an androgen binding protein (ABP) in rat testis and epididymis, *Steroids 21:*593–607.

Root, A., Steinberger, E., Smith, K., Steinberger, A., Russ, D., Somers, L., and Rosenfeld, R. (1972), Isosexual pseudoprecocity with testicular adenoma, *J. Pediatr. 80:*264–268.

Samuels, L. T., Short, J. G., and Huseby, R. A. (1964), The effect of diethylstilbestrol on testicular 17α-hydroxylase and 17 demolase activities in BALB/c mice, *Acta Endocrinol. 45:*487–497.

Sapsford, C. S. (1963), The development of the Sertoli cell of the rat and mouse: its existence as a mononucleate unit, *J. Anat. 97:*225–238.

Smith, P. E. (1927), The diabilities caused by hypophysectomy and their repair, *JAMA 88:*158–161.

Steinberger, A. (1973), Effect of gonadotropins on the replication of Sertoli cells in immature and immature hypophysectomized rats, *Biol. Reprod. 9:*61–62.

Steinberger, A., and Steinberger, E. (1965), Differentiation of rat seminiferous epithelium in organ culture, *J. Reprod. Fertil. 9:*243–248.

Steinberger, A., and Steinberger, E. (1966), Stimulatory effect of vitamins and glutamine on the differentiation of germ cells in rat testes organ culture grown in chemically defined media, *Exp. Cell Res. 44:*429–443.

Steinberger, A., and Steinberger, E. (1967), Factors affecting spermatogenesis in organ cultures of mammalian testes. *J. Reprod. Fertil (suppl.) 2:*117–124.

Steinberger, A., and Steinberger, E. (1970), *In vitro* growth and development of mammalian testes, in: *The Testis,* Vol. II, pp. 363–391 (A. D. Johnson, W. R. Gomes, and N. L. VanDemark, eds.), Academic Press, New York.

Steinberger, A., and Steinberger, E. (1971), Replication pattern of Serotoli cell in maturing rat testis *in vivo* and in organ culture, *Biol. Reprod. 4:*84–87.

Steinberger, A., and Steinberger, E. (1973), Hormonal control of mammalian spermato-genesis, in: *The Regulation of Mammalian Reproduction,* Vol. 3, pp. 139–150 (S. J. Segal, R. Crozier, P. A. Corfman, and G. P. Condliffe, eds.), Charles C Thomas, Springfield, Ill.

Steinberger, A., Steinberger, E., and Perloff, W. H. (1964), Mammalian testes in organ culture, *Exp. Cell Res. 36:*19–27.

Steinberger, A., Ficher, M., and Steinberger, E. (1969), Bioconversion of progesterone in organ culture of testicular tissue, *Fed. Proc. 28:*773.

Steinberger, A., Ficher, M., and Steinberger, E. (1970), Studies of spermatogenesis and steroid metabolism in cultures of human testicular tissue, in: *The Human Testis,* pp. 333–352 (E. Rosemberg and C. A. Paulsen, eds.), Plenum Press, New York.

Steinberger, E. (1971), Hormonal control of mammalian spermatogenesis, *Physiol. Rev. 51:*1–22.

Steinberger, E. (1974), Maturation of male germinal epithelium, in: *NIH Conference on the Control of the Onset of Puberty, Airlie, Va.,* pp. 386–402, John Wiley and Sons, New York.

Steinberger, E., and Chowdhury, A. K. (1973), Effect of C-21 steroids on spermatogenesis in hypophysectomized rats, *Endocrine Soc., Chicago,* abst. 98.

Steinberger, E., and Duckett, G. E. (1965), Effect of estrogen or testosterone on initiation and maintenance of spermatogenesis in the rat, *Endocrinology 76:*1184–1189.

Steinberger, E., and Duckett, G. E. (1967), Hormonal control of spermatogenesis, *J. Reprod. Fertil. 2:*75–87.

Steinberger, E., and Ficher, M. (1973), Effect of hypophysectomy and gonadotropin treatment on metabolism of ^{3}H-progesterone by rat testicular tissue, *Steroids 22:*425–443.

Steinberger, E., and Nelson, W. O. (1955), Effect of hypophysectomy, cryptorchidism, estrogen and androgen upon the level of hyaluronidase in the rat testis, *Endocrinology 56:*429–444.

Steinberger, E., and Steinberger, A. (1969), The spermatogenic function of the testes, in: *The Gonads,* pp. 715–737 (K. W. McKerns, ed.), Appleton-Century-Crofts, New York.

Steinberger, E., and Steinberger, A. (1972), The testis: Growth vs. function, in: *Regulation of Organ and Tissue Growth,* pp. 299–314. (R. G. Goss, ed.), Academic Press, New York.

Steinberger, E., Steinberger, A., and Perloff, W. H. (1964a), Studies on growth in organ culture of testicular tissue from rats of various ages, *Anat. Rec. 148:*581–589.

Steinberger, E., Steinberger, A., and Perloff, W. H. (1964b), Initiation of spermatogenesis *in vitro, Endocrinology 74:*788–792.

Steinberger, E., Steinberger, A., and Ficher, M. (1970), Study of spermatogenesis and steroid metabolism in cultures of mammalian testes, *Rec. Progr. Hormone Res. 26:*547–588.

Steinberger, E., Root, A., Ficher, M., and Smith, K. D. (1973), The role of androgens in the initiation of spermatogenesis in man, *J. Clin. Endocrinol. Metabol. 37:*743–751.

Vernon, R. G., Kopec, B., and Fritz, I. B. (1973), Studies on the distribution of the high-affinity testosterone-binding protein in rat seminiferous tubules, *J. Endocrinol.* *57:*ii.

Walsh, E. L., Cuyler, W. K., and McCullagh, D. R. (1934), Physiologic maintenance of male sex glands; effect of androtin on hypophysectomized rats, *Am. J. Physiol.* *107:*508–512.

Williams-Ashman, H. G., and Reddi, A. H. (1971), Actions of vertebrate sex hormones, *Ann. Rev. Physiol.* *33:*31–82.

Wilson, J. D., and Loeb, P. M. (1965), Intra-nuclear localization of testosterone-1, 2-H in the preen gland of the duck, *J. Clin. Invest.* *44:*1111.

Woods, M. C., and Simpson, M. E. (1961), Pituitary control of the testis of the hypophysectomized rat, *Endocrinology* *69:*91–125.

12

Genetic Aspects of Spermatozoa

R. A. Beatty
A.R.C. Unit of Animal Genetics
Department of Genetics
Edinburgh, U.K.

The spermatozoon is a life form of particular interest, since it is typical of nearly all animals, is a highly specialized cell posing many problems in developmental biology, has a genetic constitution differing from that of the soma, and is a transmitter of genetic information between generations.* Genetic departures from the somatic genotype involve not only haploidy but also the existence of altered gene relations brought about by crossing-over and meiotic segregation.

The phenotype of a spermatozoon is subject to two potential forms of genetic control: (1) a "diploid effect" mediated by the diploid genome of the soma and premeiotic germ cell and (2) a "haploid effect" mediated by its own haploid genetic content after meiosis. Irrespective of the form of control, spermatozoan dimensions certainly have an extremely high heritability (Beatty, 1970), and dimensions can be changed in a desired direction by a genetic selection program (Woolley, 1970).

The "diploid effect" is paramount. "Haploid effects," though they must be rare, are of great fundamental and applied interest. In an apparently well-attested example in mice (Braden, 1972), the fertility of individual spermatozoa appeared to depend on their own genetic content at the T-locus. An exception to Mendel's law of random assortment of the gametes resulted: an experimental challenge succeeded in altering the relative fertility of spermatozoa in accor-

---

*The genetics of the spermatozoon has been reviewed recently (Beatty, 1970, 1971, 1973a,b), and the proceedings of a symposium on the subject have been published (Beatty and Gluecksohn-Waelsch, 1972). These publications were relied on for detailed references and for preparing this brief introduction.

dance with their specific content of *T*-locus alleles and therefore constituted a novel way of controlling the process of genetic transmission.

When spermatozoan phenotype varies in accordance with genetic content, the possibility arises of the deliberate discouragement, or even the physical removal, of genetically deleterious spermatozoa from semen. Such possibilities, if realizable, could well be of interest in a medical context. Indeed, in the work on *T*-locus mice, a simple experimental treatment, believed to act through the spermatozoa, reduced the incidence among progeny of a hereditary and disastrous defect for a mouse. Perhaps something of this nature will be feasible one day in man. In the rabbit (Beatty and Fechheimer, 1972), a limited, though regular, physical removal of the genetically deleterious diploid spermatozoa from semen has become possible. Such spermatozoa are deleterious because, if fertile, they would lead to a triploid abortus or even (in man) to an occasional malformed-born triploid. In domestic animals, ordinary Y spermatozoa are "deleterious" in the economic sense because they produce an unwanted incidence of male offspring, and there has been much work in developing experimental techniques designed to reduce the proportion of fertilizing Y spermatozoa (Kiddy and Hafs, 1971; Beatty, 1974).

The work now to be described began with a long-standing interest in the etiology of the chromosomal abnormalities in animals that can cause up to 10% fetal wastage (Fechheimer, 1972). Progress in evaluating the causes of one particular form of abnormality, triploidy, was held up because one essential piece of information was lacking: the relative numbers of XX, XY, and YY diploid spermatozoa. The discovery of the fluorescent "F-bodies" that mark the Y chromosome in the human sperm head (Pearson and Bobrow, 1970; Barlow and Vosa, 1970; Sumner *et al.*, 1971) suddenly brought about the possibility of directly estimating the numbers of the three types of diploid spermatozoa, at least in human spermatozoa. This estimate has been attempted and will be discussed in the next section. Further evidence comes from study of the relative numbers of XXX, XXY, and XYY human triploid fetuses, considered in a final section. The combined evidence from F-body studies and from study of triploids provides an explanation of the numbers of F-bodies in haploid, diploid, and tetraploid human spermatozoa and an estimate of the proportions of the three sex chromosome karyotypes of diploid spermatozoa, of the three karyotypes of triploid, and of the modes of origin of triploid conceptuses in the human.

THE NUMBERS OF XX, XY, AND YY DIPLOID HUMAN SPERMATOZOA: F-BODY EVIDENCE

The object of this work was to attempt an estimate of the numbers of XX, XY, and YY diploid spermatozoa in semen of normal men. The method was to count the numbers of spermatozoa containing either 0, 1, 2, or $\geqslant 3$ of the fluorescent F bodies that mark the Y chromosomes in mature human spermatozoa. Spermatozoa were viewed with dark-ground fluorescence microscopy, using an FITC blue-light fluorescence exciting filter and an FITC barrier filter, the light source being an HBO 200-W UV microscope lamp with the ultraviolet stopped by a filter. Details of the procedure are given by Beatty (1974).

Spermatozoa were classed not only by the number of F-bodies within their heads but also by three visually judged size classes: Small (S), Medium (M), and Large (L). In animal material, M and L correspond very closely with diploid (2N) and tetraploid (4N). It became apparent during the present work that M and L in human material do not correspond too well with 2N and 4N, and a corrective parameter g had to be introduced during analysis, as described below.

A full random sampling of the whole spermatozoan population would have been desirable, but few M and L would then have been encountered. Sampling was therefore in the form of three subsets, with random selection of spermatozoa within subsets. In each microscope slide, 500 Small spermatozoa were scored by the number of F-bodies (subset 1). Another 1000 spermatozoa were then classed as Small or Medium, ignoring Large spermatozoa and F-bodies (subset 2). A further 50 spermatozoa were classed as Medium or Large (ignoring Small spermatozoa), and their F-body contents were scored at the same time (subset 3). There were 11 microscope slides, prepared from the semen of seven normal volunteers. The results, pooled over slides, are listed in Table I.

Since the numbers of Small and Medium are known from subset 2, and the numbers of Medium and Large from subset 3, the data can be adjusted by simple arithmetic proportion to give the equivalent of a full random sampling of the whole sperm population. This is shown in Table II in the form of percentages (the "predicted values" in parentheses will be considered later and can be ignored for the moment).

The data in Table II raise many problems which prevent us from answering

TABLE I. Counts of Spermatozoa from Normal Men[a]

F-bodies	S (Small)	M (Medium)	L (Large)
OF	3,102	157	12
1F	2,192	244	22
2F	177	82	16
≥3F	29	11	6
Unclassed F	10,666	334	

[a]Classed by number of F-bodies and sperm size. The data comprise three independent sub-sets enclosed in "boxes" and described in the text.

TABLE II. Data as Percentages of Sperm Types: Predicted Values in Parentheses

F-bodies	S	M	L	Total
0F	54.50 (53.95)	0.96 (1.18)	0.07 (0.03)	55.53 (55.16)
1F	38.51 (38.20)	1.50 (1.49)	0.13 (0.10)	40.14 (39.79)
2F	3.11 (4.12)	0.50 (0.41)	0.10 (0.14)	3.71 (4.67)
≥3F	0.51 (0.24)	0.07 (0.07)	0.04 (0.07)	0.62 (0.38)
	96.63 (96.51)	3.03 (3.15)	0.34 (0.34)	100%(100)

our main enquiry by making a simple correspondence between 0F, 1F, and 2F Medium spermatozoa on the one hand, and XX, XY, and YY diploid spermatozoa on the other hand. Haploid X and Y spermatozoa should be equal in number, but the numbers of 0F and 1F Small spermatozoa are far from equal. Further, (if Medium spermatozoa are diploid) the numbers of 0F and 2F Medium spermatozoa should be equal, but are not. The numbers of 2F Small spermatozoa seem unreasonably high. (If such spermatozoa are really YY, due to nondisjunction at the second meiotic division, then 3.11 of these spermatozoa among 100 scored would mean a nondisjunction of 3.11 among 25 secondary Y spermatocytes, i.e., an unacceptable incidence of 12.44%. Hence, not all of the 2F Small spermatozoa can really be YY.) Ordinary cytogenetic expectation has no place for spermatozoa with ≥3 F-bodies, nor for 0F and 1F Large spermatozoa (if Large spermatozoa are really tetraploid). Finally, Medium spermatozoa (3.03%) cannot all be truly diploid, since DNA measurements give an incidence of 1.0% diploids (Sumner, 1971).

A mathematical model of the meiotic process was set up and, from the data various parameters were estimated that could collectively explain the data and answer the problems just mentioned. It is important to note that the introduction of a given parameter does not presuppose that the parameter has any real existence; if it does not have a real existence, the calculation may well assign to it a value of zero. Because this first model will undoubtedly have to be improved in future work, it does not seem worthwhile to give a lengthy formal description of it. Instead, the parameters and their estimated values will be listed briefly (Table III) and the table will be amplified by the following detail.

Parameter a (the percentage nondisjunction of sex chromosomes at the first meiotic division) and parameter b (the percentage nondisjunction of X chromosomes at the second meiotic division) both vanish when spermatozoa are classed by the number of F-bodies and are omitted from the table. Parameters a and b cannot therefore be estimated from the data, and, correspondingly, whatever their values, they will not bias the estimates of the other parameters. They will become useful only if the X chromosome in the sperm head can be marked visually in some way.

TABLE III. Parameters and Values[a]

c	—	% ND of Y, M_{II} (assume zero)
d	25.74	% F-bodies not recognized
q	2.81	% chromosome doubling at M_I
r	1.22	% chromosome doubling at M_{II}
s	1.15	% obligatory tetraploids
g	1.20	% $1N$ (Small) sperm misclassed as Medium sperm
m	0.118	mean adventitious F-bodies per haploid sperm; $\times 2$ for $2N$ sperm; $\times 4$ for $4N$ sperm

[a]ND, nondisjunction.

Parameter c is the percentage nondisjunction of the Y chromosome at the second meiotic division. For the present purposes, its value was set at zero, a simplification not thought to introduce significant bias in relation to the main objective of the analysis (study of diploid spermatozoa).

Parameter q (2.81%) is the percentage of chromosome doubling at the first meiotic division (failure of cytokinesis). The doubling should yield XY diploid spermatozoa (if we accept the standard view that there is no crossing over between human X and Y and that X and Y separation is therefore prereductional).

Parameter r (1.22%) is the percentage of chromosome doubling at the second meiotic division (failure of cytokinesis). The resulting spermatozoa should be XX and YY in equal number. Simultaneous operation of q and r should yield XXYY tetraploid spermatozoa.

Parameter s (1.15%) is the percentage of obligatory tetraploidy, visualized as a predestination of a spermatogonium to double chromosomally at both meiotic divisions. This is also equivalent to supposing that the circumstances causing chromosome doubling in a cell at the first division are liable to persist and give an extra chance of further doubling at the second division.

Parameter d (25.74%) is the percentage of F-bodies not scored for technical or other reasons. This has also been called "observational distortion" (Beatty, 1974). Some such parameter is obviously necessary in order to allow for the marked excess of 0F over 1F Small spermatozoa.

Parameter m (0.118) estimates the mean number of "adventitious F-bodies" per spermatozoon, not truly F-bodies, but appearing to be such. Anyone accustomed to observing F-bodies will be familiar with occasions when there is uncertainty as to whether one is seeing an F-body or an artifact. The adventitious F-bodies are assumed to be spread randomly over spermatozoa in Poisson distribution. For instance, if we consider 0F haploid spermatozoa and follow the terms of the Poisson distribution a proportion $1/e^m$ will be correctly scored, a proportion m/e^m will acquire one adventitious F-body and be misclassed as 1F, a proportion $m^2/2e^m$ will acquire two adventitious bodies and be misclassed as 2F spermatozoa, and so on. In similar fashion, a proportion of truly 1F spermatozoa will acquire one adventitious body, and so on. Similar proportions exist for spermatozoa that are truly 2F, 3F, and so on. It was assumed that the heads of diploid and tetraploid spermatozoa, respectively twice and four times the volume of haploids, would have correspondingly greater chances of displaying adventitious F-bodies, so that m is replaced by $2m$ for diploids and by $4m$ for tetraploids.

Parameter g (1.20%) allows for the inexact correspondence (in human material) between the numbers of visually scored Small, Medium, and Large spermatozoa and the numbers of $1N$, $2N$, and $4N$. It is known from unpublished DNA measurements made with Mr. Andrew Carothers of this Department that Small spermatozoa are haploid but that Medium ones contain diploids and haploids. The following model was employed: if p_1, p_2, and p_3 ($\Sigma p = 1.0$) are the true proportions of $1N$, $2N$, and $4N$ spermatozoa, then the visually observed size classes would be in the following proportions: Small $[gp_1]$; Medium $[g(1-g)p_1 + gp_2]$; Large $[(1-g)^2 p_1 + (1-g)p_2 + p_3]$. In other words, it is believed that Small spermatozoa are truly haploid, Medium are a mixture of haploids and diploids, and Large are a mixture of haploids, diploids, and tetraploids. The treatment of the Large spermatozoa in this model is somewhat formalistic, but it does make some kind of allowance for a rather minor element of the data.

These parameters were then estimated from the data of Table I, their values being those that gave the best fit with the data (minimum χ^2 discrepancy between observation and expectation). The laborious calculation was stopped when the iterative process led to little further decrease in discrepancy. Their values have already been listed in the text and in Table III. When inserted in the mathematical structure of the model, these estimates yield predicted figures shown in parentheses in Table II. By inspection, there seems to be a satisfactory fit between expectation and observation, though some significant discrepancy remains that will require further study. However, the fit is good enough to suggest that the analysis has been reasonably successful and that the estimates of the parameters may be not far from the truth.

Finally, the effect of the three "nuisance factors" d, m, and g was removed by calculation to produce the best estimate that can be made of the true proportions of XX, XY, and YY diploid spermatozoa, as shown in Table IV. It will be seen that XY diploids, arising from chromosome doubling at the first meiotic division, constitute the major class (70.06%), while XX and YY diploids (each 14.97%) are smaller classes attributable to chromosome doubling at the second meiotic division. In Table IV, the identity of the chromosome classes has been marked as "approximate" because, for instance, an XXY spermatozoon would be treated by the calculation as if it were XY. The numbers of such unusual types of spermatozoa should, however, be low.

The estimate of 70.06% XY diploid spermatozoa has a key relevance to the

TABLE IV. Diploid Sperm: Estimated Percentages of Chromosome Classes After Correction for Nonrecognized F-Bodies, Misclassification of Size Class, Adventitious Spots

~ XX	14.97	
~ XY	70.06	(±⩾7.0)
~ YY	14.97	
	100.0%	

interpretation of the data on human triploids in the next section. A minimal standard error of ± (⩾7.0) has been attached to it; the true standard error cannot be smaller.

THE ETIOLOGY OF TRIPLOIDY AMONG HUMAN FETUSES

A wholly independent line of evidence from triploid human fetuses that provides estimates of the relative numbers of XX, XY, and YY diploid spermatozoa and also throws some light on the etiology of triploidy will now be considered. The initial data consist of three figures from Carr (1971); the numbers of XXX, XXY, and XYY triploids are 26, 44, and 4. It is assumed that they have equal viability. This is supported by a lack of correlation between fetal age and the proportions of the three karyotypes (Carr, 1971).

Possible origins of triploids are summarized in section A of Table V. The first type of origin is estimated by P, the percentage of triploids arising by digyny (XX diploid eggs, meeting equal numbers of haploid X or Y spermatozoa, should produce XXX and XXY triploids in equal numbers). The parameter Q estimates the percentage of triploids arising after fertilization with diploid spermatozoa produced at the first male meiotic division (100% of such spermatozoa should be XY diploids, and all triploids should be XXY). The parameter R estimates the percentage of triploids arising by fertilization with diploid spermatozoa produced at the second male meiotic division (there should be equal numbers of XX and YY diploid spermatozoa, giving a 50:50 ratio of XXX and XYY triploids). Finally (the parameters being arranged to total 100), $(100 - P - Q - R)$ estimates the percentage of triploids arising as a result of dispermy [The random expectation is fertilization by $(X + X)$, $(X + Y)$, and $(Y + Y)$ pairs of spermatozoa in 25:50:25 ratio, giving XXX, XXY, and XYY triploids in the same ratio.] It will be noted that the percentage of triploids arising by diandry (the sum of the

TABLE V. Numbers of Human Triploid Fetuses[a]

Triploid sex chromosomes	Digyny P	Diandry			Data
		$2N$ sperm M_I Q	$2N$ sperm M_{II} R	Dispermy $100 - P - Q - R$	
A. Expected % ratios					
XXX	50	0	50	25	
XXY	50	100	0	50	
XYY	0	0	50	25	
B. Solution with minimum (zero) dispermy: numbers					
XXX	22	0	4	0	26
XXY	22	22	0	0	44
XYY	0	0	4	0	4
Σ	44	22	8	0	74
$\%\Sigma$	59.5	29.7	10.8	0	100%
C. Solution with maximum dispermy: numbers					
XXX	22	0	0	4	26
XXY	22	14	0	8	44
XYY	0	0	0	4	4
Σ	44	14	0	16	74
$\%\Sigma$	59.5	18.9	0	21.6	100%

[a] Data from Carr (1971).

percentages for fertilization by diploid spermatozoa and for dispermic fertilization) is $[Q + R + (1 - P - Q - R)] = (1 - P)$, with the same standard error as that of P.

The problem, then, is to account for the data by finding values of P, Q, R and $(100 - P - Q - R)$ (each with its expected ratio of the three karyotypes) so that the data are fitted exactly. With three observations, we can estimate only two parameters. A maximum likelihood solution gives an explicit estimate of the percentage of triploids attributable to digyny $[P = 59.5 \pm (SE\ 13.1)\%]$ and also of the percentage due to diandry $[(1 - P) = 40.5\ (\pm SE\ 13.1)\%]$. The remaining parameter has to be a combination of the main parameters in which we are interested. A convenient combination is the difference $(Q - R)$, which has a value of 18.9 $(\pm SE\ 11.4)\%$. The estimate of $(Q - R)$ approaches formal statistical significance in comparison with its standard error and suggests that a larger series of observations might show more definitely that Q exceeds R. Q, R, and $(100 - P - Q - R)$ cannot be estimated explicitly. However, certain limits can be assigned to them from the maximum likelihood expressions, but it happens that these limits can also be worked out by the following direct appeal to the data. The truth must lie somewhere between the assumption, on the one hand, that none of the four XYY triploids is attributable to dispermy (as in section B of Table V) and the assumption, on the other hand, that all the XYY triploids are attributable to dispermy (as in section C of Table V). It can readily be visualized that in both sections B and C of the table, the numbers entered are the only possible ones corresponding to the various ratios of karyotypes under each type of origin and also adding up exactly to the observations. The %Σ figures are estimates of P, Q, R, and $(100 - P - Q - R)$ according to the two assumptions about the role of dispermy in sections B and C of the table.

The range of possibilities for the value of the parameters is set out in Fig. 1 in the form of a nomogram. The data are fitted exactly if we draw any vertical line through the four plotted lines and read off the intercept points on the scale. So, from the evidence of triploids alone, we have an explicit estimate of a 59.5% incidence of triploidy caused by digyny (the remaining 40.5% being due to diandry). The other parameters are smaller and cannot be estimated explicitly.

At this point, the key evidence from F-bodies considered in an earlier section of this chapter will be recalled, i.e., where the numbers of XY diploid spermatozoa (arising by chromosome doubling at the first meiotic division) were estimated to be 70.06% of all diploid spermatozoa. If these XY spermatozoa fertilize a haploid egg, the numbers of triploids (XXY) so produced should be 70.06% of the total numbers of triploids arising after fertilization with diploid spermatozoa. In other words, a vertical line must be drawn in Fig. 1 giving intercepts with the Q and R plotted lines such that $100 \, Q/(Q + R)$ is 70.06. The point at which this occurs is indicated by the arrowed vertical line. It will be seen that the dispermy plotted line is intercepted at a value close to zero (the actual intercept is a small irrational value of -5%, which cannot correspond to reality, but could easily arise through sampling error).

The conclusion from the joint evidence of triploid fetuses and spermatozoan F-bodies is therefore that the best estimate of the true value of the percentage of triploids due to dispermy is zero, and the best solution of the whole problem is that given in the %Σ row of section B of Table V. Using round numbers, the final conclusion is

60% of triploids attributable to digyny.
40% of triploids attributable to diandry:
    30% attributable to fertilization by diploid (XY) spermatozoa that arose after chromosome doubling at the first male meiotic division.

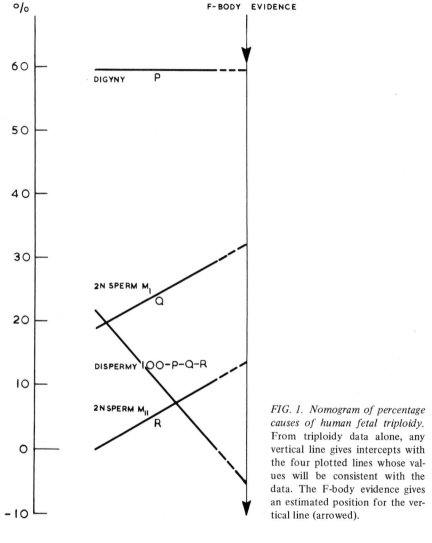

FIG. 1. Nomogram of percentage causes of human fetal triploidy. From triploidy data alone, any vertical line gives intercepts with the four plotted lines whose values will be consistent with the data. The F-body evidence gives an estimated position for the vertical line (arrowed).

10% attributable to fertilization by diploid spermatozoa (XX and YY in equal numbers) that arose after chromosome doubling at the second male meiotic division.

~0% attributable to dispermic fertilization.

We may also express the results in section B of Table V in such a way as to show the relative magnitudes of the causes of triploidy separately for each karyotype:

XXX: 85% digyny, 15% fertilization by XX diploid spermatozoa.
XXY;   50% digyny, 50% fertilization by XY diploid spermatozoa.
XYY: 100% fertilization by diploid YY spermatozoa.

It must be emphasized that these figures estimating the relative roles of the causes of triploidy are the best that can be produced, but they remain highly approximate. The best estimates are those for digyny and diandry, but even these have a SE of 13.1.

DISCUSSION

This quantitative inquiry into sex chromosomes and ploidies of human spermatozoa and fetuses and the etiology of triploids must be regarded as highly preliminary. It is, however, an attempt to integrate the facts so far available and may at the least have some epistemological value. Unless an effort is made to face up to the numerous interconnected qualitative and quantitative problems, no real answer can be given to any individual problem. It is justifiable for the following reasons to think that the present approach has some general validity:

1. There is a large measure of success in accounting for the numbers of spermatozoa classified by their content of F-bodies (0, 1, 2, and $\geqslant 3F$) and also by their visually appraised size (Small, Medium, and Large).
2. Medium-sized spermatozoa are estimated to include not only diploids but a proportion of misclassed haploids. This agreed with the results of DNA observations on Medium spermatozoa.
3. The wholly independent arguments from F-bodies and from human triploid fetuses concur in indicating that XY diploid spermatozoa (70%) (arising after chromosome doubling at the first meiotic division) are commoner than the XX and YY diploid spermatozoa (each 15%) arising after chromosome doubling at the second meiotic division.
4. The combined evidence from F-bodies and human triploid fetuses merges without significant conflict to give a complete explanation of the origin of human triploids in terms of digyny and of fertilization by diploid spermatozoa, the role of dispermy being estimated as nil. The relative numbers of XXX, XXY, and XYY triploid karyotypes are completely explained.
5. When the observational data are challenged with the biometrical model, apparently sensible answers emerge. No parameters lead in an obviously wrong direction or have significant irrational values of $>100\%$ or $<0\%$. Since haploid X and Y spermatozoa must be nearly equal in number (Fechheimer and Beatty, 1974; Kaufman, 1973), yet 0F spermatozoa are much commoner than 1F, it is essential to suppose that for technical

or other reasons many Y chromosomes are not represented by observable F-bodies; the estimate is 25% not represented. As a matter of observation, "adventitious F-bodies," not true F-bodies representing Y chromosomes, must sometimes be encountered; the estimate is a mean of 0.118 adventitious F-bodies per haploid sperm head (double that value being assumed for diploid spermatozoa, four times for tetraploids).

The results provide what is apparently the first evidence that diploid mammalian spermatozoa are fertile.

In experimental animals, there is evidence (reviewed by Schindler and Mikamo, 1970) that delayed fertilization leads both to dispermy and to the production of triploid fetuses, and it has been a natural inference that the dispermy was the cause of the triploidy. There is also a subsidiary argument that delayed fertilization yields "overripe" eggs whose physiological condition encourages dispermy. Schindler and Mikamo used this argument in accounting for the origin of some human triploid fetuses. The present work suggests that dispermy is not a significant cause of triploidy and that the main causal chain may be delayed fertilization → "overripe" eggs → digyny → triploidy.

A reduction in the incidence of triploid conceptuses would obviously be desirable in the human subject, since late triploid abortuses are distressing objects and the occasional malformed triploid at term is even more distressing. Triploidy in domestic animals is probably a cause of fetal wastage of some economic significance. The present results suggest that 60% of the problem in man is caused by digyny at the time of fertilization, and this may be caused in part by delayed fertilization. Forty percent of the problem is apparently caused by diandry, and this in turn is attributable to a defect in the testis—the production of diploid spermatozoa. Little is known about the etiology of diploid spermatozoa, except that they are typical of very young breeding males of the rabbit and their incidence is subject to strain variation (Beatty and Fechheimer, 1972), while in man also the incidence may possibly be higher in the younger subject (Sumner, 1971). In the rabbit work, it was regularly possible, though to a limited degree, to carry out a physical removal of some of the diploid spermatozoa by means of a centrifugation technique applied to semen.

SUMMARY

Dependence of the phenotype of spermatozoa on their individual genetic contents is a matter of both fundamental and applied interest. When such dependence exists, the experimental discouragement or physical removal of genetically deleterious spermatozoa can be attempted. Some successes in animal material have been listed.

The Y-chromosome content of mature human spermatozoa is known to be reflected by phenotypically observable fluorescent "F-bodies," and the double genome of diploid spermatozoa is reflected by their observed double size. A study of these forms of dependence of sperm phenotype on genotype, integrated with a published record of the incidence of sex chromosome karyotypes in triploid human fetuses, has led to the following preliminary conclusions and estimates:

1. Some diploid spermatozoa are fertile. The incidence of dispermic fertilization is close to zero.
2. XX, XY, and YY diploid spermatozoa occur in the ratio of 15:70:15.
3. Sixty percent of triploids arise through digyny (two sets of maternal chromosomes), 40% through diandry (two sets of paternal chromosomes).
4. The 40% triploids of diandric origin can be subdivided provisionally into 30% after fertilization by XY diploid spermatozoa arising after chromosome doubling at the first male meiotic division, 10% after fertilization by diploid spermatozoa (XX and YY in equal number) arising after chromosome doubling at the second male meiotic division, and 0% attributable to dispermic fertilization.
5. The sire is responsible for the 40% incidence of triploids of diandric origin, because the incidence is attributable wholly to fertilization by diploid spermatozoa arising by cytological accident in the testis.

Biometrical models underlying the study have been outlined, and certain "nuisance factors" were estimated and used to make corrections.

ACKNOWLEDGMENTS

This work was supported by a grant from the Ford Foundation. I would like to thank Mr. V. J. Coulter, Mr. M. D. Parnham, and Mr. J. Foster for technical assistance. I am greatly indebted to Dr. R. V. Short, Director of the M.R.C. Unit for Reproductive Biology, and to Dr. J. V. T. H. Hamerlynck and Mr. D. W. Richardson of that Unit for access to normal human semen samples.

REFERENCES

Barlow, P., and Vosa, C. G. (1970), The Y chromosome in human spermatozoa, *Nature (Lond.) 226:*961.

Beatty, R. A. (1970), The genetics of the mammalian gamete, *Biol. Rev. 45:*73–120.

Beatty, R. A. (1971), Phenotype of spermatozoa in relation to genetic content, in: *Sex ratio at birth—Prospects for Control Symposium of the American Society of Animal Science, Albany, N.Y.,* 1971 (C. A. Kiddy and H. D. Hafs, eds.), pp. 10–18.

Beatty, R. A. (1973a), Sperm diversity within the species, in: *Proceedings of the Interna-*

tional Symposium on the Functional Anatomy of the Spermatozoon, Wenner-Gren Centre, Stockholm, Aug. 29–31, Pergamon Press, Oxford, in press.

Beatty, R. A. (1973b), The phenogenetics of spermatozoa in: *Proceedings of the International Symposium on the Biology of the Male Gamete, Cambridge, Sept. 5–7,* Biological Journal of the Linnean Society (J. G. Duckett and P. A. Racey, eds.), Academic Press, New York, in press.

Beatty, R. A. (1974), Separation of X and Y spermatozoa, *Bibliogr. Reprod. 23(1):* 1.

Beatty, R. A., and Fechheimer, N. S. (1972), Diploid spermatozoa in rabbit semen and their experimental separation from haploid spermatozoa, *Biol. Reprod. 7:*267–277.

Beatty, R. A., and Gluecksohn-Waelsch, S. (eds.) (1972), *Proceedings of the International Symposium on the Genetics of the Spermatozoon, Edinburgh, Aug. 1971,* 406 pp., Department of Genetics, University of Edinburgh, and Albert Einstein College of Medicine, New York.

Braden, A. W. H. (1972), *T*-locus in mice; segregation distortion and sterility in the male, in: *Proceedings of the International Symposium on the Genetics of the Spermatozoon, Edinburgh, Aug. 1971,* (R. A. Beatty and S. Gluecksohn-Waelsch, eds.) pp. 289–305.

Carr, D. H. (1971), Chromosome studies in selected spontaneous abortion: Polyploidy in man, *J. Med. Genet. 8:*164–174.

Fechheimer, N. S. (1972), Causal basis of chromosome abnormalities, *J. Reprod. Fertil. (suppl.) 15:*79–98.

Fechheimer, N. S., and Beatty, R. A. (1974), Chromosome abnormalities and sex ratio in rabbit blastocysts, *J. Reprod. Fertil., 37:*331–341.

Kaufman, M. H. (1973), Analysis of the first cleavage division to determine the sex ratio and incidence of chromosome anomalies at conception in the mouse, *J. Reprod. Fertil. 35:*67–72.

Kiddy, C. A., and Hafs, H. D. (eds.) (1971), *Sex Ratio at Birth—Prospects for Control Symposium of the American Society of Animal Science, Albany, N.Y.,* Published by American Society of Animal Science, 104 pp.

Pearson, P. L., and Bobrow, M. (1970), Fluorescent staining of the Y-chromosome in meiotic stages of the human male, *J. Reprod. Fertil. 22:*117–119.

Schindler, A. M., and Mikamo, K. (1970), Triploidy in man, *Cytogenetics 9:*116–130.

Sumner, A. T. (1971), Frequency of polyploid spermatozoa in man, *Nature (Lond.) 231:*49.

Sumner, A. T., Robinson, J. A., and Evans, H. J. (1971), Distinguishing between X, Y and YY-bearing human spermatozoa by fluorescence and DNA content, *Nat. New Biol. 229:*231–233.

Woolley, D. M. (1970), Selection for the length of the spermatozoan midpiece in the mouse, *Genet. Res. (Camb.) 16:*261–275.

13

Response of Spermatogonia of the Mouse to Hycanthone: A Comparison With the Effect of Gamma Rays

E. F. Oakberg

Biology Division
Oak Ridge National Laboratory
Oak Ridge, Tennessee

The identification of the stem cell of the seminiferous epithelium has been recognized as a requirement for understanding spermatogenesis since the description of spermatogonia by von La Valette (1876) and the first use of the term "stem cell" by Benda (1887) and Regaud (1901). Various models of spermatogonial stem cell renewal have been proposed since the classical study of Regaud (1901), but the most significant advances in characterization of the stem cells and stem cell renewal have occurred in the last decade. (For a review of the literature, see Huckins, 1972; Clermont, 1968; and Roosen-Runge, 1962.) The model presented here is the one proposed by Huckins (1971a) on the basis of morphological, quantitative, and cell kinetic studies of tubule whole mounts in the rat and by Oakberg (1971a) on the basis of long-term ^{3}H-thymidine labeling in the mouse.

The stem cell is characterized as an isolated (A_{is} or A_s) spermatogonium with a small, spherical, or ovoid nucleus in whole mounts (Huckins, 1971a) and oval or elongate nucleus in cross-section (Oakberg, 1971a). Cells comparable to A_s spermatogonia have been described in all species examined either with electron microscope or careful light microscope studies. The interphase chromatin is finely granular, the nucleolus inconspicuous, and the overall staining with hematoxylin darker than for other type A spermatogonia. Cell-cycle properties

This research was sponsored by the U. S. Atomic Energy Commission under contract with the Union Carbide Corporation.

of the A_s spermatogonia are variable (Huckins, 1971b), and there is no evidence (Huckins, 1972; Oakberg, 1971a) to support the existence of a noncycling A_0 population, as proposed by Clermont and Bustos-Obregon (1968). The stem (A_s) spermatogonia are also characterized by high resistance to radiation and chemicals (Oakberg, 1971b, 1974).

According to the model of Huckins (1971a, 1972) and of Oakberg (1971a), the isolated A_s (A_{is}) spermatogonia undergo two types of division. In one, the daughter cells move far apart, cytokinesis is complete, and two stem cells result. In the second type of division, the daughter cells remain connected by a cytoplasmic bridge to form the A_{pr} spermatogonia. Division of the A_{pr} spermatogonia generates irregular chains of 4, 8, 16, or even 32 A_{a1} spermatogonia connected by cytoplasmic bridges. It is important to remember that nuclear morphology of the A_{pr} and A_{a1} spermatogonia is the same as that of the A_s. At stages V–VIII of the cycle of the seminiferous epithelium (Huckins, 1971b), the nuclei of the A_{a1} become larger, the chromatin more finely dispersed, and the nucleoli more prominent as they transform into the A_1 spermatogonia, which divide at stage IX to form the A_2 spermatogonia. Successive divisions at stages XI and I give rise to the A_3 and A_4 spermatogonia, respectively, and division of the A_4 at stage II produces the In (intermediate) spermatogonia (Huckins, 1972). In agreement with Monesi (1962a), there is no evidence for formation of anything but In spermatogonia by the division of the A_4 cells in stage II. Finally, division of the In spermatogonia at stage IV gives rise to the B spermatogonia, which divide at stage VI to form preleptotene spermatocytes, which immediately enter meiotic prophase. The isolated A_s (A_{is}) spermatogonium, therefore, is the cell whose survival is requisite for recovery of fertility after treatments which deplete the seminiferous epithelium.

The mechanisms regulating complete cytokinesis of stem cell divisions, as opposed to "pair" and "chain" formation, are obscure. It is significant that all spermatogonia more advanced than the A_s are connected by cytoplasmic bridges. This is an important factor in the synchronization of the members of a chain of cells. However, there must be other factors which control the approximate synchrony of the several chains of cells occurring within a given segment of the tubule. The occurrence of bridges between spermatogonia has been observed in several mammalian species: rat (Dym and Fawcett, 1971), mouse (Huckins and Oakberg, 1971; Schleiermacher and Schmidt, 1973), monkey (Gondos and Zemjanis, 1970), and man (Rowley et al., 1971). Care must be exercised in interpretation of electron microscope photographs, and the claim that the A_s spermatogonia also are connected by bridges (Schleiermacher and Schmidt, 1973) may not exclude the possibility of misclassification of A_{pr} and A_{a1} cells. Not only do members of a "chain" show synchrony in division and differentiation, they also respond as a unit to radiation. If one member of the "chain" is lethally damaged, the entire group of connected cells degenerates (Huckins and Oakberg, 1971).

TECHNIQUES

Characterization of the spermatogonial response to experimental procedures depends on accurate cell classification, identification of the stages of the cycle of the seminiferous epithelium, and timing of spermatogenesis. Histological and cytological preparations must be both excellent and consistent in order to distinguish between the various types of A spermatogonia. This is especially important in the identification of A_s spermatogonia.

Our standard procedure is to fix specimens for 6 h in Zenker-formol, wash them for 12 h in running tap water, treat them with iodine to remove the $HgCl_2$, and then use $Na_2S_2O_3 \cdot 5H_2O$ to remove the traces of iodine. This permits use of the PAS staining of the acrosome for identification of the stage of the cycle of the seminiferous epithelium, and it also allows good autoradiographs (Kopriwa and Huckins, 1972). The morphological appearance of the A spermatogonia revealed by this technique is the best we have obtained in any autoradiographs.

The procedure developed for study of radiation effects is to allow cell death to occur and to score the surviving cells in a standard sample of tubule stages. Data then are expressed as experimental/control ratios. Our assumption that the rate of spermatogenesis has not been altered appears reasonable in view of the demonstration that radiation does not affect the rate of spermatocyte and spermatid development (Edwards and Sirlin, 1958) and our observation that the synchrony between spermatogonial divisions and spermatid stage is not affected. An effect comparable to the 2-h radiation-induced mitotic delay reported by Monesi (1962b) would not affect our results. A more serious problem is that cell death among the A_1 spermatogonia usually is not expressed until stage VIII or IX of the spermatogenic cycle, even though the initial damage may have occurred as much as 96 h earlier. Thus in counts of the total A spermatogonia, repopulation is under way before cell degeneration has run its course, and the particular manner in which these factors interact to give a minimum value is dose dependent (Oakberg, 1959). Such problems are likely to be more serious with chemicals, and the rapid recovery after treatment with hycanthone is a good example of the difficulties involved in evaluating the total spermatogonial response.

Spermatogenesis is a dynamic process, and cells which survive radiation or chemicals continue to divide and differentiate. Failure to distinguish between cell-stage treated and cell-stage scored has led to considerable confusion in the literature. For example, decrease in number of preleptotene spermatocytes 72 h after irradiation does not indicate sensitivity of the preleptotene stage, but, instead, is the result of killing A_4 and In spermatogonia. Likewise, damage to late A_3 and early A_4 spermatogonia will be expressed as a decrease in number of type B spermatogonia in stage VI tubules 72 h after treatment. The cell-type treated and cell-type scored remain the same only for A_s spermatogonia.

RADIATION RESPONSE

The A_2–A_4 spermatogonia are uniformly sensitive to radiation, and damage to these cells is primarily expressed by degeneration during late interphase or very early prophase of the first postirradiation division (Oakberg, 1959). Since these cells are irreversibly committed to differentiation, their loss is reflected in depletion of more advanced stages. Enumeration of cells derived from the sensitive A_2–A_4 spermatogonia has been useful in the investigation of low doses of radiation, study of the effects of dose rate, and comparison of radiations of different quality (Oakberg and Clark, 1961).

In radiation studies, we have emphasized the importance of the stem cells because they persist throughout reproductive life, and genetic damage to the stem cell likewise persists. Differentiating cells, including the A_{pr}–A_{a1}, A_1–A_4, In, and B spermatogonia, spermatocytes, and spermatids subjected to acute radiation exposure are rapidly eliminated from the reproductive tract either by the process of degeneration or by maturation. With protracted irradiation, differentiating cells accumulate a small dose owing to their short life span, whereas stem cells can accumulate a large exposure.

The A_s spermatogonia are the most resistant of the spermatogonial types; they are the only survivors after doses of 150 R or more. Our radiation dose–response curves were done before the recent studies on germ cell renewal (Huckins, 1971a; Oakberg, 1971a). Consequently, the A_s cells were combined with all types of A spermatogonia in scoring. However, the linear dose–response curve observed for the 100–1000 R range (Oakberg, 1964) constitutes a stem cell response. Reappearance of the A_{pr} and A_{al} spermatogonia occurs within 72 h after doses of ~100 R, suggesting that some of the A_s survivors already were "programmed" at the time of irradiation. After doses of 500–1000 R, "pairs" and chains appear at 8.5 days or at cycle one of the seminiferous epithelium after irradiation. If ^{3}H-thymidine is injected prior to irradiation and one waits 8.5 days to be certain one is scoring cells treated as A_s spermatogonia, the percentages of labeled A_s spermatogonia are 8% for control and 16% for 100 and 500 R (Oakberg, 1971b). The cycle of the seminiferous epithelium of the mouse has been divided into 12 stages on the basis of spermatid development (Oakberg, 1956). Each stage is further characterized by specific cellular associations of spermatogonia and spermatocytes. The mechanisms which preserve this synchrony are unknown. It is significant that the A_s spermatogonia which survive radiation are randomly distributed among the 12 stages of the cycle and that the different spermatogonial types reappear in the predicted, normal association with resistant spermatocytes and spermatids that survived the radiation.

The appearance of numerous 3H-thymidine-labeled cells among the spermatogonia surviving irradiation (Oakberg, 1964, 1971b) refutes the concept of an A_0 (noncycling) spermatogonial population. The survivors cannot be predominantly of the A_0 type, and the data are consistent with this fact. Instead of stimulation of division among the A_0 to replenish the depleted spermatogonial population as proposed by Dym and Clermont (1970), our data demonstrate that the surviving cells already were in cycle at the time of irradiation. Depletion of differentiating spermatogonia may trigger an enhanced division rate of the A_s, but it does not stimulate an inactive population. The mechanism of stem cell renewal used here is extremely important in evaluation of genetic effects. If the model of Clermont and Bustos-Obregon (1968) is correct, then there is a possibility that sensitive $A_1 - A_4$ spermatogonia could indefinitely contribute to the gamete pool at doses below 100 R. The model of stem cell renewal which the data of Huckins (1971a) and Oakberg (1971a) support, however, indicates that all long-term fertility and genetic effects trace to radiation-resistant stem cells.

HYCANTHONE

Although many chemicals—especially the alkylating agents—have been termed "radiomimetic," it has long been known that this is a misnomer; the response of the testis to chemicals mimics the radiation response only in part and with significant differences if the total pattern is considered. Even the responses to such closely similar compounds as n-propyl methanesulfonate and isopropyl methanesulfonate can be quite different (Ehling et al., 1972).

Mutagenic activity of hycanthone had been claimed for microorganisms (Hartman et al., 1971) and for cells in tissue culture (Clive et al., 1972). Chromosome breakage by hycanthone also had been observed in vivo (Green et al., 1973). A test for specific locus mutations in the mouse (Russell and Kelly, 1973), however, was negative, and the obvious question arose as to whether hycanthone actually reached the stem spermatogonia. Demonstration of a cytotoxic action of injected hycanthone on spermatogonia would indicate that the compound, or an active metabolite of it, was, in fact, reaching the spermatogonia.

The hycanthone was suspended in cold, balanced Hank's solution and was injected either intraperitoneally (i.p.) or intramuscularly (i.m.). Mice were killed at 3 and 5 days after injection, and the number of spermatogonia was scored in a comparable sample of tubules in treated and control animals.

The dose curves for the 72-h data after i.p. injection are given in Fig. 1. A continuous increase in sensitivity occurs with progression from the stem (A_s) to

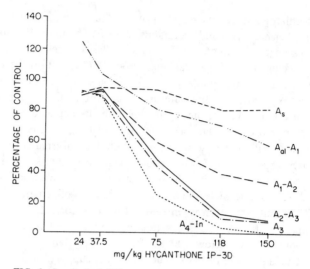

FIG. 1. Survival of different types of spermatogonia 72 h after intraperitoneal injection of hycanthone.

the A_4–In spermatogonia. The i.m. data for 72 h (Fig. 2), however, reveal differences from i.p. injection which appear to be cell-type specific. Survival for A_s spermatogonia after i.m. injection is higher at all doses, and the difference is significant (F = 4.83, df 1 and 30, $P < 0.05$). No marked effect of injection route was observed for A_{a1}–A_1 and A_1–A_2 spermatogonia, though survival was slightly higher for the i.m. group. Survival for the low (24 and 37.5 mg/kg) and

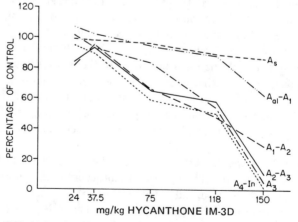

FIG. 2. Survival of different types of spermatogonia 72 h after intramuscular injection of hycanthone.

high (150 mg/kg) doses was the same after i.p. and i.m. injection for A_2, A_2-A_3, and A_4-In spermatogonia. At 75 and 118 mg/kg, however, survival was significantly higher for A_2-A_3 and A_4-In spermatogonia, and also at 118 mg/kg for A_2 cells. These results suggest that for spermatogonial types including late A_2 through early In, repair (or protective) mechanisms are equally effective for i.p. and i.m. routes at 24 and 37.5 mg/kg, more effective for i.m. injection at 75 and 118 mg/kg, and ineffective for both i.m. and i.p. routes at 150 mg/kg. Three patterns of spermatogonial response to hycanthone are demonstrated by these data: (1) the characteristic pattern of the A_s; (2) the characteristic pattern of the A_{a1}, A_1, and early A_2; and (3) the pattern of the late A_2, A_3, A_4, and early In. Therefore, the target cell is an important site of drug inactivation and/or resistance, in addition to enzyme systems of the liver and elsewhere in the body. These results demonstrate the advisability of more than one dose in testing of chemicals; completely different interpretations of the i.p. vs. i.m. effect would have been obtained if only one dose, instead of a range of doses, had been used.

The data for 5 days are not given here because recovery was so rapid that the loss of A_{pr}, A_{a1}, and A_1 observed at 72 h had already been replaced. The number of A_s cells was lower than at 72 h, presumably because of increased rates of differentiation into the A_{pr} spermatogonia.

Demonstration of a reduction in numbers of spermatogonia after hycanthone injection shows that hycanthone or toxic metabolites reach the spermatogonia. This loss occurs through cell degeneration, since many necrotic spermatogonia were observed 15 h after injection. Spermatogonial type, dose, route of injection, and time of observation are all significant variables in the response. Since hycanthone usually is given as a single injection, it can be considered analogous to an acute X-ray exposure. Therefore, the A_s (stem) spermatogonia are the most important cells in terms of both fertility and genetic effects. Since even the lowest number of the A_s spermatogonia present was 70% of control (150 mg/kg at 5 days), no prolonged effect on fertility would be expected. Also, effects of cell selection on mutation frequency have not been observed at such high cell survival. The doses used here are many times those used in humans, and it is doubtful that an effect of hycanthone on spermatogonia of man could be detected after clinical doses. Furthermore, the effects measured here represent *somatic* damage, which is rapidly repaired by surviving spermatogonia.

RADIATION–HYCANTHONE COMPARISON

Certain aspects of the response of spermatogonia to hycanthone are similar to those of radiation: the high incidence of cell necrosis at 15 h, the high sensitivity of A_2-In spermatogonia, and the resistance of spermatocytes and spermatids. Important differences also occur, the most marked being the difference between the lethal dose and spermatogonial killing. For example, both 600

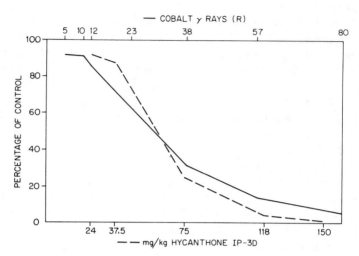

FIG. 3. Comparison of hycanthone and γ-rays over a comparable dose response range for A_4–In spermatogonia.

R of X-rays and 150 mg/kg of hycanthone have similar animal toxicity, yet survival of type A spermatogonia after these doses is 34% for hycanthone and only ~3 for X-rays.

Although it is not possible to make comparisons for all spermatogonial types owing to the different method of scoring used for A_s–early A_3 cells in the radiation data, survival of A_3, late A_3–early A_4, and late A_4–early In cells can be compared. Data for γ-ray exposure giving comparable survival showed a lower relative effectiveness for hycanthone at low doses and a greater effectiveness at high doses. Data for the A_4–In spermatogonia, shown in Fig. 3, are representative of A_3 and A_3–A_4 cells also. Spermatogonia exposed as A_s–A_2 and scored as A_s–A_4 cells can be combined for the hycanthone data to make the comparison shown in Fig. 4. In contrast to the result obtained for A_3–In cells, A_s–A_2 spermatogonia show a lower effectiveness at all doses. Therefore, the difference in sensitivity between A_3–In and earlier (A_s–A_2) spermatogonia observed with γ-rays is even greater with hycanthone. This results in a more rapid regeneration of the seminiferous epithelium after hycanthone.

The data presented here and the comparison of hycanthone with γ-rays demonstrate some of the parameters which must be considered in a thorough evaluation of the effect of any noxious agent on sensitive tissues and cells. The understanding of normal gametogenesis, identification of cells, and techniques developed over many years are the most important contributions of our radiation studies to the evaluation of the effects of drugs and chemicals on spermatogonia. Dose, route of administration, cell type, time of observation, and endpoint scored all are important parameters to be considered in evaluating the

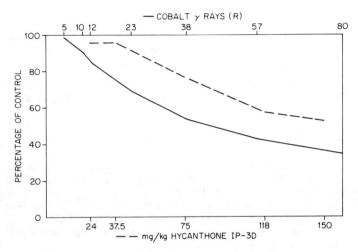

FIG. 4. Comparison of hycanthone and γ-ray survival for A_S–A_2 spermatogonia plotted on same scale used in Fig. 3.

effect of chemicals and drugs. Reliance on limited data can be very misleading; significantly different conclusions on the effect of hycanthone on mouse spermatogonia would have been reached if only a portion of the present data had been available.

SUMMARY

The stem cell of the seminiferous epithelium has been identified as a type A spermatogonium with an oval, darkly staining nucleus in cross-sections and a spherical or ovoid shape in tubule whole mounts. The stem spermatogonia occur as single, isolated cells, in contrast to the groups of differentiating spermatogonia which form "chains" of cells connected by cytoplasmic bridges. Some stem cells have very long cell-cycle times (8+ days in the mouse); others have cycles only slightly longer than the 26–28 h characteristic of differentiating spermatogonia. The spermatogonial stem cells are further characterized by high resistance to radiation and noxious agents, in general. The cell-specific response characteristic of radiation also was observed after hycanthone injection for A_3, A_4, and intermediate (In) spermatogonia. The killing of A_S and A_1 spermatogonia by hycanthone, however, was much less than would have been predicted for radiation doses giving comparable survival for A_3, A_4, and In spermatogonia. Dose, route of administration (i.p. or i.m.), time of observation, and cell stage all were important variables in the response to hycanthone. Whereas the use of a specific cell type, time of observations, end point, and dose may be useful in demonstrating the action of a chemical, extreme care must be used in estimating possible hazards to the organism from such information. Failure to observe mutagenicity of hycanthone in the mouse has raised the obvious question of whether the drug reaches the germ cells. The cytotoxic effect demonstrated by the data presented here indicates that either hycanthone or toxic metabolites of the drug do reach the spermatogonia in significant quantities. The hycanthone was kindly supplied by Sterling-Winthrop Research Institute, Rensselaer, N.Y.

REFERENCES

Benda, C. (1887), Untersuchungen über den Bau des funktionierenden Samenkanälchens einiger Säugetiere und Folgerungen für die Spermatogenese dieser Wirbeltierklasse, *Arch. Anat. Microse. Morpholol. Exp. 30:*49–110.

Clermont, Y. (1968), Différenciation et evolution des cellules sexuelles 1. La lignée male. Cinétique de la spermatogenèse chez les Mammifères, in: *La Physiologie de la Reproduction chez les Mammifères,* pp. 7–60, (A. Jost, ed.) Editions du Centre National de la Recherche Scientifique, Paris.

Clermont, Y., and Bustos-Obregon, E. (1968), Re-examination of spermatogonial renewal in the rat by means of seminiferous tubules mounted "in toto," *Am. J. Anat. 122:*237–248.

Clive, D., Flamm, W. G., and Machesko, M. R., (1972), Mutagenicity of hycanthone in mammalian cells, *Mutat. Res. 14:*262–264.

Dym, M., and Clermont, Y. (1970), Role of spermatogonia in the repair of the seminiferous epithelium following X-irradiation of the rat testis, *Am. J. Anat. 128:*265–282.

Dym, M., and Fawcett, D. W. (1971), Spermatogonial intercellular bridges, *Anat. Rec. 169:*309.

Edwards, R. G., and Sirlin, J. L. (1958), The effect of 200r of X-rays on the rate of spermatogenesis and spermiogenesis in the mouse, *Exp. Cell Res. 15:*522–528.

Ehling, U. H., Doherty, D. G., and Malling, H. V. (1972), Differential spermatogenic response of mice to the induction of dominant-lethal mutations by *n*-propyl methanesulfonate and isopropyl methanesulfonate, *Mutat. Res. 15:*175–184.

Gondos, B., and Zemjanis, R. (1970), Fine structure of spermatogonia and intercellular bridges in *Macaca nemestrina, J. Morphol. 131:*431–446.

Green, S., Sauro, F. M., and Legator, M. S. (1973), Cytogenetic effects of hycanthone in the rat, *Mutat. Res. 17:*239–244.

Hartman, P. E., Levine, K., Hartman, Z., and Berger, H. (1971), Hycanthone: A frameshift mutagen, *Science 172:*1058–1060.

Huckins, C. (1971a), The spermatogonial stem cell population in adult rats I. Their morphology, proliferation, and maturation, *Anat. Rec. 169:*533–558.

Huckins, C. (1971b), The spermatogonial stem-cell population in adult rats II. A radioautographic analysis of their cell cycle properties, *Cell Tissue Kinet. 4:*313–334.

Huckins, C. (1972), Spermatogonial stem cell behavior in rodents, in: *Biology of Reproduction, Basic and Clinical Studies,* Vol. III, pp. 395–421 (J. T. Velardo and B. A. Kasprow, eds.), Pan American Congress of Anatomy, New Orleans.

Huckins, C., and Oakberg, E. F. (1971), Cytoplasmic connections between spermatogonia seen in whole-mounted seminiferous tubules from normal and irradiated mouse testes, *Anat. Rec. 169:*344.

Kopriwa, B. M., and Huckins, C. (1972), A method for the use of Zenker-formol fixation and the periodic acid Schiff staining technique in light microscope radioautography, *Histochemie 32:*231–244.

Monesi, V. (1962a), Autoradiographic study of DNA synthesis and the cell cycle in spermatogonia and spermatocytes of mouse testis using tritiated thymidine, *J. Cell Biol.* *14:*1–18.

Monesi, V. (1962b), Relation between X-ray sensitivity and stages of the cell cycle in spermatogonia of the mouse, *Radiat. Res. 17:*809–838.

Oakberg, E. F. (1956), A description of spermiogenesis in the mouse and its use in analysis of the cycle of the seminiferous epithelium and germ cell renewal, *Am. J. Anat. 99:*391–413.

Oakberg, E. F. (1959), Initial depletion and subsequent recovery of spermatogonia of the mouse after 20 R of gamma rays and 100, 300, and 600 R of X-rays, *Radiat. Res. 11:*700–719.

Oakberg, E. F. (1964), The effects of dose, dose rate and quality of radiation on the dynamics and survival of the spermatogonial population of the mouse, *Jap. J. Genet. 40:*119–127.

Oakberg, E. F. (1971a), Spermatogonial stem-cell renewal in the mouse, *Anat. Rec. 169:*515–532.

Oakberg, E. F. (1971b), A new concept of spermatogonial stem-cell renewal in the mouse and its relationship to genetic effects, *Mutat. Res. 11:*1–7.

Oakberg, E. F. (1974), Effects of radiation on the testis, in: *Handbook of Physiology.*

Oakberg, E. F., and Clark, E. (1961), Effect of dose and dose rate on radiation damage to mouse spermatogonia and oocytes as measured by cell survival, *J. Cell. Comp. Physiol. (suppl. 1) 58:*173–182.

Regaud, C. (1901), Études sur la structure des tubes séminiferes et sur la spermatogénèse chez les Mammifères, *Arch. Anat. Microse. Morphol. Exp. 4:*101–156.

Roosen-Runge, E. C. (1962), The process of spermatogenesis in mammals, *Biol. Rev. 37:*343–377.

Rowley, M. J., Berlin, J. D., and Heller, C. G. (1971), The ultrastructure of four types of human spermatogonia, *Z. Zellforsch. Mikrosk. Anat. 112:*139–157.

Russell, W. L., and Kelly, E. M. (1973), Ineffectiveness of hycanthone in inducing specific locus mutations in mice, *Mutat. Res. 21:*14.

Schleiermacher, E., and Schmidt, W. (1973), The local control of mammalian spermatogenesis, *Humangenetik 19:*75–98.

von La Valette, St. George (1876), Über die Genese der Samenkörper. I, *Arch. Anat. Microse. Morphol. Exp. 1:*403–414.

14

Ultrastructure of the Mammalian Sperm Head During Differentiation and Maturation

Mario H. Burgos

Instituto de Histología y Embriología
Facultad de Ciencias Médicas, U.N.C.
Mendoza, Argentina

The changes which transform the relatively simple nucleus of the spermatid into the highly specialized sperm head take place mainly in the seminiferous tubule. The strategy is very similar in all the numerous species of mammals studied. Final maturation is attained in the sperm pathway, especially during the journey along the epididymis.

The intratesticular phase (spermatid differentiation) involves many steps, either sequential or simultaneous; these are organization of the acrosome, condensation of the nuclear material, changes in the nuclear envelope, formation of the basal plate, migration of perinuclear cytoplasm, and shaping of the sperm head.

THE ACROSOME

The differentiation of the acrosome starts at the Golgi complex. Three stages have been described in most mammals studied. The first is called the *Golgi phase:* during this phase, the Golgi complex acquires a remarkable development close to one of the nuclear poles. A single layer of rough endoplasmic reticulum (RER) cisternae appears on top of the Golgi complex. They have a characteristic asymmetrical distribution of components. On their outer wall the cisternae show typical ribosomes, whereas the wall facing the Golgi is smooth. Between the RER cisternae and the Golgi complex are small vesicles occasionally fused with the RER cisternae or with the Golgi cisternae. On the basis of what is known about RER–Golgi relationships, it is tempting to postulate that the intermedi-

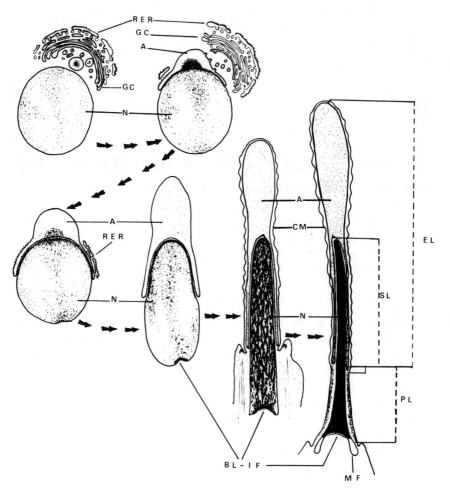

FIG. 1. *Diagram of the differentiation of the head of the guinea pig spermatid.* Arrows indicate direction of events. The Golgi complex (GC) is prominent and has on top a layer of rough endoplasmic reticulum (RER). The acrosomal vesicle (A) with the acrosomal granule approaches and covers one pole of the nucleus (N). The chromatin condenses gradually, and the nuclear envelope shows two places of higher density, one under the acrosome and the other at the implantation fossa (IF) or basal lamina (BL). The lateral sides of the acrosomal cap show cisternae of the RER closely related. With elongation of the spermatid, the nucleus changes shape and increases condensation. The acrosome forms a prominent anterior portion and a dense equatorial segment. A subacrosomal (SL) and an epiacrosomal (EL) lamina remain from the former cytoplasm. Both layers become continuous with the postacrosomal lamina (PL). The nuclear envelope forms membrane folds (MF) at the caudal end.

ate vesicles pinch off from the RER cisternae to fuse with the Golgi cisternae. Larger vesicles are also seen between the Golgi cisternae and the nuclear pole. They contain an electron-dense material which gradually becomes conglomerated into dense granules. During this stage, one can frequently see several granules, enclosed in a vesicle, which apparently fuse into a single conglomerate, the acrosomal granule, and its envelope, the acrosomal vesicle. Gradually both components approach the nuclear pole and establish contact with it through a thin layer of cytoplasm devoid of organelles (Fig. 1).

The origin of the acrosome was originally related to the synthetic activity of the Golgi complex. There is no doubt that the acrosomal vesicle starts as a component of the Golgi complex and that the PAS-positive reaction of the acrosomal granule is due to a carbohydrate moiety synthesized or added in the Golgi cisternae. But in the light of what is known, the protein component of the acrosome which makes up some of its enzymes has to be related to the activity of the RER. Recent observations in favor of such assumption are, as mentioned above, the presence of a layer of RER cisternae on top of the Golgi complex and of intermediate vesicles between both organelles (Fig. 2).

In the second stage, the *cap phase,* the acrosomal vesicle contacts the nucleus more widely; it increases in size by the coalescence of new Golgi vesicles. As a result, the anterior third of the nucleus becomes flattened. The acrosomal granule also acquires a hemispherical shape. The tension of the vesicle later decreases, coincident with a migration of the Golgi complex and surrounding cytoplasm. The vesicle then collapses on the nuclear pole, like a double-layered stocking cap, the head cap (Fig. 1).

Recent observations show that the rough endoplasmic reticulum is often closely apposed to the equatorial portion of the acrosomal cap (Figs. 1 and 3). Ribosomes are implanted in a single layer on the membranes of the RER cisternae and clustered between the acrosome and the RER. Ribosomes are also frequently seen on the equatorial acrosomal surface. The acrosomal lumen at this level shows strands of a filamentous material mostly perpendicular to the acrosomal wall and coincident with the ribosomal sites (Fig. 3).

Detergent extraction of the acrosomal content gives a proteinase, which is PAS positive (Garner, 1973) and probably responsible for the acrosomal PAS-positive reaction, and a complex of hyaluronidase and the zona-lysing enzyme, acrosin (Yang, 1973). The latter has been associated with the inner acrosomal membrane on the equatorial segment (Srivastava, 1973).

The above mentioned observations of the Golgi complex and RER in close relationship to the acrosomal vesicle and granule allow us to postulate two mechanisms of origin and concentration of the proteins synthesized in the RER. One reaches the acrosomal vesicle through the Golgi complex and the other directly through the acrosome outer membrane. This may indicate that enzymes

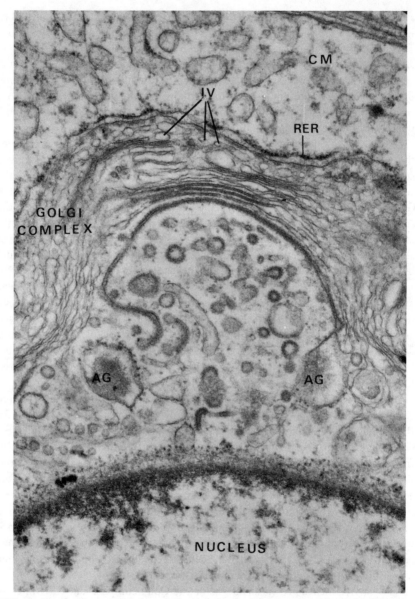

FIG. 2. Electromicrograph of a portion of the cytoplasm and nucleus of a guinea pig spermatid. A layer of rough endoplasmic reticulum (RER) cisternae appears on top of the Golgi complex. Intermediate vesicles are indicated (IV). Proacrosomal granules (AG) are enclosed in vesicles, one of which appears to pinch off the inner Golgi cisterna. The nucleus shows an ill-defined contour due to the plane of section and to the accumulation of dense particles (ribosomes?).

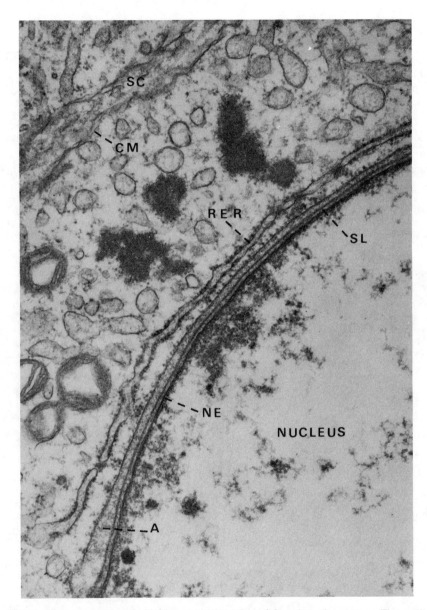

FIG. 3. Electron micrograph of the equatorial portion of the guinea pig acrosome. The rough endoplasmic reticulum (RER) forms cisternae parallel to the acrosome. Clusters of ribosomes are seen between both organelles as well as implanted in the outer acrosomal membrane. The lumen of the acrosome (A) contains a granulofilamentous material which in some places appears to be perpendicular to the outer membrane. The nuclear envelope (NE) thickens, and a dense subacrosomal layer (SL) is recognized. The cell membrane (CM) is in close contact with a Sertoli cell process (SC).

with a carbohydrate moiety come through the Golgi complex and pure protein enzymes directly from the RER.

In the third stage, *the acrosomal phase,* the nucleus regains its ovoid shape and the acrosomal granular material remains heaped up at the anterior pole of the nucleus (rodents, guinea pig, cat, and rabbit) or spread over the narrow cleft of the cap (man and monkey) (Figs. 1 and 4.).

The shape of the acrosome varies in different species. The variations mainly concern the thickened anterior segment, where the acrosomal granula heaps up or spreads over the nuclear pole. In some species the apical segment of the acrosome is small and simple (man, monkey, boar, bull, rabbit, and bat), in

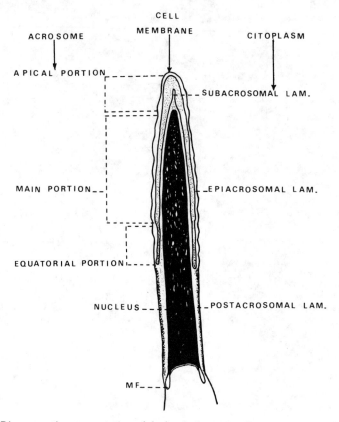

FIG. 4. Diagrammatic representation of the head of a mammalian spermatozoon (monkey). It shows the three regions of the acrosome and the three layers or laminae of the cytoplasmic derivatives, epiacrosomal, subacrosomal, and postacrosomal. The cell membrane is loosely detached from the underlying acrosome and is smooth contoured and closely adherent to the postacrosomal lamina. The nucleus is extremely dense and shows numerous small cavities. The nuclear envelope forms the caudal membrane folds (MF).

others it is much larger and more elaborate (guinea pig, chinchilla, and ground squirrel).

Little is known about the factors involved in the shape and volume of the acrosome. After leaving the germinal epithelium, the acrosome shows no apparent change in man (Bedford, personal communication), little change in rabbit and monkey (Bedford and Nicander, 1971), and remarkable changes in guinea pig and chinchilla (Fawcett, 1970). These changes occur during the epididymal journey and have been ascribed to intrinsic morphogenetic factors. However, new evidence indicates the presence of epididymal factors which induce the final acrosomal shape in the guinea pig (Blaquier et al., 1972).

THE NUCLEUS

During the acrosomal phase, after regaining its oval shape the nucleus begins to show changes in content, envelope, and shape. The nucleus in most mammals studied stretches and flattens slightly, and the granulofilamentous chromatin condenses to form coarse filaments and thin bands which shorten and thicken into dense granules or coarse lamellae. The granules or lamellae fuse together, to end up as a dense homogeneous mass with no discernible structure (Burgos and Fawcett, 1956a,b; Koehler, 1970). (Fig. 1).

During condensation of the nuclear material, the nuclear matrix gradually decreases, and almost disappears in most mammals. In the nucleus of the mature spermatozoon, only small cavities remain in the condensed chromatin. The way in which the nuclear matrix diffuses out of the condensing chromatin is not well understood. The nuclear envelope shows lacunar dilatation of the perinuclear cisternae and occasional vacuolization of the nucleoplasm. These large vacuoles apparently fuse with the inner membrane of the nuclear envelope and empty their content into the perinuclear cisterna.

Nuclear pores may also be related to the elimination of the nuclear sap into the cytoplasm. Nuclear pores, as will be discussed later, change in number and place during the nuclear condensation.

Coincident with the condensation and reorganization of the chromatin, the spermatid nucleus takes the shape characteristic of the species.

The initial shape of the spermatid nucleus is commonly oval or spherical, but the final shape varies widely in different species. Mammals usually show an ovoid flattened head, globular forms are common in fishes, and elongated tapering heads are the rule in amphibia. As an exception to the ovoid shape of the mammalian sperm, laboratory rodents have sickle-shaped sperm heads. The shape of the sperm is probably determined by a specific, genetically controlled pattern of aggregation of the molecular subunits of DNA and protein during condensation of the chromatin (Fawcett et al., 1971), and not as a consequence of modeling forces. On the other hand, microtubules have been implicated in the elongation and shaping of the spermatid nucleus in the rat (Kessel and Spaziani, 1969), mouse (Illison, 1969), insect (Shoup, 1966; Kessel, 1970), domestic fowl (McIntosh and Porter, 1967), and lizard (Clark, 1967).

THE NUCLEAR ENVELOPE

The nuclear envelope during the various phases of differentiation of the spermatid shows the following changes: During the Golgi phase, it is a well-defined double membranous structure with irregular lumen and some scattered pores. When the acrosomal vesicle contacts and spreads over the nucleus, the intervening membranes of the nuclear envelope become denser; so does the nuclear cisterna, which regularly becomes 200 Å wide. The inner membrane becomes ill-defined due to adherence of granulofilamentous chromatin. Nuclear pores are always absent from this region covered by the acrosome, but become evident and more numerous in the rest of the nuclear envelope. As nuclear condensation proceeds, pores tend to increase in number and to concentrate in some places of the nuclear envelope. They appear occasionally related to the chromatoid body or to cisternae of the RER. Streamers of dense material are frequently seen in the nuclear pores. They have been interpreted as an apparent passage of RNA from the nucleus to the cytoplasm anticipating nuclear condensation and providing for continuing protein synthesis in the cytoplasm at later stages of development (Fawcett and Phillips, 1967).

On the other hand, the presence of basic arginine-rich protein in the chromatoid body and the well-known increase in basic nuclear proteins during condensation of chromatin (Alfert, 1956, 1957; Block and Hew, 1960; Block, 1962; Block and Brach, 1964; Das, 1963) led to speculations that the proximity of the chromatoid body to the area where nuclear pores concentrate may be related to passage of basic proteins from the chromatoid body to the nucleus during nuclear condensation (Sud, 1961).

As nuclear condensation proceeds, the two membranes of the nuclear envelope, which can be resolved only at high magnification, become closely apposed, with virtual obliteration of the original perinuclear cisterna. Around almost all the nuclear surface, the nuclear envelope is closely applied to the condensed chromatin except at the laterocaudal surface, where it is often reflected to form a long membranous fold which enters into the neck region (Fig. 1).

Pores are generally lacking in the nuclear envelope at this stage of the nuclear condensation. They have been found occasionally in the redundant portion that extends back into the neck region and at the caudal surface of the nucleus.

A final differentiation which occurs at the caudal surface of the nucleus is the close apposition of the two layers of the nuclear envelope, which practically erases the perinuclear cisterna; its continuity is interrupted by regularly spaced densities binding both membranes together. The membranes of the nuclear envelope are dense and ill-defined owing to the close adherence of chromatin to the inner membrane. On the outer surface of the nuclear envelope, a layer of dense material is deposited to form the basal plate lining the concavity of the caudal surface of the nucleus or "implantation fossa," which provides attachment to the connecting piece.

THE CYTOPLASMIC COMPONENT

During differentiation of the late spermatid, two layers of cytoplasm remain in the future head of the spermatozoon. One is a perinuclear layer, which after the acrosome phase appears as two continuous layers: the "subacrosomal" and the "postacrosomal." The other layer, after the nuclear rotation which places the Golgi complex and the periacrosomal cytoplasm backward, remains below the cell membrane as a thin layer of pale cytoplasmic matrix devoid of organelles (Fig. 4). This layer is gradually compressed, during the spermatid elongation, between the cell membrane and the outer acrosomal surface and is confluent with the postacrosomal layer. As there is no reference to or name for this layer, we propose to call it the "epiacrosomal" layer. In most mammals, this layer is difficult to preserve for electron microscopy and frequently shows a tendency to swell in an irregular scalloped way and with the cell membrane loosely apposed to the acrosomal surface. The opposite is true for the cell membrane which covers the postacrosomal region. Here the cell membrane is smooth and closely adherent to the underlying material. Recent scanning electron microscope observations of the head of the guinea pig sperm show the presence of scattered blebs on the acrosomal surface which may be the tridimensional appearance of the scalloped swellings seen in thin sections. This fact may also correlate well with the acrosomal vesiculation which occurs during fertilization.

The subacrosomal layer has received more attention. Different authors refer to it as the "apical body" (Hadek, 1963; Bedford, 1964), "perforatorium" (Blandau, 1951; Leblond and Clermont, 1952), "subacrosomal material" (Nicander and Bane, 1966), "rod" (Friend, 1936), or, more recently and widely used, the "subacrosomal space" (Fawcett, 1965). Without debating which is the best term, it is pertinent to mention that in the sperm of amphibia (Burgos and Fawcett, 1956b) and birds (Nagano, 1961) a cluster of dense fibers called the "perforatorium" is found in the subacrosomal layer. No comparable structure is found in mammalian spermatozoa (Fawcett and Phillips, 1969).

The subacrosomal layer becomes evident in the early cap phase and is well defined at the early phase of nuclear condensation. This layer shows extreme variability of shape in different species; it is present as a thin layer in human late spermatids (Burgos, unpublished) and apparently absent in mature human spermatozoa (Bedford, 1967). The subacrosomal layer is minimal in the cat and horse (Nicander and Bane, 1966), well developed in rodents, and moderate in the guinea pig, chinchilla, bat (Fawcett, 1970), and rabbit (Bedford, 1964). The subacrosomal layer appears almost empty in the guinea pig, but in other species, notably the rabbit, it shows a substance of appreciable density.

The postacrosomal layer of cytoplasm together with the subacrosomal layer forms the perinuclear cytoplasm. It becomes apparent when the manchette vanishes and the mitochondrial helix forms in the midpiece. At this stage, the cell membrane approaches the nuclear envelope and a narrow cytoplasmic layer remains as a perinuclear cylinder between nucleus and cell membrane. A dense material probably related, at least topographically, to the former microtubular manchette and dense nuclear ring is deposited on the inner aspect of the cell membrane and apparently contributes to reinforcement of the cell membrane, which is closely adherent to the cytoplasmic layer.

The fact that this postacrosomal layer is a perinuclear cylindrical layer which does not continue over the caudal aspect of the nucleus and is not a caplike structure indicates that the former term "postnuclear cap" is inadequate. Fawcett (1970) proposes instead the term "postacrosomal lamina."

The freeze-etching technique shows in the rabbit postacrosomal region an array of small depressions and cordlike stria parallel to the long axis of the head and associated with the implantation fossa (Koehler, 1970).

The functional significance of the perinuclear cytoplasmic layer is not clearly understood. It has been shown to possess enzymatic activity (Teichmann and Bernstein, 1969), and Bedford (1970) suggested that it activates the mechanism of rapid disintegration of the compact sperm nucleus within the egg ooplasm.

RELATIONSHIP WITH SERTOLI CELLS

The entire process of spermatid differentiation takes place in apical recesses of the Sertoli cells. The outline of the spermatids elongates; so do the deep recesses which they occupy on the surface of the Sertoli cells. In the places of contact between both types of cells is a special type of junction. It is found only on the Sertoli side and consists of a layer of filaments associated with subsurface cisternae of smooth endoplasmic reticulum.

During the first stages of spermatid differentiation, the apical recesses become so deep that the acrosome of the elongated spermatid get close to the Sertoli cell nucleus; then during stage V (Clermont's classification) in most rodents, the apical recesses unfold and push the late spermatid into the lumen. During this ascending motion, the mitochondrial sheet is formed, the nucleus becomes denser, the nuclear envelope closely adherent to the nucleus is ill-defined and forms a postnuclear membrane redundance, and the acrosome acquires the final stage of differentiation and is covered by a thin cytoplasmic layer and by the cell membrane. Most of the cytoplasm becomes concentrated behind the nuclear region of the spermatid. Elongated branches of the Sertoli cell penetrate and anchor the periphery of this migrating cytoplasm and retain it during the ascending motion. These two opposite tensions have been interpreted as strip-teasing the excess cytoplasm and are apparently one of the main causes of the formation of the residual body and final spermatid shaping (Sapsford and Rae, 1969).

During spermiation, there is apparently no further change in spermatid morphology outside the rupture of the thin cytoplasmic bridge which connects the midpiece with the residual body. The ascending motion which pushes the spermatids into the lumen is not clearly understood. In the so-called spontane-ous spermiation which occurs during sexual abstinence, the unfolding of the apical recesses is due to simple motion of the Sertoli cell cytoplasm (Fawcett and Phillips, 1970) or to swelling of the smooth endoplasmic cisternae and cytoplas-mic matrix (Burgos et al., 1973) which surround the implanted spermatid head.

After spermiation, the wide and almost erased apical recesses appear sur-rounded by elongated prolongations of the Sertoli cell cytoplasm which accom-pany the late spermatids released into the lumen. At this stage, it is pertinent to call them spermatozoa. The Sertoli cell surface shows an extracellular coating of thin filamentous material which was previously in contact with the spermatid surface.

SPERM MATURATION

The differentiation of spermatids into spermatozoa is essentially complete at spermiation, but in several rodents changes have been observed with the electron microscope in the head of the spermatozoa during the epididymal transit. One of the most notable remodeling changes occurs in the guinea pig acrosome. At spermiation in the testis as well as in the caput epididymidis, the acrosome is a flat, crescent-shaped structure (Fig. 5) which covers the anterior part of the nucleus. The spermatozoa obtained from the cauda epididymidis have a spoon-shaped acrosome with a curled edge like a hook (Fig. 6) (Fawcett and Hollen-berg, 1963). This remarkable change is apparently due to an extrinsic maturation factor present in the caudal portion of the epididymis which is androgen dependent (Blaquier et al., 1972).

In other rodents, similar changes in acrosome shape have been reported, such as in the chinchilla (Fawcett and Phillips, 1970) and the white-tailed rat (Bedford and Nicander, 1971) and to a lesser degree in the rabbit (Bedford, 1965).

The ultrastructural appearance of the mammalian sperm nucleus remains constant after spermiation until it contacts the ooplasm at fertilization (Barros and Franklin, 1968; Piko, 1969; Bedford, 1970). The investigation of disulfide crosslinks in mammalian spermatozoa shows the establishment of linkages in the nucleus during sperm maturation in the epididymis (Calvin and Bedford, 1971);

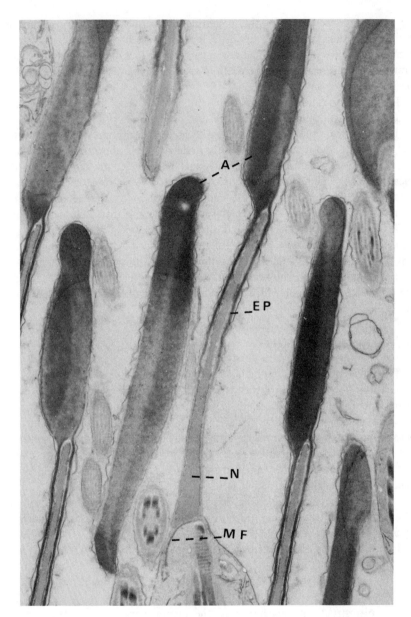

FIG. 5. Micrograph of guinea pig spermatozoa in the caput epididymidis. The acrosomes (A) are flat and elongated; they show different densities after PTA–chromium stain. The equatorial portion (EP) is dense, and the nucleus (N) appears homogeneous and pale. The cauda membrane fold (MF) is covered by a dense basal plate.

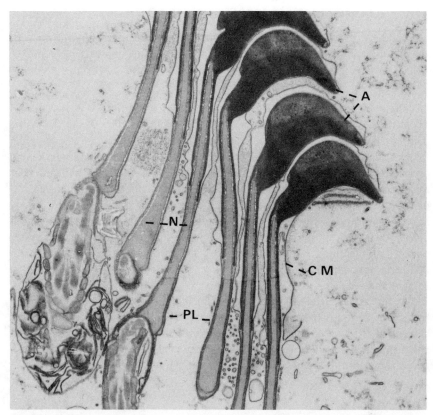

FIG. 6. *Micrograph of guinea pig spermatozoa in the cauda epididymidis.* The acrosomes (A) are spoonlike in shape and stacked in piles. They show different densities with the PTA–chromium stain and a loosely attached cell membrane (CM) over the acrosomal cap. In the postacrosomal region, the cell membrane is smooth and well adherent to the postacrosomal lamina (PL). The nucleus (N) is homogeneous and pale.

these changes apparently are independent of the epididymal milieu. The perinuclear cytoplasmic material beneath the acrosome and in the postacrosomal region also becomes stabilized by establishment of disulfide bonds during the passage of sperm from caput to cauda epididymidis (Calvin and Bedford, 1971).

Changes in density of the outer leaflet of the cell membrane over the whole head in rabbit and monkey have been reported as the spermatozoa reach the distal portion of the epididymal body (Bedford and Nicander, 1971).

The cell surface of mammalian spermatozoa is negatively charged. This charge increases with epididymal maturation of spermatozoa (Bedford, 1963; Cooper and Bedford, 1971; Yanagimachi *et al.*, 1972).

THE MATURE MAMMALIAN SPERM HEAD

The head of the mature mammalian spermatozoon is formed by the nucleus, the acrosome, the cytoplasmic derivatives, and the cell membrane.

The Nucleus

The nucleus is found to be extremely dense by electron microscopy, devoid of resolvable fine structures other than a variable number of small cavities distributed at random through the condensed chromatin; they are known as the "nuclear vacuoles," although they do not have a limiting membrane. In human sperm, these vacuoles are so large that they are easily visualized with the light microscope. The two membranes of the nuclear envelope are almost coalescent, and the perinuclear cisterna is largely obliterated. They can be resolved only at high magnification. The nuclear nevelope is closely applied to the condensed chromatin except at the junction between the lateral and the caudal surface, where both membranes are often reflected away from the condensed chromatin and form a membranous fold of variable length extending into the neck region (Figs. 1 and 4).

At the caudal surface of the nucleus, which has a concavity, the implantation fossa, the two closely apposed layers of the nuclear envelope leave a narrow space that is traversed by uniformly distributed densities which appear to bind the membranes together. On the outer surface of this structure, a layer of dense material constitutes the basal plate (Figs. 1 and 5).

The Acrosome

The mammalian acrosome presents a great variation in volume and shape. In man, monkey, bull, boar, rabbit, and bat the acrosome is relatively small, but in guinea pig, chinchilla, and ground squirrel it is much larger and has an elaborated and species-characteristic shape (see Fawcett, 1970).

The acrosomal content is amorphous, with frequent differences in density. By use of a special stain (PTA and chromium; Morré, 1973), it is possible to recognize heterogeneity where the combined lead–uranyl stain shows homogeneity (Fig. 6).

Three portions have been recognized: the apical segment, the main segment, and the equatorial segment (Fawcett, 1970). The apical segment extends beyond the anterior margin of the nucleus; the main segment extends back over the anterior half of the nucleus, then abruptly decreases in thickness and forms the equatorial segment, which extends to the caudal portion of the acrosomal cap. This last portion is of higher density than the rest of the acrosome (Fig. 4).

The apical and main segments have been related to the dispersal of the cumulus (Austin, 1963; Bedford, 1967), and the equatorial segment and the inner membrane of the acrosome appear to be involved in the lysis of the zona pellucida.

The Cytoplasmic Derivatives and the Cell Membrane

In three places derivatives of the former cytoplasm of the spermatid remain after the differentiation of the spermatozoon (Figs. 1 and 4). One derivative is found between the acrosome and the anterior pole of the nucleus, the "subacrosomal layer" or "subacrosomal space." This layer contains a small amount of amorphous material of low density. In human sperm, its volume is insignificant. In rodents, however, there is a relatively large pyramidal subacrosomal accumulation of the amorphous material. Another layer is found over the anterior portion of the head between the acrosomal cap and the overlying cell membrane. This layer, which is insignificant in volume, tends to swell, leaving the cell membrane loosely detached from the underlying acrosome. The third layer is the postacrosomal layer (postnuclear cap). It is continuous with the two previous layers and contributes to form with the subacrosomal one a continuous perinuclear layer. The cell membrane is smooth contoured and closely adherent to the underlying material, which usually appears amorphous or less frequently with some regular pattern of periodic ridges (Fawcett and Ito, 1965).

These cytoplasmic layers appear to play a role during the process of fertilization; the epiacrosomal layer disappears during the acrosome vacuolization, and the other two remain, apparently as triggers of the disintegration of the compact sperm nucleus within the egg ooplasm (Bedford, 1970).

REFERENCES

Alfert, M. (1956), Chemical differentiation of nuclear proteins during spermatogenesis in the salmon, *J. Biophys. Biochem. Cytol.* 2:109–114.

Alfert, M. (1957), Some cytochemical contributions to genetic chemistry, in: *The Chemical Basis of Heredity,* pp. 186–194 (W. D. McElroy and B. Glass, eds.), Johns Hopkins Press, Baltimore.

Austin, C. R. (1963), Acrosome loss from the rabbit spermatozoan in relation to entry into the egg, *J. Reprod. Fertil.* 6:313.

Barros, C., and Franklin, L. E. (1968), Behavior of the gamete membranes during sperm entry into the mammalian egg. *J. Cell Biol.* 37:C13–C18.

Bedford, J. M. (1963), Changes in the electrophoretic properties of rabbit spermatozoa during passage through the epididymis, *Nature (Lond.)* 200:1178–1180.

Bedford, J. M. (1964), Fine structure of the sperm head in ejaculate and uterine spermatozoa of the rabbit, *J. Reprod. Fertil.* 7:221–228.

Bedford, J. M. (1965), Changes in fine structure of the rabbit sperm head during passage through the epididymis, *J. Anat.* 99:891–906.

Bedford, J. M. (1967), Observations on the fine structure of spermatozoa of the bush baby (*Galago senegalensis*), the African green monkey (*Cercopithecus aethiops*) and man, *Am. J. Anat.* 121:443–460.

Bedford, J. M. (1970), Sperm capacitation and fertilization in mammals, *Biol. Reprod. (suppl.)* 2:128–158.

Bedford, J. M., and Nicander, L. (1971), Ultrastructural changes in the acrosome and sperm membranes during maturation of spermatozoa in the testis and epididymis of the rabbit and monkey, *J. Anat.* 108:527–543.

Blaquier, J. A., Cameo, M. S., and Burgos, M. H. (1972), The role of androgens in the maturation of epididymal spermatozoa in the guinea pig, *Endocrinology.* 90:839–842.

Blandau, R. J. (1951), Observations on the morphology of rat spermatozoa mounted in media of different refractive indices and examined with the phase microscope, *Anat. Rec.* 109:271.

Block, D. P. (1962), Histone synthesis in non-replicating chromosomes, *J. Histochem. Cytochem.* 10:137–144.

Block, D. P., and Brach, S. D. (1964), Evidence for the cytoplasmic synthesis of nuclear histone during spermiogenesis in the grasshopper *Chortophaga veridifasciata* (De Geer), *J. Cell Biol.* 22:237–340.

Block, D. P., and Hew, H. Y. C. (1960), Schedule of spermatogenesis in the pulmonate snail *Helix aspersa,* with special reference to histone transition, *J. Biophys. Biochem. Cytol.* 7:515–532.

Burgos, M. H., and Fawcett, D. W. (1955), Studies on the fine structure of the mammalian testis. I. Differentiation of the spermatid in the cat (Felis domestica), *J. Biophys. Biochem. Cytol.* 1:287–300.

Burgos, M. H., and Fawcett, D. W. (1956), An electron microscope study of spermatid differentiation in the toad *Bufo arenarum* Hensel, *J. Biophys. Biochem. Cytol.* 2:223–240.

Burgos, M. H., Sacerdote, F. L., and Russo, J. (1973), Mechanism of sperm release, in: *The Regulation of Mammalian Reproduction,* pp. 166–182 (S. J. Segal, R. Crozier, P. A. Corfman, and P. G. Condliffe, eds.), Charles C Thomas, Springfield, Ill.

Burgos, M. H., Vitale-Calpe, R. and Russo, J. (1968), Effect of LH in the seminiferous tubule at the subcellular level, in: *Gonadotropins,* p. 213 (E. Rosemberg, ed.), Geron-X, Los Altos, California.

Calvin, H. I., and Bedford, J. M. (1971), Formation of disulphide bonds in the nucleus and accessory structures of mammalian spermatozoa during maturation in the epididymis, *J. Reprod. Fertil. (suppl.)* 13:65–75.

Clark, A. W. (1967), Some aspects of spermiogenesis in a lizard, *Am. J. Anat.* 121:369–400.

Cooper, G. W., and Bedford, J. M. (1971), Acquisition of surface charge by plasma membrane of mammalian spermatozoa during epididymal maturation, *Anat. Rec.* 169:300–301.

Das, N. K. (1963), Chromosomal and nucleolar RNA synthesis in root tips during mitosis, *Science* 140:1231–1233.

Fawcett, D. W. (1965), The anatomy of the mammalian spermatozoon with particular reference to the guinea pig, *Z. Zellforsch. Mikrosk. Anat.* 67:279–296.

Fawcett, D. W. (1970), A comparative view of sperm ultrastructure, *Biol. Reprod. Suppl.* 2:90–127.

Fawcett, D. W., Anderson, W. A., and Phillips, D. M. (1971), Morphogenetic factors influencing the shape of the sperm head, *Develop. Biol.* 26:220–251.

Fawcett, D. W., and Hollenberg, R. (1963), Changes in the acrosome of guinea pig spermatozoa during passage through the epididymis, *Z. Zellforsch. Mikrosk. Anat.* 60:276–292.

Fawcett, D. W., and Ito, S. (1965), The fine structure of bat spermatozoa, *Am. J. Anat.* 116:567–610.

Fawcett, D. W., and Phillips, D. M. (1967), Further Observations on mammalian spermio-genesis, *J. Cell Biol. 35:*152A.

Fawcett, D. W., and Phillips, D. M. (1969).Observations on the release of spermatozoa and on changes in the head during passage through the epididymis, *J. Reprod. Fert. (suppl.)* *6:*405–418.

Friend, G. F. (1936), The sperm of the British Muridae, *Quart. J. Microsc. Sci. 78:*419–443.

Garner, D. L. (1973), Partial characterization of bovine acrosomal proteinase, *Biol. Reprod.* *9:*71A.

Hadek, R. (1963), Study on the fine structure of rabbit sperm head, *J. Ultrastruct. Res.* *9:*110–122.

Illison, L. (1969), Spermatozoal head shape in two inbred strains of mice and their F_1 and F_2 progenies, *Anat. J. Biol. Sci. 22:*947.

Kessel, R. G. (1970), Spermiogenesis in the dragonfly with special reference to a considera-tion of the mechanisms involved in the development of cellular asymmetry, in: *Com-parative Spermatology,* pp. 531–549 (B. Baccetti, ed.), Academic Press, New York.

Kessel, R. G., and Spaziani, E. (1969), Nuclear morphogenesis in rat spermatids, *J. Cell* *Biol. 43:*67A.

Koehler, J. K. (1970), Freeze-etching studies on spermatozoa with particular reference to nuclear and post-nuclear cap structure, in: *Spermatologia Comparata,* Vol. 137, pp. 515–522 (B. Baccetti, ed.), Accademia Naz. dei Lincei.

LeBlond, C. P., and Clermont, Y. (1952), Spermiogenesis of rat, mouse, hamster and guinea pig as revealed by the Periodic acid–fuchsin sulfurous acid technique, *Am. J. Anat.* *90:*167–215.

McIntosh, J. R., and Porter, K. R. (1967), Microtubules in the spermatids of the domestic fowl, *J. Cell Biol. 35:*153–173.

Mooré, D. J. (1973), An electron-dense stain for identifying isolated fragments of plasma and acrosome membranes from porcine sperm, *Biol. Reprod. 9:*101A.

Nagano, T. (1961), The structure of the cytoplasmic bridges in dividing spermatocytes of the rooster, *Anat. Rec. 141:*73–79.

Nicander, L., and Bane, A. (1966), Fine structure of the sperm head in some mammals with particular reference to the acrosome and the sub-acrosomal substance, *Z. Zellforsch.* *Mikrosk. Anat. 72:*496–515.

Piko, L. (1969), Gamete structure and sperm entry in mammals, in: *Fertilization, Compara-tive Morphology, Biochemistry and Immunology,* Vol. II, pp. 325–404 (C. B. Metz and A. Monroy, eds.), Academic Press, New York.

Sapsford, C. S., and Rae, C. A. (1969), Ultrastructural studies on Sertoli cells and sperma-tids in the bandicoot and ram during the movement of mature spermatids into the lumen of the seminiferous tubule, *Aust. J. Zool. 17:*415–445.

Shoup, J. R. (1967), Spermiogenesis with special reference to nuclear differentiation in wild type and in male sterility mutant of *Drosophila melanogaster, J. Cell. Biol. 32:*663–676.

Srivastava, P. N. (1973), Location of the zona lysin, *Biol. Reprod. 9:*84A.

Sud, B. N. (1961), Morphological and histochemical studies of the chromatoid body and related elements in spermatogenesis of the rat, *Quart. J. Microsc. Sci. 102:*495–505.

Teichmann, R. J., and Bernstein, M. H. (1969), Regional differentiation in the head of human and rabbit spermatozoa, *Anat. Rec. 163:*343A.

Yanagimachi, R., Noda, Y. D., Fujimoto, M., and Nicolson, G. L. (1972), The distribution of negative surface charges on mammalian spermatozoa, *Am. J. Anat. 135:*497–520.

Yang, C. H. (1973), Separation and properties of hyaluronidase from ram sperm acrosomes, *Biol. Reprod. 9:*71A.

15

Ultrastructure of the Sperm Tail

Henning Pedersen
Laboratory of Reproductive Biology
Department of Obstetrics and Gynecology
Rigshospitalet, University of Copenhagen
Copenhagen, Denmark

Ultrastructural studies of the sperm tail from a wide variety of mammalian species have confirmed the basically uniform picture demonstrated in early light-microscopic investigations and have also contributed the description of many new details, such as the axoneme, the coarse fibers, and the fibrous sheath. At the same time it has been found that differences in several substructural details often allow species determination from the ultrastructural picture of the sperm tail. In several species, the substructure of the sperm tail has been described in considerable detail. However, at the present time, it is still not possible to infer a functional model for flagellar motility from the morphological picture. Many biochemical and cytochemical studies have thrown new light on details of these mechanisms, but a composite functional anatomy, as known for muscle contraction, still awaits description.

The following deals mainly with the human sperm, although complete description of the human sperm tail is not attempted (for general review, see Fawcett, 1970). Rather, an attempt is made to describe a few details characteristic of the human spermatozoon and to describe in detail some structures which are probably not unique for this species. Their functional significance will be discussed, with full awareness of the many weaknesses presented by the suboptimal preservation of such delicate structures.

MIDDLE PIECE

The cytoplasm of the human middle piece extends anteriorly to engulf the basal portion of the nucleus (Fig. 1) and is sharply demarcated there by a close circumferential union of the cell membrane with the nuclear envelope, the

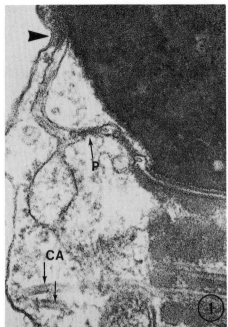

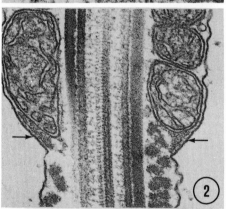

FIG. 1. Anteriorly the cytoplasm of the middle piece is sharply demarcated by the "striated band," which is a close union of the cell membrane with the nuclear envelope (arrowhead). The redundant nuclear envelope with its nuclear pores (P) encloses a light, structureless nucleoplasm. In mature sperm, remnants of the centriolar adjunct (CA) are often seen (95,000✕.) From Pedersen 1972a).

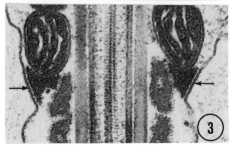

FIG. 2. Posteriorly the middle piece. is sharply separated from the principal piece by the presence of the annulus. In human spermatozoa, the annulus is a relatively inconspicuous structure (arrows).(70,000✕.)

FIG. 3. In mice, the annulus (arrows) is a well-developed, dense structure closely apposed to the cell membrane. (60,000✕.)

"striated band" (Pedersen, 1972a). The "redundant nuclear envelope" thus begins more anteriorly than in other species so far studied. It contains nuclear pores (Fig. 1) arranged in a regular hexagonal pattern (Pedersen, 1972a), and the adjacent nucleoplasm is light and nearly structureless. It is still uncertain whether this morphology reflects the presence of any nucleocytoplasmic interaction in the mature sperm, an idea possibly supported by autoradiographic studies (Salisbury and Hart, 1970).

Posteriorly, the content of the middle piece is also rather sharply demarcated by the presence of the annulus (Jensen's ring), a circumferential dense material closely apposed to the cell membrane and immediately posterior to the mitochondrial helix (Figs. 2 and 3). Substantial morphological and biochemical evidence leaves no doubt that the middle piece is the site of energy production for sperm motility, but it is still uncertain where the energy sources are, how they are transported, and how the energy is transferred to the motor apparatus.

While the distal centriole of the developing flagellum disappears during spermiogenesis, the proximal centriole persists in the mature sperm. In species with flattened sperm heads, it has been repeatedly reported that the longitudinal axis of the centriole is roughly in the plane of the flattened head, or inclined a few degrees with respect to the plane of the head. This relation is more difficult to determine in the almond-shaped human sperm head, but it is probably the same. In longitudinal sections, the centriole is seen in an eccentric position and is inclined a few degrees with respect to the longitudinal axis of the flagellum. In cross-sections, its triplets have a fixed orientation with respect to the axis of the flagellum. Thus a line passing through the triplet nearest the implantation plate and between the two triplets on the opposite side of the centriole coincides rather closely with the longitudinal axis of the flagellum. Because of this consistent relationship, a system of numbering the triplets can be adopted (Pedersen, 1972b) (Fig. 9) to provide a more detailed description of the complicated morphogenesis of the connecting piece. Structures reminiscent of the centriolar adjunct (Fig. 10)—described in considerable detail by Fawcett and Phillips (1969)—are not infrequently found in mature human spermatozoa (Fig. 1), and sometimes remnants of the distal centriole may be found in ejaculated human spermatozoa.

Based mainly on morphological evidence, the centriole is considered to be the structure from which ciliary and flagellar motility is initiated, but the basic mechanisms are still largely unknown. Thus the middle piece of mammalian spermatozoa is the unit of energy production and conversion into highly coordinated motility. Again, the basic mechanisms involved are still largely unknown.

PRINCIPAL PIECE

With some variation in details, the principal piece of mammalian spermatozoa is characterized by the presence of the fibrous sheath, a structure basically

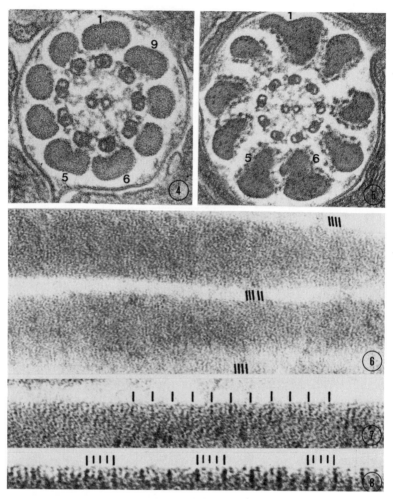

FIG. 4. On cross-sections, the coarse fibers are rounded, dense, homogeneous structures. In human spermatozoa, fibers Nos. 1, 9, 5 and 6 are thicker than the others, the difference being most pronounced in their anterior extremities. Human spermatozoa have no satellite fibrils. (112,500×.)

FIG. 5. In most other mammalian spermatozoa, as in those of the monkey Macaca arctoides shown here, there are well-developed satellite fibrils, cross-sections of which are seen on the mesial aspects of the coarse fibers. (66,000×.)

FIG. 6. In very thin longitudinal sections of the coarse fibers, they are found to be finely cross-striated with a period of 40 Å. The striations are inclined a few degrees with respect to the longitudinal axis of the fibers. (262,500×.) From Pedersen (1972b).

FIG. 7. Near the abaxial surface of the coarse fibers, more dense lines demarcate a major period of 160 Å. Of the three intraperiod lines, the one in the middle appears slightly thicker than the neighboring ones. (328,500×.) From Pedersen (1972b).

FIG. 8. A print-translation technique (Pedersen 1972b) has been applied to part of Fig. 10 in order to illustrate more clearly the findings described. (450,000×.) From Pedersen (1972b).

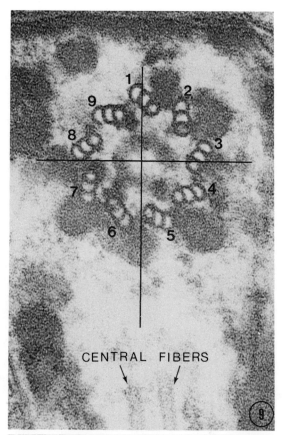

FIG. 9. The centriole has a constant orientation with respect to the axis of the flagellum, and it is perpendicular to the plane of the central fibers. This consistent relationship allows a system of numbering the single triplets, as indicated. The triplet nearest to the implantation plate is No. 1. The triplet whose C-fiber is connected with the A-fiber or triplet No. 1 is designated No. 2. (190,000×.) From Pedersen (1972b).

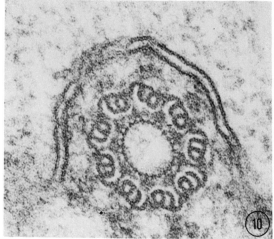

FIG. 10. The centriolar adjunct, here from Macaca arctoides, *disappears almost completely during late spermiogenesis.* However, as illustrated in Fig. 1, remnants of its tubules might be found in mature human spermatozoa. (153,900×.)

similar in all species. The longitudinal columns of the human sperm are relatively inconspicuous, and, characteristically, the semicircular ribs are less regularly arranged than in most other species. The longitudinal columns are found in a dorsal and a ventral position and have, throughout most of their length, a laminar connection with two of the doublets (Nos. 3 and 8) of the axoneme (Fig. 11). Relatively little attention has been paid to the composition of the fibrous sheath. Usually it is considered a cytoskeleton with a supportive or elastic function. A total lack of the fibrous sheath has been described in the spermatozoa of a patient with severe asthenospermia (Pedersen et al., 1971). This finding does not, however, elucidate the function of the fibrous sheath in sperm movement, since such spermatozoa also have abnormal middle pieces and coarse fibers.

END PIECE

In the end piece, the axoneme is covered by the cell membrane and lacks other characteristic structures. The axoneme becomes highly modified as it tapers down in this part of the tail (Pedersen, 1972b) and loses any morphological evidence of active motility.

COARSE FIBERS

With only a few exceptions, the coarse fibers are paraflagellar structures unique to the mammalian sperm tail. They are found only in the anterior end of the tail, make close contact anteriorly with the paracentriolar connecting piece and extend posteriorly for a varying length into the principal piece. In the human spermatozoon these fibers are relatively inconspicuous and also relatively short, extending only a few microns into the principal piece. The lateral coarse fibers, Nos. 1, 9, 5, and 6 (for numbering, see Fig. 11), on cross-sections are a little thicker than the others (Figs. 4 and 5). Distally, they have a relatively well-defined successive termination, so that the first coarse fibers to terminate are Nos. 3 and 8. The next fibers to terminate are Nos. 4, 2, and 7, followed by Nos. 5 and 6. The last fibers to terminate are Nos. 1 and 9 (Pedersen, 1974). For some time the coarse fibers were considered to be homogeneous structures, except for the presence in some species of a cortical and a medullary zone, as seen on cross-sections. In replicas of mouse sperm, Wooley (1971) found a coarse, striated pattern on the outer surface of the coarse fibers. Thus the homogeneous coarse fibers with a coarse, regular striation on the outer surface appeared to be morphologically different from the elements of the connecting piece, which were very finely cross-striated (Fawcett and Phillips, 1969). However, it has been demonstrated that very thin sections of coarse fibers from human spermatozoa show a fine cross-striation of the fibers (Pedersen, 1972b) basically similar to the

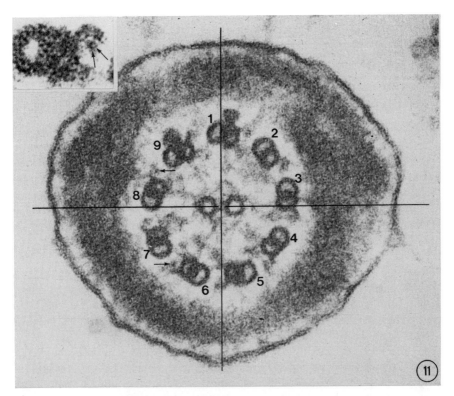

FIG. 11. In this cross-section of the principal piece of a human spermatozoon, the traditional numbering of the doublets is indicated. On the mesial aspect of the curved outer arm, a sharply demarcated dot can often be recognized, possibly representing the cross-section of a thin, longitudinal thread. As illustrated, the substructure of these delicate elements is difficult to evaluate in greater detail. (204,000×, inset 410,400×.)

substructure described for the connecting piece by Fawcett and Phillips (1969). Logitudinal sections of the coarse fibers show thin lines 40 Å apart and inclined a few degrees with respect to the axis of the tail, so that the continued direction of these lines makes flattened spirals around the tail (Fig. 6). Near the abaxial surface of the coarse fibers, somewhat thicker lines—160 Å apart—demarcate a major period. Within this major period, there are three thinner lines spaced at 40 Å intervals. Of these, the middle line appears slightly thicker than the others (Figs. 7 and 8). A quite similar substructure has also been observed in coarse fibers of spermatozoa of *Macaca arctoides* and mice (Pedersen, unpublished).

An active role in flagellar motility has been attributed to the coarse fibers, but, at present, supporting evidence appears to be largely circumstantial (Fawcett, 1970) since the techniques involved are still capricious. From cinematographic studies, it appears that species with thick and long coarse fibers usually have coarse and slow movements. Human sperm, with its relatively inconspicuous coarse fibers, have highly undulating and quick movements, leaving the impression that human sperm coarse fibers have merely a supportive or elastic function. The question is, however, still unresolved.

AXONEME

The general axonemal substructure is well known and has been dealt with in several previous works. Here, some attention will be given to the substructure of the axonemal matrix, based mainly on observations of the human spermatozoon. The numbering of the doublets, as adopted from original works on cilia and flagella (Afzelius, 1959), is indicated in Fig. 11. As illustrated in Fig. 9, a plane interconnecting the two central fibers of the axoneme will be perpendicular to the longitudinal axis of the centriole, which is roughly in the plane of the flattened sperm head. Thus doublets No. 3 and 8 are found in a dorsal and a ventral position and are connected with the longitudinal columns of the fibrous sheath by two longitudinal laminae (Fig. 11). From a purely morphological point of view, one would expect a movement of the tail from side to side to meet with least resistance since the ribs of the fibrous shealth should easily give way to such a movement, wheras the dorsal and ventral longitudinal columns would be expected to be more resistant to longitudinal changes.

The axonemal matrix is rather difficult to resolve in detail with the present technique of sperm preservation for electron microscopy. The two central fibers appear to be interconnected by regularly spaced ribs, 135 Å apart, and oriented perpendicular to the fibers (Figs. 12 and 13). It has also been demonstrated that the two central fibers are surrounded by two evenly spaced spiral threads, 135 Å apart, which have points of contact with the central fibers at exactly the same level as the ribs interconnecting the two fibers (Pedersen, 1970) (Figs. 13–15). These spiral threads are connected to the doublets by evenly spaced lines—270 Å apart—the so-called spokes, which are arranged in spiraling planes around the central fibers (Pedersen, 1970) (Figs. 14 and 16). Moreover, it appears that one spiral thread provides the doublets with spokes in half of the axoneme, as divided by the plane of the central fibers. The doublets in the other half of the axoneme receive their spokes from the other spiral thread. These central spiral threads and their associated spokes have been referred to as the "axial spiral complex" (Pedersen, 1970), which extends anteriorly to the posterior extremity of the modified "distal centriole" and posteriorly to the end piece. In the end piece it is modified together with the successive termination of the general axonemal substructure.

At the present time, the function of the "axial spiral complex" is unknown. Based on biochemical and morphological observations, it has been speculated that this complex might play a role in the transmission of the activating impulse

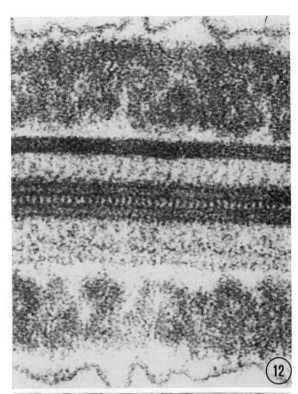

FIG. 12. The two central fibers are seen to be interconnected by regularly spaced ribs, 135 Å apart and oriented perpendicular to the axis of the fibers. (148,000×.)

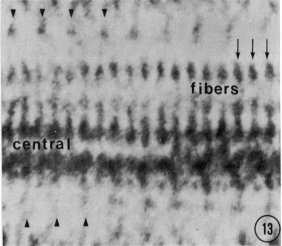

FIG. 13. By means of a special print-translation technique (Pedersen, 1972b), these small structures are more clearly visualized. This section is in the plane of the two central fibers, and it is seen that the points of contact of the two spiral threads of the central sheath (arrows) are found at exactly the same level as the ribs interconnecting the central fibers. On each side of the axoneme, the spokes (arrowheads) are connected to every second spiral thread. They are perpendicular to the axis of the flagellum, which is in accordance with their arrangement in the form of spiraling planes around the flagellum (for detailed discussion, see Pedersen, 1970). (358,000×.)

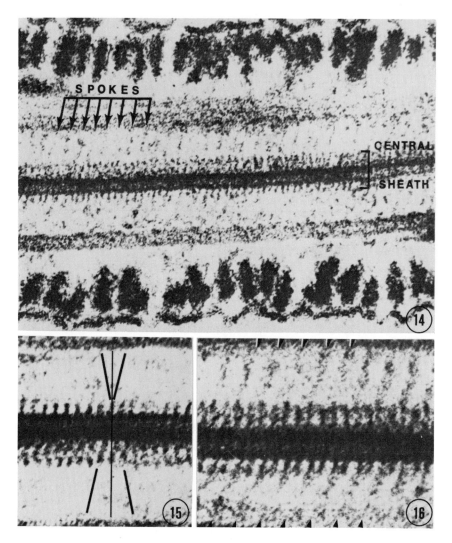

FIG. 14. The spokes are regularly spaced with a maximum inclination equal to the maximum inclination of the spiral threads of the central sheath and with a center-to-center distance of 270 Å. (135,000×.) From Pedersen (1970).

FIG. 15. The geometrical arrangement of the threads of the central sheath seems to indicate the presence of two spiral threads equally spaced around the central fibers. (260,000×.) From Pedersen (1970).

FIG. 16. The spokes in half of the axoneme are connected to every second spiral thread, and the spokes in the other half of the axoneme are connected to the other spiral thread. The implication of this finding is discussed in the text. (287,000×.) From Pedersen (1970).

for flagellar motility (Pedersen, 1970). In this role it seems to give satisfactory answers to some of the basic questions regarding the pattern of flagellar motion. If one spiral thread, beginning in the centriole region, is considered impulse-transmitting, it could provide half (one side) of the axoneme with the activating impulse mediated by the spokes. The other side of the axoneme could then be controlled by the other spiral thread. Thus a timely asynchrony in the two spiral threads would naturally cause an undulating movement of the tail. At the same time, a successive activation of the doublets would be expected to result in a twisting movement of the flagellum. These two components of the movements have been recognized for several years, but they have been difficult to explain on the basis of the apparently symmetrical structure of the flagellum.

With respect to the central fibers, the coherent stability of which is secured by the ribs, a system supporting and carrying the axial spiral complex would be in accordance with the fact that this central component is morphologically the most variable one in cilia and flagella from various sources (Baccetti, 1970). The presence of a spiral-like structure around the central component of flagella from various sources has been described, with apparently some variance in dimensions. It is, however, connected to the outer doublets by a system of spokelike structures (for review, see Pedersen, 1970).

Based on various techniques, increasing evidence now seems to point to the doublets—more specifically, to the arms (Gibbons, 1963, 1965, 1968; Gibbons and Row, 1965)—as being the site of the contractile elements of cilia and flagella (for review, see Pedersen, 1970, 1974). A detailed understanding of the substructure of this outer complex has met with difficulties, since it is rather difficult to preserve meticulously. An example is the substructure of the outer arm, which is generally considered to be curved with a hooklike appendage on its free end. This impression was mainly gained from earlier works with the Markham print-translation technique (Allen, 1968). However, sufficiently often another picture is seen (Fig. 11, inset): a uniformly curved arm, which on its mesial aspect encloses a sharply demarcated dot. Obviously, such a detail would easily be obscured by the technique mentioned. The dark dot, free of the arm itself, might represent the cross-section of a thin, longitudinal thread running on the mesial aspect of the arms. This question awaits resolution.

Great attention is focused on the arms as the probable sites of contractile elements. Thus it might be relevant to report a finding in the spermatozoa of a patient from this department. He presented an unusual seminal picture where all the usual parameters were normal, except for one thing: his spermatozoa were all totally immobile; a finding confirmed by several semen analyses during the last 2 yr. The ultrastructure of his spermatozoa showed one major defect: a total absence of arms on the doublets (Fig. 17). In a testicular biopsy, the same defect was observed in the spermatids (Pedersen and Rebbe, unpublished).

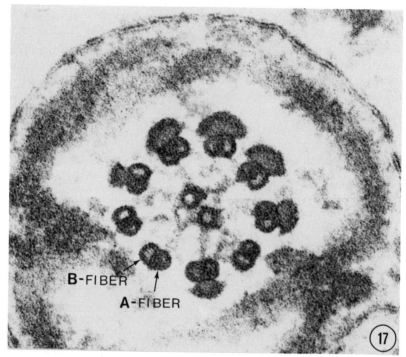

FIG. 17. This cross-section of the principal piece of a spermatozoon from a sterile patient whose spermatozoa were all immobile illustrates the total lack of arms on the doublets. The rest of the flagellum, including the axonemal matrix, is normal. The same finding was encountered in spermatids from this patient. (225,000×.)

CONCLUSION

A meticulous evaluation of the structure and functional morphology of the spermatozoon still meets with basic difficulties, some of which have been pointed out. In the wide aspect of human reproduction, this is only a facet. However, to understand the processes involved, to affect or control them, and to treat their pathology, greater basic knowledge is indispensable.

REFERENCES

Afzelius, B. A. (1959), Electron microscopy of the sperm tail: Results obtained with a new fixative, *J. Biophys. Biochem. Cytol. 5:*269–278.

Allen, R. D. (1968), A reinvestigation of cross-sections of cilia, *J. Cell Biol. 37:*825–831.

Baccetti, B. (1970), *Comparative Spermatology,* Academic Press, New York.

Fawcett, D. W. (1970), A comparative view of sperm ultrastructure, *Biol. Reprod. (suppl.) 2:*90–127.

Fawcett, D. W., and Phillips, D. M. (1969), The fine structure and development of the neck region of the mammalian spermatozoon, *Anat. Rec. 165:*153–184.

Gibbons, I. R. (1963), Studies on the protein components of cilia from *Tetrahymena pyriformis, Proc. Natl. Acad. Sci. (U.S.A.) 50:*1002–1010.

Gibbons, I. R. (1965), Chemical dissection of cilia, *Arch. Biol. 76:*317–352.

Gibbons, I. R. (1968), The biochemistry of motility, *Ann. Rev. Biochem. 37:*521–546.

Gibbons, I. R., and Rowe, A. J. (1965), Dynein: A protein with adenosine triphosphatase activity from cilia, *Science 149:*424–426.

Pedersen, H. (1970), Observations on the axial filament complex of the human spermatozoon, *J. Ultrastruct. Res. 33:*451–462.

Pedersen, H. (1972a), The postacrosomal region of the spermatozoa of man and *Macaca arctoides, J. Ultrastruct. Res. 40:*366–377.

Pedersen, H. (1972b), Further observations on the fine structure of the human spermatozoon, *Z. Zellforsch. Mikrosk. Anat. 123:*305–315.

Pedersen, H. (1974), The human spermatozoon: An electron microscopical study including comparative details of *Macaca arctoides* spermatozoa, *Dan. Med. Bull. 21(suppl.1):*1–35.

Pedersen, H., Rebbe, H., and Hammen, R. (1971), Human sperm fine structure in a case of severe asthenospermia-necrospermia, *Fertil. Steril. 22:*156–164.

Salisbury, G. W., and Hart, R. G. (1970), Gamete aging and its consequences, *Biol. Reprod. (suppl.) 2:*1–13.

Wooley, D. M. (1971), Striations in the peripheral fibers of rat and mouse spermatozoa, *J. Cell Biol. 49:*936–939.

16

Chemical and Structural Analysis of Mammalian Spermatozoa

W. E. Gall, C. F. Millette, and G. M. Edelman

The Rockefeller University
New York, New York

The distinctive structure of the spermatozoon and several well-defined sequences of events in fertilization have been elucidated by ultrastructural studies. Morphological investigations have, for example, revealed the role of the acrosome in the penetration of the protective layers surrounding the egg (Bedford, 1968) and have also revealed the fate of the different segments of the spermatozoon after formation of the male pronucleus (Stefanini *et al.*, 1969). Biochemical studies have identified a number of hydrolytic enzymes in the acrosome and have indicated their function in the fertilization process (Stambaugh and Buckley, 1969; Allison and Hartree, 1970). A large number of other enzymatic activities have been observed in the spermatozoon (Garbers *et al.*, 1973; Jones and Mann, 1973), but the function and the location in the cell of these molecular constituents have not yet been defined. Although histochemical studies have indicated that the plasma membrane of the sperm cell is topologically specialized, e.g., in relation to the charge of the membrane (Yanagimachi *et al.*, 1973) and the localization of at least some glycoprotein or glycolipid moieties (Nicolson and Yanagimachi, 1972), the biochemical characterization of any spermatozoal membrane component has not yet been completed. A detailed map at the molecular level will be essential for understanding the function of this specialized cell.

We have begun to develop a number of methods to carry out biochemical mapping of mammalian spermatozoa. Chemical dissection procedures have been found to provide homogeneous populations of spermatozoal subcellular components in a rapid, reproducible, and specific manner (Millette *et al.*, 1973). In addition, studies on the distribution of surface membrane constituents have been initiated using a series of molecular probes (Edelman and Millette, 1971). These and similar approaches using antibodies and lectins should help to aid in the identification of those molecular components in particular regions of the cell which are important both for the maintenance of cellular integrity and for fertilization.

Biochemical analysis of the spermatozoon would be considerably simplified by an initial fractionation of subcellular components. Previous attempts to dissect the sperm cell have concentrated on physical means to disrupt the spermatozoal structure (Iverson, 1965), although notable success has been achieved with the use of cationic detergents to remove sperm acrosomes containing their enzymatic complement (Hartree and Srivastava, 1965). The additional methods of chemical dissection allow the fractionation of spermatozoal heads, intact tails, tails without mitochondria, and whole sperm without mitochondria in quantities sufficient for biochemical study.

Cleavage of spermatozoal heads from tails can be achieved by brief treatment with endopeptidases, particularly trypsin. Exposure of mouse or rat spermatozoa to 0.1 mg/ml trypsin in phosphate-buffered saline (pH 7.4) for 15 s at 25°C resulted in the cleavage of more than 95% of the cells (Fig. 1). Human, rabbit, or guinea pig spermatozoa were not affected by this procedure; however, spermatozoa from these species could be cleaved by first incubating the cells with 0.1 M dithiothreitol or 0.1 M 2-mercaptoethanol in phosphate-buffered saline for 30 min at 25°C prior to washing in fresh phosphate-buffered saline. Treatment with trypsin at a concentration of 0.05 mg/ml was then sufficient to insure cleavage of 90–95% of the cells (Millette et al., 1973). Initial incubation with trypsin, followed by addition of reducing agent, did not cause cleavage of human, rabbit, or guinea pig spermatozoa. In all cases, cleavage was not observed in the presence of soybean or lima bean trypsin inhibitor.

Mammalian spermatozoa can also be cleaved at the junction of the head and the tail by alteration of the pH of the suspension buffer without the addition of extraneous proteolytic enzyme. Incubation of mouse cells at pH 1.8 in citrate–phosphate buffer for 5 min at 25°C caused cleavage of about 40% of the spermatozoa (Fig. 2a); further incubation did not appreciably increase the proportion cleaved. Sperm from the other mammalian species examined were also cleaved by acid treatment, although the proportion of cleaved cells and the optimum pH for cleavage varied from species to species (Millette et al., 1973). Cells were not cleaved when exposed to alkaline buffers with a pH below 11, but in more strongly alkaline solutions the percentage of affected spermatozoa increased rapidly (Fig. 2b). The maximum percentage of cells cleaved by alkaline treatment ranged from 69% for rat spermatozoa to 95% for guinea pig spermatozoa. When examined by light microscopy, spermatozoa incubated in strongly

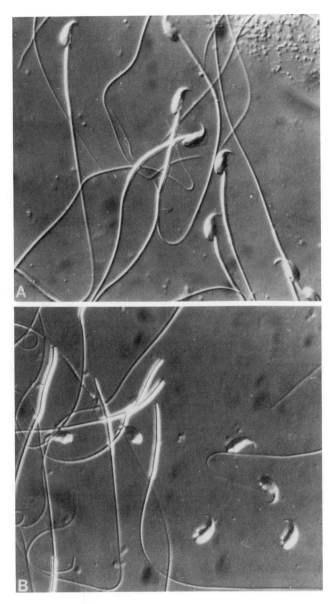

FIG. 1. NCS mouse spermatozoa in phosphate-buffered saline, pH 7.4. (A) Before and (B) after treatment with 0.05 mg/ml trypsin for 15 s at 25°C. (1,690×, Nomarski optics.)

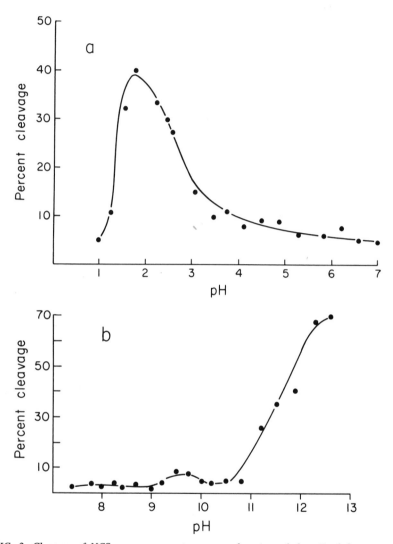

FIG. 2. *Cleavage of NCS mouse spermatozoa as a function of the pH of the suspension buffer.* (a) Phosphate–citrate buffer (0.05 M citrate, 0.01 M phosphate) was used for pH values between 1.0 and 7.0. (b) Tris buffer (0.01 M) was used for pH values between 7.4 and 12.6. Percent cleavage was measured after incubation for 5 min at 25°C.

alkaline solutions showed curled flagella, and the flagella often appeared to be partially dissolved. These effects were especially noticeable in mouse cells.

Ultrastructural examinations were conducted in order to assess the specificity of these cleavage methods. The effects on mouse spermatozoa of treatment with trypsin, acid, and base are shown in Fig. 3. Tryptic cleavage occurs at an apparently specific location in the neck of the cell, and the basal plate remains

FIG. 3. Effects of cleavage techniques on NCS mouse spermatozoa. (a) Head and neck of untreated spermatozoon. (18,240×.) (b) Spermatozoal head after treatment with 0.05 mg/ml trypsin. The acrosome, the membrane folds along the posterior end of the head, and the basal plate are intact. The plasma membrane surrounding the head appears to be relatively undamaged. (22,674×.) (c) Spermatozoal head after treatment with citrate–phosphate buffer at pH 1.8. The acrosome is destroyed, the plasma membrane is vesiculated, and there is no adherent basal plate. (34,656×.) (d) Spermatozoal head after treatment with tris buffer at pH 12.6. The acrosome is destroyed and the plasma membrane is severely damaged, but the basal plate remains. (25,296×.)

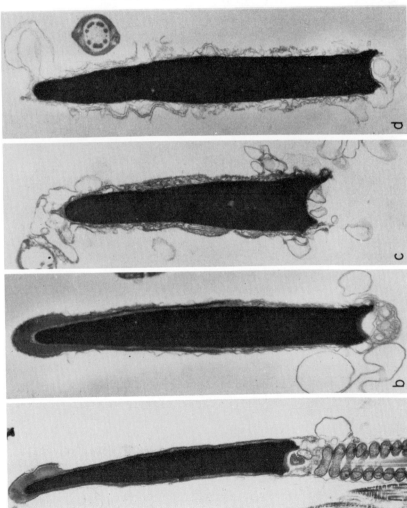

with the head (Fig. 3b). Little damage to the plasma membrane overlying either the head or the tail is observed. The neck structures, including the mitochondria and the connecting piece, appear intact and adherent to the flagellar filaments. The redundant nuclear membrane at the base of the head also appears intact. Freeze-fracture studies on mouse and guinea pig spermatozoa indicate that the complex patterns of intramembranous particles characteristic of the different spermatozoal membranes (Fig. 4) are not affected by the trypsin treatment.

In contrast to the enzymatic cleavage, exposure of spermatozoa to acid or base caused damage to the plasma membranes of both the head and tail regions and dissolution of the acrosome (Fig. 3c,d). Incubation with base resulted in cleavage at the same point as was detected after trypsin treatment. Treatment with acid, however, caused cleavage at a different point, resulting in the separation of the basal plate from the head, with the basal plate remaining attached to the tail structures.

Chemical dissection of the midpiece region was accomplished by the incubation of cells with reducing agents. After incubation of mouse or guinea pig spermatozoa in 0.1 M dithiothreitol at $37°C$ in phosphate-buffered saline for 90 min, more than 95% of the spermatozoa showed midpieces with swollen or partially detached mitochondria (Fig. 5), and about 10% had no adherent mitochondria. Gentle agitation of the cell suspension for 15 s completely removed the mitochondria from more than 96% of the cells (Fig. 5C). Some cleavage of heads from tails occurred during the agitation, but the extent of this cleavage was usually less than 5%. Occasionally separation of the central flagellar filaments in the midpiece region was observed, but the principal-piece and endpiece segments of the tail were not noticeably affected.

Preparative fractionation of spermatozoal components after chemical dissection has been accomplished by differential centrifugation in sucrose solutions using a procedure based on that of Stambaugh and Buckley (1969). Up to 2 ml of a cell suspension in phosphate-buffered saline (about 10 million cells/ml) is layered on a discontinuous sucrose gradient, with a total volume of 20 ml, made up of 5 ml of 65% sucrose, 15 ml of 60% sucrose, and 5 ml of 55% sucrose. The sucrose solutions are prepared in 0.05 M tris hydrochloride, pH 7.5. After centrifugation for 30 min at 600g, tails are recovered from the top interface of the 55% sucrose layer and heads are collected as a diffuse band in the 55% sucrose layer. Isolated heads were obtained in 65–75% yield with less than 5% contamination by tails. Fractionated tails were obtained in the same yield with less than 3% contamination with heads. A similar procedure can be used to purify spermatozoa without mitochondria after treatment with dithiothreitol alone or exposure to both trypsin and dithiothreitol as described above. These preparations are suitable for further biochemical studies on the localization of spermatozoal components.

Preliminary experiments to determine the distribution of various protein

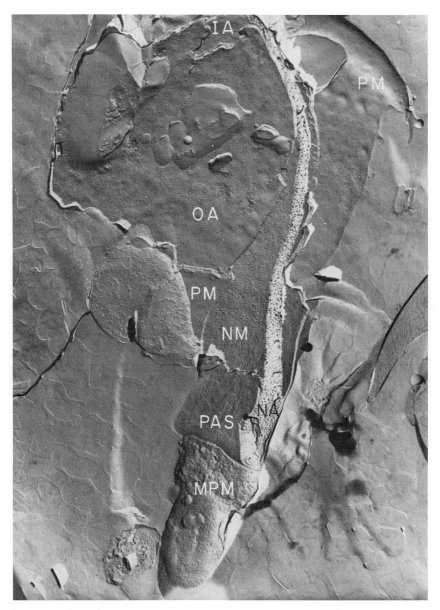

FIG. 4. Freeze-fracture replica of a guinea pig spermatozoon showing the distribution of intramembranous particles characteristic of each of the different spermatozoal membranes. PM, Plasma membrane; OA, outer acrosomal membrane; IA, inner acrosomal membrane; NM, nuclear membrane; NA, nucleic acid; PAS, postacrosomal sheath membrane; MPM, plasma membrane overlying the midpiece. (17,787X.)

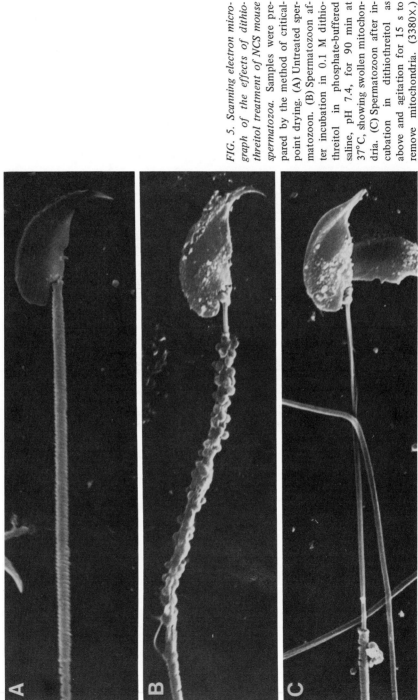

FIG. 5. Scanning electron micrograph of the effects of dithiothreitol treatment of NCS mouse spermatozoa. Samples were prepared by the method of critical-point drying. (A) Untreated spermatozoon. (B) Spermatozoon after incubation in 0.1 M dithiothreitol in phosphate-buffered saline, pH 7.4, for 90 min at 37°C, showing swollen mitochondria. (C) Spermatozoon after incubation in dithiothreitol as above and agitation for 15 s to remove mitochondria. (3380X.)

components of the spermatozoon have been conducted in conjunction with the chemical dissection methods. After solubilization of cellular components by treatment with dithiothreitol and sodium dodecylsulfate (Hernandez-Montes *et al.*, 1973) and sonication, extracts of intact NCS mouse sperm, isolated heads, and isolated tails were separated by polyacrylamide gel electrophoresis in sodium dodecylsulfate (Laemmli, 1970). As shown in Fig. 6, extracts of whole spermatozoa yielded a large number of proteins, while extracts of fractionated spermatozoal tails yielded a less complex pattern, although some components not observed in the extracts of the intact cells were revealed. The examination of fractionated spermatozoal head preparations in this system failed to indicate the presence of any protein components in significant quantity. Additional investigations are required to identify the nucleoprotein constituents of the mouse spermatozoon and to resolve this difficulty.

The effects of removal of the spermatozoal midpiece and plasma membrane have also been examined using gel electrophoresis (Fig. 7). Although the band patterns obtained both from the supernatant fluid after treatment with dithiothreitol and from the treated cells themselves are quite complex, a number of significant differences can be noted. These studies provide an opportunity for the localization of specific proteins found in intact spermatozoa and may yield information concerning the physiological function of these components.

A number of lines of evidence suggest that the constituents of the spermatozoal surface are of primary importance in the physiological function of this cell. Knowledge of the nature and distribution of these membrane components may be important in molecular descriptions of the fertilization process. For example, membrane components responsible for the specific recognition of the ovum may be localized to a particular region of the surface, e.g., the acrosome. Several different kinds of molecular probes have been used to examine the spermatozoal surface. For example, by use of colloidal iron it has been shown that the charge distribution over the surface is not uniform and that this distribution changes during sperm maturation (Bedford *et al.*, 1971).

A wide variety of carbohydrate-binding proteins called lectins are available from the seeds of leguminous plants (see Lis and Sharon, 1973), and we have utilized these as probes of the spermatozoal surface. Experiments have been carried out using both fluorescence microscopy (with fluorescein-labled lectins) and electron microscopy (with ferritin-labeled lectins). Several lectins which bind specifically to mannosyl or glucosyl groups have been used, and the results indicate that receptors for these lectins have polar distributions on the surface of the cell. Concanavalin A binds predominantly to the acrosomal region of mouse spermatozoa, with much less binding to the midpiece and tail portions (Fig. 8A). However, lectins with a similar carbohydrate-binding specificity obtained from the green pea, yellow pea, and lentil show different labeling patterns. The lectin from the green pea binds to the tail and the nonacrosomal regions of the head, while lectins from the yellow pea and the lentil label the entire surface of the

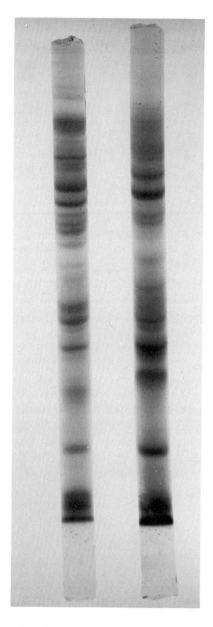

FIG. 6. Polyacrylamide gels showing proteins obtained from the solubilization of
whole NCS mouse spermatozoa (left) and
spermatozoal tails fractionated after trypsin
treatment (right).

cell. These observations suggest that lectin binding to cell surfaces may have
requirements in addition to the presence of appropriate sugar moieties; until the
nature of these requirements is understood, a detailed chemical interpretation of
the binding results is premature.

Ultrastructural investigations with ferritin-conjugated lectins also reveal a

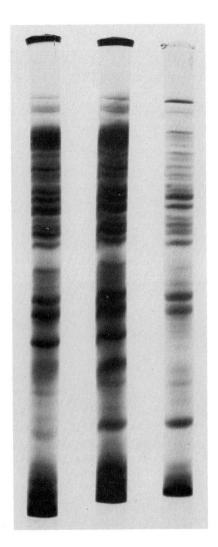

FIG. 7. Polyacrylamide gels showing proteins obtained from the solubilization of NCS mouse spermatozoa after treatment with 0.1 M dithiothreitol to remove mitochondria (left) and from the supernatant after treatment (right). Extract from untreated spermatozoa is shown in the center.

localized distribution of carbohydrates on mammalian spermatozoa. As shown in Fig. 9, wheat germ agglutinin (which has a binding specificity for N-acetylglucosamine) binds strongly to the midpiece and tail regions of the cell, but only weakly to the acrosome and postacrosomal regions of the plasma membrane on the spermatozoal head. In contrast, a lectin isolated from the red lentil (with a specificity similar to that of concanavalin A) is seen on the tail, midpiece, and acrosomal regions of spermatozoa, but does not bind to the post acrosomal areas of the surface membrane (Fig. 10). Binding of ferritin–wheat germ agglutinin and of ferritin–red lentil lectin appears to be specific, for it is completely inhibitable by N-acetylglucosamine and mannose, respectively.

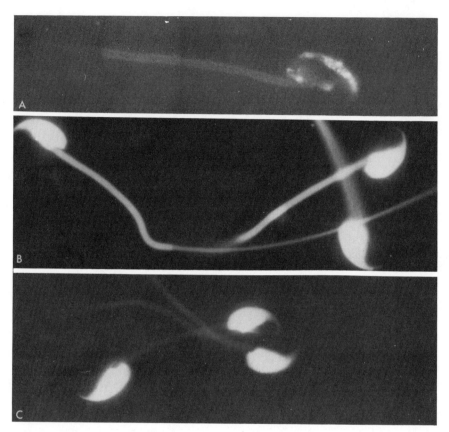

FIG. 8. Binding of (A) fluorescein-labeled concanavalin A, (B) 8-anilino-1-naphthalenesulfonic acid, and (C) ethidium bromide to NCS mouse spermatozoa in phosphate-buffered saline, pH 7.4. Observation by combined fluorescence and phase contrast microscopy indicated that the acrosome was unlabeled with ethidium bromide. (829×.)

The polar distribution of receptors for concanavalin A has been confirmed by quantitative measurements of the number of binding sites on isolated heads and tails from mouse spermatozoa (Table I). Most of the binding sites are found on the isolated heads, although the tails show significant binding. Measurements of the number of binding sites for a number of other lectins are also given in Table I. It should be noted that while the density of receptor sites may vary considerably, as was indicated in the labeling experiments described above, the total number of binding sites for various lectins is relatively constant. It is pertinent to note that our observations of the labeling patterns obtained with the various lectins reveal differences in the postacrosomal region of the head, the region which first contacts the ovum.

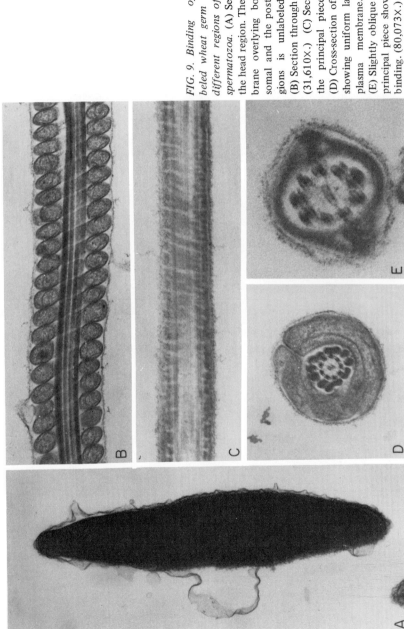

FIG. 9. Binding of ferritin-labeled wheat germ agglutinin to different regions of NCS mouse spermatozoa. (A) Section through the head region. The plasma membrane overlying both the acrosomal and the postacrosomal regions is unlabeled. (33,900X.) (B) Section through the midpiece. (31,610X.) (C) Section through the principal piece. (54,684X.) (D) Cross-section of the midpiece showing uniform labeling of the plasma membrane. (39,990X.) (E) Slightly oblique section of the principal piece showing extensive binding. (80,073X.)

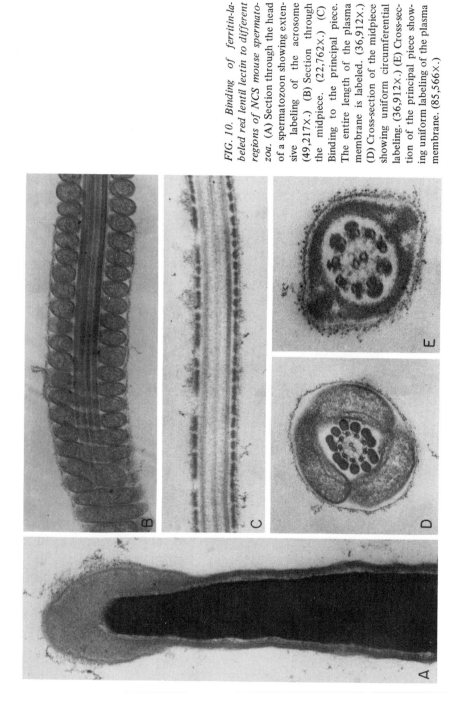

FIG. 10. Binding of ferritin-labeled red lentil lectin to different regions of NCS mouse spermatozoa. (A) Section through the head of a spermatozoon showing extensive labeling of the acrosome (49,217×.) (B) Section through the midpiece. (22,762×.) (C) Binding to the principal piece. The entire length of the plasma membrane is labeled. (36,912×.) (D) Cross-section of the midpiece showing uniform circumferential labeling. (36,912×.) (E) Cross-section of the principal piece showing uniform labeling of the plasma membrane. (85,566×.)

TABLE I. Quantitation of Lectin Binding to
Mouse Spermatozoa

Cell type	Lectin	Sites per cell[a]
Sperm	Concanavalin A	4.9×10^7
Sperm tails[b]	Concanavalin A	2.5×10^6
Sperm heads[b]	Concanavalin A	7.9×10^6
Sperm	Green pea	1.0×10^7
Sperm	Lentil	7.4×10^6
Sperm	Wheat germ	7.0×10^6
Sperm	Red lentil	5.5×10^6
Sperm	Yellow pea	5.5×10^6

[a]Increasing aliquots of ^{125}I-labeled lectin were incubated with cells (10^6 cells/ml) to insure the
saturation of receptor sites. Similar incubation was
done in the presence of free saccharide inhibitor as
a control for nonspecific binding. Values represent
the average of duplicate determinations.

[b]Prepared after trypsin treatment.

The labeling of mammalian spermatozoa by low molecular weight molecular probes has also been investigated. The fluorescent probe 8-anilino-1-naphthalenesulfonic acid (ANS) binds to the entire surface of the spermatozoal membrane (Fig. 8B). In addition, binding of ANS by motile spermatozoa resulted in the instantaneous cessation of motion. Nonmotile cells were also labeled by incubation of cells in 1 mM ANS in phosphate-buffered saline. Similar results were obtained with mouse, rabbit, rat, guinea pig, and human spermatozoa.

In attempts to develop specific molecular probes for intracellular components of spermatozoa, we have observed that ethidium bromide (Bauer and Vinograd, 1968) binds strongly to the DNA of the spermatozoal head. Incubation of spermatozoa in 1 mM ethidium bromide in phosphate-buffered saline resulted in the intense fluorescence of the sperm head (Fig. 8C) without affecting spermatozoal motility. The midpiece and tail regions of the cells were not significantly labeled by this procedure. In contrast to acridine orange (Bishop and Smiles, 1963), ethidium bromide does not label the acrosome of mouse or human spermatozoa and so may be useful as a label for the male gamete in *in vitro* fertilization studies.

In summary, fractionation of subcellular components of spermatozoa, obtained by specific chemical techniques, provides the opportunity to analyze molecular constituents in localized regions of gametic cells. Studies with molecular probes of known specificity indicate that the plasma membrane is nonuniform in the expression of carbohydrate groups, and it is possible that these reagents will be useful for the isolation of surface components by affinity techniques for further characterization. Finally, the application of similar procedures to the complex events of spermatogenesis should aid our understanding of this process. Chemical dissection of spermatozoa at different stages of development may reveal a temporal sequence of the appearance of certain intracellular structures and plasma membrane components. The isolation of protein components from mature sperm and the production of antibodies directed against these components may allow the specific interruption of spermatogenesis and fertilization in order to clarify the mechanisms of the molecular events involved in these physiological processes.

ACKNOWLEDGMENTS

This work was supported in part by USPHS Grant HD07014 from the National Institutes of Health, by Grant RF70095 from the Rockefeller Foundation, and by grants from the National Science Foundation.

REFERENCES

Allison, A. C., and Hartree, E. F. (1970), Lysosomal enzymes in the acrosome and their possible role in fertilization, *J. Reprod. Fertil. 21:*501–515.
Bauer, W., and Vinograd, J. (1968), The interaction of closed circular DNA with intercalative dyes. I. The superhelix density of SV40 DNA in the presence and absence of dye, *J. Mol. Biol. 33:*141–171.
Bedford, J. M. (1968), Ultrastructural changes of the sperm head during fertilization in the rabbit, *Am. J. Anat. 123:*329–357.
Bedford, J. M., Cooper, G. W., and Calvin, H. I. (1971), Post-meiotic changes in the nucleus and membranes of mammalian spermatozoa, in: *Proceedings of the International Symposium on the Genetics of the Spermatozoon,* pp. 69–89 (R. A. Beatty and S. Gluecksohn-Waelsch, eds.) University of Edinburgh Press, Edinburgh.
Bishop, M. W. H., and Smiles, J. (1963), Differentiation of the acrosome in living mammalian spermatozoa and spermatids by fluorescence microscopy, *J. Reprod. Fertil. 6:*297–303.
Edelman, G. M., and Millette, C. F. (1971), Molecular probes of spermatozoon structures, *Proc. Natl. Acad. Sci. (U.S.A.) 68:*2436–2440.
Garbers, D. L., First, N. L., and Lardy, H. A. (1973), Properties of adenosine 3′,5′-monophosphate–dependent protein kinases isolated from bovine epididymal spermatozoa, *J. Biol. Chem. 248:*875–879.
Hartree, E. F., and Srivastava, P. N. (1965), Chemical composition of the acrosomes of ram spermatozoa, *J. Reprod. Fertil. 9:*47–60.
Hernandez-Montes, H., Iglesias, G., and Mujica, A. (1973), Selective solubilization of mammalian spermatozoa structures, *Exp. Cell Res. 76:*437–440.
Iverson, S. (1965), Volume of untreated and ultrasonically-treated bull, boar, and human spermatozoa electronically determined, *J. Reprod. Fertil. 9:*197–202.
Jones, R., and Mann, T. (1973), Lipid peroxidation in spermatozoa, *Proc. Roy. Soc. Lond. Ser. B 184:*103–107.
Laemmli, U. K. (1970), Cleavage of structural proteins during the assembly of the head of bacteriophage T4, *Nature (Lond.) 227:*680–685.
Lis, H., and Sharon, N. (1973), The biochemistry of plant lectins (phytohemagglutinins), *Ann. Rev. Biochem. 42:*575–600.

Millette, C. F., Spear, P. G., Gall, W. E., and Edelman, G. M. (1973), Chemical dissection of mammalian spermatozoa, *J. Cell Biol. 58:*662–675.

Nicolson, G. L., and Yanagimachi, R. (1972), Terminal saccharides on sperm plasma membranes: Identification by specific agglutinins, *Science 177:*276–279.

Stambaugh, R., and Buckley, J. (1969), Identification and subcellular localization of the enzymes effecting penetration of the zona pellucida by rabbit spermatozoa, *J. Reprod. Fertil. 19:*423–432.

Stefanini, M., Oura, C., and Zamboni, L. (1969), Ultrastructure of fertilization in the mouse. 2. Penetration of sperm into the ovum, *J. Submicrosc. Cytol. 1:*1–32.

Yanagimachi, R., Noda, Y. D., Fujimoto, M., and Nicolson, G. L. (1973), The distribution of negative surface charges on mammalian spermatozoa, *Am. J. Anat. 135:*497–520.

17

Inhibition of Spermatogenesis

J. Frick and G. Bartsch

Department of Urology
University of Innsbruck
Innsbruck, Austria

For the past several years, we have investigated the question of how to achieve reversible inhibition of spermatogenesis in man without affecting libido and potency. The studies to be reported here indicate that this long-sought method of contraception may be perfected in the next few years. Preliminary trials carried out at the University of Innsbruck (Frick, 1973) and at the University of Bahia (Coutinho and Melo, 1973) revealed that spermatogenesis in men bearing subdermal testosterone implants could be suppressed by progestational steroids administered orally without loss of libido. The studies in Innsbruck were expanded, and in this chapter we will include data on young men suffering from congestive prostatitis, hematospermia, subfertility, and varicocele and also on older men with benign prostatic hypertrophy. In the older age group, alterations in testicular morphology were taken as parameters of the effect of the progestin treatment.

MATERIALS AND METHODS

All patients enrolled in the present study were either young men with various urological disorders such as congestive prostatitis, subfertility, varicocele, and hematospermia, or older men with benign prostatic hypertrophy.

For all patients who received testosterone substitution therapy, the hormone (Serva Company, Heidelberg) was administered through subdermal silastic capsules (Dow Corning Corporation, Midland, Michigan, No. 602-261). The length of each capsule was 20 mm, inside diameter was 1.58 mm, and outside diameter was 2.41 mm. The surface area of each capsule was about 150 mm^2, and the contents weighed between 22 and 23 mg. The release of testosterone per capsule per 24 h was about 55 mg.

The data regarding release of material (all *in vivo* in the human male) were calculated by gravimetric investigation of the contents of capsules that had been implanted for different periods of time. Identification of the contents of these retrieved capsules by thin-layer chromatography indicated that the steroid remains unchanged in chemical structure during implantation.

The capsules were gas-sterilized in ethylene oxide after packing in small plastic bags.

The encapsulated compounds were inserted under the right or left mammilla using a trochar, after local anesthesia (Fig. 1). Capsules containing norethindrone or norethandrolone (both obtained from Prodotti Gianni, Milan) were filled by ourselves. Silastic capsules filled with megestrol acetate were manufactured by the British Drug House, London, and were provided by the Population Council, New York. Medroxyprogesterone acetate depot was manufactured by Farmitalia, Milan. R2323 (13-ethyl-17α-ethynyl-17 hydroxy-gona-4,9,11-triene-3-one) tablets were manufactured by Laboratories Roussel France, and provided by the Population Council, New York, Norethisterone tablets, 25 mg, were manufactured by Astra, Sweden.

Plasma testosterone levels were measured by radioimmunoassay (Bartke *et al.*, 1973). The antiserum was a gift of the Population Council, New York. For LH determination, a modified solid-phase radioimmunoassay developed by Crosignani *et al.* (1970) was used. The immunological material was a gift from

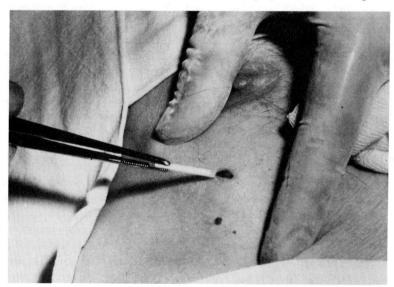

FIG. 1. *Subcutaneous insertion of the silastic capsule.*

the National Institutes of Health, Bethesda, Maryland. For both assays, the blood was taken from each individual at a standard time in the morning between 10:00 and 12:00 a.m. The values for testosterone represent duplicate determinations and those for LH triplicate determinations (Frick, 1973; Johansson and Nygren, 1973).

CLINICAL EXPERIENCE

Our clinical efforts concentrated on five different groups of patients, as follows.

Group I

The first group consisted of five patients aged 27–38. Table I shows the medication schedule, sperm count, sperm motility, and plasma testosterone and LH levels for each patient before and during treatment.

Subjects No. 2 and 3 reached azoospermia within the first 6 weeks of treatment; subjects No. 1, 4, and 5 showed lowered sperm counts, but in these cases it is possible that there were irregularities in the ingestion of individual norethisterone tablets. Twelve weeks after the treatment started or 9 weeks after discontinuing oral administration of norethisterone, while retaining the implants, all patients again had an increasing number of sperm. The plasma testosterone and LH levels did not change significantly during this treatment. The individuals noted no alterations in their sexual behavior.

Group II

In the second group, there were four young men aged 25–32 and three men 66, 68, and 73 yr old. The subjects were treated with 25 mg norethisterone daily for 3 wk. In addition, each man received six subcutaneous implants of megestrol acetate and four subcutaneous implants of testosterone at the outset of the treatment period.

Three of the four young men had a drop in sperm count 6 wk after treatment started (Table II). Subject No. 4 showed an inexplicable increase from 71 million to 126 million. The sperm motility, plasma testosterone, and LH levels showed no significant alterations. In the three older men, the therapeutic effect was assessed by pre- and post-treatment testicular biopsies. As seen in Table II, the histological findings were similar in all three cases. None of the seven men noticed any change in libido, erections, or sexual activity. In the young age group, there were doubts about the correct daily taking of the tablets. The drop in the sperm count would have been much more significant than was found in this group if the progestine had been taken correctly for 3 wk.

TABLE I. Effects of 25 mg Norethisterone Daily (Orally) in Conjunction with Six Norethindrone Implants and Three Testosterone Implants on Sperm Count, Sperm Motility, Plasma Testosterone Level, and Plasma LH Level (group I)

Patient no.	Age (yr)	Sperm count (million/ml)			Sperm motility (%)			Plasma testosterone (μg/100 ml)			Plasma LH (mU/ml)		
		Pretreatment	6 wk	12 wk	Pretreatment	6 wk	12 wk	Pretreatment	6 wk	12 wk	Pretreatment	6 wk	12 wk
1	31	16	10	21	53	55	64	0.35	0.30	0.31	5.1	4.2	3.8
2	36	38	0	3	28	0	56	0.35	0.31	0.30	5.1	3.8	9.6
3	27	23	0	2	15	13	48	0.17	0.14	0.23	4.5	3.2	4.5
4	28	29	7	11	31	23	22	0.33	0.25	0.48	6.2	5.1	5.3
5	38	51	31	23	33	23	55	0.31	0.31	0.32	4.5	4.0	4.0

TABLE II. Effects of 25 mg Norethisterone Daily (Orally) in Conjunction with Six Megestrol Acetate and Four Testosterone Implants on Sperm Count, Sperm Motility, Plasma Testosterone Level, and Plasma LH Level (group II)

Patient no.	Age (yr)	Sperm count (million/ml)			Sperm motility (%)			Plasma testosterone (μg/100 ml)			Plasma LH (mU/ml)		
		Pretreatment	6 wk	12 wk	Pretreatment	6 wk	12 wk	Pretreatment	6 wk	12 wk	Pretreatment	6 wk	12 wk
1	26	143	86	42	40	48	39	0.49	0.46	0.49	5.0	6.6	4.0
2	25	28	14	47	65	47	56	0.46	0.60	0.77	9.7	9.8	13.0
3	32	150	68	41	45	48	53	0.34	0.33	0.33	6.6	5.0	5.0
4	31	71	126	221	32	33	23	0.33	0.49	0.44	4.0	6.7	5.5
5[a]	66							0.25	0.32	–	13.8	9.8	–
6[a]	69							0.34	0.42	–	18.2	13.6	–
7[a]	73							0.40	0.55	–	9.8	8.6	–

[a]Testicular biopsy pretreatment: There were normal, wide, not sclerosed tubules with all steps of spermatogenesis. The interstitial tissue seemed to be normal, and interstitial cells were quite frequent. Testicular biopsy after treatment: The diameter of the tubules was reduced, and the tubular epithelium was generally devoid of germinal elements. Also, there was disorganization and depopulation of the seminal epithelium. Leydig cells seemed to be reduced and atrophic.

Group III

The third group consisted of six young men aged 26–39 who had fertility problems. The subjects were treated with 100 mg medroxyprogesterone acetate depot and four silastic capsules of testosterone, subcutaneously implanted.

Between the sixth and the twelfth week after treatment started, four of the six patients exhibited azoospermia. Patients Nos. 2 and 4 showed a drop in sperm count (Table III). For all subjects except No. 2, we have no explanation of this; the sperm motility showed alterations which were proportional to those of the sperm counts. The plasma testosterone levels were slightly reduced in all cases 6 wk after treatment started, except in subject No. 5. Only patient No. 4 had a significant reduction ($>$ 50%) in plasma LH level after 12 wk of treatment. All patients complained of decrease in libido and sexual activity during the first 3 wk of treatment and then noticed a gradual normalization of these parameters.

Group IV

In the fourth group, five men aged 63–74 and suffering from benign prostatic hypertrophy were treated with 100 mg medroxyprogesterone acetate depot intramuscularly along with six implants of megestrol acetate and four implants of testosterone inserted subcutaneously under the left and right mammillae. The parameter chosen to demonstrate the effect of this progestin–testosterone combination therapy on spermatogenesis was the morphological change seen in testicular biopsies before and 6–8 wk after treatment started.

The pretreatment biopsies in all cases revealed normal tubules with normal spermatogenesis. The distribution of Leydig cells was normal (Fig. 2). Between 6 and 8 wk after treatment started, the second biopsies were taken. They showed a lack of germinal elements in the tubules. The diameter of the tubules was not decreased, and the Leydig cells appeared partially atrophic and diminished (Fig. 3). The plasma LH levels did not alter significantly in the first weeks of the treatment period (Table IV), while the plasma testosterone levels decreased moderately except in subject No. 3. In spite of the age of the patients, they affirmed normal sexual activity and noted no changes of libido or potency during treatment.

Group V

The five patients of the fifth group, aged 32–62, were treated with R2323 orally, 50 mg twice a week for 6 wk and then 25 mg twice a week. The patients took the tablets on Tuesdays and Fridays. In addition, four silastic capsules of testosterone were implanted subcutaneously under the right mammilla on day 0. Three of the younger men came to our clinic because of hematospermia; patient No. 4 was a subfertile man and patient No. 5 had benign hypertrophy of the prostate.

TABLE III. Effects of 100 mg Medroxyprogesterone Acetate Depot (i.m.) in Conjunction with Four Testosterone Implants on Sperm Count, Sperm Motility, Plasma Testosterone Level, and Plasma LH Level (group III)

Patient no.	Age (yr)	Sperm count (million/ml)			Sperm motility (%)			Plasma testosterone (μg/100 ml)			Plasma LH (mU/ml)		
		Pretreatment	6 wk	12 wk	Pretreatment	6 wk	12 wk	Pretreatment	6 wk	12 wk	Pretreatment	6 wk	12 wk
1	27	17	0.95 (million/ml)	0	37	8	0	0.34	0.29	0.28	7.2	7.2	7.2
2	32	39	17	15	17	28	45	0.44	0.39	0.25	6.9	8.2	8.5
3	39	33	9	0	46	3	0	0.40	0.22	0.27	9.8	9.2	7.6
4	37	23	10	6	53	42	30	0.43	0.14	0.24	9.8	6.8	4.2
5	39	11	0	4	40	0	14	0.43	0.59	0.50	12.3	18.0	14.0
6	26	20	0	17	28	0	38	0.34	0.28	0.33	8.0	10.7	10.0

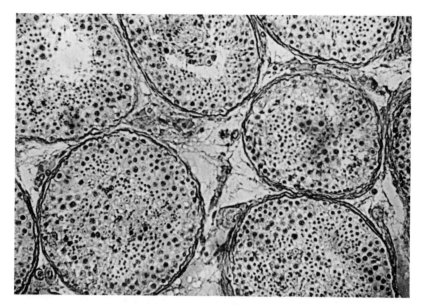

FIG. 2. Pretreatment testicular biopsy material from a 63-yr-old man (group IV). Stained with hematoxylin and eosin. (90×.)

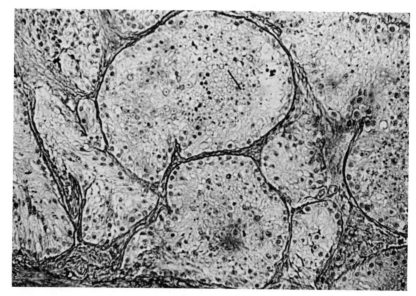

FIG. 3. Second testicular biopsy material from the same 63-yr-old man as in Fig. 2 obtained 7 wk after treatment started. Stained with hematoxylin and eosin. (90×.)

TABLE IV. Effects of 100 mg Medroxyprogesterone Acetate Depot (i.m.) in Conjunction with Six Megestrol Acetate Implants and Four Testosterone Implants on Plasma Testosterone Level and Plasma LH Level (group IV)[a]

Patient no.	Age (yr)	Plasma testosterone (μg/100 ml)			Plasma LH (mU/ml)		
		Pretreatment	6 wk	12 wk	Pretreatment	6 wk	12 wk
1	68	0.44	0.24	–	9.8	7.9	–
2	63	0.39	0.37	–	10.2	6.9	–
3	70	0.11	0.32	–	10.7	10.2	–
4	74	0.55	0.34	–	8.6	7.5	–
5	68	0.54	0.20	0.35	4.4	9.7	8.2

[a]Testicular biopsy pretreatment: Normal wide tubules with all steps of spermatogenesis. Interstitial tissue seemed to be normal; Leydig cells were frequent. Testicular biopsy after treatment: The tubules were generally devoid of germinal elements, also there was disorganization and depopulation of the seminal epithelium. Some of the germinal cells were necrotic. Leydig cells were atrophic.

The sperm analysis of subjects No. 1, 2, and 4 showed azoospermia between 6 and 12 wk after treatment started. Patient No. 3 had a decrease in sperm count during the same period of time, but he did not reach azoospermia. However, he confessed that he took only about 50% of the tablets. The pretreatment testicular biopsy of the 62-yr-old man showed normal spermatogenesis and normal Leydig cells (Fig. 4). The second biopsy, taken during the seventh week of treatment, revealed a total arrest of spermatogenesis; the Leydig cells were diminished and partly atrophic (Fig. 5). The most interesting point in this series was the drastic decrease in plasma testosterone levels in all cases, about 80% in the first 6 wk of treatment. The levels remained low when the R2323 dose was decreased by one-half 6 wk after treatment had started. The plasma LH levels dropped in the same manner and showed a reduction of about 50% or more 12 wk after treatment had started (Table V). The R2323 medication did not affect blood counts or serum electrolytes during the 3 months that they were studied. Patients No. 1 and 5 showed an increase of SGOT and SGPT between the sixth and the twelfth week of treatment and also had increased amounts of urobilinogen in the urine. The data on fat metabolism are conflicting and do not permit any clear conclusions. Three patients in this group exhibited weight gains of as much as 4 kg within the first 8 wk of treatment. Two complained about intensive perspiration at night, and one also about heartburn. In spite of very low plasma testosterone levels, the patients had more or less normal frequencies of sexual activity during the first 6 wk of treatment, but later libido and erections decreased appreciably.

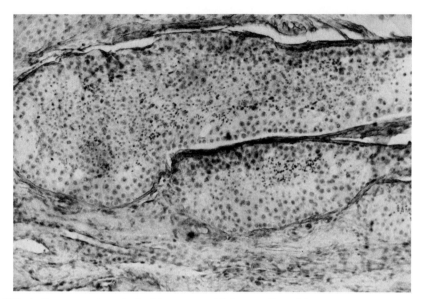

FIG. 4. *Pretreatment testicular biopsy material from a 62-yr-old man (group V).* Stained with hematoxylin and eosin. (90×.)

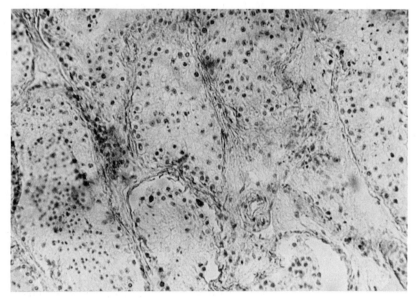

FIG. 5. *Seven weeks post-treatment biopsy material from the same 62-yr-old man as in Fig. 4.* Stained with hematoxylin and eosin. (90×.)

TABLE V. Effects of 100 mg R2323 Weekly (Orally) for 6 wk and Followed by 50 mg R2323 Weekly on Sperm Count, Sperm Motility, Plasma Testosterone Level, and Plasma LH Level (group V)[a]

Patient no.	Age (yr)	Sperm count (million/ml)			Sperm motility (%)			Plasma testosterone (μg/100 ml)			Plasma LH (mU/ml)		
		Pretreatment	6 wk	12 wk	Pretreatment	6 wk	12 wk	Pretreatment	6 wk	12 wk	Pretreatment	6 wk	12 wk
1	40	63	1	0	39	0	0	0.35	0.0065	0.04	8.5	8.5	4.0
2	58	10	0	0	20	0	0	0.39	0.06	0.008	43.5	9.7	5.5
3	39	80	55	35	50	41	49	0.33	0.05	0.07	11.0	5.5	2.4
4	32	3	0	—	10	0	—	0.23	0.06	—	8.8	4.4	—
5	62							0.44	0.03	—	23	5.0	—

[a]Testicular biopsy pretreatment: Normal wide tubules with all steps of spermatogenesis. Interstitial tissue seemed to be normal. Testicular biopsy after treatment: Tubules were generally devoid of germinal elements; except in Sertoli cells and spermatogonia, there was a total arrest of spermatogenesis. The interstitial tissue seemed fibrotic. Leydig cells were atrophic.

DISCUSSION

From this study and other studies already published, it is evident that we are on the way to devising a medical treatment for reversible inhibition of spermatogenesis without undue side-effects (Coutinho and Melo, 1973; Johansson and Nygren, 1973; Rivarola et al., 1968; Skoglund and Paulsen, 1973; Heller et al., 1958; McLeod and Tietze, 1964).

It still would seem that we do not yet know either the the optimal progestine–testosterone combination or the optimal dosage regimen. As we have seen from this study and from the work carried out by Coutinho and Melo (1973) and Johansson and Nygren (1973), relatively high doses of progestins are needed to obtain a complete arrest of spermatogenesis. Obviously, what other changes may occur in men during long-term treatment with high doses of progestin must be carefully investigated. In the very few men in our study who were treated with R2323, we saw alterations in the blood levels of liver enzymes and an increased secretion of urobilinogen in the urine even within the first weeks of treatment. A further fact that should be mentioned is that plasma testosterone levels and sexual activity are not always correlated.

The subcutaneous implantation of silastic capsules containing testosterone seems a practical way for exogenous androgen administration over long periods of time. This mode of application guarantees a relatively constant uptake of the hormone. But as our data show it might be necessary in some subjects to implant additional capsules to maintain normal sexual behavior.

ACKNOWLEDGMENTS

This work was undertaken as part of the contraceptive development research program sponsored and coordinated by the International Committee for Contraception Research of the Population Council. The ICCR program is funded by the Ford and Rockefeller Foundations.

REFERENCES

Bartke, A., Steele, R. E., Musto, N., and Caldwell, B. V. (1973), Fluctuations in plasma testosterone levels in adult male rats and mice, *Endocrinology 92:*1223.

Coutinho, E. M., and Melo, J. F. (1973), Successful inhibition of spermatogenesis in man without loss of libido: A potential new approach to male contraception, *Contraception 8:*207–217.

Crosignani, P. G., Mishell, D. R., Nakamura, R., et al. (1970), A method of solid phase radioimmunoassay utilizing polypropylene discs, *J. Clin. Endocrinol. Metabl. 30:*153–160.

Frick, J. (1973), Control of spermatogenesis in men by combined administration of progestin and androgen, *Contraception 8:*191–206.

Frick, J., Marberger, M., Jr., and Marberger, H. (1974), Hormonal therapy with steroid filled silastic rubber implants, *Urol. Int., 29:*81–92.

Heller, C. G., Laidlaw, W. M., Harvey, H. T., and Nelson, W. O. (1958), Effects of progestational compounds on the reproductive processes of the human male, *Ann. N.Y. Acad. Sci. 71:*649–665.

Johansson, E. D. B., and Nygren, K. G. (1973), Depression of plasma testosterone levels in men with norethindrone, *Contraception 8:*219–226.

McLeod, J., and Tietze, C. (1964), Control of reproductive capacity, *Ann. Rev. Med. 15:*299–314.

Rivarola, M. A., Camacho, A. M., and Migeon, C. J. (1968), Effect of treatment with medroxyprogesterone acetate (Provera) on testicular function, *J. Clin. Endocrinol. 28:*679–684.

Skoglund, R. D., and Paulsen, C. A. (1973), Danazol–testosterone combination: A potentially effective means for reversible male contraception. A preliminary report, *Contraception 7:*357.

Ovum Development and Ovulation

18

Central Nervous System and Ovulation

W. Ladosky

Department of Biodynamics
Federal University of Pernambuco
Recife, Brazil

and

J. G. L. Noronha

Department of Physiology
Catholic University of Paraná
Curitiba, Brazil

Gorski (1966, 1967) and Barraclogh and Haller (1970) identified the preoptic area (POA) of the hypothalamus as the area responsible for the ovulatory surge of luteinizing hormone (LH) which is characteristic of the female pattern of gonadotropin release. The median eminence of the hypothalamus would be the final pathway for pituitary stimulation. Previous studies by Harris and Jacobsohn (1952) and Nikitovitch-Winer and Everett (1959), in which the anterior pituitary gland (AP) was transplanted into different parts of the brain, demonstrated that the graft was able to maintain structure and function of the gonads only when connected to the median basal hypothalamus (MBH) at a point corresponding to the arcuate nucleus (AN).

Using a small knife placed stereotaxically, Halász and Pupp (1965) and Halasz and Gorski (1967) cut the neural connection between the POA and MBH. They were able to demonstrate that the MBH–AP island is able to maintain a follicular ovary but cannot form or maintain the corpora lutea. Authors agree that the basic consequence of frontal deaferentiation is a lowering of LH release

This work was supported with Grants from The Population Council of New York (Grant M70.142C) and from the Conselho Nacional de Pesquisas.

(Tima and Flerkó, 1967). Two levels of hypothalamic control of the pituitary gland are consequently proposed:

1. A "basal" level corresponding to the deafferented MBH, represented by the AN–AP complex. Here LH would be produced only in a basal tonic pattern, resulting in an anovulatory sterility syndrome.
2. A "control" level in which the POA would induce a cyclic pattern of activity in the MBH–AP complex.

During the period of sexual differentiation in the rat (days 1–4), the presence of testosterone from the testis of the male or testosterone injected into females would induce changes in the threshold of the POA area. This could reduce POA sensitivity to positive feedback of estrogen and render it inactive (Barraclough and Gorski, 1961). The AN would then be left as the only structure to control liberation by the pituitary. As a consequence, the pituitary would no longer be the ovulatory source of LH, as compared to animals whose APO–AN connection was cut by frontal deafferentation (Halász and Gorski, 1967). Although the blocked POA activity in the male gives a lower and constant level of LH in blood (Zeilmaker, 1962), castration induces a significant increase of LH in blood in both sexes which may become higher in the male (Paesi et al., 1955; Gans, 1959; van Rees, 1964). On the other hand, the ovary grafted into the spleen of male rats (Biskind, 1941; Ladosky, 1965) or female rats made sterile by neonatal treatment with estrogen or testosterone (Ladosky, 1965) shows large and active corpora lutea without any sign of cyclic change. These corpora lutea disappear if a direct connection is made between the grafted spleen and the systemic circulation. This connection bypasses the liver and therefore reinstates the negative feedback to the pituitary.

With respect to male or sterilized rats, we may think of the MBH–AP complex as freed of the POA influence as well as the negative feedback from the gonadal hormones. In this situation, the island is able to liberate an amount of LH great enough to induce and maintain ovulation.

THE THREE-LEVEL HYPOTHESIS

The "two-level" control theory did not adequately explain the increase of LH after castration, nor did this theory account for the liberation of the brain from negative feedback even in those rats whose POA had been inactivated by deafferentation or neonatal testosterone. It was therefore decided to repeat the experiments of Halász and Gorski (1967). The frontal cut, made according to the technique described by Halász and Pupp (1965), was located immediately behind the nucleus suprachiasmaticus (ScN) in order to prevent any possible influence by this structure. It was made not only in intact female rats, as in the previous experiments, but also in castrated males and females containing an

TABLE I. Incidence of Corpora Lutea (CL) in the Ovarian Spleen Graft Before and After a Frontal Medial Basal Hypothalamic Deafferentation (FMBHD)

	Before FMBHD		After FMBHD	
Group[a]	CL/rat	LH (ng/ml ± SE)	CL/rat	LH (ng/ml ± SE)
Control males	12/12	721.28 ± 82.18	12/12	752.44 ± 80.41
Control females	10/10	1118.25 ± 250.01	9/9	1265.56 ± 300.75
Androgenized females	10/10	780.62 ± 81.67	10/10	815.72 ± 88.72

[a] All animals were castrated 15 days before grafting.

ovary in the spleen. Blood was taken from the jugular vein under ether anesthesia 20–25 days after the graft, and a small piece of the grafted tissue was collected for histological examination. At the same surgical session, a cut was made between the POA and the MBH, just behind the ScN, in order to isolate the AN. Fifteen days after deafferentation, the rats were sacrificed under ether, blood was collected from the jugular vein for LH assay, and grafts were recovered for histological study.

As seen in Table I, deafferentation does not modify the histological aspect of an ovary grafted in the spleen of male or female rats. The blood level of LH is also not significantly altered. Based on results obtained from the ovarian ascorbic acid depletion (OAAD) test for assay of LH in blood and pituitary gland, Halász and Gorski (1967) stated that the extended frontal cut did not interfere with the pituitary LH response to castration. However, they have criticized their work on the basis of the small number of pituitaries and the large variation in LH values. Therefore, it cannot be concluded that the pituitary response to castration is precisely normal in the deafferentiated animals. They also decided not to take castrated animals into consideration when constructing their two-level control theory.

By use of a much more precise method for LH dosage (RIA), it was observed that when the MBH is freed from the negative feedback of gonadal hormones it is able to stimulate LH production by the pituitary gland to levels tenfold greater than before. This response is not altered by frontal deafferentation (Table II).

The fully luteinized ovary grafted into the spleen of a castrated deafferented rat confirms that the AN–AP complex is producing LH in amounts great enough to induce and maintain luteinization. Contrary to what was previously stated, these results suggest that when the MBH is liberated from the negative influence

TABLE II. LH in Blood of Rats with FMBHD Before and
After Castration

Group	Number of animals	Before castration (ng/ml ± SE)	After castration[a] (ng/ml ± SE)
Males	7	45.32 ± 13.64	728.13 ± 75.92
Females	9	34.16 ± 11.34	1168.15 ± 285.63
Androgenized females	8	66.26 ± 10.70	853.76 ± 108.96

[a]Blood collected 20 days after castration.

of the gonadal steroids it is able to maintain a high level of LH release by the pituitary. This high level is sufficient for ovulation. Since the ovaries grafted into the spleen show a set of fully developed corpora lutea but lack developing follicles as well as degenerating CL, it may be concluded that, under these conditions, LH is liberated in an acyclic manner in spite of its presence at an ovulatory level. Primary experiments with giving a daily dosage of LH to female castrated rats, deafferented or not, having an ovary in the spleen (Fig. 1) confirm this idea.

Lisk (1960) and Ramirez et al. (1964) have demonstrated that implantation of estrogen in the arcuate nucleus blocks the estrus cycle and induces uterine atrophy. Using minute amounts of 17β-estradiol diluted 1/20 in cholesterol, Ladosky and Sakata (1969) observed an anovulatory syndrome, with the ovaries showing ripening follicles only when the mixture was implanted in the arcuate nucleus. This did not occur when the diluted estradiol was implanted in other structures of the MBH. For this reason, it is suggested that the AN is the main structure altered after deafferentation of the MBH.

On the basis of the experiments described above and on those done by Halász and Pupp (1965) and Halász and Gorski (1967), a three-level hypothesis for neural control of the pituitary gland is suggested. The first level would correspond to "liberated" AN activity and is represented by the castrated male and female rat. In this situation, the AN may stimulate the AP to an excessively high level of activity, characterized by a large amount of LH released into blood. Since frontal deafferentation does not significantly introduce any alteration in this case, one may suggest that the POA is not playing any role. However, since LH is being released in an acyclic fashion, the question remains as to why the POA-controlled cyclic activity has disappeared. One possible explanation is that the liberated AN has so high a LH-releasing activity that the POA influence is secondary to it. According to our experience, deafferentation of a normal female

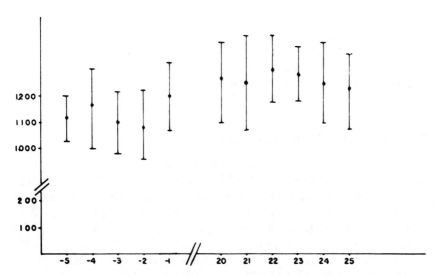

FIG. 1. *LH levels in castrated female rats bearing an ovary in the spleen.* Assays were done 5 days prior to and beginning at 20 days after deafferentation.

results in a drop of LH concentration in blood by one-half (Table III), the new value almost corresponding to that of the male. Since castration increases LH in blood tenfold, this new level is probably too high to respond to a further stimulatory influence from the POA.

The second and third levels would correspond to the "basal" and "cyclic" control, as previously suggested. At the second level, the "basal" of Halász and Gorski (1967), the AN−AP complex is under the influence of sex steroids, but is disconnected from the APO. The complex would liberate a tonic basal level of LH, being unable, however, to induce ovulation. As seen in Table III, after

TABLE III. Influence of Deafferentation on Blood LH of Intact Rats

Group	Number of animals	Before FMBHD (ng/ml ± SE)	Number of animals	After FMBHD[a] (ng/ml ± SE)
Males	12	49.04 ± 18.63	7	45.32 ± 13.64
Females	15	82.12 ± 12.15	9	39.16 ± 16.34
Androgenized females	8	64.16 ± 12.07	7	54.16 ± 13.15

[a]Twenty days after operation.

deafferentation, LH in plasma decreases in the intact female rat to a level corresponding to that in the intact male. In the intact male, the frontal cut does not modify the level of LH secretion. This supports the hypothesis by Barraclough and Gorski (1961) and Gorski and Barraclough (1963) that the ovulatory surge of LH is caused by the POA and that the process of sexual differentiation is related to the activity of the POA.

ROLE OF SEROTONIN AS MEDIATOR

There is increasing evidence that serotonin plays an inhibitory role in the control of ovulation. An increase of 5-hydroxytryptamine (5-HT) in the brain by pharmacological treatment impedes ovulation after gonadotropin treatment in prepubertal rats (Kordon et al., 1969). Intraventricular injection of 5-HT decreases LH secretion (Schneider and McCann, 1970; Porter et al., 1971) and interferes with spontaneous ovulation (Domanski et al., 1972). Systemic injection of monoamine oxidase inhibitors (MAOI) blocks ovulation (Meyerson and Sawyer, 1968; Labhsetwar, 1971). In vitro serotonin inhibits oxygen consumption by the hypothalamus, but not by the cortex (Campos and Ladosky, 1972), an action which is controlled by the presence of sex steroids (Ladosky and Campos, 1972). Fuxe (1965) made extensive use of a fluorescence technique to visualize monoaminergic neurons coming to the MBH. With this method, he demonstrated the presence of serotoninergic neurons coming near or within the ScN, an area which supposedly stimulates ovulation (Critchlow, 1958).

More recently, p-chlorophenylalanine (PCPA) has been widely used as a tool to destroy serotonin at its terminals in the brain (Koe and Weissman, 1966). Authors agree that after PCPA there is an increase of LH secretion, as well as a block of prolactin release. These results, taken together, mean that liberation of LRF and PIF has been blocked (Miller et al., 1970; Labhsetwar, 1972; Porter et al., 1972). When the hypothalamus is depleted of 5-HT by an injection of 400 mg/kg of PCPA, it shows a higher oxygen consumption than that seen in control saline-treated animals (Ladosky and Campos, unpublished results). Labhsetwar (1972), in a large revision, discussed the possibility that 5-HT could be acting not only at a hypothalamic level but also on the ovary.

To elucidate this point, we used 5,6-dihydroxytryptamine (5,6-DHT) instead of PCPA. This drug not only acts much more specifically to destroy serotoninergic terminals but also exerts a longer effect (Baumgarten et al., 1971). Fifty nanograms of 5,6-DHT was infused through a steel cannula placed stereotaxically in the third ventricle. Fifteen days later, the animals were bled for LH radioimmunoassay, and the ovary was recovered for histological study.

Table IV shows that after 5,6-DHT perfusion of the third ventricle a spectacular rise of LH occurs in the plasma—even in castrated rats. Since such a

TABLE IV. Influence of 5,6-DHT LH Release in Intact and Castrated Rats

Group	Number of animals	Sham (ng/ml ± SE)	Number of animals	Perfused (ng/ml ± SE)
Intact males	12	49.04* ± 18.13	8	>3000
Castrated males	9	712.31 ± 97.16	9	>3000
Intact females	15	82.12 ± 12.15	12	2850 ± 425
Castrated females	13	1368.50 ± 317.75	9	>3000

*Nanogram per milliliter.

high increase was not expected, the calibration curve for RIA of LH was done only up to 3000 ng/ml. For this reason, measurement of LH could be done only at this level. When 5,6-DHT was infused in sterile rats, the rise of LH in the blood was followed by ovulation with many fully developed corpora lutea (Table V and Figs. 2–4).

These results strengthen the idea not only that 5-HT is the mediator for inhibitory impulses coming to the MBH to block ovulation, but also that the destruction of serotonin at the arcuate nucleus stimulates the pituitary gland to release a very large amount of LH. This is further evidence that the MBH is able, when free from inhibition, to maintain a high stimulation for LH release.

The fact that LH is increased in male and androgenized female rats after administration of 5,6-DHT suggests that 5-HT is really acting on the AN, the final pathway for ovulation, and not on the other areas responsible for the ovulatory surge. Furthermore, the augmented LH release in deafferented rats means that the ScN and the POA are not involved in this mechanism. This fact also strengthens the idea that the arcuate nucleus is able, *per se,* to liberate a large amount of LH in a steady fashion.

The question of the source of 5-HT arises. The results of Halász and Gorski (1967) which show that posterior deafferentation does not induce significant changes in the ovulatory pattern suggest that fibers coming from the mammillary bodies or the amygdala are not playing any important role as far as LH liberation is concerned. There remains, however, a possibility that the tract coming from the hypocampus, the medial corticohypothalamic tract (Raisman and Field, 1971), could be carrying 5-HT. Further histochemical studies are necessary to clarify this point.

Another possibility, not to be lightly discarded, is that 5-HT from the pineal

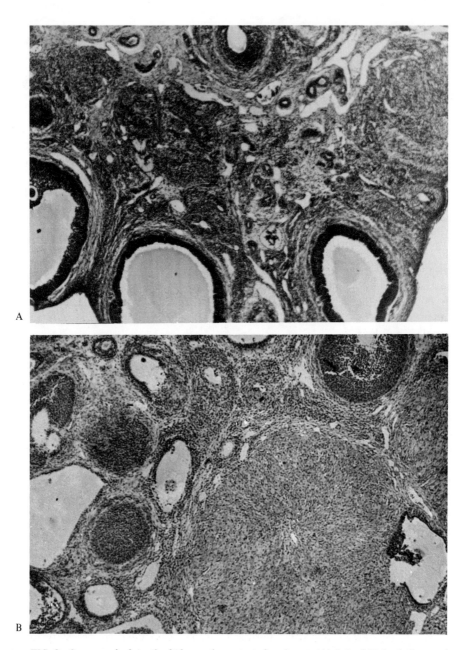

FIG. 2. Ovary grafted in the kidney of a castrated male rat. (A) Only follicles before and (B) fully developed corpora lutea 15 days after 5,6-DHT perfusion in the third ventricle.

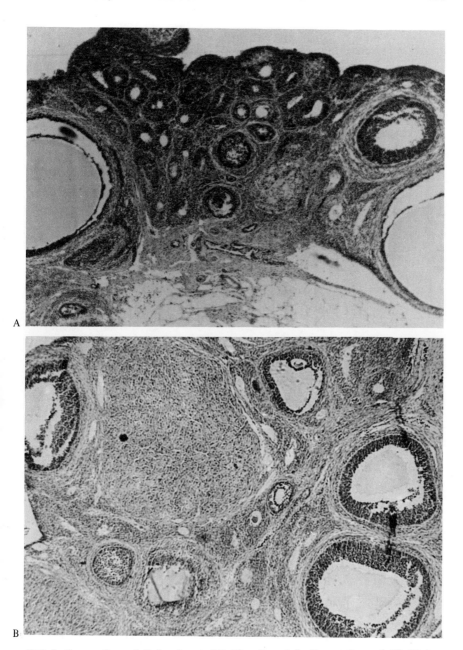

FIG. 3. Ovary of an adult female rat. (A) After frontal deafferentation and (B) 15 days after infusion of 5,6-DHT in the third ventricle.

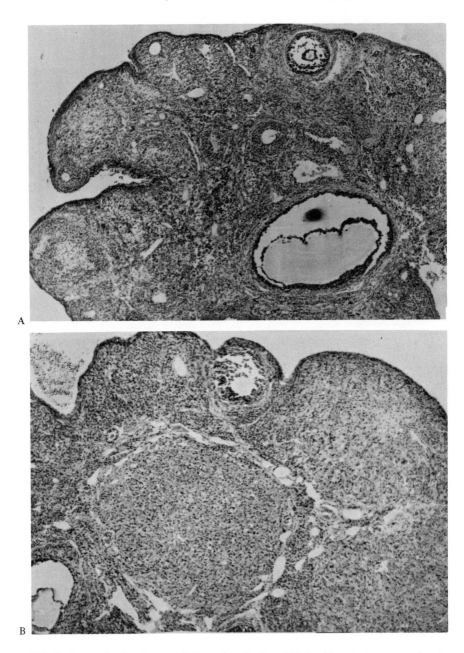

FIG. 4. Ovary of a female rat. (A) Treated at the day of birth with testosterone propionate and (B) 15 days after infusion of 5,6-DHT in the brain.

TABLE V. Ovulation and LH Liberation in Sterile Rats after 5,6-DHT Infusion in the Third Ventricle

Group	Ovulated/treated	LH before (ng/ml ± SE)	LH after (ng/ml ± SE)
Males bearing an ovary	12/12	49.04 ± 19.83	>3000
Androgenized females	8/8	64.16 ± 12.07	>3000
Deafferentated females	15/15	34.16 ± 16.34	>3000

gland is acting on the AN. As has been demonstrated by Mess *et al.* (1972), Tima *et al.* (1973), and Mess *et al.* (1973), the pineal gland exerts an inhibitory role on ovulation due to a blockade of LH secretion. Whether this action is mediated through serotonin or melatonin is a question which needs to be answered. The ovulation inhibitory effect of melatonin was demonstrated by Reiter and Sorrentino (1970, 1971). Fraschini, Mess and Martini (1968) injected PMS-treated infantile rats with pharmacological doses of melatonin and observed interference with ovulation. They concluded that melatonin probably acts through the mesencephalic reticular formation and the hypothalamus. Domanski *et al.* (1972) reported a blockade of ovulation in sheep after infusion of melatonin in the third ventricle, and we have observed that, as with serotonin, melatonin is able to reduce hypothalamic oxygen consumption (Ladosky and Campos, 1972). As Anton-Tay (1971) reported, a close relationship between 5-HT and melatonin exists, the latter causing an increase of the former, and the possibility remains that pineal melatonin is working through serotonin. However, since 5,6-DHT selectively blocks the synthesis of 5-HT, any inhibitory influence of the pineal would be stopped at the level of the AN when serotonin no longer exists.

The results herein described are consistent with the hypothesis that the arcuate medial basal hypothalamus is able to maintain a high level of LH secretion by the pituary gland at a steady state. This "liberated" level may be significantly increased if serotonin synthesis or liberation is impeded at the AN. If a negative feedback by gonadal steroids is on the action and the AN is not submitted to the influence of the POA, LH liberation by the pituitary gland drops to the "basal" level suggested by Halász and Gorski (1967). Even in this situation, if serotonin synthesis or liberation is blocked at the AN, LH rises significantly. These results confirm those previously reported by Campos and Ladosky (1972) who suggested that the negative feedback works through serotonin. When the POA is working on the AN, a cyclic pattern of LH liberation is instituted. This confirms previous results of Barraclough and Gorski (1961) and Halász and Gorski (1967).

SUMMARY

Previous studies in which anterior neural connections of the medial basal hypothalamus (MBH) were cut posteriorly to the optic chiasma suggested two levels for the control of gonadotropic hormone release by the pituitary gland: (1) the MBH–pituitary gland complex, which would release LH in a tonic fashion and result in ripening follicles only, in the ovaries, and (2) the nervous structure responsible for the cyclic release of LH by the pituitary, lying on the anterior hypothalamus (Halász and Gorski, 1967).

In this study, female rats showed constant estrus and a decrease in blood LH after frontal deafferentation. However, if they were castrated, LH rose to levels comparable to those of castrated non-deafferented animals. When these castrated rats had an ovary implanted in the spleen, they showed fully developed corpora lutea but no signs of cyclic activity. Similarly treated male rats showed the same response; if a bridge was made between the abdominal wall and the grafted ovary, ripening follicles were again observed.

Female rats rendered acyclic by either neonatal treatment with testosterone or a frontal cut isolating the MBH were infused in the third ventricle with 5,6-dihydroxytryptamine–a substance which blocks long-lasting serotonin production in nerves. These rats showed corpora lutea and a rise in LH blood level much above that observed in castrated animals. The same results were observed in castrated male rats with an ovary grafted in the anterior chamber of the eye.

It is therefore concluded that (1) the arcuate–pituitary island, freed from negative feedback of estrogen or testosterone, is able to maintain a tonic release of LH at levels inducing ovulation, which may be considered as a basic level of activity; (2) negative feedback acting on the MBH reduces LH release to a tonic level which is incapable of inducing ovulation; (3) some structures anterior to the chiasma are indispensable to cyclic release of LH; and (4) serotonin may be the inhibitory mediator for LH release. Sufficient evidence does not exist to suggest serotonin production in the MBH or in the medial forebrain bundle.

REFERENCES

Anton-Tay, F. (1971), Pineal–brain relationships, in: *The Pineal Gland,* pp. 213–277 (G. E. W. Wolstenholme and J. Knight, eds.), A Ciba Foundation Symposium, Churchill Livingstone, London.

Barraclough, C. A., and Gorski, R. (1961), Evidence that the hypothalamus is responsible for androgen-induced sterility in the female rat. *Endocrinology 68:*68–79.

Barraclough, C. A., and Haller, E. W. (1970), Positive and negative feed-back effect of estrogen on pituitary LH synthesis and release in normal and androgen sterilized female rats, *Endocrinology 86:*542–555.

Baumgarten, H. G., Bjørklund, A., Lachenmayer, L., Nobin, A. and Stenevi, U. (1971), Long-lasting selective depletion of brain serotonin by 5,6-dihydroxytryptamine, *Acta Physiol. Scand. (suppl.) 373:*5–15.

Biskind, G. R. (1941), The inactivation of estradiol and estradiol benzoate in castrated female rats, *Endocrinology* 28:894–896.

Campos, D. G. J., and Ladosky, W. (1972), Some aspects of the influence of serotonin on the metabolism of the hypothalamus as related to sex hormones, *Neuroendocrinology* 9:133–141.

Critchlow, B. V. (1958), Blockade of ovulation in the rat by mesencephalic lesions, *Endocrinology* 63:596–610.

Domanski, E., Przekop, F., and Skubiszewski, B. (1972), The effect of indolamines (melatonin and serotonin) on the function of the hypothalamic centers controlling the process of ovulation in sheep, in: *Symposium on Differentiation and Neuroendocrine Regulation in the Hypothalamo-Hypophysial-Gonadal System* (G. Doerner, ed.), Berlin.

Fraschini, F., Mess, B., and Martini, L. (1968), Pineal gland, melatonin and the control of luteinizing homrone secretion, *Endocrinology* 82:919–924.

Fuxe, K. (1965), Evidence for the existence of monoamine neuron in the central nervous system. IV. Distribution of monoamine nerve terminals in the central nervous system, *Acta Physiol. Scand. (suppl.)* 64:37–85.

Gans, E. (1959), The FSH content of serum of intact and of gonadectomized rat and rats treated with sex hormones, *Acta Endocrinol.* 32:362–372.

Gorski, R. A. (1966), Localization and sexual differentiation of the nervous structures which regulate ovulation, *J. Reprod. Fertil. (suppl.)* 1:67–88.

Gorski, R. A. (1967), Localization of the neural control of luteinization in the feminine male rat (FALE), *Anat. Rec.* 157:63–69.

Gorski, R. A., and Barraclough, C. A. (1963), Effects of low dosage of androgen on the differentiation of hypothalamic regulatory control of ovulation in the rat, *Endocrinology* 73:210–216.

Halász, B., and Gorski, R. A. (1967), Gonadotrophic hormone secretion in female rats after partial or total interruption of neural afferents to the medial basal hypothalamus *Endocrinology* 80:608–622.

Halász, B., and Pupp, L. (1965), Hormone secretion of the anterior pituitary gland after physical interruption of all nervous pathway to the hypophysiotrophic area, *Endocrinology* 77:553–562.

Harris, G. W., and Jacobsohn, D. (1952), Functional grafts of the anterior pituitary gland, *Proc. R. Soc. Lond. Ser. B* 139:263–276.

Koe, B. K., and Weissman, A. (1966), Chlorophenylalanine: A specific depletion of brain serotonin, *J. Pharmacol. Exp. Therap.* 154:499–516.

Kordon, C., Javoy, F. Vassent, G., and Glowinski, J. (1969), Blockade of superovulation in the immature rat by increased brain serotonin, *Eur. J. Pharmacol.* 4:169–174.

Labhsetwar, A. P. (1971), Effects of serotonin on spontaneous ovulation: A theory for the dual hypothalamic control of ovulation, *Acta Endocrinol.* 68:334–344.

Labhsetwar, A. P. (1972), Role of monoamines in ovulation: Evidence for a serotoninergic pathway for inhibition of spontaneous ovulation, *J. Endocrinol.* 54:269–275.

Ladosky, W. (1965), Pituitary gonadotrophic activity in rats castrated shortly after birth and grafted with an ovary in the spleen, *Endokrinologie* 48:279–285.

Ladosky, W., and Campos, D. G. J. (1972), Influence of biogenic amines on hypothalamic metabolism during the period of sexual differentiation, in: *Symposium on Differentiation and Neuroendocrine Regulation in the Hypothalamo-Hypophysial-Gonadal System,* (G. Doerner, ed.), Berlin.

Ladosky, W., and Sakata, K. (1969), Influência do estrogênio implantado em núcleos do hipotálamo sôbre o contrôle da ovulação, in: IXth Congress Latin American Association of Physiological Sciences (W. T. Beraldo, ed.), Belo Horizonte (MG), Brazil.

Lisk, R. D. (1960), Estrogen-sensitive centers in the hypothalamus of the rat, *J. Exp. Zool.* *145:*197–208.

Mess, B., Trentini, G., and Tima, L. (1972), Influence of the pineal body on gonadotrophin secretion, in: *Symposium on Differentiation and Neuroendocrine Regulation in the Hypothalamo-Hypophysial-Gonadal System,* (G. Doerner, ed.), Berlin.

Mess, B., Tima, L., and Trentini, G. P. (1973), The role of pineal principles in ovulation, *Prog. Brain Res. 39:* in press.

Meyerson, B. J., and Sawyer, C. (1968), Monoamines and ovulation in the rat, *Endocrinology 83:*170–176.

Miller, F. P., Cox, R. H., Snodgrass, W. R., and Maickel, R. P. (1970), Comparative effects of *p*-chlorophenylalanine and *p*-chloro-*N*-methylamphetamine on rat brain norepinephrine, serotonin, and 5-hydroxyindole-3-acetic acid, *Biochem. Pharmacol. 19:*435–442.

Nikitovich-Winer, M., and Everett, J. W. (1959), Histo-cytologic changes in grafts of rat pituitary on the kidney and upon retransplantation under the diencephalon, *Endocrinology 65:*357–368.

Paesi, F. J. A., de Jongh, S. E., Hoogstra, M. J., and Engelbregt, A. (1955), The follicle-stimulating hormone-content of the hypophysis of the rat as influenced by gonadectomy and estrogen treatment, *Acta Endocrinol. 19:*49–60.

Porter, J. C., Mical, R. S., and Cramer, O. M. (1971), Effect of serotonin and other indoles on the release of LH, FSH, and prolactin, *Gynecol. Invest. 2:*13–22.

Raisman, G., and Field, P. M. (1971), Anatomical considerations relevant to the interpretation of neuroendocrine experiments, in: *Frontiers in Neuroendocrinology,* (L. Martini and W. Ganong, eds.), Oxford University Press, London.

Ramirez, V. D., Abrams, R. M., and McCann, S. M. (1964), Effect of estradiol implants in the hypothalamo-hypophysial region of the rat on the secretion of luteinizing hormone, *Endocrinology 75:*243–248.

Reiter, R., and Sorrentino, S. (1970), Early photoperiodic conditions and pineal antigonadal function in male hamsters, *Int. J. Fertil. 15:*163–170.

Reiter, R., and Sorrentino, S. (1971), Inhibition of lutenizing hormone release and ovulation in PMS-treated rats by peripherally adminstered melatonin, *Contraception 4:*385–392.

Schneider, H. P. G., and McCann, S. M. (1970), Mono- and indolamines and control of LH secretion, *Endocrinology 86:*1127–1133.

Tima, L., and Flerkó, B. (1967), Ovulation induced by autologous pituitary extracts in persistent oestrus rats, *Endocrinol. Exp. 1:*193–199.

Tima, L., Trentini, G. P., and Mess, B. (1973), Effect of serotonin on ovulation induced by pinealectomy in anovulatory frontal-deafferented rats. *Neuroendocrinology,* in press.

van Rees, G. P. (1964), Interplay between steroid sex hormones and secretion of FSH and ICSH, in: *Major Problems in Neuroendocrinology,* pp. 322–345 (E. Bajusz and G. Jasmin, eds.) Karger, Basel.

Zeilmaker, G. H. (1962), Luteotrophic hormone secretion in the male rat, *Acta Endocrinol. (suppl.) 67:*70.

19

Mechanism of Action
of Luteinizing Hormone-Releasing Hormone

Fernand Labrie, Georges Pelletier, Pierre Borgeat,
Jacques Drouin, Muriel Savary, Jean Côté,
and Louise Ferland

MRC Group in Molecular Endocrinology
Centre Hospitalier de l'Université Laval
Quebec, Canada

After more than 10 yr of research in many laboratories, the neurohormone controlling gonadotropin secretion was isolated from porcine (Schally *et al.*, 1971a,b,c) and ovine (Amos *et al.*, 1971) hypothalami and characterized as a decapeptide having the following structure: (pyro)Glu-His-Trp-Ser-Tyr-Gly-Leu-Arg-Pro-Gly-NH$_2$ (Matsuo *et al.*, 1971a; Baba *et al.*, 1971; Burgus *et al.*, 1971). This peptide stimulates the release of both luteinizing hormone (LH) and follicle-stimulating hormone (FSH) under a wide variety of experimental conditions (Schally *et al.*, 1971a,b,c,d,e; Amos *et al.*, 1971; Borgeat *et al.*, 1972; Baba *et al.*, 1971; Burgus *et al.*, 1971; Guillemin, 1972) and has been called the LH- and FSH-releasing hormone (Schally *et al.*, 1971a) or the gonadotropin-releasing factor (Guillemin, 1972).

Although some useful information about the mechanism of action of luteinizing hormone-releasing hormone (LH-RH) could be obtained from studies performed with different preparations of the purified neurohormone, the availability of synthetic LH-RH (Matsuo *et al.*, 1971b; Monahan *et al.*, 1971; Geiger *et al.*, 1971) and of its analogues opened new possibilities for studies of the mechanism of action of this neurohormone. Before describing these, it seems of interest to briefly present our data on the localization of LH-RH in dense granules of the median eminence.

This work was supported by the Medical Research Council of Canada.

IMMUNOHISTOCHEMICAL LOCALIZATION OF LH-RH IN NERVE ENDINGS OF THE RAT MEDIAN EMINENCE

Much evidence indicates that the median eminence contains high levels of LH-RH (Ishii, 1970; Kobayashi *et al.,* 1970; Clementi *et al.,* 1971; Krulich *et al.,* 1971). This area contains numerous axon endings of the arcuate-tuberoinfundibular tract situated in close proximity to the primary capillary loops of the hypothalamohypophyseal portal blood system. These nerve endings of the external zone of the median eminence are morphologically similar to each other and contain synaptic vesicles and "dense-cored vesicles" or membrane-bound granules of different sizes (60–150 nm) (Halász and Pupp, 1965; Ishii, 1970; Kobayashi *et al.,* 1970; Clementi *et al.,* 1971).

However, no direct evidence of storage of releasing hormones in these

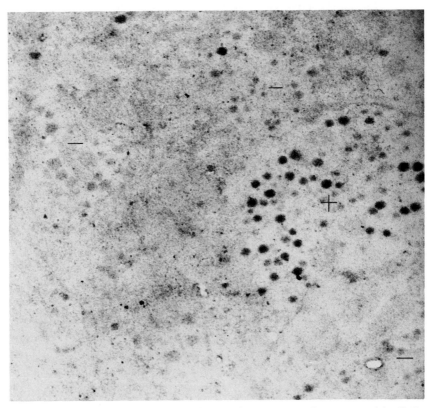

FIG. 1. Portion of the palisade layer of rat median eminence. In one axon (+), all the granules are immunohistochemically stained. Other axons contain unstained granules (–) which may be visualized by their own density and probably also some osmiophilia. No counterstain; glutaraldehyde fixation. (37,200X.) From Pelletier *et al.* (1974).

granules had been obtained. The availability of synthetic LH-RH (Matsuo *et al.*, 1971b) made possible the production of antibodies against the neurohormone (Arimura *et al.*, 1973). In order to gain a better understanding of the mechanisms of packaging and release of LH-RH, it was felt important, as a first step, to identify the structures containing LH-RH in the median eminence using an immunohistochemical technique performed essentially as described by Sternberger (1972).

As shown in Fig. 1, nerve terminals containing immunohistochemically reactive granules were consistently found in the external palisade layer of the median eminence. No positive reaction was found in the internal zone of the median eminence, which contains mainly the tracts from the supraoptic and paraventricular nuclei. The specificity of the staining is demonstrated by the lack of staining in 80–90% of the nerve terminals of the external zone of the median eminence and the absence of staining in control sections when normal rabbit serum or rabbit LH-RH antiserum absorbed with LH-RH was used instead of the anti-LH-RH serum.

These positive nerve terminals were observed randomly distributed in the palisade layer, i.e., the outermost area of the external zone, and account for 10–20% of all granule-containing nerve endings in the medial part of the median eminence. The diameter of positive granules ranges from 75 to 95 nm. This first demonstration of the presence of LH-RH in small secretory granules of the median eminence confirms the hypothesis that hypothalamic releasing hormones are stored in the small secretory granules contained in the nerve fibers located at the proximity of the primary capillaries of the pituitary portal plexus (Scott and Knigge, 1970).

STIMULATORY EFFECT OF SYNTHETIC LH-RH ON BOTH SYNTHESIS AND RELEASE OF LH AND FSH

Chronic treatment (6 days) of adenohypophyseal cells in monolayer culture with increasing concentrations of synthetic LH-RH leads to a progressive increase of LH release into the culture medium and to a marked depletion of the intracellular LH content measured at the end of the experiment (Fig. 2A,B). Total radioimmunoassayable LH (tissue plus culture medium) is increased fourfold (from 6505 ± 735 to 23,695 ± 715 ng) by 3×10^{7} M LH-RH, while an initial dose of 1×10^{-10} M leads to a 75% increase of total LH (10,495 ± 895 ng) over control (Fig. 2C).

Since the cell content of LH at day 0 was 10,630 ± 60 ng (equivalents LH-RP-1) and 2290 ± 570 ng of the hormone was found to be released spontaneously during the first 24 h of incubation, approximately 20% of the intracellular content of LH is released daily under our culture conditions. In the presence of 10^{-6} M LH-RH, 15,870 ± 330 ng of LH was found in the culture

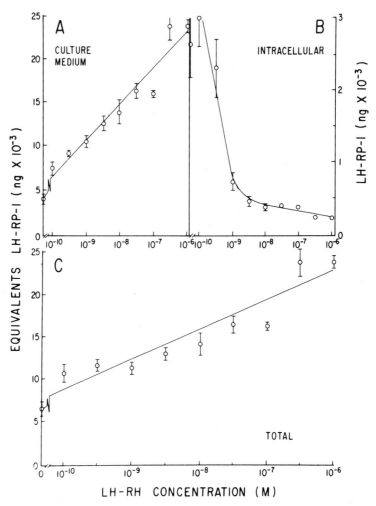

FIG. 2. *Effect of chronic treatment (6 days) of anterior pituitary cells in monolayer culture with increasing concentrations of synthetic LH-RH on (A) LH release, (B) intracellular content of LH, and (C) total (tissue plus culture medium) radioimmunoassayable LH.* Cells were cultured for 7 days before beginning the experiment. The culture medium was removed after the first 24 h of incubation in the presence or absence of increasing concentrations of LH-RH, and the new medium was left for the following 5 days. Results are presented as mean ± SD of data obtained from triplicate dishes. LH content at day 0 was 10,630 ± 60 ng LH (equivalents NIAMD-Rat-LH-RP-1). From Labrie *et al.* (1973).

medium during the first 24 h, thus indicating that increased LH synthesis had already occurred during that period. In the same experiment, the total FSH content (tissue plus culture medium) was raised from 3910 ± 290 ng to 7110 ± 410 ng FSH at a concentration of 1×10^{-10} M LH-RH (Labrie *et al.*, 1973).

Under our culture conditions, the daily release of FSH (1355 ± 155 ng) represents approximately 80% of the intracellular hormone content at day 0 (1630 ± 60 ng). These data indicate a fourfold higher rate of turnover of FSH than of LH. Since 4090 ± 630 ng of FSH were released during the first 24 h of incubation in the presence of 3×10^{-7} M LH-RH, it appears that the synthesis of FSH is also markedly stimulated during this short period of incubation with the neurohormone.

These data indicate clearly that synthetic LH-RH, besides stimulating the release of LH and FSH, leads to a marked stimulation of the synthesis of these two hormones. The increased synthesis occurs in the first 24 h of incubation in the presence of LH-RH. This increased synthesis may be a direct action of the neurohormone or may occur secondarily to a depletion of the pituitary stores of the hormones. These results are in agreement with those reported recently by Vale *et al.* (1972) and support data obtained using rat anterior pituitary organ cultures, where purified (Mittler *et al.*, 1970; Redding *et al.*, 1972) and synthetic (Redding *et al.*, 1972) gonadotropin-releasing hormones have been found to stimulate both release and synthesis of LH and FSH. Kobayshi *et al.* (1963) have also reported that addition of saline extracts of hypothalami to monolayer cultures of rat adenohypophysis led to an increase of total gonadotropins measured by bioassay.

Although it is difficult to rule out the possibility of a decreased lysosomal or autophagic activity under the influence of the releasing hormone, it appears most likely that synthetic LH-RH not only stimulates the release of both LH and FSH but also leads to a fairly rapid increase of the rate of synthesis of these two hormones.

EFFECT OF CYCLIC AMP DERIVATIVES AND THEOPHYLLINE ON LH AND FSH RELEASE

Effect of N^6-Monobutyryl Cyclic AMP, N^6-2'-O'-Dibutyryl Cyclic AMP, and Theophylline on LH Release

Figure 3 shows the stimulatory effect of 5 mM mbcAMP, 5 mM dbcAMP, or 5 mM theophylline on LH release during five successive 2-h incubations of rat anterior pituitary cells in monolayer culture. mbcAMP at 5mM leads to a maximal 47-fold stimulation (1900 ± 329 vs. 40 ± 11 ng/ml) of LH released during the second period of incubation with a progressive decrease to a fourteen-

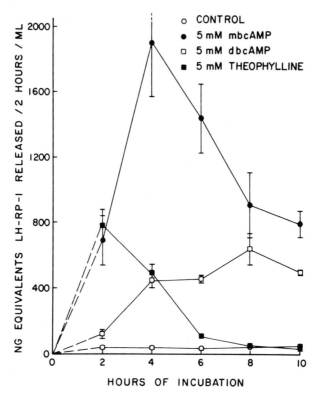

FIG. 3. Effect of N^6-monobutyryl cyclic AMP (mbcAMP), N^6,2'-O-dibutyryl cyclic AMP (dbcAMP), and theophylline on LH release from anterior pituitary cells in monolayer culture. Cells from female rat anterior pituitaries were incubated for 5 days before beginning the experiment. Cells were then incubated in a volume of 3 ml for five successive 2-h incubation periods in the presence or absence of 5 mM mbcAMP, 5 mM dbcAMP, or 5 mM theophylline. Results are expressed as mean ± SD of data obtained from duplicate dishes. From Drouin and Labrie (1974).

fold stimulation observed between 8 and 10 h of incubation with the cyclic AMP derivative. dbcAMP at 5 mM leads to an approximately constant ten- to fourteenfold stimulation of LH release measured between the second and tenth hour of incubation. The maximal effect of 5 mM theophylline is more rapid, an eighteenfold stimulation of LH release being observed during the first 2 h of incubation with a progressive decrease to basal levels after 6 h.

Using rat hemipituitaries, and a high concentration of cyclic AMP (15 mM), Jutisz (1970) has reported an approximately 50% stimulation of LH release during the first 90 min of incubation with the cyclic nucleotide.

Effect of Cyclic AMP and Theophylline on FSH Release

A possible role of cyclic AMP in the control of FSH release was suggested by the finding of a potentialization by theophylline of the effect of a crude preparation of FSH-releasing hormone on FSH release (Jutisz and De La Llosa, 1969). Theophylline alone had no effect on hormone release.

ULTRASTRUCTURAL CHANGES ACCOMPANYING CHRONIC TREATMENT OF GONADOTROPHS IN CELL CULTURE WITH LH-RH

We had previously studied the ultrastructural changes accompanying a relatively short-term (up to 6 h) effect of mbcAMP on GH, PRL, and ACTH release in rat anterior pituitary gland *in vitro* (Pelletier *et al.*, 1972). Although the cyclic nucleotide stimulated exocytosis in somatotrophs and mammotrophs and a progressive degranulation as well as a hypertrophy of the Golgi apparatus in these two cell types, no striking modification of gonadotrophs was detected in these studies. Chronic treatment of anterior pituitary cells in monolayer culture with LH-RH has been shown to increase both synthesis and release of gonadotropic hormones (Labrie *et al.*, 1973). Since no data are available on the morphology of adenohypophyseal cells in monolayer culture, it seemed important to study at the electron microscope level the modifications induced by LH-RH after 6 days of incubation.

In control cultures, well-granulated gonadotrophs were identified on the basis of the size of their secretory granules and the presence of dilated rough endoplasmic reticulum (RER) cisternae. The other granulated cell types were identified as somatotrophs, mammotrophs, thyrotrophs, and corticotrophs. In cultures exposed to 1×10^{-8} M LH-RH for 6 days (Fig. 4), typical control gonadotrophs were replaced by markedly hypertrophied cells. These enlarged cells were classified as gonadotrophs on the basis of their dilated RER cisternae and large irregularly shaped nucleus located at the periphery of the cytoplasm. They usually contained a few small secretory granules or were completely degranulated, while the Golgi apparatus was usually well developed. Such depletion of secretory granules agrees well with the observed decrease in FSH and LH content (Fig. 2, Labrie *et al.*, 1973). That this depletion of secretory granules had not been observed in gonadotrophs after 6 h of incubation of pituitary halves in the presence of mbcAMP (Pelletier *et al.*, 1972) could be due to a phenomenon which occurs only after a long-term stimulation. The presence of a well-developed Golgi apparatus suggests that granules are discharged rapidly from this organelle into the extracellular space. The hypertrophy of the nucleus and the high content of dilated cisternae of the rough ER are probably related to

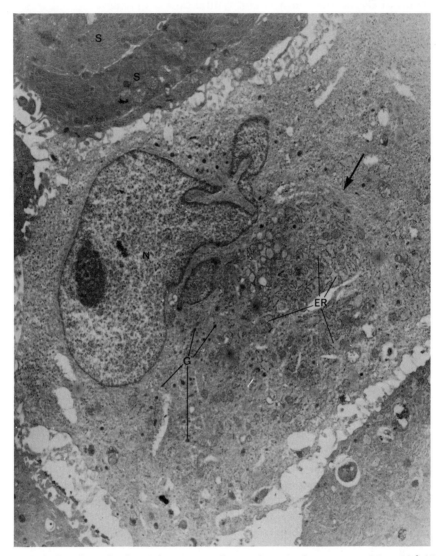

FIG. 4. *Gonadotroph after 6 days in monolayer culture in the presence of 1 × 10⁻⁸ M LH-RH.* The cell is markedly hypertrophied. In the cytoplasm, the diluted cisternae of the rough endoplasmic reticulum (ER) are abundant and a few secretory granules (G) are present. The nucleus (N) is large and irregular and located at the periphery of the cell. A bundle of microfilaments (→) can be observed. Note the presence of two well-granulated somatotrophs (S). (6,630×.)

the increased LH and FSH synthesis. Bundles of microfilaments dispersed in the cytoplasm were not infrequently observed.

The enlargement of gonadotrophs after a long-term stimulation with LH-RH in tissue culture agrees well with the hypertrophy of gonadotrophs observed *in vivo* after castration (Farquhar, 1971). It should, however, be mentioned that the gonadectomy cells have an increased number of granules and a more dilated RER. Specificity of the stimulatory effect of LH-RH has been confirmed at the morphological level by the absence of modifications of the other cell types.

PARALLEL STIMULATORY EFFECT OF LH-RH AND SOME OF ITS ANALOGUES ON CYCLIC AMP ACCUMULATION AND LH AND FSH RELEASE

Although the observation of a stimulatory effect of theophylline, mbcAMP, and dbcAMP (Fig. 3) on LH release was suggestive of a role of cyclic AMP in the control of gonadotropin secretion, definitive proof of the role of the adenylate cyclase system as mediator of the action of LH-RH could be obtained only by measurements of adenohypophyseal adenylate cyclase activity or cyclic AMP concentrations under the influence of the neurohormone.

Concentrations of synthetic LH-RH ranging from 5 to 100 ng/ml lead to a 160–250% increase over control of anterior pituitary cyclic AMP concentrations (Borgeat *et al.,* 1972). A close correlation is found between the rates of LH and FSH release and changes of adenohypophyseal cyclic AMP concentrations as a function of both time of incubation and increasing concentrations of the neurohormone. The concentration of LH-RH required for half-maximal stimulation of cyclic AMP accumulation and LH release is between 0.1 and 1 ng/ml or between 1×10^{-10} and 1×10^{-9} M (Borgeat *et al.,* 1972).

In the presence of 10 mM theophylline, the stimulatory effect of LH-RH on cyclic AMP accumulation is similar to that observed in the absence of the cyclic nucleotide phosphodiesterase inhibitor, thus indicating that the releasing hormone exerts its effect by activation of adenylate cyclase rather than by inhibition of phosphodiesterase. Since the release of GH, TSH, PRL, and ACTH is not affected by LH-RH and cyclic AMP stimulates the release of all six adenohypophyseal hormones (Lemay and Labrie, 1972; Labrie *et al.,* 1973), the observed changes of cyclic AMP concentrations indicate specific stimulation of adenylate cyclase activity in LH- and FSH-secreting cells of the adenohypophysis. In fact, an increased cyclic AMP concentration in any anterior pituitary cell type would be expected to lead to increased release of the corresponding hormone. Since gonadotrophs correspond to about 7% of anterior pituitary cells in male rats, the threefold stimulation of cyclic AMP concentration in total pituitaries would correspond to a 45-fold specific stimulation of cyclic AMP accumulation in

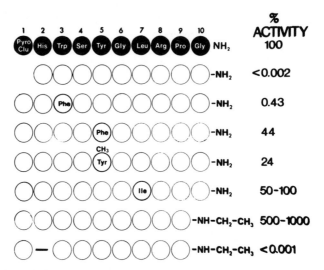

FIG. 5. *Relative biological activity of LH-RH and some of its analogues:* des(pyro)Glu-LH-RH, [Phe³]LH-RH, [Phe⁵]LH-RH, [*O*-methyl-Tyr⁵]LH-RH, [Ile⁷]LH-RH, desGly¹⁰-LH-RH-ethylamide, and desHis²-desGly¹⁰-LH-RH-ethylamide. A close correlation was found between changes of intracellular levels of cyclic AMP in the presence of increasing concentrations of the various analogues and LH and FSH release in rat anterior pituitary tissue *in vitro.*

gonadotrophs. Kaneko *et al.* (1973) have also reported that synthetic LH-RH (1 µg/ml) increased cyclic AMP levels in rat anterior pituitary gland *in vitro.*

The potential importance of LH-RH analogues in the control of fertility has led to the synthesis of a wide variety of analogues of the decapeptide by several laboratories. Such analogues have already provided much information on the structure–function relationships of the LH-RH molecule (Coy *et al.*, 1973a; Monahan *et al.*, 1973) and offer the opportunity of investigating the relative potency of these compounds on cyclic AMP accumulation and hormone release. The finding of a close correlation between their effect on these two parameters would add strong support for the role of cyclic AMP as mediator of the intracellular effects of the releasing hormone.

The LH-RH analogues used for such a study and their relative potencies on LH release measured by different laboratories using *in vitro* and *in vivo* tests (Schally *et al.*, 1972; Coy *et al.*, 1973a,b; Fujino *et al.*, 1972a,b; Yanaihara, 1973) are shown in Fig. 5. It can be seen that the biological activity of these compounds ranges from less than 0.001% (des-His²-desGly¹⁰-LH-RH-ethylamide) to 500–1000% (desGly¹⁰-LH-RH-ethylamide) of the activity of LH-RH itself. When increasing concentrations of these compounds were tested on cyclic AMP accumulation and LH and FSH release in rat hemipituitaries *in vitro,* a close correlation was consistently found among the values of these three parameters (Borgeat *et al.,* 1974).

Such a close parallelism between changes of intracellular cyclic AMP concentrations and hormone release add strong support to the already obtained evidence for a role of the cyclic nucleotide as mediator of LH-RH action (Borgeat *et al.,* 1972; Labrie *et al.,* 1973). These data also add strong support to the previous observations made both *in vivo* and *in vitro* of simultaneous release of both LH and FSH by a single neurohormone (Schally *et al.,* 1971a,b,c,d,e; Amos *et al.,* 1971; Baba *et al.,* 1971; Kastin *et al.,* 1970; Milhaud *et al.,* 1971).

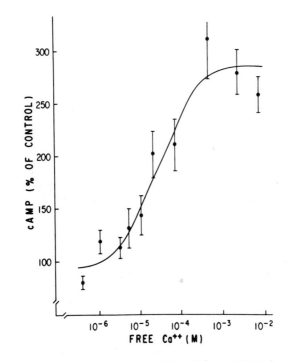

FIG. 6. *Effect of increasing concentrations of free Ca^{2+} on LH-RH-induced cyclic AMP accumulation in male rat pituitary gland.* Three pituitary halves were used in each group. Adenohypophyseal tissue was first incubated for 60 min at 37°C in an atmosphere of 5% CO_2–95% O_2 in 1 ml of KRBG before incubation for 3½ h in the presence or absence of various concentrations of Ca^{2+} as described in Borgeat *et al.* (1972). LH-RH (100 ng/ml), theophylline (10 mM), and EGTA (2 mM) were present in all groups. The indicated concentrations of free Ca^{2+} were obtained by addition of $CaCl_2$.

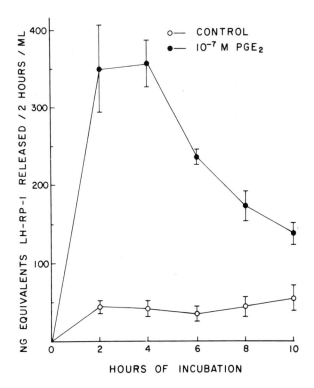

FIG. 7. Effect of PGE$_2$ on LH release from anterior pituitary cells in monolayer culture.
Experimental conditions were as in Fig. 3 except for the presence of 1×10^{-7} M PGE$_2$ in
the appropriate groups. From Drouin and Labrie (1974).

REQUIREMENT OF Ca^{2+} FOR ACTIVATION OF ANTERIOR PITUITARY ADENYLATE CYCLASE BY LH-RH

Since Ca^{2+} was reported to be required for the stimulation of LH release induced by a hypothalamic extract presumably containing LH-RH (Samli and Geschwind, 1968; Wakabayashi *et al.*, 1968), it was felt of interest to study a possible requirement of Ca^{2+} at a step preceding activation of adenylate cyclase.

Removal of Ca^{2+} from the incubation medium by addition of 2 mM EGTA had no significant effect on the basal level of cyclic AMP but led to an approximately 75% inhibition of the stimulation observed in the presence of LH-RH.

The more precise requirements of Ca^{2+} for activation of adenohypophyseal adenylate cyclase by LH-RH are shown in Fig. 6. Half-maximal stimulation of adenylate cyclase activation is observed at 5×10^{-5} M free Ca^{2+}, while maximal stimulation is found at 1×10^{-4} M. Analogous data have been obtained for the action of ACTH on adrenocortical adenylate cyclase (Lefkowitz et al., 1970). These data indicate that Ca^{2+} is required at a step preceding activation of adenylate cyclase by LH-RH. Such an early site of action of Ca^{2+} would then be added to the already suspected late site of requirement of Ca^{2+} during high-K^+-induced release of LH (Samli and Geschwind, 1968; Wakabayashi et al., 1969).

EFFECT OF PROSTAGLANDINS ON THE RELEASE OF LH AND FSH

It is well known that prostaglandins stimulate adenylate cyclase activity in various systems (Wolfe and Shulman, 1969; Peery et al., 1971; Sato et al., 1972) including the anterior pituitary gland (Zor et al., 1969a), and a few studies suggest that prostaglandins may well control intracellular cyclic AMP levels (Ramwell and Shaw, 1970; Zor et al., 1969b; Butcher and Baird, 1968; Kuehl et al., 1970).

Figure 7 shows that 1×10^{-7} M PGE$_2$ leads to an approximately tenfold stimulation of LH release during the first two 2-h incubation periods of pituitary cells in monolayer culture with a progressive decrease to a 2.5-fold stimulation of hormone release between the eighth and the tenth hour of incubation.

Coupled with the observation of an inhibition of LH release by indomethacin, a PG synthetase inhibitor, or 7-oxo-13-prostynoic acid, a PG antagonist, and the stimulatory effect of PGE$_1$ and PGE$_2$ on anterior pituitary cyclic AMP formation (Borgeat, Drouin, and Labrie, unpublished data), the present finding of a marked stimulation of LH release by PGE$_2$ suggests that PGs may play an important role in the action of LH-RH in the anterior pituitary gland.

REFERENCES

Amos, M., Burgus, R., Blackwell, R., Vale, W., Fellows, R., and Guillemin, R. (1971), Purification of amino acid composition and N-terminus of the hypothalamic luteinizing hormone-releasing factor (LRF) of ovine origin, Biochem. Biophys. Res. Commun. 44:205.

Arimura, A., Sato, H., Kumasaka, T., Wonobec, R. B., Debeljuk, L., Dunn, J. D., and Schally, A. V. (1973), Production of antiserum to LH-releasing (LH-RH) associated with marked atrophy of the gonads in rabbits; characterization of the antibody and development of a radioimmunoassay for LH-RH, Endocrinology, 93:1092.

Baba, Y., Matsuo, H., and Schally, A. V. (1971), Structure of the porcine LH- and FSH-releasing hormone. II. Confirmation of the proposed structure by conventional sequential analysis, Biochem. Biophys. Res. Commun. 44:459.

Borgeat, P., Chavancy, G., Dupont, A., Labrie, F., Arimura, A., and Schally, A. V. (1972), Stimulation of adenosine 3',5'-cyclic monophosphate accumulation in anterior pituitary gland in vitro by synthetic luteinizing hormone-releasing hormone, Proc. Natl. Acad. Sci. (U.S.A.) 69:2677.

Borgeat, P., Labrie, F., Côté, J., Ruel, F., Schally, A. V., Coy, D. H., Coy, E. H., and Yanaihara, N. (1974), Parallel stimulation of cyclic AMP accumulation and LH and FSH release by analogs of LH-RH *in vitro, J. Mol. Cell. Endocrinol. 1:7.*

Burgus, R., Butcher, M., Ling, N., Monahan, M., Rivier, J., Fellows, R., Amos, M., Blackwell, R., Vale, W., and Guillemin, R. (1971), Structure moléculaire du facteur hypothalamique (LRF) d'origine ovine contrôlant la sécrétion de l'hormone gonadotrope hypophysaire de luténisation (LH), *C.R. Acad. Sci. (Paris) 273:*1611.

Butcher, R. W., and Baird, C. E. (1968), Effects of prostaglandins on adenosine 3',5'-monophosphate levels in fat and other tissues, *J. Biol. Chem. 243:*1713.

Clementi, F., Ceccarelli, B., Cerati, E., Demonte, M. L., and Pecile, A. (1971), Subcellular organization of the median eminence, in: *Advances in Cytopharmacology,* Vol. 1, p. 331, Raven Press, New York.

Coy, D. H., Coy, E. J., and Schally, A. V. (1973a), Structure–activity relationships in the luteinizing hormone-releasing hormone (LH-RH) in: *Proceedings of the 55th Meeting of the Endocrinology Society,* p. A-145.

Coy, D. H., Coy, E. J., and Schally, A. V. (1973b), Luteinizing hormone-releasing hormone: Solid-phase synthesis of a 5-phenylalanine analog possessing high biological activity, *J. Med. Chem. 16:*83.

Drouin, J., and Labrie, F. (1974), in preparation.

Farquhar, M. G. (1971), Processing of secretory products by cells of the anterior pituitary gland, in: *Memoirs of the Society of Endocrinologists,,* Vol. 19, p. 79 (H. Hellers and K. Lederis, eds.), Cambridge University Press, Cambridge.

Fujino, M., Kobayashi, S., Obayashi, M., Shinagawa, S., Fukuda, T., Kitada, C., Nakayama, R., Yamasaki, I., White, W. F., and Rippel, R. H. (1972a), Structure–activity relationship in the *c*-terminal part of luteinizing hormone-releasing hormone (LH-RH), *Biochem. Biophys. Res. Commun. 49:*863.

Fujino, M., Kobayashi, S., Obayashi, M., Fukuda, T., Shinagawa, S., Yamasaki, I., Nakayama, R., White, W. F., and Rippel, R. H. (1972b), Synthesis and biological activities of analogs of luteinizing hormone-releasing hormone (LH-RH), *Biochem. Biophys. Res. Commun. 49:*698.

Geiger, R., Konig, W., Wissman, H., Geisen, K., and Enzman, F. (1971), Synthesis and characterization of a decapeptide having LH-RH/FSH-RH activity, *Biochem. Biophys. Res. Commun. 45:*767.

Guillemin, R. (1972), Physiology and chemistry of the hypothalamic releasing factors for gonadotropins: A new approach to fertility control, *Contraception 6:*1.

Halász, B., and Pupp, L. (1965), Hormone secretion of the anterior pituitary gland after physical interruption of all nervous pathways to the hypophysiotropic area, *Endocrinology 77:*553.

Ishii, S. (1970), Association of luteinizing hormone-releasing factor with granules separated from equine hypophysial stalk, *Endocrinology 86:*207.

Jutisz, M. (1970), Régulation de la sécrétion gonadotrope adénohypophysaire par les hormones hypothalamiques, in: *Mécanismes de'Actions Intracellulaires des Hormones,* p. 93 (R. Vokaer, ed.), Mason & Cie, Paris.

Jutisz, M., and De La Llosa, M. P. (1969), Adenosine 3',5'-monophosphate cyclique, un intermédiaire probable de l'action de l'hormone hypothalamique TRF, *C.R. Acad. Sci. (Paris) 268:*1636.

Kaneko, T., Saito, S., Oka, H., Oda, T., and Yanaihara, N. (1973), Effects of synthetic LH-RH and its analogs on rat anterior pituitary cyclic AMP and LH and FSH release, *Metabolism 22:*77.

Kastin, A. J., Schally, A. V., Gual, G., Midgley, A. R., Jr., Bowers, C. Y., and Gomez-Perez,

F. (1970), Administration of LH-releasing hormone to selected subjects, *Am. J. Obstet. Gynecol. 108:*177.

Kobayashi, H., Kobayashi, T., Kigawa, I., Mizuno, M., and Amenomori, Y. (1963), Influence of rat hypothalamic extract on gonadotropin activity of cultivated anterior pituitary cells, *Endocrinol. Jap. 10:*16.

Kobayashi, H., Matsui, T., and Ishii, S. (1970), Functional electron microscopy of the hypothalamic median eminence, *Int. Rev. Cytol. 29:*281.

Krulich, L., Quijada, M., Illner, P., and McCann, S. M. (1971), The distribution of hypothalamic hypophysiotropic factors in the hypothalamus of the rat, *Proc. Int. Union Physiol. Sci. 9:*326.

Kuehl, F. A., Jr., Humes, J. L., Tarnoff, J., Cirillo, V. J., and Ham, E. A. (1970), Prostaglandin receptor site: Evidence for an essential role in the action of luteinizing hormone, *Science 169:*883.

Labrie, F., Pelletier, G., Lemay, A., Borgeat, P., Barden, N., Dupont, A., Savary, M., Côté, J., and Boucher, R. (1973), Control of protein synthesis in anterior pituitary gland, in: *6th Karolinska Symposium on Research Methods in Reproductive Endrocrinology,* pp. 301–340 (E. Diczfalusy, ed.).

Lefkowitz, R. J., Roth, J., and Pastan, I. (1970), Effects of calcium on ACTH stimulation of the adrenal: Separation of hormone binding from adenyl cyclase activation, *Nature (Lond.) 228:*864.

Lemay, A., and Labrie, F. (1972). Calcium-dependent stimulation of prolactin release in rat anterior pituitary *in vitro* by N^6-monobutyryl adenosine 3′,5′-monophosphate, *FEBS Letters 20:*7.

Matsuo, H., Baba, Y., Nair, R. M. G., Arimura, A., and Schally, A. V. (1971a), Structure of the porcine LH- and FSH-releasing hormone. I. The proposed amino acid sequence, *Biochem. Biophys. Res. Commun. 43:*1334.

Matsuo, H., Arimura, A., Nair, R. M. G., and Schally, A. V. (1971b), Synthesis of the porcine LH- and FSH-releasing hormone by the solid-phase method, *Biochem. Biophys. Res. Commun. 45:*822.

Milhaud, G., Rivaille, P., Garnier, P., Chaussain, J. L., Binet, E., and Job, J. C. (1971), Synthèse de la LH-RH et effet sélectif sur la libération de l'hormone lutéotrophique chez l'homme adulte, *C.R. Acad. Sci. (Paris) 273:1858.*

Mittler, J. C., Arimura, A., and Schally, A. V. (1970), Release and synthesis of luteinizing hormone and follicle-stimulating hormone in pituitary cultures in response to hypothalamic preparations, *Proc. Soc. Exp. Biol. Med. 133:*1321.

Monahan, M., Rivier, J., Burgus, R., Amos, M., Blackwell, R., Vale, W., and Guillemin, R. (1971), Synthèse totale par phase solide d'un décapeptide qui stimule la sécrétion des gonadotropines hypophysaires LH et FSH, *C.R.H. Acad. Sci. 273:*508.

Monahan, M., Vale, W., Rivier, C., Grant, G., and Guillemin, R. (1973), Analogues of LRF with inhibitory action of greater potency than the natural decapeptide hormone, in: *Proceedings of the 55th Meeting of the Endocrinology Society,* p. A-145.

Peery, C. V., Johnson, G. S., and Pastan, I. (1971), Adenylcyclase in normal and transformed fibroblasts in tissue culture, *J. Biol. Chem. 246:*5785.

Pelletier, G., Lemay, A., Béraud, G., and Labrie, F. (1972), Ultrastructural changes accompanying the stimulation effect of N^6-monobutyryl adenosine 3′,5′-monophosphate on the release of growth hormone (GH), prolactin (PRL) and adrenocorticotropic hormone (ACTH) in rat anterior pituitary gland *in vitro, Endocrinology 91:*1355.

Pelletier, G., Labrie, F., Puviani, R., Arimura, A., and Schally, A. V. (1974), Electron microscope immunohistochemical localization of luteinizing hormone-releasing hormone in the rat median eminence, *Endocrinology, 95:*314.

Ramwell, P. W., and Shaw, J. E. (1970), Biological significance of the prostaglandins, *Rec. Progr. Hormone Res. 26:*139.

Redding, T. W., Schally, A. V., Arimura, A., and Matsuo, H. (1972), Stimulation of release and synthesis of luteinizing hormone (LH) and follicle stimulating hormone (FSH) in tissue cultures of rat pituitaries in response to natural and synthetic LH and FSH releasing hormone, *Endocrinology 90:*764.

Samli, M., and Geschwind, I. I. (1968), Some effects of energy-transfer inhibitors and of Ca^{++}-free or K^+-enhanced media on the release of luteinizing hormone (LH) from the rat pituitary gland *in vitro, Endocrinology 82:*225.

Sato, S., Szabo, M., Kowalski, K., and Burke, G. (1972), Role of prostaglandin in thyrotropin action of thyroid, *Endocrinology 90:*343.

Schally, A. V., Baba, Y., Arimura, A., Redding, T. W., and White, W. F. (1971a), Evidence for peptide nature of LH- and FSH-releasing hormones, *Biochem. Biophys. Res. Commun. 42:*50.

Schally, A. V., Arimura, A., Baba, Y., Nair, R. M. G., Matsuo, H., Redding, T. W., and Debeljuk, L. (1971b), Isolation and properties of the FSH- and LH-releasing hormone, *Biochem. Biophys. Res. Commun. 43:*393.

Schally, A. V., Nair, R. M. G., Redding, T. W., and Arimura, A. (1971c), Isolation of the luteinizing hormone and follicle-stimulating hormone-releasing hormone from porcine hypothalami, *J. Biol. Chem. 246:*7230.

Schally, A. V., Kastin, A. J., and Arimura, A. (1971d), Hypothalamic follicle-stimulating hormone (FSH) and luteinizing hormone (LH)-regulating hormone: Structure, physiology and clinical studies, *Fertil. Steril. 22:*703.

Schally, A. V., Arimura, A., Kastin, A. J., Matsuo, H., Baba, Y., Redding, T. W., Nair, R. M. G., Debeljuk, L., and White, W. F. (1971e), Gonadotropin-releasing hormone: One polypeptide regulates secretion of luteinizing and follicle-stimulating hormones, *Science 173:*1036.

Schally, A. V., Arimura, A., Carter, W. H., Redding, T. W., Geiger, R., Konig, W., Wessman, H., Jaeger, G., Sandow, J., Yanaihara, N., Yanaihara, C., Hashimoto, T., and Sakagami, M. (1972), Luteinizing hormone-releasing hormone (LH-RH) activity of some synthetic polypeptides. 1. Fragments shorter than decapeptide, *Biochem. Biophys. Res. Commun. 48:*366.

Scott, D. E., and Knigge, K. M. (1970), Ultrastructural changes in the median eminence of the rat following differentiation of the basal hypothalamus, *Z. Zellforsch. 105:*1.

Sternberger, J. A. (1972), The unlabeled-antibody-peroxidase and the quantitative immunouranium methods in light and electron immunohistochemistry, in: *Techniques of Biochemical and Biophysical Morphology,* p. 67 (D. Glick and R. M. Rosenbaum, eds.), Wiley, New York.

Vale, W., Grant, G., Amoss, M., Blackwell, R., and Guillemin, R. (1972), Culture of enzymatically dispersed anterior pituitary cells: Functional validation of a method, *Endocrinology 91:*562.

Wakabayashi, K., Schneider, H. P. G., Watanabe, S., Crighton, D. B., and McCann, S. M. (1968), Studies on the mechanism of action of the gonadotrophin releasing factors on the pituitary, *Fed. Proc. 27:*269.

Wakabayashi, K., Kamberi, I. A., and McCann, S. M. (1969), *In vitro* response of the rat pituitary to gonadotropin releasing factors and to ions, *Endocrinology 85:*1046.

Wolfe, S. M., and Shulman, N. R. (1969), Adenyl cyclase activity in human platelets, *Biochem. Biophys. Res. Commun. 35:*265.

Yanaihara, N., Hashimoto, I., Yanaihara, C., Tsuji, K., Kenmochi, Y., Ashizawa, F., Kaneko, T., Ika, H., Saito, S., Arimura, A., and Schally, A. V. (1973), Synthesis and biological evaluation of analogs of luteinizing hormone-releasing hormone (LH-RH) modified in position 2, 3, 4 or 5, *Biochem. Biophys. Res. Commun. 52:*64.

Zor, U., Kaneko, T., Schneider, H. P. G., McCann, S. M., Lowe, I. P., Bloom, G., Borland, B., and Field, J. B. (1969a), Stimulation of anterior pituitary adenyl cyclase activity and adenosine 3', 5'-cyclic phosphate by hypothalamic extract and prostaglandin, *Proc. Natl. Acad. Sci. (U.S.A.) 63:*918.

Zor, U., Kaneko, T., Lowe, I. P., Bloom, G., and Field, J. B. (1969b), Effect of thyroid-stimulating hormone and prostaglandins on thyroid adenyl cyclase activation and cyclic adenosine 3', 5'-monophosphate, *J. Biol. Chem. 244:*5189.

20

Protein Synthesis Machinery in Growing Oocytes of Mice

Roberto B. García, Claudio Benech, and J. Roberto Sotelo

Instituto de Investigación de Ciencias Biológicas
Departamento de Ultraestructura Celular and Laboratorio de Biofísica
Montevideo, Uruguay

Few morphological evaluations of the ribosome population in eukaryotic cells have been made (Rifkind *et al.,* 1964; Boynton *et al.,* 1972). However, this methodological approach can provide interesting information which can be used as a source of reference for further investigations on the machinery of protein synthesis involved in differentiation, growth, and/or maturation of several cell lines. Among slow-growing cells, the oocyte is a suitable model, and presently there is much information on the work of this machinery in female germ cells. Most of this information, however, has been obtained from lecithical oocytes of amphibia and echinoderms (Davidson, 1968). Mammalian oocytes (alecithical), although less adequate for a direct biochemical approach than those just mentioned, can be a valuable material for a quantitative morphological analysis, particularly if one takes advantage of the wave of oocyte growth which starts shortly after birth (see below).

In the early 1950s, several researchers used the basophilic properties of the cytoplasm to grossly evaluate the concentration and distribution of RNA in growing oocytes (Vincent and Dornfeld, 1948; Brachet, 1950, 1957; Dalcq, 1950, 1953, 1955). The ultraviolet absorption of the oocyte cytoplasm was used for a similar purpose (Austin and Braden, 1953; Hedberg, 1953).

These investigations were the first attempts to relate in a quantitative way

This investigation was partially supported by an "Acción de Refuerzo (U 16) del Programa Regional del Consejo Interamericano para la Educación, la Ciencia y la Cultura (CIECC) de la Organización de los Estados Americanos."

"cytoplasmic RNA" and the process of protein synthesis in the mammalian oocyte. Later, autoradiographic methods were used to explore the dynamics of both nuclear RNA turnover and the transference of RNA to cytoplasm in defined stages of oocyte growth (Oakberg, 1968; Baker *et al.*, 1969).

Electron microscope techniques offer the possibility of developing a different approach. The rationale for this approach is that ribosomes in polysomes are the morphological expression of the fraction of the ribosome population actually engaged in protein synthesis (Warner *et al.*, 1963; Wettstein *et al.*, 1963). Therefore, a comparative study of the number of ribosomes per cell, the percentage of ribosomes in polysomes, the length of polysomes, and the ribosome density in the cytoplasm can be tentatively proposed as an expression of how the translational apparatus of oocytes is working.

The present investigation consisted of a systematic counting of the ribosome values in growing oocytes of prepubertal mice. Prepubertal animals were selected for the following reasons: (1) the oocyte population is very homogeneous at birth; (2) since a growth wave starts shortly after and simultaneously involves a large number of oocytes, the progression of growth can be correlated with definite ages of the animals, and a large number of prepubertal animals of the same age provide oocytes at a similar growth stage; (3) most of the oocytes not involved in the first growth wave remain quiescent during prepubertal life (primordial oocytes).

MATERIAL AND METHODS

Prepubertal white mice of the IICB-Montevideo colony were used. Animals were sacrificed at the following ages: 2, 4–5, 7–8, 11, 14, and 21 days postpartum (four animals for each age). The ovaries were fixed by dropping 2.5% glutaraldehyde in 0.1 M phosphate buffer into the abdominal cavity, removing them after 5 min, and placing them in a vial containing the same fixative for 2 h. The next steps, postosmication, dehydration, and embedding (Durcupan ACM), were performed as usual. In some cases fixation was carried out only in 1% osmium tetroxide in Veronal buffer. The two types of samples did not show any obvious differences in the distribution of the ribosome population. Sectioning was performed with either the MT1 or the MT2 Sorvall ultramicrotome. Sections mounted on one-hole grids or in 400-mesh grids were stained with saturated uranyl acetate, followed or not by lead citrate, and were examined in a Siemens Elmiskop I.

Light microscopy: Each sample was explored in alternate, adjacent, thick and thin sections. The former (stained with 1% methylene blue in 1% borax) were examined under the light microscope for the purpose of discriminating (1) areas containing primordial oocytes and (2) areas containing growing oocytes. They were then recorded photographically in order to determine the average size of the oocytes. These measures are used to express in the graphics the maximum growth attained for each age.

Electron microscopy: Electron microscope recordings of 500–600 Å ultra-thin sections were made in two different ways: (1) equatorial sections of oocytes at the 2-day stage and primordial oocytes at later stages were mapped, and montages were made after adequate enlarging (20,000 × 4); (2) growing oocytes (large) were scanned radially, and electron micrographs which covered a wide-diameter band of the oocyte were taken. Electron micrographs taken at random from serial sections of oocytes were also recorded in order to compare different depths. An average of ten oocytes were recorded for each age and growth stage.

Parameters of the ribosome population: The following evaluations were made on randomly selected areas of 1 μm^2 of oocyte cytoplasm devoid of membrane-bound organelles (called "cytoplasmic background"): (1) *ribosome density,* defined as the total number of ribosomes counted in the sample (single ribosomes plus ribosomes integrating polysomes); (2) *percentage of ribosomes in polysomes,* calculated from the total number mentioned in (1); (3) *polysome lengths,* measured by counting the maximum and minimum number of ribosomes forming single polysomes. As a certain number of polysomes are transected, the last magnitude should be diminished by thin sectioning. The factor by which real polysome lengths are underestimated can be calculated according to the method proposed by Perl (1964). However, in the present investigation this factor was not taken into consideration (see Results).

Calculation of the cytoplasmic background: Contours of equatorial sections of oocytes were traced on homogeneous paper. Their nuclei and membrane-bound organelles were also traced, and later eliminated by differential weight.

RESULTS

At the 2-day stage, most of the primary oocyte population has already passed through the pachytene phase of meiosis, which is recognized by the gradual disappearance of synaptonemal complexes. At this transitional period (pachytene to diplotene), some remnants of these are still found in a small number of oocytes. The nuclear diameter/oocyte diameter ratio changes after 3–4 days postpartum, which means that cytoplasmic growth is under way. Distribution of organelles at the pregrowth period is as follows: the nucleus is eccentric, the Golgi components form a large body located at the widest side of the cytoplasm, mitochondria are mostly located in the neighborhood of the Golgi bodies, and the endoplasmic reticulum is represented by numerous vesicles, 0.1 μm in diameter, evenly distributed in the cytoplasm. A few multivesicular bodies and lamellated bodies can be found near the Golgi bodies or elsewhere in the cytoplasm.

TABLE I. Mean Values of Ribosome Densities, Percentage of Ribosomes in Polysomes, and Polysome Length at Various Ages of Primordial and Growing Oocytes

Age (days)	Ribosome densities		Ribosome % in polysomes		Length of polysomes	
	Primordial	Growing	Primordial	Growing	Primordial	Growing
2	335 ± 35		> 95		15–50	
4–5	135 ± 20	111 ± 19	75–80	55–65	4–12	4–12
7–8	123 ± 8	152 ± 21	55–65	>95	same	same
11	116 ± 7	79 ± 4	same	same	same	same
14	119 ± 14	72 ± 8	same	same	same	same
21	112 ± 13	63 ± 6	same	same	same	same

As growth starts and progresses, the distribution of organelles follows a pattern similar to the one in mammalian oocytes, as described by van der Stricht (1923) and redescribed by Sotelo and Porter (1959) after electron microscope examination of rat oocytes. The cytoplasmic material distributes progressively in two layers: perinuclear and cortical. The former contains mostly mitochondria, multivesicular bodies, and a few Golgi components; the latter contains a large amount of Golgi bodies, mitochondria, and clusters of multivesicular bodies surrounded by microvesicles. In mice, at the beginning of oocyte growth, the endoplasmic reticulum vesicles become larger, and some of them show a few studded particles on their surface. Later these vesicles become elongated and form stacks of three to six lamellae, located either in the cortical layer or in the perinuclear layer. The space between both layers shows an amorphous matrix in which few mitochondria or other organelles are dispersed. Sometimes short bundles of filaments of low electron density occur in the cytoplasm and increase in number with age. (Specimens older than 21 days have not been checked in this regard.)

During cytoplasmic growth, the nuclear diameter change is so small, in comparison to the increase of the oocyte diameter that it can be considered stationary. At all the stages observed, nucleoli appear as large and well-developed bodies integrated by fibrillar and granular components.

Table I shows the mean values of the ribosome population (ribosome densities, percentages of ribosomes in polysomes, polysome lengths), as counted in early and in growing oocytes. Six ages are listed: the first one corresponds to the homogeneous oocyte population undergoing passage from pachytene to diplotene. At the following ages listed, two classes of oocyte populations have already divided: one integrated by growing oocytes and the other which is formed by the so-called primordial oocytes.

The values recorded for oocytes at pachytene–diplotene are the highest observed among all the stages studied. With regard to polysomes, it is assumed that a certain number of them have been transected during sectioning. However, as seen in the last two right-hand columns, transection does not affect comparison of results, since the polysome length values are at least four times higher than those observed at the other stages (Figs. 1 and 2).

During transition to dictyate (from 2 to 4 days postpartum), all parameters fall to lower values. From the percentage of ribosomes in polysomes, it is inferred that the number of single ribosomes is very high (almost 35%) (Fig. 3).

At the beginning of growth (4–5 days postpartum), no obvious changes in the ribosome population values are observed. Shortly afterwards (from 7–8 days postpartum onwards), a progressive decrease of the ribosome density is noted. The percentage of ribosomes in polysomes rises to the higher level found at the pachytene–diplotene stage (>95%), but polysome lengths stay the same, as in transition to dictyate (4–12 ribosomes) (Fig. 4). In comparison, the values of the three parameters in primordial oocytes are as low as those observed in transition to dictyate all during the prepubertal period.

Table II shows the magnitude of the areas of cytoplasmic background, as calculated from equatorial sections. The percentages of cytoplasmic background after elimination of the organelles as well as the percentages of the latter are listed according to age.

TABLE II. Magnitude of the Areas of Cytoplasmic Background and of Organelles in Growing Oocytes

Age (days)	Cytoplasmic background (%)	Organelles (%)	Cytoplasmic background (equatorial area in μm^2)
2	78,66	21,33	175
4–5	84,58	15,40	753
7–8	87,72	12,28	877
11	91,25	8,74	1623
14	92,78	7,22	4239
21	89,31	10,68	7426

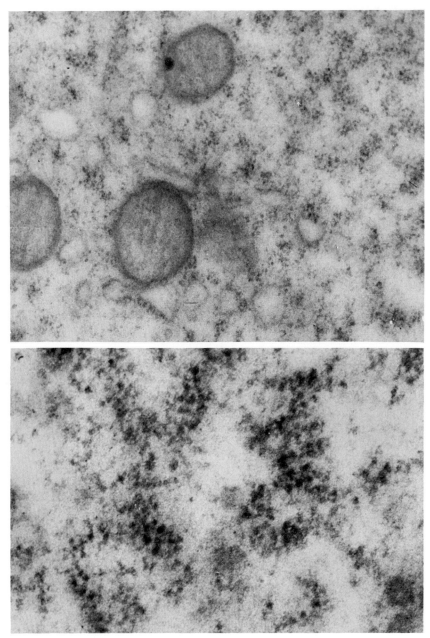

FIGS. 1 and 2. At 2 days postpartum, the oocyte cytoplasm shows a high ribosome density and polysomes formed of about 15–50 ribosomes. Figure 1 is a low-magnification picture (55,000×) in which the large number of these elements is obvious, whereas Fig. 2 illustrates polysome lengths (140,000×).

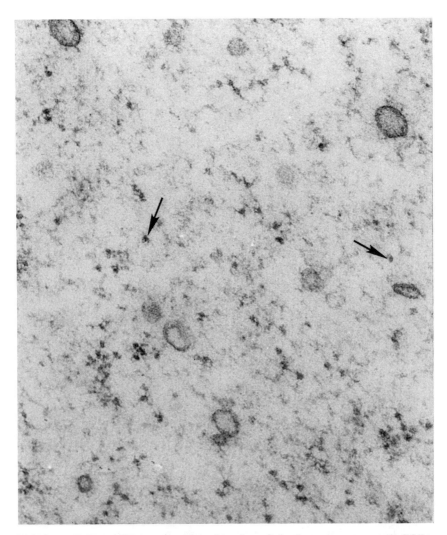

FIG. 3. *At diplotene–dictyate transition, the values of the three parameters studied fall to lower levels, and single ribosomes (arrows) are more numerous than in the preceding stage (>35%).* The figure shows a field in which single ribosomes predominate. The same conditions occur in primordial oocytes of later stages (4–5 days postpartum). (110,000×.)

Figure 5 expresses the relation between ribosome density and increase of cytoplasmic background. The hyperbolic curve shown ($r = 0.986$, $p < 0.01$) suggests that a "dilution" of the ribosome population occurs during the 21-day period of oocyte growth. However, if this curve is compared to a theoretical one calculated on the basis that the total number of ribosomes per oocyte remains constant during the same period, a significant difference between the two curves

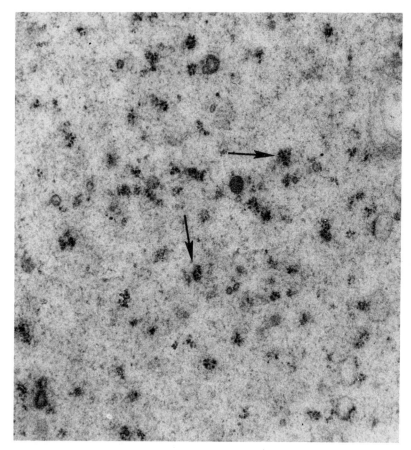

FIG. 4. *In growing oocytes, polysomes (arrows) are short (4–12 ribosomes) and are spaced in the cytoplasm.* Single ribosomes are nearly absent (<5%) (40,000×). The photographs of Figs. 1–4 were selected as representative of the four main stages studied: pachytene–diplotene, diplotene–dictyate, primordial, and growing oocytes.

is found (null hypothesis test: $t = 2.92, p < 0.05$). It is therefore inferred that an increase in the total number of ribosomes per oocyte has occurred during this growth period.

The total number of ribosomes forming polysomes (R in Fig. 6) is calculated in equatorial sections by multiplying the average number of ribosomes in polysomes per μm^2 by the area of cytoplasmic background recorded for each age. In Fig. 6, the R values are plotted against age. For the ages corresponding to the dictyate phase, growing and primordial oocytes are distinguished for comparison. The curves show (1) the decrease in the number of ribosomes in polysomes at the transition to dictyate, (2) the stability of this number in primordial oocytes, and (3) the increase of ribosomes during oocyte growth. At the last age recorded, this increase amounts to about eight times the initial value.

DISCUSSION

Some of the results of research using basophilia or ultraviolet absorption to recognize the distribution and content of RNA in the oocyte cytoplasm differ from those obtained by electron microscope recordings of the ribosome population. On

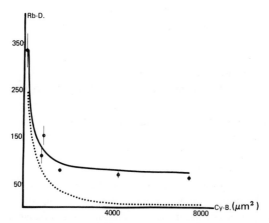

FIG. 5. *Pattern of ribosome density decrease vs. cytoplasmic background during oocyte growth.* Rb-D., Ribosome density; Cy-B., cytoplasmic background area. Solid line, Dilution pattern from recorded values. Rb-D. (rib./μm^2) = 65.997 + 4.77 (10^4 /area) ($r = 0.986, p <$ 0.01). Dotted line, Dilution pattern calculated on the basis of a constant ribosome population. Rb-D. (rib./μm^2) = 5.91 (10^4 /area). Null hypothesis test: $t = 2.92, p < 0.05$.

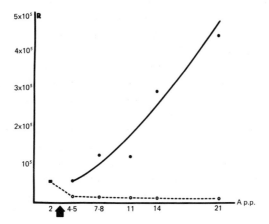

FIG. 6. *Total number of ribosomes forming polysomes.* R, Number of ribosomes in polysomes; A, animal age (days postpartum). ■, Pachytene–diplotene oocytes, ●, growing oocytes (first wave); ○, primordial oocytes; arrow, diplotene–dictyate transition.

the basis of the repartition of cytoplasmic basophilia, Dalcq (1950) and his colleagues (Jones-Seaton, 1950; de Geeter, 1954) hypothesized that differentiation of egg polarity is apparent before fertilization (growth period). This assumption was not substantiated by other researchers. For instance, Austin and Braden (1953) found that ultraviolet absorbance reaches similar levels in all parts of the oocyte cytoplasm. The observations reported in this chapter show that the distribution of ribosomes and polysomes in the cytoplasm is uniform at all stages of oocyte growth. In addition, a comparison of the intensity of cytoplasmic basophilia with the increase of protein synthesis activity demanded by cell growth has been done in the past. Jacoby (1962) summarized the reports published in this regard and, after analyzing the Ishida (1952), Hedberg (1953), and Dalcq (1955) papers concluded that "there appears to be a lack of uniformity among different species as regards the RNA-linked mechanism of protein increase in the growing oocyte." The RNA concentration was observed to decrease in some cases, to increase in others, or even to remain constant. It appears likely that the procedures employed or the samples used in each case were not the most adequate for an accurate evaluation.

Autoradiographic studies made by Oakberg (1968) suggest that rRNA synthesis occurs all along oocyte growth, that is, up to the onset of antrum formation. The pattern of incorporation and movement of labeled uridine found by Baker *et al.* (1969) using electron microscope autoradiography seems to be similar to the one reported by Oakberg.

The line of investigation followed in the present study is based on the fact that the rates of protein synthesis in eukaryotic cells can be correlated with the ribosomal–polysomal profiles in precise phases of the cell cycle. Part of this research was done on somatic cells of various origins (cultured mouse fibroblasts, Zetterberg and Killander, 1965; frog pepsinogenic cells, van Venrooij *et al.*, 1973; mouse liver cells, Mellet, 1973), part on eggs of echinoderms at prefertilization and/or early development (Hultin and Morris, 1968; Rinaldi and Monroy, 1969; Mirkes, 1972), and part on slime mold spores (Feit *et al.*, 1971). At this point, it is pertinent to state that when protein synthesis is correlated with the ribosome population, it must be evaluated by taking into account two specific parameters: the ribosome content (called "ribosomal capacity") and the readout velocities of polysomes (called "ribosomal efficiency"). Data have been reported which suggest that changes in the rate of protein synthesis can take place by variations in the readout velocities only (rat liver cells, von der Decken, 1967; rat skeletal muscle, Millward *et al.*, 1973). In addition, the possibility of the existence, in the cell model studied, of an inactive form of polysomes (supposedly kept as storage or reserve of "masked" mRNAs for further use) must be taken into consideration. It has been claimed that these inactive polysomal structures occur in the sea urchin egg (Spirin and Nemer, 1965) and in the *Ascaris* egg (Kaulenas and Fairbairn, 1966).

Electron microscope research carried out by Burkholder *et al.* (1971) on whole-mount preparations of preovulatory mice oocytes showed that a lattice-like structure exists in their cytoplasm. Cytochemical tests performed on this material indicated that part of the constituents of the lattice are sensitive to RNase. In consequence, the authors suggested that this kind of structural organization may represent a highly ordered aggregate of ribosomes. They also suggested that this material may be a storage form of preprogrammed ribosomes to be used during early development. In the material studied for the investigation reported here, whorled bundles of filaments of low electron density were observed. They occurred in oocytes long before ovulation could have taken place (12–14 days postpartum). Weakley (1967, 1968) found ordered structures (reported in the form of lamellae) in the golden hamster. Vázquez-Nin and Sotelo (1967) described the occurrence of ordered lamellae in oocytes (supposed to be atretic) of rats aged 6–60 days postpartum. These structures were less frequently found in animals older than 30 days postpartum. Following the studies of Mazanec and Dvorák (1963), who stated that elements of this kind might be polysomes, Dvorák *et al.* (1972) found lamellae in oocytes and segmenting eggs of rats. In contrast to these studies, Sotelo and Porter (1959) found them neither in oocytes of adult animals nor in segmenting eggs. Enzymatic tests were not carried out on these structures (except those described by Burkholder *et al.*, 1971).

It is obvious that morphological examination (as in the present investigation) provides data on the so-called ribosomal capacity only. Whether the numerical data collected are representative of real values depends on the procedure used. It seems clear that the more reliable technique would be serial sectioning and serial recording of cells. However, as serial recording of large cells (diameter greater than 50 μm) involves a considerable amount of work, it was decided to use electron micrographic montages covering significant areas of oocyte cytoplasm. The main condition facilitating this approach is that ribosomes, as well as the polysomes formed by their aggregation, occur evenly in the cytoplasm. Therefore, the statistical analysis based on these counts is considered reliable.

Assuming that the methodological approach correctly represents the real values of the selected parameters, Fig. 6 expresses the variations of the so-called ribosomal capacity. According to this proposition, the progressive increase in the total number of ribosomes forming polysomes during oocyte growth may be interpreted as a response necessary to support the rise in synthetic activity demanded by the building up of cytoplasm. It is important to stress that the fall in ribosome–polysome values, which seems to occur at the transition to dictyate, implies a significant functional change in the cell program. It is not known how the cell program becomes changed, or which factor triggers the change at transition to dictyate. As a hypothesis to be tested in further studies, it can be suggested that different mRNAs are in translation prior to and during dictyate.

The fall in polysome lengths at the beginning of dictyate is, at present, the only detectable morphological sign that makes this hypothesis tenable. The starting point selected for this investigation (2 days postpartum) permitted the detection of this change. After dictyate, two different oocyte populations separate neatly, and the separation occurs coincidently with the fall. The ribosome content and distribution remain stabilized in primordial oocytes at the levels attained at the fall and contrast with the progressive increase as shown by the curve obtained from growing oocytes. It is assumed that when each primordial oocyte starts to grow at a later period of life, its own curve must parallel those observed in prepubertal oocyte growth.

It has been observed that eukaryotic cells contain a pool of single ribosomes. Kabat and Rich (1969) provided evidence that this pool does not participate in the protein synthesis cycle. They suggested that single ribosomes may be a storage site of mRNAs, which may be reincorporated to form active polysomes. They also suggested that the cycling of ribosome particles involved in protein synthesis occurs as a ribosome subunit–polysome cycle, as it has been reported to occur in bacteria (Algranati *et al.*, 1973). In relation to this point, it is noted that a large number of single ribosomes is one of the characteristics of primordial oocytes. Whether these ribosomes correspond to a pool similar to the one claimed by Kabat and Rich is yet to be determined. As a matter of fact, in standard electron micrographs of thin-sectioned cells, it is not possible to recognize units other than the 200–240 Å electron-dense particles, currently defined by electron microscopists as single ribosomes. Nevertheless, the possibility of the existence of smaller particles (subunits) cannot be discarded.

The present electron microscope study can be compared with earlier investigations on the distribution of the so-called cytoplasmic RNA in mammalian oocytes. It has been stated that there is no agreement as to whether RNA concentration increases, decreases, or remains constant during oocyte growth. The main point in this discussion is that the constancy or the decrease in RNA concentration does not match the rise of protein synthesis activity demanded during oocyte growth (see Jacoby, 1962). The discrepancy, however, may be more apparent than real and can be attributed to different factors. On the one hand, different species may show different patterns of oocyte growth, which means a different timing in RNA turnover and protein synthesis; on the other hand, the criterion used in the 1950s was to directly correlate the variations of RNA concentration (as recognized by staining or ultraviolet absorbance) and protein synthesis activity. Figure 5 shows a "dilution" of the ribosome concentration (decrease of the ribosome density) that, at first view, might seem parallel to the decrease in the "cytoplasmic RNA" concentration reported by earlier researchers. However, the same data indicate that the total number of ribosomes per oocyte increases during oocyte growth.

SUMMARY

Oocytes of prepubertal mice (2–21 days postpartum) were taken as a model to study the distribution of ribosomes during cell growth. Electron microscope techniques, involving the mapping of oocytes at magnifications ranging from 60,000 to 80,000X, were used to determine the following parameters: ribosome density per μm^2 of cytoplasm, global percentage of ribosomes forming polysomes, and minimum and maximum values of polysome lengths. The values of each parameter were plotted against oocyte size and age.

The curves obtained indicate that (1) the values of the three parameters fall to a lower level at the diplotene–dictyate transition period; (2) after the first phase of growth, the total number of ribosomes per oocyte increases, and the percentage of ribosomes in polysomes increases as well, with polysome lengths being the same as in early dictyate, (3) the ribosome population of primordial oocytes does not show changes while they are in a quiescent state.

Comparison of these data suggests that (1) mRNAs active at late diplotene differ from those active at advanced periods of growth and (2) the increase in the total number of ribosomes forming polysomes during oocyte growth may represent the morphological expression of a progressive rise in protein synthesis.

ACKNOWLEDGMENT

We are indebted to R. Wettstein for critical reading of this paper.

REFERENCES

Algranati, I. D., Gonzalez, N. S., Garcia-Patrone, M., Perazzolo, C. A., and Azam, M. E. (1973), The ribosome cycle in bacteria, in: *Gene Expression and Its Regulation* (Proceedings of the Eleventh International Latin American Symposium), pp. 327–338 (F. T. Kenney, B. A. Hamkalo, G. Favelukes, and J. T. August, eds.), Plenum Press, New York.

Austin, C. R., and Braden, A. W. H. (1953), The distribution of nucleic acids in rat eggs in fertilization and early segmentation. I. Studies on living eggs by ultraviolet microscopy, *Aust. J. Exp. Biol. Med. Sci. 6:*324–333.

Baker, T. G., Beaumont, H. M., and Franchi, L. L. (1969), The uptake of tritiated uridine and phenylalanine by the ovaries of rats and monkeys, *J. Cell Sci. 4:*655–675.

Boynton, J. E., Gillha, N. W., and Chabot, J. F. (1972), Chloroplast ribosome deficient mutants in the green alga, *Chlamydomonas reinhardi,* and the question of chloroplast ribosome function, *J. Cell Sci. 10:*267–305.

Brachet, J. (1950), *Chemical Embryology* (translated by L. G. Barth), Interscience, New York.

Brachet, J. (1957), *Biochemical Cytology,* Academic Press, New York.

Burkholder, G. D., Comings, D. E., and Okada, T. A. (1971), A storage form of ribosomes in mouse oocytes, *Exp. Cell Res. 69:*361–371.

Dalcq, A. M. (1950), The morphogenetic organization of the oocyte and follicle in some mammals, including man, in: *International Anatomy Congress,* Oxford, pp. 49–50 (abst.).

Dalcq, A. M. (1953), Fixation de l'oeuf des mammiféres et répartition, dans celui-ci, des acides ribonucléiques, *C.R. Soc. Biol. (Paris) 147:*1259–1261.

Dalcq, A. M. (1955), Processes of synthesis during early development of rodent's eggs and embryos, *Stud. Fertil. 7:*113–122.

Davidson, E. H. (1968), *Gene Activity in Early Development,* Academic Press, New York.

de Geeter, L. (1954), Etudes sur la structure de l'oeuf vierge et les prémiers stades du developpement chez le cobaye et le lapin, *Arch. Biol. (Paris) 65:*363–436.

Dvorák, M., Kukletova, M., and Stastna, J. (1972), Ultrastructure and occurrence of lamellar structures in ovarian and segmenting ova in rat, *Scr. Med. 45:*35–45.

Feit, I. N., Chu, L. K., and Iverson, R. M. (1971), Appearance of polyribosomes during germination of spores in cellular slime mold, *Dyctiostelium purpureum, Exp. Cell Res. 65:*439–444.

Hedberg, F. (1953), The chemical composition of the human ovarian oocyte, *Acta Endocrinol. (Copenhagen) (suppl. 15) 14:*1–89.

Hultin, T., and Morris, J. E. (1968), The ribosomes of encysted embryos of *Artemia salina* during cryptobiosis and resumption of development, *Develop. Biol. 17:*143–164.

Ishida, K. (1952), Histochemical studies of rat ova with special reference to glycogen of them after ovulation, *Tohoku J. Ag. Res. 4:*133–139.

Jacoby, F. (1962), Ovarian histochemistry, in: *The Ovary,* Vol. I, pp. 189–245 (Sir Solly Zuckerman, ed.), Academic Press, New York.

Jones-Seaton, A. (1950), Étude de l'organisation cytoplasmique de l'oeuf des rongeurs, principalement quant á la basophilie ribonucléique, *Arch. Biol. (Paris) 61:*291–444.

Kabat, D., and Rich, A. (1969), The ribosomal subunit–polyribosome cycle in protein synthesis of embryonic skeletal muscle, *Biochemistry 8:*3742–3749.

Kaulenas, M. S., and Fairbairn, D. (1966), Ribonuclease-stable polysomes in the egg of *Ascaris lumbricoides, Develop. Biol. 14:*481–490.

Mazanec, K., and Dvorák, M. (1963), On the submicroscopical changes in the segmenting ovum in the albino rat, *Cs. Morfol. 11:*103–108.

Mellet, J. (1973), Étude de l'effectif ribosomique du foie chez la souris normale et chez la souris naine, *Biochimie 55:*189–194.

Millward, D. J., Garlick, P. J., James, W. P. T., Nnanyelugo, D. O., and Ryatt, J. S. (1973), Relationship between protein synthesis and RNA content in skeletal muscle, *Nature (Lond.) 241:*204–205.

Mirkes, P. E. (1972), Polysomes and protein synthesis during development of *Ilyanassa obsoleta, Exp. Cell Res. 74:*503–508.

Oakberg, E. F. (1968), Relationship between stage of follicular development and RNA synthesis in the mouse oocyte, *Mutat. Res. 6:*155–165.

Perl, W. (1964), Correction of polyribosome distributions as observed in cell sections by electron microscopy, *J. Cell Biol. 22:*613–621.

Rifkind, R. A., Danon, D., and Marks, P. A. (1964), Alterations in polyribosomes during erythroid cell maturation, *J. Cell Biol. 22:*599–611.

Rinaldi, A. M., and Monroy, A. (1969), Polyribosome formation and RNA synthesis in the early postfertilization stages of the sea urchin egg, *Develop. Biol. 19:*73–86.

Sotelo, J. R., and Porter, K. R. (1959), An electron microscope study of rat ovum, *J. Biophys. Biochem. Cytol. 5:*327–342.

Spirin, A. S., and Nemer, M. (1965), Messenger RNA in early sea urchin embryos: Cytoplasmic particles, *Science 150:*214–217.

van der Stricht, O. (1923), Étude comparée des ovules des mammiféres aux différentes périodes de l'ovogénése d'aprés les travaux du Laboratoire d'Histologie et d'Embryologie de l'Université de Gand, *Arch. Biol. (Liége) 33:*229–300.

van Venrooij, W. J., Poort, C., and Geuze, J. J. (1973), The effects of fasting and feeding in the protein synthesis rate and polyribosomal profile of frog pepsinogenic cells, *J. Cell Sci. 12:*903–909.

Vazquez-Nin, G. H., and Sotelo, J. R. (1967), Electron microscope study of the atretic oocytes of the rat, *Z. Zellforsch. 80:*518–533.

Vincent, W. S., and Dornfeld, E. J. (1948), Localization and role of nucleic acids in the developing rat ovary, *Amer. J. Anat. 83:*437–469.

von der Decken, A. (1967), Evidence for regulation of protein synthesis at the translation level in response to dietary alterations, *J. Cell. Biol. 33:*657–663.

Warner, J. R., Knopf, P. M., and Rich, A. (1963), A multiple ribosomal structure in protein synthesis, *Proc. Natl. Acad. Sci. (U.S.A.) 49:*122–129.

Weakley, B. S. (1967), Investigations into the structure and fixation properties of cytoplasmic lamellae in the hamster oocyte, *Z. Zellforsch. 81:*91–99.

Weakley, B. S. (1968), Comparison of cytoplasmic lamellae and membranous elements in the oocytes of five mammalian species, *Z. Zellforsch, 85:*109–123.

Wettstein, F. O., Staehelin, T., and Noll, H. (1963), Ribosomal aggregate engaged in protein synthesis. Characterization of the ergosome, *Nature (Lond.) 197:*430–435.

Zetterberg, A., and Killander, D. (1965), Quantitative cytophotometric and autoradiographic studies on the rate of protein synthesis during interphase in mouse fibroblasts *in vitro, Exp. Cell Res. 40:*1–11.

21

Follicular Maturation, Ovulation, Luteinization and Menstruation in the Baboon

Nobuyoshi Hagino

Department of Neurophysiology
Southwest Foundation for Research and Education

and

Department of Anatomy
University of Texas
Health Science Center at San Antonio
San Antonio, Texas

The baboon is a spontaneously ovulating animal; length of the menstrual cycle and ovarian function are similar to those in the human (Ross *et al.*, 1970), with an average cycle length of approximately 30 days. In the baboon (Fig. 1), changes in the perineal sex skin are a convenient indicator of ovarian activity (Gillman, 1940). The swelling of perineal sex skin increases to a maximum after menstruation, remains until ovulation, and declines approximately 2 days after ovulation. The perineal sex skin remains in a quiescent stage until the next menstruation. Vaginal epithelial cornification appears at both the ovulatory phase (Hagino and Goldzieher, 1970; Hendrickx, 1971) and the premenstrual phase (beginning 3 days before menstruation); however, there is no complete vaginal cornification during the early follicular phase or quiescent stage.

An experimental approach to the physiology of menstruation dates from the observation of Allen (1927) that uterine bleeding occurs in castrated monkeys following the discontinuance of estrogen treatment. The mechanism of estrogen withdrawal or estrogen deprivation in induction of menstruation in experimental animals has been reviewed by Hisaw and Hisaw (1961). In the baboon, the plasma concentration of estrogens is lower during menstruation; the plasma concentration of progestins is also lower (Fig. 2).

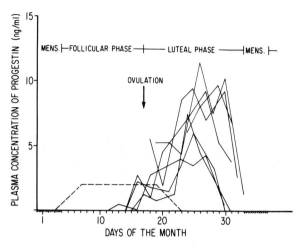

FIG. 1. Plasma concentration of progestins in seven baboons. The plasma progestins rise during the ovulatory stage and during the luteal phase and decline at the time of menstruation (Mens.). Vertical axis represents plasma concentration of progestins (ng/ml) and horizontal axis represents days of the month. The changes of perineal sex skin are shown on the horizontal axis by a dashed line. The swelling of perineal sex skin increases to a maximum after menstruation, remains until ovulation, and declines approximately 2 days after ovulation. The perineal sex skin remains in a quiescent stage until the next menstruation. Plasma concentration of progestins remains undetectable or less than 0.5 ng/ml between menstruation and the preovulatory stage.

Removal of the baboon corpus luteum immediately after luteinization (2 or 3 days after ovulation) advances the onset of the following menstruation; however, after injections of 5 mg progesterone the regular length of the luteal period is maintained. Furthermore, removal of corpus luteum after the midluteal phase does not advance the following menstruation (Hagino and Goldzieher, 1970). In castrated monkeys, progesterone induces uterine bleeding at intervals of about 8 days, provided the treatment is started immediately after menstrual bleeding has been induced either by removal of the ovaries or by withdrawal of estrogen or progesterone (Krohn, 1951). This also applies to progesterone-withdrawal bleeding in the baboon. Sufficient progesterone may be present to induce menstruation even in the absence of ovulation, and this progesterone may arise from extraovarian sources, such as the adrenal cortex (Venning and Browne, 1937). A possible explanation for periodic bleeding in monkeys on a constant submaintenance dose of estrogen may be the influence of progesterone from the adrenal cortex (Zuckerman, 1941).

Administration of desoxycorticosterone in large doses can inhibit estrogen-withdrawal bleeding in castrated monkeys (Zuckerman, 1951) and induce phases of uterine bleeding in rapid succession in normal monkeys (Krohn, 1951).

A single injection of 4 mg triamcinolone acetonide (a synthetic corticosteroid) at the time of menstruation advances the onset of the following menstruation in the baboon. After injections of triamcinolone at menses for two to seven consecutive cycles, the cycle length remains quite consistent and regular. By contrast, injection of 50 mg cortisol has no effect (Fig. 3) (Hagino, 1972). Injection of triamcinolone at menses suppresses the plasma concentration of progestins as well as estrogens (except in two of five baboons studied which showed an extremely high value of plasma estrogens); however, in this situation, menstruation occurs an average of 15 days after injection (Table I).

Following appropriate treatment with HMG, a dose of LH induces ovulation in hypophysectomized women, but menstruation occurs 5 or 6 days after administration of LH (Vande Wiele *et al.*, 1970). In triamcinolone-treated baboons, injections of 300 μg LHRH (LH-releasing hormone) for 4 days immediately after menstruation release LH and cause menstrual flow 7 or 8 days after the last injection.

The periodicity (biorhythm) of sleep and wakefulness is a synchronized phenomenon of interoceptive activity and exteroceptive factors. This interoceptive activity can be dependent on either the intrinsic rhythm of individual cell activity or the rhythmic activation of the central nervous system, including the

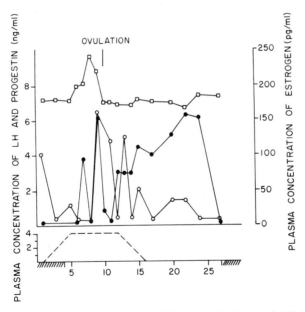

FIG. 2. Plasma concentrations of estrogens (□), progestins (●), and LH (○) during the menstrual cycle in the baboon. Vertical axes represent the plasma concentrations of estrogens (right) and progestins and LH (left). Horizontal axis represents days in menstrual cycle. Dotted line represents degree of turgescence of perineal sex skin. Menstruation is indicated by shaded areas on horizontal axis.

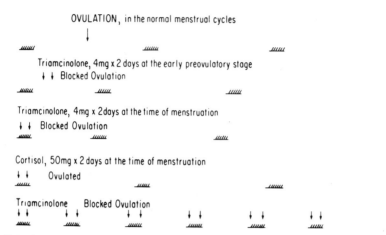

FIG. 3. A summary of the experiments. Menstruation (shaded areas) occurs regularly in about a 30-day period. Ovulation in the normal menstrual cycle occurs in the middle of the cycle. Administration of 4 mg triamcinolone for 2 days at the early preovulatory stage blocks ovulation and advances the onset of the next menstruation. Furthermore, the same regimen at the time of menstruation also blocks ovulation and advances the onset of the next menstruation. However, the second following menstrual cycle after treatment appears normal. Administration of 50 mg cortisol for 2 days at the time of menstruation does not interfere with ovulation and the menstrual cycle. The last line shows that administration of 4 mg triamcinolone for 2 days at the time of six consecutive menses blocks ovulation. However, the actual length of the menstrual cycle is regular.

TABLE I. Effect of Triamcinolone Treatment (4 mg/baboon) on Plasma Concentrations of Estrogens and Progestins

Animal No.		Plasma concentrations of estrogens (pg/ml) and progestins (ng/ml) measured every other day from menses to menses				
1	Estrogens	0	0	0	0	0
	Progestins	0.5	0.5	0.5	0.5	0.5
2	Estrogens	0	0	0	0	0
	Progestins	0.5	0.5	0.5	0.5	0.5
3	Estrogens	459	540	0	0	
	Progestins	0.5	0.5	0.5	0.5	
4	Estrogens	0	259	462	171	
	Progestins	0.5	0.9	2.3	0.9	
5	Estrogens	386	465	556	539	427
	Progestins	0.5	0.5	0.5	0.5	0.5

autonomic nervous system. The hypothalamic outflow to the peripheral autonomic nervous system through the reticular formation in the brain stem is also
responsible for interoceptive activity, such as endocrine function. The endocrine
feedback action is known to have a regulatory effect on the hypothalamic
outflow (Sawyer, 1970) and may be responsible for the appearance and periodicity of paradoxical sleep (Kawakami and Sawyer, 1959). Therefore, the periodicity (biorhythm) of sleep and wakefulness may correspond to the periodicity of
gonadotropin secretion, while pituitary hormones regulate the biorhythm of
sleep and wakefulness (Kawakami *et al.*, 1972).

Under a controlled lighting schedule (light on at 5 A.M. and off at 7 P.M.),
baboons show circadian variation of EEG slow wave sleep and paradoxical sleep
with the peak of sleep at midnight (Hagino and Yamaoka, 1974). The special
appearance of EEG paradoxical sleep during the daytime increases at menstruation and ovulation (Fig. 4). Two major elevations in the plasma concentration of
LH have been found at the times of menstruation and ovulation in the baboon
(Fig. 2) and the rhesus monkey (Niswender and Spies, 1973).

Increased plasma concentration of LH appears to be correlated with EEG
paradoxical sleep in the daytime and appears at an average of 15-day intervals in
30-day menstrual cycles; in addition, injection of triamcinolone at consecutive
menses induces an average 15-day anovulatory menstrual cycle in the baboon
(Hagino, 1972). These facts imply that the autonomic nervous system may have
an important role in the regulation of menstruation; spinal transection induces
menstruation (Markee *et al.*, 1936) and hypothalamic surgery of preopticotuber-

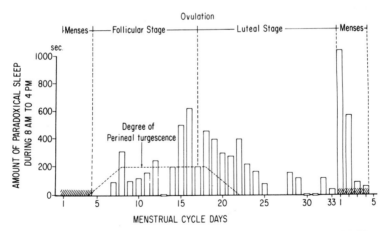

*FIG. 4. The appearance of paradoxical sleep during daytime (8 A.M. to 4 P.M.) in the
baboon under a controlled lighting schedule (light on at 5 A.M. and off at 7 P.M.).* Vertical
axis represents the amount of paradoxical sleep during 8 A.M. to 4 P.M. Horizontal axis
represents menstrual cycle days. Dotted line represents degree of turgescence of perineal sex
skin. Menstruation is indicated by shaded areas.

al efferents produces amenorrhea with persistent vaginal cornification in the baboon (unpublished data).

It may be reasonably hypothesized that the normal menstrual cycle is primarily under the control of ovarian estrogens and progestins; it is equally clear that menstruation does not result from a specific hormonal action.

FOLLICULAR DEVELOPMENT

The swelling of perineal sex skin begins shortly after menstruation. Inspection of the ovary by laparoscopy shows that follicular maturation can be recognized shortly after menstruation and progresses visibly until ovulation. The plasma concentration of total estrogens begins to rise shortly after menstruation and continues to increase until the time of LH release (Fig. 2). In our study, we found the peak of plasma estrogens to appear prior to the LH peak in three of six baboons, at the same time in two baboons, but 24 h afterward in one baboon. In addition, the plasma concentration of estrogen declines within 48 h. This finding is similar to the results of Mishell *et al.* (1971).

The plasma concentration of progestins rises 24 h prior to LH release, and the peak of plasma progestins appears after the LH peak and declines within 24

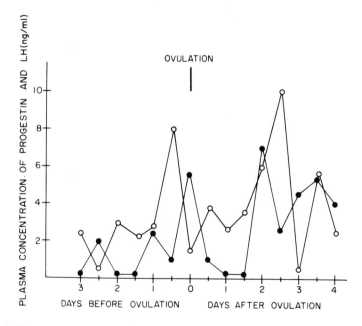

FIG. 5. *Plasma concentrations of progestins (●) and LH (○) at the midcycle ovulatory stage.* Blood samples were collected daily at 8 A.M. and 3 P.M. Vertical axis represents the plasma concentrations of progestins and LH. Horizontal axis represents days before ovulation (O) and days after ovulation.

TABLE II. Effect of Laparoscopic Surgery on Plasma Concentrations of Progestins and LH

Animal No.	Plasma LH or progestins	Day prior to operation	Minutes after general anesthesia		Time after abdominal incision		
			10	40	30 min	60 min	24 h
1439	Progestins	6.1	6.0	19.2	19.8	8.7	8.0
	LH	1.3	1.0	1.0	4.0	7.5	1.0
S728	Progestins	–	4.0	43.3	32.3	42.9	6.5
	LH	3.2	1.0	5.0	4.0	9.5	1.8
4247	Progestins	3.5	4.8	4.0	4.5	3.0	4.0
	LH	3.7	–	5.5	3.7	15.5	1.3

Plasma concentrations of progestins (ng/ml) and LH (ng/ml)

h (Fig. 5). Ovarian vein blood contains a higher concentration of 17-OH-progesterone prior to LH release (Strott et al., 1969), and, further, surgical stress facilitates the increase in plasma progestins prior to LH release (Table II). Adrenal progestin plays an important role in the time sequence of LH release in female rats (Hagino et al., 1973a, 1973b).

One day prior to ovulation, the blood supply at the surface of the follicle increases, except in a small avascular region near the central portion of the follicle wall which protrudes from the ovary. This region is surrounded by a fine network of small vessels which evidently corresponds to the stigma. At this stage in the ovarian cycle, the estrogens remain high or begin to decline, and plasma LH reaches a maximum. In addition, plasma progestins remain low. Rupture of the follicle occurs 10–24 h after the LH peak (Yussman and Taymor, 1970), and release of the ovum through the small avascular region is associated with degenerative changes in the collagen of the follicular wall (Espey, 1967). On the following day, stigma and luteinization can be recognized. The swelling of perineal sex skin begins to decline and plasma progestins begin to increase (Fig. 1).

With the above information in mind, an attempt was made to rationalize the correlation of circulating hypothalamic hormone (LHRH) with LH release in the baboon. This experiment was performed in conjunction with Dr. A. Arimura, Endocrine and Polypeptide Laboratory, VA Hospital, New Orleans, Louisiana. The distribution peak of administered LHRH reaches a maximum within 4 min during the follicular or luteal phase (Fig. 6), which is comparable to that in humans (Keye et al., 1973). When baboons receive 100 μg LHRH subcutaneously, the disappearance of LHRH in plasma ($t1/2 = 4.7$ min) is also comparable to that in humans.

Significant differences in the response of pituitary LH release to administered LHRH exist between baboons in the follicular development stage and
those in the luteal phase. Injection of 100 μg LHRH does not facilitate LH
release immediately in the follicular phase, but does facilitate LH release in the
luteal phase. However, injection of 200 μg LHRH during follicular development
does tend to elicit pituitary release of LH. In the human, similar differences in
response of pituitary LH release to LHRH exist between the follicular development stage and luteal phase (Nillius and Wide, 1971; Yen *et al.,* 1972a). The first
peak in plasma concentration of LH is concomitant with the plasma concentration of exogenously administered LHRH, but the second peak appears 15 min
after LHRH injection (Fig. 6). The first peak of plasma LH is elicited by a

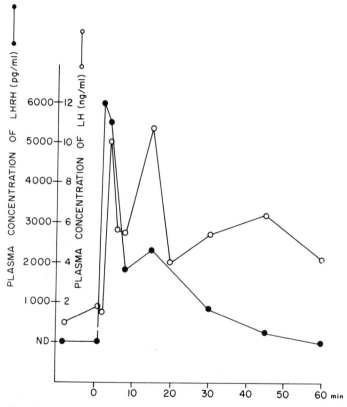

FIG. 6. *Correlation of plasma concentration of exogenously administered 100 μg LHRH (●)
with the plasma concentration of LH (○) in a normal adult female baboon (No. 0161) in the
luteal phase.* Vertical axes represent the plasma concentration of administered LHRH and
the plasma of LH. Horizontal axis represents minutes before and after administration of
LHRH.

TABLE III. Effect of LHRH on LH Release

Stage of ovarian cycle	Animal No.	Before LHRH injection	Plasma concentration of LH after LHRH injection (ng/ml)							
			15 min	30 min	45 min	60 min	90 min	120 min	180 min	24 h
Follicle	0269	1.1	11.5	1.1	5.0	2.5	3.3	7.5	11.5	3.5
	2567	3.2	6.5	7.5	8.0	8.5	13.5	1.1	2.5	5.5
Preovulatory	0269	5.0	16.5	21.0	23.0	4.0	25.5	27.5	16.0	1.5
	2656	4.0	5.0	7.0	14.0	6.0	23.0	12.5	9.0	4.0
Luteal	0260	1.3	6.3	2.4	11.5	7.5	12.0	12.0	1.7	1.1
	2567	2.3	15.0	8.0	4.5	4.3	11.5	10.5	4.1	2.3
	2656	3.4	2.1	3.5	4.0	2.8	14.0	2.6	1.1	1.1

sufficient concentration of plasma LHRH, but the second peak may be elicited by the effect of an accumulation of administered LHRH in the plasma. A third LH peak appears within 90 or 120 min, even though the injected LHRH has already disappeared within 60 min (Table III). In the LHRH-injected group, as well as the saline-injected group, plasma concentrations of estrogens and progestins are increased (Table IV). Since the technique of radioimmunoassay for plasma LHRH used in this study does not detect endogenous LHRH, the effect of exogenous LHRH on endogenous LHRH secretion cannot be substantiated. A possible explanation for the increased plasma concentration of LH within 90 or 120 min after LHRH injection may be that the effect of circulating estrogens and progestins on the pituitary is increased by exposure to exogenous LHRH. Saline injection does not result in a third LH peak, even though plasma concentrations of estrogens and progestins are increased.

The rhesus monkey is relatively insensitive to administered LHRH (Arimura et al., 1973; Ehara et al., 1972); nevertheless, pituitary LH does respond to LHRH when it is administered at the ovulatory phase (Arimura et al., 1974; Krey et al., 1973). These results suggest that endogenous LHRH and circulating estrogens and progestins exert their effect on the pituitary together with exogenously administered LHRH to facilitate LH release.

After injection of 2 mg triamcinolone at menstruation, perceptible follicular maturation begins an average of 13 days after onset of the menstrual flow. Two days before deturgescence of the perineal sex skin, the follicle does not show the full maturation normally observed. Two days after deturgescence, stigma formation and luteinization are not observed and plasma progestins are suppressed (Table V).

In baboons, injection of 100 μg LHRH at the follicular phase increases the

TABLE IV. Effect of 100 μg LHRH on Plasma Concentration of Estrogens

Stage of ovarian cycle	Animal No.	Before LHRH injection	Plasma concentration of estrogens after LHRH injection (pg/ml)							
			15 min	30 min	45 min	60 min	90 min	120 min	180 min	24 h
Follicular phase	0269	94	115	121	119	105.5	136	147.5	149.5	100
	2656	110	126.5	145	114	109	122.5	120.5	109.0	–
Preovulatory phase	0269	133.5	132	138	133	137	143	143	151.5	105
	2656	285	235	120	241	271	246	226	245	184
Luteal phase	0269	101	113	101	118.5	134.5	117.5	106.5	124	128.5
	2656	159	150	81.5	155	156.5	140	193.5	201.5	137.5

plasma concentration of estrogens (Table IV). In addition, LHRH is known to release FSH in experimental animals (Monahan *et al.*, 1971; Schally *et al.*, 1971) and man (Kastin *et al.*, 1972; Yen *et al.*, 1972b). Subcutaneous injections of 300 μg LHRH for 4 days immediately after menstruation do not override the blockade of follicular maturation by triamcinolone. However, treatment with this regimen causes menstruation immediately and resets a new menstrual cycle (follicular and luteal phase). Because of this situation, only two of five baboons were found to ovulate during the following cycle, judged by plasma concentrations of progestins, but three other baboons maintained regular follicular and luteal phases.

A possible explanation for the reset of new follicle maturation by LHRH administration may be the facilitation of atresia in presently maturing follicles and/or the initiation of follicle maturation in other resting follicles. In the human, injection of estrogens at an early follicular phase facilitates LH release and may reset new follicle maturation (Yen and Tsai, 1972). The details need to be investigated further.

These results imply that the onset of follicular maturation may begin its sequence at the time of menstruation; therefore, disruption or delay of follicular development at menses alters the time schedule of follicular maturation and subsequently causes an atresic follicle.

TABLE V. Effect of Triamcinolone Treatment (2 mg/ baboon) on Plasma Progestins

Animal No.	Treatment regimen	Plasma concentration of progestins (ng/ml) measured every other day from expected ovulation to menstruation				
1	Control	1.8	8.5	9.5	7.0	2.5
	Triamcinolone[a]	0.5	0.5	0.5	0.5	0.5
2	Control	1.6	7.1	5.0	1.8	0.5
	Triamcinolone	0.5	0.5	2.4	2.2	0.5
3	Control	2.3	4.5	2.3	4.7	0.5
	Triamcinolone	1.5	3.0	3.3	2.8	0.5
4	Control	1.8	2.3	2.0	3.1	2.6
	Triamcinolone	0.5	0.5	0.5	0.5	0.5
5	Control	1.8	5.5	7.9	1.4	1.3
	Triamcinolone	1.4	7.8	0.5	0.8	0.5
6	Control	6.8	8.3	5.9	5.2	4.1
	Triamcinolone	3.8	2.7	2.9	0.5	0.5

[a] 2 mg of triamcinolone acetonide was given at the time of menstruation.

OVULATION

A definite criterion for ovulation is the recognition of an ovum. In our study, we observed an ovum in flushed solution in only two of ten baboons, even though eight other baboons showed normal stigma and corpus luteum formation at laparotomy. Therefore, the following criteria have been proposed for detection of ovulation in the baboon:

1. Recognition of regular changes of perineal sex skin and observation of menstrual cycles.
2. Recognition of cervical secretion and vaginal cornification.
3. Determination of elevated plasma LH for approximately 3 days at midcycle.
4. Observation of stigma and corpus luteum.
5. Characteristic distribution of plasma concentration of progestins in the luteal phase.

The daily changes in perineal sex skin and vaginal smear, together with the concentrations of plasma LH and/or progestins, provide a presumptive indicator of ovulation. Observation of the stigma and/or corpus luteum by laparotomy or laparoscopy is required to confirm ovulation.

In normally cycling female baboons, inspection of the ovary by frequent laparoscopy shows that follicular maturation can be recognized shortly after menstruation and progresses visibly until ovulation. Stigma formation as well as luteinization is found the following day.

In triamcinolone-treated baboons (2 mg injected at menstruation), frequent laparoscopic examination shows that perceptible follicular maturation appears an average of 13 days after onset of menstrual flow. Two days before deturgescence of the perineal sex skin, the follicle does not show the full maturation normally observed. However, at the time of deturgescence both stigma and luteinization are observed by laparoscopy. Judging from the plasma concentration of progestins, these baboons show normal luteinization. This is inconsistent with previous results which indicate that injection of triamcinolone at menses blocks ovulation and luteinization.

In triamcinolone-treated baboons, when laparoscopic surgery is performed only once at the stage of deturgescence (after expected ovulation), stigma and corpus luteum formation are not observed. Laparoscopic surgery tends to increase the plasma concentrations of progestins and LH (Table II).

The possible explanation of induction of ovulation by laparoscopic surgery in triamcinolone-treated baboons may be facilitation of LH release by surgical stress (Aono et al., 1972; Carstensen et al., 1973). Therefore, frequent examination of the ovary by laparoscopy is not an adequate method to detect the time sequence of ovulation in primates and man.

LUTEINIZATION

In the baboon, the plasma concentration of progestins rises before the LH surge and ovulation. However, plasma progestins decline at the time of ovulation. Another progestin peak appears after ovulation (Fig. 5), and consequently a postovulatory LH peak also appears (TABLE VI). Following the postovulatory LH peak, plasma progestins continue to increase until the midluteal phase and decline at the time of premenstruation (beginning 3 days before menstruation). In the baboon, like the monkey (Knobil, 1973; Stabenfeldt and Hendrickx, 1972), plasma progesterone rises only after ovulation.

A dose of human pituitary LH induces ovulation in hypophysectomized women under appropriate pretreatment with HMG (Vande Wiele *et al.*, 1970), but following a short rise the plasma progesterone reverts to its base value. When the ovulatory dose of LH is followed by a small "maintenance" dose of LH, the appropriate elevation of progesterone is observed and the regular length of luteal phase is maintained. In *Macaca fascicularis,* administration of anti-LH serum for 4 consecutive days after midcycle results in a sharp decline in progesterone concentration, failure to return to normal values after cessation of treatment, and shortening of cycle lengths by 5–9 days (Moudgal *et al.*, 1972). A midcycle rise in LH has been observed in both bioassay and radioimmunoassay; the postovulatory LH peak might be related to a facilitation of LH secretion by a rapid rise in progesterone concentration (Neill *et al.*, 1967), or erratic elevations in immunoreactive LH may occur occasionally during the luteal phase of normal cycles (Midgley and Jaffe, 1968).

These results imply that luteinization begins shortly after ovulation and continues until the midluteal stage. In addition, an increased plasma concentra-

TABLE VI. Plasma Concentration of LH During Ovulation

	Plasma concentration of LH (ng/ml)									
	Days before ovulation			Day of ovulation	Days after ovulation					
Animal No.	3	2	1		1	2	3	4	5	6
0229	4.3	9.5	18.5	6.6	1.3	*6.1*	1.1	1.1	1.1	
1657	1.1	1.1	6.5	5.5	4.8	1.1	*5.1*	1.1	2.1	
4247	8.5	–	8.5	5.0	1.8	2.5	3.4	1.1	2.9	*8.0*
0759			6.0	1.1	2.5	*6.5*	5.5			
1439			15.0	1.1	1.1	*11.0*	3.7	1.1	1.1	
0946			12.0	2.2	9.5	4.0	7.0	7.5	*10.0*	1.0

tion of LH after ovulation (postovulatory LH surge) may have an important role in the maintenance of the corpus luteum and its continuing function.

After consecutive injections of Nembutal (sodium pentobarbital, 35 mg/kg body weight) in the afternoon (1 and 4 P.M.) of the day prior to anticipated ovulation, swelling of the perineal sex skin is disrupted and the postovulatory rise of plasma progesterone is diminished (Hagino and Yamaoka, 1974). Histological examination reveals an atresic follicle rather than a corpus luteum. Deafferentation of diffused forebrain preopticotuberal efferents posterior to the medial preoptic area produces anovulation, amenorrhea, and persistent vaginal cornification (unpublished data).

Although a midcycle rise in FSH has been reviewed (Ross et al., 1970), the above results suggest that the blockade of LH release rather than FSH release suppresses luteinization. Follicles incubated with FSH alone do not luteinize (Ross et al., 1970). These facts imply that FSH has no major role in the process of luteinization.

Prolactin is also known to have a luteotropic effect on the ovary (Astwood, 1941; Evans et al., 1941). Synthetic thyroid-releasing hormone (TRH) has been shown to stimulate release of prolactin as well as thyroid-stimulating hormone (TSH) in experimental animals and man. A possible relationship

TABLE VII. Effect of TRH on Plasma Concentration of Progestins: (TRH Treatment 2 Days Prior to Expected Ovulation)

Animal No.	Treatment regimen			Plasma concentration of progestins (ng/ml) during luteal phase measured every other day from deturgescence to menstruation					
	Control	Saline	TRH[a]						
1	+			2.8	9.2	1.7	6.3	3.4	1.9
		+		7.3	8.0	4.2	5.8	5.5	0.9
			+	0.5	0.5	0.5	0.5	3.0	0.5
2	+			1.8	2.5	4.1	1.5	0.5	
		+		2.3	2.0	3.1	2.6	1.3	
			+	0.5	0.5	0.5	1.9	0.5	
3	+			3.6	1.8	4.7	2.1	2.1	0.5
		+		3.8	2.3	7.0	5.5	2.4	0.5
			+	2.7	0.5	0.9	1.7	1.5	3.5
4	+			2.0	3.6	2.3	1.0		
			+	3.5	0.5	1.8	0.5		
5	+			8.5	9.5	7.0	19.2	2.5	
			+	2.1	1.3	6.7	2.2	0.5	

[a]Thyrotrophin releasing hormone: daily injections of 40 μg of TRH were given at preovulatory stage.

exists between the secretion of prolactin and the absence of ovulation in lactation (Keettel and Bradbury, 1961) and galactorrhea (Boroditsky and Faiman, 1973) in women. Prolactin secretion might promote a prolonged period of postpartum infertility in the nursing mother. TRH stimulation of prolactin secretion prompted us to study the influence of TRH on ovulatory function in the baboon. This experiment was performed in conjunction with Dr. A. V. Schally, Endocrine and Polypeptide Laboratory, VA Hospital, New Orleans, Louisiana.

The results show that TRH exerts a suppressing effect on luteinization when administered before ovulation in the baboon (Table VII). Previous studies (Hagino and Yamaoka, 1974) demonstrated that sodium pentobarbital treatment at the time of ovulation disrupts both turgescence of perineal sex skin and vaginal cornification and suppresses progesterone secretion. Further, examination of the ovary revealed an atresic follicle. Immediate deturgescence of perineal sex skin, disruption of vaginal cornification, and suppression of plasma progestins following TRH treatment indicate that TRH is involved in the regulation of luteinization in the baboon. Therefore, our attention was directed to identification of the agent responsible for suppression of progestin secretion in TRH-treated baboons. Stimulation of prolactin release by synthetic TRH (Bowers *et al.,* 1971; Stevens *et al.,* 1973) suggests that prolactin, produced by TRH injections, may be responsible for suppression of progestin secretion, while prolactin stimulates regression of the corpus luteum under certain circumstances (Malven and Sawyer, 1966). Injections of LHRH bring about a resumption of the postovulatory rise in plasma progestin in TRH-treated baboons (Table VIII and Fig. 7). These results imply that either alteration of the hypothalamic hormone itself or pituitary hormone secretion induced by TRH injection may be responsible for suppression of progestin secretion. Given this situation, a relationship may also exist between administered TRH and LHRH and the luteinization. The mechanisms of this relationship remain to be elucidated.

Administration of TRH during expected ovulation suppresses luteinization. However, preliminary data show that TRH facilitates luteinization only when ovulation occurs prior to TRH administration.

Removal of the corpus luteum shortly after ovulation advances the following menstruation and ovulatory cycle, while removal of corpus luteum after the midluteal phase has no effect (Hagino and Goldzieher, 1970). Administration of 5 mg progesterone brings about resumption of regular luteal phase length in baboons having the corpus luteum removed. Even when injections of human pituitary LH in small maintenance doses are continued beyond 14 days, plasma progesterone begins to drop 9 to 11 days after ovulation (Jewelewicz *et al.,* 1970).

The mechanism of degeneration of the corpus luteum in the normally cycling ovary remains unknown. It may be inferred that a certain period of luteinization of the corpus luteum is necessary to set in motion the onset of the following menstruation and ovulatory cycle in the baboon.

TABLE VIII. Effect of LHRH on Plasma Concentration of Progestins in TRH-Treated Baboons

Animal No.	Control	TRH[a]	LHRH[b]	Plasma concentration of progestins (ng/ml) during luteal phase measured every other day from deturgescence to menstruation					
1	+			2.8	9.2	1.7	6.3	3.4	1.9
		+		0.5	0.5	0.5	0.5	3.0	0.5
		+	+	2.1	4.8	4.2	7.6	3.5	1.7
3	+			3.6	1.8	4.7	2.1	2.1	0.5
		+		2.7	0.5	0.9	1.7	1.5	3.5
		+	+	3.7	4.5	4.0	3.8	2.5	0.8
6	+			1.6	7.1	5.0	1.8	0.5	
		+	+	2.3	4.4	5.5	3.6	0.5	
7	+			10.2	13.4	14.8	6.2	5.2	1.8
		+	+	7.2	12.5	15.2	13.8	7.7	2.3
8	+			2.4	2.3	2.6	0.8	0.5	
		+	+	4.5	2.7	4.4	0.5	0.5	

[a]Thyrotrophin releasing hormone: daily injections of 40 μg of TRH were given at prevoulatory stage for 4 days.

[b]Luteinizing hormone releasing hormone: daily injections of 300 μg of LHRH were given simultaneously with TRH, plus LHRH an additional 4 days.

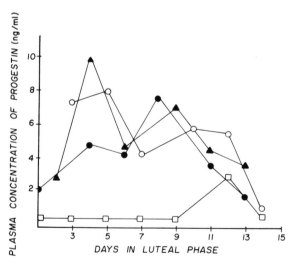

FIG. 7. Plasma concentration of progestins following treatments at the ovulatory stage in the baboon (No. 1). ○, Saline, 4 days; □, 40 μg TRH, 4 days; ●, 40 μg TRH and 300 μg LHRH, 4 days simultaneously, plus LHRH on additional 4 days; ▲, 2 mg prolactin, 4 days.

CONCLUSIONS

The use of the baboon as a model in the analysis of periodicity of ovulatory cycles in the human is still in its incipient stage. The normal menstrual cycle is primarily under control of ovarian estrogens and progestins: it is clear that menstruation does not result from a specific hormonal action. An increase in plasma concentration of LH is observed at menstruation and ovulation: these LH peaks appear to be correlated with EEG paradoxical sleep. The onset of follicular maturation may begin its sequence at the time of menstruation and continues until midcycle. The midcycle LH peak appears prior to ovulation, and circulating plasma estrogens and progestins promote LH release and ovulation. Luteinization of the corpus luteum and progesterone secretion appear to be maneuvered by postovulatory circulating LH. The mechanism of corpus luteum degeneration remains unknown. However, a certain period of luteinization of the corpus luteum is necessary to set in motion the onset of the following menstruation and ovulatory cycle. Given this situation, regularity of menstruation is critical for the onset of the following follicular maturation, ovulation, and luteinization in the baboon.

The purpose of these investigations was to examine the periodicity of the ovulatory cycle in the baboon and to study species similarities and differences which may be of fundamental importance in interpretation and extrapolation of data obtained in humans—a relatively vast body of information compared to that available on the nonhuman primates.

ACKNOWLEDGMENTS

The author wishes to express his gratitude to Drs. Yamaoka and T. Koyama for their association; to Drs. A. V. Schally and A. Arimura (Endocrine and Polypeptide Laboratory, VA Hospital, New Orleans, Louisiana) for their collaboration; and to Mrs. E. M. Menchaca for determination of plasma LH and steroids. Synthetic LHRH (AY-24.031) was supplied by Dr. Givner (Ayerst Research Laboratory, Montreal, Canada). The author is especially grateful to Mr. Lonnie C. Pleasant for preparing the animals for this experiment and to Mrs. O. Mascorro for preparing this manuscript. This study was supported by NIH Contract 69-2133 and Grant GB 28817X of the NSF. An in-house grant from Southwest Foundation for Research and Education, San Antonio, Texas, also supported this project.

REFERENCES

Allen, E. (1927), Menstrual cycle of monkey, *Macacus rhesus:* Observations on normal animals, effects of removal of ovaries and effects of injections of ovarian and placental extracts into spayed animals, *Contrib. Embryol. Carnegie Inst. Wash. 19:*1.

Aono, T., Kurachi, K., Mizutani, S., Hamanaka, Y., Uozumi, T., Nakasima, A., Koshiyama, K., and Matsumoto, K. (1972), Influence of major surgical stress on plasma levels of testosterone, luteinizing hormone and follicle-stimulating hormone in male patients, *J. Clin. Endocrinol. Metabl. 35:*535.

Arimura, A., Spies, H. G., and Schally, A. V. (1973), Relative insensitivity of rhesus monkeys to the LH-releasing hormone (LH-RH), *J. Clin. Endocrinol. Metabl. 36:*372.

Arimura, A., Spies, H. G., and Schally, A. V. (1974), Immunoreactive LH-releasing hormone in plasma: midcycle elevation in women, *J. Clin. Endocrinol. Metabl. 38:*510.

Astwood, E. B. (1941), Regulation of corpus luteum function by hypophysial luteotrophin, *Endocrinology 28:*309.

Boroditsky, R. S., and Faiman, C. (1973), Galactorrhea-amenorrhea due to primary hypo-thyroidism, *Am. J. Obstet. Gynecol. 116:*661.

Bowers, C. Y., Friesen, H. G., Hwang, P., Guyda, H. J.. and Folkers, K. (1971), Prolactin and thyrotropin release in man by synthetic pyroglutamyl-histidyl-prolinamide, *Biochem. Biophys. Res. Commun. 45:*1033.

Carstensen, H., Amer, B., Amer, I., and Wide, L. (1973), The postoperative decrease of plasma testosterone in man, after major surgery, in relation to plasma FSH and LH, *J. Steroid Biochem. 4:*45.

Ehara, Y., Ryan, K. J., and Yen, S. S. C. (1972), Insensitivity of synthetic LRF in LH-release of rhesus monkey, *Contraception 6:*465.

Espey, L. L. (1967), Ultrastructure of the apex of the rabbit Graafian follicle during the ovulatory process, *Endocrinology 81:*267.

Evans, H. M., Simpson, M. E., Lyons, W. R., and Turpeinen, K. (1941), Anterior pituitary hormones which favor production of traumatic uterine placentomata, *Endocrinology 28:*933.

Flerkó, B. (1970), Control of follicle-stimulating hormone and luteinizing hormone secretion, in: *Hypothalamus,* pp. 351–364 (L. Martini, M. Motta, and F. Franschini, eds.), Academic Press, New York.

Gillman, J. 1940), Effect of multiple injections of progesterone on turgescent perineum of baboon *(Papio porcarius), Endocrinology 26:*1072.

Hagino, N. (1972), The effect of synthetic corticosteroids on ovarian function in the baboon, *J. Clin. Endocrinol. Metab. 35:*716.

Hagino, N., and Goldzieher, J. W. (1970), Regulation of gonadotrophin release by the corpus luteum in the baboon, *Endocrinology 87:*413.

Hagino, N., and Yamaoka, S. (1974), Role of biorhythm of sleep and wakefulness in the periodicity of gonadotropin secretion in the baboon (non-human primate), in: *Biological Rhythm in Neuroendocrine Activity* (M. Kawakami, ed.), Igaku Shoin Ltd., Tokyo, pp. 326–337.

Hagino, N., Markovsky, T. C., Parker, M. H., and Menchaca, E. M. (1973a), Role of adrenal progesterone on initiation of ovulation in rats, *Fed. Proc. 32:*283.

Hagino, N., Tsuchihashi, S., Parker, M. H., Menchaca, E. M., and Yamaoka, S. (1973b), Role of the ACTH-adrenal progestin on LH release upon mPOA stimulus, in: *Abstracts of the 55th Annual Meeting of the Endocrine Society,* Chicago, p. A-117.

Hendrickx, A. G. (1971), Reproduction, in: *Embryology of the Baboon,* pp. 3–30, University of Chicago Press, Chicago.

Hisaw, F. L., and Hisaw, F. L., Jr. (1961), Action of estrogen and progesterone on the reproductive tract of lower primates, in: *Sex and Internal Secretions,* Vol. 1, p. 556 (W. C. Young, ed.), Williams and Wilkins, Baltimore.

Jewelewicz, R., Warren, M., Dyrenfurth, I., and Vande Wiele, R. L. (1970), in: *Proceedings of the 17th Meeting of the Society for Gynecological Investigation,* p. 14.

Kastin, A. J., Schally, A. V., Gual, C., and Arimura, A. (1972), Release of LH and FSH after administration of synthetic LH-releasing hormone, *J. Clin. Endocrinol. Metab. 34:*753.

Kawakami, M., and Sawyer, C. H. (1959), Induction of behavioral and electroencephalographic changes in the rabbit by hormone administration of brain stimulation, *Endocrinology 65:*631.

Kawakami, M., Yamaoka, S., and Yamaguchi, T. (1972), Influence of light and hormones upon circadian rhythm of EEG slow wave and paradoxical sleep, in: *Advances in Climatic Physiology,* pp. 349–366 (S. Itoh, K. Ogata, and H. Yoshimura, eds.), Igaku Shoin Ltd., Tokyo,, Springer-Verlag, New York.

Keettel, W. C., and Bradbury, J. T. (1961), Endocrine studies of lactation amenorrhea, *Am. J. Obstet. Gynecol. 82:*995.

Keye, W. R., Jr., Kelch, R. P., Niswender, G. D., and Jaffe, R. B. (1973), Quantitation of endogenous and exogenous gonadotropin releasing hormone by radioimmunoassay, *J. Clin. Endocrinol. Metab. 36:*1263.

Keyes, P. L. (1969), Luteinizing hormone: Action on the Graafian follicle *in vitro, Science 164:*846.

Knobil, E. (1973), On the regulation of the primate corpus luteum, *Biol. Reprod. 8:*246.

Krey, L. C., Butler, W. R., Weiss, G., Weick, R. F., Dierschke, D. J., and Knobil, E. (1973), Influences of endogenous and exogenous gonadal steroids on the actions of synthetic LRF in the rhesus monkey, in: *Hypothalamic Hypophysiotropic Hormones,* pp. 1–428 (C. Gual and E. Rosemberg, eds.), International Congress Series 263, Excerpta Medica, Amsterdam.

Krohn, P. L. (1951), Induction of menstrual bleeding in amenorrhoeic and normal monkeys by progesterone, *J. Endocrinol. 7:*310.

Malven, P. V., and Sawyer, C. H. (1966), Formation of new corpora lutea in mature hypophysectomized rats, *Endocrinology 78:*1259.

Markee, J. E., Davis, J. H., and Hinsey, J. C. (1936), Uterine bleeding spinal monkeys, *Anat. Rec. 64:*231.

Midgley, A. R., Jr., and Jaffe, R. B. (1968), Regulation of human gonadotropins. IV. Correlation of serum concentrations of follicle stimulating and luteinizing hormones during the menstrual cycle, *J. Clin. Endocrinol. Metabl. 28:*1699.

Mikhail, G. (1970), Hormone secretion by the human ovaries, *Gynecol. Invest. 1:*5.

Mishell, D. R., Jr., Nakamura, R. M., Crosignani, P. G., Stone, S., Kharma, K., Nagata, Y., and Thorneycroft, I. H. (1971), Serum gonadotropin and steroid patterns during the normal menstrual cycle, *Am. J. Obstet. Gynecol. 111:*60.

Monahan, M., Rivier, J., Burgus, R., Amoss, M., Blackwell, R., Vale, W., and Guillemin, R. (1971), Synthese totale par phase solide d'un decapeptide que stimule la secretion des gonadotropines hypophysaires LH et FSH, *C.R. Acad. Sci. (Paris) 273:*508.

Moudgal, N. R., Macdonald, G. J., and Greep, R. O. (1972), Role of endogenous primate LH in maintaining corpus luteum function of the monkey, *J. Clin. Endocrinol. Metab. 35:*113.

Neill, J. D., Johansson, E. D. B., Datta, J. K., and Knobil, E. (1967), Relationship between the plasma levels of luteinizing hormone and progesterone during the normal menstrual cycle, *J. Clin. Endocrinol. Metabl. 27:*1167.

Nillius, S. J., and Wide, L. (1972), Variation in LH and FSH response to LH-releasing hormone during the menstrual cycle, *J. Obstet. Gynecol. Brit. Commonw. 79:*865.

Niswender, G. D., and Spies, H. G. (1973), Serum levels of luteinizing hormone, follicle-stimulating hormone and progesterone throughout the menstrual cycle of rhesus monkeys, *J. Clin. Endocrinol. Metab. 37:*326.

Ross, G. T., Cargille, C. M., Lipsett, M. B., Rayford, P. L., Marshall, J. R., Strott, C. A., and

Rodbard, D. (1970), Pituitary and gonadal hormones in women during spontaneous and induced ovulatory cycles, *Rec. Progr. Hormone Res. 26:*1–62.

Sawyer, C. H. (1970), Some endocrine applications of electrophysiology, in: *Hypothalamus,* pp. 83–102 (L. Martini, M. Motta, and F. Fraschini, eds.), Academic Press, New York.

Schally, A. V., Arimura, A., Kastin, A. J., Matsuo, H., Baba, Y., Redding, T. W., Nair, R. M. G., Debeljuk, L., and White, W. F. (1971), Gonadotropin-releasing hormone: One polypeptide regulates secretion of luteinizing and follicle-stimulating hormones, *Science 173:*1036.

Schally, A. V., Arimura, A., and Kastin, A. J. (1973), Hypothalamic regulatory hormones, *Science 179:*341.

Stabenfeldt, G. H., and Hendrickx, A. G. (1972), Progesterone levels in the bonnet monkey (*Macaca radiata*) during the menstrual cycle and pregnancy, *Endocrinology 91:*614.

Stevens, V. C., Powell, J. E., and Sparks, S. J. (1973), Effects of thyroid releasing hormone (TRII) on the menstrual cycle and early gestation in the baboon, in: *Abstract of the 55th Annual Meeting of the Endocrine Society,* Chicago, A-64.

Strott, C. A., Yoshimi, T., Ross, G. T., and Lipsett, M. B. (1969), Ovarian physiology: Relationship between plasma LH and steroidogenesis by the follicle and corpus luteum; effect of HCG, *J. Clin. Endocrinol. Metab. 29:*1157.

Vande Wiele, R. L., Bogumil, J., Dyrenfurth, I., Ferin, M., Jewelewicz, R., Warren, M., Rizkallah, T., and Mikhail, G. (1970), Mechanisms regulating the menstrual cycle in women, *Rec. Progr. Hormone Res. 26:*63.

Venning, E. H., and Browne, J. S. L. (1937), Studies on corpus luteum function; urinary excretion of sodium pregnanediol glucuronidate in human menstrual cycle, *Endocrinology 21:*711.

Yen, S. S. C., and Tsai, C. C. (1972), Acute gonadotropin release induced by exogenous estradiol during the mid-follicular phase of the menstrual cycle, *J. Clin. Endocrinol. Metab. 34:*298.

Yen, S. S. C., Vandenberg, G., Rebar, R., and Ehara, Y. (1972a), Variation of pituitary responsiveness to synthetic LRF during different phases of the menstrual cycle, *J. Clin. Endocrinol. Metabl. 35:*931.

Yen, S. S. C., Rebar, R., VandenBerg, G., Naftolin, F., Ehara, Y., Engblom, S., Ryan, K. J., Guillemin, R., and Benirschke, K. (1972b), Synthetic luteinizing hormone-releasing factor: A potent stimulator of gonadotropin release in man, *J. Clin. Endocrinol. Metabl. 34:*1108.

Yussman, M. A., and Taymor, M. L. (1970), Serum levels of follicle stimulating hormone and luteinizing hormone and of plasma progesterone related to ovulation by corpus luteum biopsy, *J. Clin. Endocrinol. Metabl. 30:*396.

Zuckerman, S, (1941), Periodic uterine bleeding in spayed rhesus monkeys injected daily with constant threshold dose of oestrone, *J. Endocrinol. 2:*263.

Zuckerman, S. (1951), Hormonal basis of uterine bleeding, *Acta Endocrinol. 7:*378.

22

Physiological Studies
on the LH-and FSH-Releasing Hormone,
Its Analogues, and Antisera

A. V. Schally, A. Arimura, D. H. Coy, L. Debeljuk,
J. Vilchez-Martinez, T. W. Redding, E. J. Coy, and
W. H. Carter

Veterans Administration Hospital
New Orleans, Louisiana;
Department of Medicine
Tulane University School of Medicine
New Orleans, Louisiana

and

J. J. Reeves

Department of Animal Science
Washington State University
Pullman, Washington

A hypothalamic decapeptide which was isolated, structurally elucidated, and synthesized for the first time in our laboratory in 1971 (Schally *et al.*, 1971a,c; Baba *et al.* 1971; Matsuo *et al.*, 1971a,b) has been shown to be a powerful stimulator of the release of luteinizing hormone (LH) and follicle-stimulating hormone (FSH) in laboratory and domestic animals, some birds and fishes, and human beings (Schally *et al.*, 1971b, 1972a, 1973a). This decapeptide was designated by us as the LH- and FSH-releasing hormone (LH-RH/FSH-RH). We proposed that this hypothalamic hormone could be responsible for controlling the release of both FSH and LH from the anterior pituitary gland (Schally *et al.*, 1971b). The time courses for the release of LH and FSH *in vitro*, induced by the synthetic or natural hormone, are identical (Schally *et al.* 1972b, 1973a).

Occasional divergence of LH and FSH release in the human menstrual cycle, in the estrus cycle in other animals, and in certain pathological conditions can be explained in part by interactions where sex steroids such as estrogens stimulate LH release and inhibit FSH release in response to LH-RH while some androgens have the opposite effect (Schally *et al.*, 1973b; Debeljuk *et al.*, 1974). The possibility of the presence in hypothalamic tissue of another hormone which predominantly or solely releases FSH cannot be excluded at present. Nevertheless, the ovulation which can be induced in rats, golden hamsters, rabbits, sheep, and amenorrheic women after treatment with natural and synthetic LH-RH demonstrates that this decapeptide may release enough FSH to cause ovarian follicular maturation. In any case, the detection by radioimmunoassay of a peak of LH-RH during the preovulatory surge of LH and FSH in sheep (Kerdelhue *et al.*, 1973) and women (Arimura *et al.*, 1974b) suggests that this decapeptide is probably the hypothalamic mediator responsible for stimulating the release of the ovulatory quota of LH and FSH.

In addition to describing the induction of ovulation in animals with LH-RH, we would like to report the most recent studies carried out in our laboratory on this substance, its synthetic analogues, and antisera to it.

INDUCTION OF OVULATION IN ANIMALS WITH LH-RH

Ovulation in Rats

Adult female Sprague-Dawley rats weighing between 230 and 280 g were used. They were kept at near-constant temperature. Artificial lighting was controlled by an automatic time switch which gave 14 h of light per 24 h, starting at 5:30 A.M. and ending at 7:30 P.M. The animals were usually kept under this condition for 7–10 days after their arrival, before examination of vaginal smears was begun. Samples of vaginal cells were taken each day by saline lavage with the aid of glass disposable pipettes. Smears of these cells were fixed in 95% methanol and stained with Giemsa's solution. From a previous week's record, it was possible to predict with sufficient accuracy the full sequence of the cycle in progress in any given animal. Rats which showed regular 4-day cycles were used. Animals in proestrus were selected by the method described by Everett (1964). In order to block spontaneous ovulation, pentobarbital (Nembutal) was injected intraperitoneally into proestrous rats shortly before 2:00 P.M. When necessary, Nembutal anesthesia was supplemented briefly with light ether anesthesia during surgical manipulation and administration of the test sample. All test samples were injected intravenously, subcutaneously, or into the carotid artery between 2:00 and 4:00 P.M. on the day of proestrus. The next morning, fallopian tubes, dissected from the ovaries and uterus, were carefully searched for ova, as described by Everett (1964).

Our earlier studies (Arimura *et al.*, 1967) demonstrated ovulation in the pentobarbital-blocked proestrous rat using highly purified LH-RH. A dose of 10 µg of this LH-RH preparation, injected over a 30 min period, induced full ovulation in rats, whereas 1–2 µg occasionally caused ovulation.

Rippel et al. (1973) induced ovulation in 5-day cycling rats by injecting 5 µg of synthetic LH-RH intravenously at 9:00 A.M. on the day of proestrus, followed by pentobarbital at 1:00 P.M. Proestrous rats injected with saline and pentobarbital did not ovulate. LH-RH given at earlier stages of the cycle failed to induce ovulation. The rise in LH occurred within 30 min of the administration of LH-RH and was similar in magnitude and duration to the levels found in a normal ovulation. Serum LH elevations after LH-RH were greater at proestrus than at metestrus or diestrus 1 or 2. Even 0.32 µg of LH-RH was able to induce 100% ovulation in these rats (200–250 g) if the injection was done at proestrus. Fujino et al. (1972, 1973) induced ovulation in the rat with synthetic LH-RH prior to 10:00 P.M. of diestrus day 2. They observed ovulation following the subcutaneous injection of 400 ng of LH-RH/100 g body weight at 2:30 P.M. of diestrus day 2. Furthermore, they also reported that proestrous rats were more responsive than diestrous animals, since only 60 ng of LH-RH/100 g body weight was necessary to cause ovulation in 90% of the rats.

Ovulation in Hamsters

Adult female golden hamsters can also be used for determining the ovulatory response to LH-RH/FSH-RH. The estrus cycle was checked by inspecting vaginal discharge, which occurred every 4 days in most of the animals. Experiments were started after the animals showed two regular 4-day cycles. At 1:00 P.M. of the day of proestrus, which preceded the day when thick vaginal discharge was observed, all hamsters were injected intraperitoneally with phenobarbital. The test sample was given between 2:00 and 4:00 P.M. The next morning the hamsters were killed, and their oviducts were inspected under a microscope for the presence of ova.

Ovulation was successfully induced in phenobarbital-blocked proestrous hamsters after the subcutaneous injection of 0.125–0.5 µg of synthetic LH-RH (Arimura et al., 1971). Animals hypophysectomized before treatment did not ovulate after LH-RH, but did ovulate following LH administration, indicating a direct effect of LH-RH on the pituitary gland.

Ovulation in Rabbits

Rabbits, estrous or untreated, have been shown to ovulate consistently after intrapituitary or intravenous administration of LH-RH (Campbell et al., 1964; Hilliard et al., 1971; Smoss et al., 1972). Adult female rabbits (New Zealand strain) were first pretreated subcutaneously with 50–100 µg of estradiol benzoate in oil daily for 3 days. Natural or synthetic LH-RH was infused directly into the pituitary or was administered either as a single rapid intravenous injection or as a 30-min infusion in the marginal ear vein. The rabbits were sacrificed 36–72 h after the injection of LH-RH and were examined for the presence of ruptured follicles in both ovaries. In some cases, visualization of the eggs was attempted after saline flushing of the fallopian tubes. Intravenous administration of 1 μg of LH-RH induced ovulation in virtually all such rabbits.

Ovulation in Sheep

LH-RH and some of its analogues can also induce ovulation in sheep (Reeves *et al.*, 1972, 1974). In one of our recent studies, five anestrous (noncycling) ewes were each treated intramuscularly with a total dose of 400 μg of synthetic LH-RH, which was given in two equal doses at a 4-h interval. Laparotomies were conducted 2 days before and 3 days after the treatment, and the presence of corpora lutea was used as an indication of ovulation. Double-antibody radio-immunoassays were used to quantitate both serum LH and serum FSH concentrations before and after treatment. The mean peak concentration of serum LH and FSH increased 300-fold and fourfold, respectively, over basal levels. The concentrations of LH and FSH were comparable to preovulatory levels reported in ewes. The mean times of the occurrence of LH and FSH peaks after intramuscular treatment with synthetic LH-RH were essentially identical (96 ± 15 and 101 ± 11 min, respectively). Ovulation occurred in three of the five LH-RH-treated ewes, as determined by the presence of corpora lutea in the ovary (Reeves *et al.*, 1972).

Ovulation in Domestic Fowl

Synthetic LH-RH will consistently induce premature ovulation in chickens if given intravenously, intramuscularly, or intracarotidally at doses of 15–20 μg (Van Tienhoven and Schally, 1972; Reeves *et al.*, 1973).

INDUCTION OF OVULATION USING ANALOGUES OF LH-RH

Because LH and FSH exert synergistic effects on induction of ovulation (Swerdloff *et al.*, 1972), ovulation-inducing activity may reflect a more integrated physiological action of the LH-RH/FSH-RH activity. This would influence the total amount of gonadotropins released, as well as the duration of elevation in the levels of these hormones in blood. One of the analogues of LH-RH, namely desGly[10]-LH-RH ethylamide, is more powerful in inducing ovulation in rats, rabbits, and sheep than LH-RH itself (Fujino *et al.*, 1972, 1973; Reeves *et al.*, 1974). Thus although the ability of desGly[10]-LH-RH ethylamide to release LH and FSH *in vivo* and *in vitro* is only 250% higher than that of LH-RH (Coy *et al.*, 1974), the ethylamide analogue is about five to ten times more active than equal doses of LH-RH in inducing ovulation in diestrous rats and rabbits and anestrous sheep (Fujino et al., 1973; Reeves et al., 1974). This augmentation in activity may be due to its increased affinity for receptor sites and/or a decrease in enzymatic inactivation as compared with LH-RH. Our recent studies show that after administration of LH-RH ethylamide to immature male rats serum LH and FSH are maintained at higher levels and for a longer time than after LH-RH. In sheep, desGly[10]-LH-RH ethylamide causes the release of perhaps 100 times as much LH as comparable doses of LH-RH.

Of course, there are major differences between the sex cycles of various species of animals and the menstrual cycle of humans, but the successful induction of ovulation in animals with LH-RH and its analogues suggests that these substances should be effective in inducing ovulation in humans. This has indeed been found to be the case in our studies conducted with Dr. Zarate in Mexico (Kastin et al., 1971; Zarate et al., 1972) and with Dr. Zanartu in Chile (Zanartu et al., 1974a,b). This topic will be discussed in Chapter 23 of this volume.

ANTISERA TO LH-RH AND RIA FOR LH-RH

Several types of antisera to LH-RH have recently been produced in rabbits and guinea pigs (Arimura and Schally, 1973; Arimura et al., 1974c; Nett et al., 1973; Jeffcoate et al., 1973; Fraser and Gunn, 1973; Kerdelhué et al., 1973). Of the male rabbits immunized against LH-RH, those which produced antibodies to LH-RH developed considerable testicular atrophy. For example, the weight of the two testes of one such rabbit was only 0.3 g, whereas the testes of a control rabbit weighed 5 g. When rabbit antisera to LH-RH were given to female rats on the morning of the day of proestrus, the preovulatory surge of LH and FSH and the ovulation were blocked (Table I). Similar results were reported by Fraser and Gunn (1973). Although antibodies to LH-RH can be produced in animals, the clinical safety of purified animal antisera to LH-RH or of complexes containing conjugated LH-RH, which are used for immunizing animals, is not known. Much additional work is needed before active or passive immunization to LH-RH can be used for controlling fertility of animals and humans. The antisera to LH-RH have been used in radioimmunoassays of LH-RH (Arimura et al., 1974c; Arimura and Schally, 1973; Nett et al., 1973; Kerdelhué et al., 1973; Jeffcoate et al., 1973; Fraser and Gunn, 1973).

A peak of LH-RH levels in plasma was detected by radioimmunoassay during the preovulatory surge of LH and FSH in sheep and women (Kerdelhué et al., 1973; Arimura et al., 1974b). In women, the mean LH-RH level at midcycle was significantly higher than that in the follicular or midluteal stage. LH-RH secretion started to increase at the beginning of the LH surge and reached a peak level at approximately the same time as the LH peak. These findings provide strong support for the concept that the preovulatory surge of LH is induced by the

TABLE I. Blockade by Anti-LH-RH Serum of Ovulation and Serum LH and FSH Rise in Cycling Rats

Treatment	Number of rats tested	Number of rats ovulated	Mean number of ova ± SE	Mean serum LH ± SD (ng/ml)	Mean serum FSH ± SE (ng/ml)
Anti-LH-RH serum[a]	4	0	0	0.8 ± 0.13[b]	145 ± 21[b]
Normal serum	4	4	12 ± 1.3	58.0 ± 13.2	720 ± 108

[a] Rabbit anti-LH-RH serum No. 742. This antiserum binds 50% of labeled LH-RH at 1:2100 dilution. One milliliter of the antiserum was injected i.v. in rats at 9:30 A.M. on the day of proestrus under ether.

[b] $P < 0.01$, as compared with the control values. Blood was collected from the jugular veins of rats under ether at 4:30 P.M. on the day of proestrus.

increased secretion of endogenous LH-RH. This also suggests that this decapeptide is probably the hypothalamic mediator responsible for stimulating the release of the amount of LH and FSH required for ovulation.

Immunological studies, supplemented by physiochemical and bioassay data, indicate that bovine, human, and rat LH-RH is identical to the porcine and ovine LH-RH (Arimura and Schally, 1973; Arimura *et al.*, 1974b).

METABOLISM AND HALF-LIFE OF LH-RH

By means of radioimmunoassays and studies with tritium-labeled LH-RH, the half-life of exogenously administered LH-RH in the rat was measured and was found to be 4–6 min. Tritiated LH-RH administered to man is rapidly degraded in the blood. Its half-life in man is about 4 min (Redding *et al.*, 1973). This finding was substantiated by direct radioimmunoassay of LH-RH (Arimura *et al.*, 1974a). Using synthetic LH-RH labeled with tritium, we were able to follow the disappearance of LH-RH in men (Redding *et al.*, 1973). One hour after injection of the labeled LH-RH almost half of the dose of radioactivity was excreted in the urine, and after 24 h almost 75% was found in the urine. One of the principal mechanisms of inactivation of LH-RH in human blood is the cleavage of (pyro)Glu-His from the *N*-terminus.

POTENTIAL ROLE OF LH-RH IN FERTILITY CONTROL: INHIBITORY ANALOGUES OF LH-RH

Continued research on LH-RH/FSH-RH, its structural analogues, and its other derivatives may lead to the development of new methods of birth control.

The two main approaches to the control of fertility would be the development of specific antisera capable of neutralizing endogenous LH-RH and the synthesis of competitive analogues of LH-RH.

The synthesis of a large number of structural analogues of LH-RH (Coy *et al.*, 1973a; Schally *et al.*, 1972a, 1973a; Fujino *et al.*, 1972, 1973; Geiger *et al.*, 1972; Yanaihara *et al.*, 1972, 1973a,b) has helped establish the structure–activity relationship of this hormone. This information has been used to guide attempts to create synthetic inhibitors of LH-RH. A contraceptive polypeptide must be devoid of significant LH-RH activity, but by competing with endogenous LH-RH for binding to the pituitary receptors, it should lead to a decrease in the secretion of LH or FSH, or both.

One analogue, desHis2-LH-RH, was reported to competitively antagonize LH-RH in a system based on dispersed rat pituitary cells cultured *in vitro*, when present in dosages 10,000 times greater than LH-RH (Vale *et al.*, 1972). However, this analogue does not inhibit the LH-RH-induced stimulation of LH release *in vivo* in rats or ovulation in rabbits (Schally *et al.*, 1973a). It was decided, nevertheless, to synthesize the corresponding peptide containing the modified C-terminus (Coy *et al.*, 1973b). *In vivo* assays for the inhibitory activity of desHis^2-desGly^{10}-LH-RH ethylamide revealed that the significant release of LH in rats induced by a standard dose of LH-RH was abolished by pretreatment with 10 μg of this peptide antagonist. Later experiments repeatedly confirmed that this peptide inhibits LH release *in vivo* at doses of 10, 1, and 0.1 μg per rat. In most cases, the inhibition was proportional to the dose. The ID$_{50}$ (the dose which causes 50% inhibition) was 14 ng. This is the first peptide which significantly reduced LH secretion *in vivo* in response to LH-RH (Vilchez *et al.*, 1974). DesHis^2-desGly^{10}-LH-RH ethylamide has also proved capable, under some conditions, of inhibiting ovulation in both rats and rabbits (Vilchez-Martinez *et al.*, 1974). This substance represents only an initial member of the first generation of antagonistic LH-RH analogues which have been synthesized, and the chances that more potent inhibitors of the hormone can be developed now appear promising. Several other LH-RH analogues, among them desHis^2-Leu^3-desGly^{10}-LH-RH ethylamide and Gly^2-Leu^3-desGly^{10}-LH-RH ethylamide, appear to be even more powerful inhibitors than the desHis^2 desGly^{10}-LH-RH ethylamide. The search for still more effective inhibitors of LH-RH must continue.

Many problems will have to be solved before a new class of birth control drugs based on various derivatives of LH-RH can be developed. In spite of their feasibility, the two principal approaches, immunological and synthetic, have not been thoroughly validated. While antisera and competitive analogues of LH-RH/FSH-RH may prove to be effective birth control agents, the available results indicate that LH-RH/FSH-RH, or its analogues, should find diagnostic and therapeutic application in clinical medicine, and they may also prove useful for stimulation of fertility in domestic animals.

SUMMARY

A polypeptide which stimulates the release of LH and FSH was isolated from porcine hypothalami, structurally identified as (pyro)Glu-His-Trp-Ser-Tyr-Gly-Leu-Arg-Pro-Gly-NH$_2$, and synthesized. A variety of studies were carried out with the natural and synthetic polypeptide named the LH- and FSH-releasing hormone (LH-RH/FSH-RH). In rats, LH-RH increased release of LH and FSH, stimulated spermatogenesis and follicular development, and induced ovulation. Stimulation of LH and FSH release and ovulation was induced by LH-RH in golden hamsters, rabbits, and sheep. LH-RH stimulated LH release in pigs and cattle. LH-RH caused LH release and ovulation in some species of fish and induced premature ovulation in chickens. Monkeys showed increases in serum LH and FSH levels after administration of LH-RH, although their response was not as good as that which can be obtained in men and women. Sex steroids greatly influence the pituitary response to LH-RH. Estrogen will inhibit the rise in FSH, but in small doses can augment that of LH in response to LH-RH. In contrast, dihydrotestosterone will inhibit the rise of LH, but can slightly enhance that of FSH in rats after administration of LH-RH. The combinations of estrogen and progesterone or estrogen and testosterone greatly decrease the response to LH-RH *in vivo* and *in vitro*. Thus part of the effect of sex steroids is undoubtedly exerted on the pituitary gland. By use of tritiated LH-RH, the half-life of LH-RH was determined to be about 6 min in the rat and 4 min in the human being. LH-RH appeared to be a fertility-stimulating agent in animals and human beings. Two approaches, based on derivatives of LH-RH, were used for the study of new methods of birth control. These approaches consisted of development of specific antisera against LH-RH and synthesis of competitive analogues of LH-RH. Immunization with LH-RH caused severe testicular atrophy in rabbits. Administration of the antisera to LH-RH suppressed the preovulatory surge of LH and FSH and blocked ovulation in rats. These antisera were used for the development of a radioimmunoassay for LH-RH which can detect as little as 0.25–0.5 ρg of the hormone in blood. Hundreds of LH-RH analogues were synthesized in order to establish the structure–activity relationship for this hormone and to find synthetic inhibitors of LH-RH. Several of these analogues, including desHis^2 desGly^{10}-LH-RH-ethylamide, blocked the response to LH-RH *in vivo* in rats, and under certain conditions inhibited ovulation in rats and rabbits. These are the first synthetic inhibitors of LH-RH found to be active *in vivo,* and the chances that effective peptide contraceptives can be developed look promising.

REFERENCES

Amoss, M., Blackwell, R., and Guillemin, R. (1972), Stimulation of ovulation in the rabbit triggered by synthetic LRF, *J. Clin. Endocrinol. Metab. 34:*434.

Arimura, A., and Schally, A. V. (1973), Production of antiserum to LH-releasing hormone (LH-RH) and development of radioimmunoassay for LH-RH, *Fed. Proc. 32:*238A.

Arimura, A., Schally, A. V., Saito, T., Muller, E. E., and Bowers, C. Y. (1967), Induction of ovulation in rats by highly purified pig LH-releasing factor (LRF), *Endocrinology 80:*515.

Arimura, A., Matsuo, H., Baba, Y., and Schally, A. V. (1971), Ovulation induced by synthetic luteinizing hormone-releasing hormone in the hamster, *Science 174:*511.

Arimura, A., Kastin, A. J., Gonzalez-Barcena, D., Siller, J., and Schally, A. V. (1974a), Disappearance of LH-releasing hormone in man as determined by RIA, *Br. Med. J.,* submitted.

Arimura, A., Kastin, A. J., Schally, A. V., Saito, M., Kumasaka, T., Yaoi, Y., Kato, N., Nishi, N., and Ohkura, K. (1974b), Immunoreactive LH-releasing hormone in plasma: Midcycle elevation in women, *J. Clin. Endoc. Metab. 38:*510.

Arimura, A., Sato, H., Kumasaka, T., Worobec, R. B., Debeljuk, L., Dunn, J. D., and Schally, A. V. (1974c), Production of antiserum to LH-RH associated with marked atrophy of the gonads in rabbits; characterization of the antibody and development of a radioimmunoassay for LH-RH, *Endocrinology, 93:*1092.

Baba, Y., Matsuo, H., and Schally, A. V. (1971), Structure of porcine LH and FSH releasing hormone. II. Confirmation of the proposed structure by conventional sequential analysis, *Biochem. Biophys. Res. Commun. 44:*459.

Campbell, H. J., Feuer, G., and Harris, G. W. (1964), The effect of intrapituitary infusion of median eminence and other brain extracts on anterior pituitary gonadotrophic secretion, *J. Physiol. 170:*474.

Coy, D. J., Coy, E. J., and Schally, A. V. (1973a), Luteinizing hormone-releasing hormone: Solid phase synthesis of a 5-phenylalanine analog possessing high biological activity, *J. Med. Chem. 16:*83.

Coy, D. H., Vilchez-Martinez, J. A., Coy, E. J., and Schally, A. V. (1973b), A peptide inhibitor of luteinizing hormone-releasing hormone (LH-RH), *J. Clin. Endocrinol. Metab. 37:*337.

Coy, D. H., Coy, E. J., Schally, A. V., Vilchez-Martinez, J. A., Debeljuk, L., Carter, W. H., and Arimura, A. (1974), Stimulatory and inhibitory analogues of luteinizing hormone releasing hormone, *Biochemistry, 13:*323.

Debeljuk, L., Vilchez-Martinez, J. A., Arimura, A., and Schally, A. V. (1974), Effect of gonadal steroids on the response to LH-RH in intact and castrated male rats, *Endocrinology, 94:*1519.

Everett, J. W. (1964), *Major Problems in Neuroendocrinology,* p. 346 (E. Bajuz and G. Jasmin, eds.), Karger, Basel.

Fraser, H. M., and Gunn, A. (1973), Effects of antibodies in male rabbit and on rat oestrous cycle, *Nature (Lond.) 244:*160.

Fujino, M., Kobayashi, S., Obayashi, M., Shinagawa, S., Fukuda, T., Kitada, C., Nakayama, R., Yamazaki, I., White, W. F., and Rippel, R. H. (1972), Structure–activity relationships in the *C*-terminal part of luteinizing hormone-releasing hormone (LH-RH), *Biochem. Biophys. Res. Commun. 49:*863.

Fujino, M., Shinagawa, S., Yamazaki, I., Kobayashi, S., Obayashi, M., Fukuda, T., Nakayama, R., White, W. F., and Rippel, R. H. (1973), (Des-Gly-NH_2[10], Pro-ethylamide[9])-LH-RH: A highly potent analog of luteinizing hormone releasing hormone, *Arch. Biochem. Biophys. 154:*488.

Geiger, R., Wissman, H., König, W., Sandow, J., Schally, A. V., Redding, T. W., Debeljuk, L., and Arimura, A. (1972), Synthesis and biological evaluation of 4-alanine lutenizing hormone releasing hormone (ALA[4]-LH-RH), *Biochem. Biophys. Res. Commun. 49:*1467.

Hilliard, J., Schally, A. V., and Sawyer, C. H. (1971), Progesterone blockade of the ovulatory response to intrapituitary infusion of LH-RH in rabbits, *Endocrinology 88:*730.

Jeffcoate, S. L., Holland, D. T., Fraser, H. M., and Gunn, A. (1973), Radioimmunoassay and identification in human urine (of LH-RH), *Nature (Lond.) 244:*161.

Kastin, A. J., Zarate, A., Midgley, A. R., Canales, E. S., and Schally, A. V. (1971), Ovulation confirmed by pregnancy after infusion of porcine LH-RH, *J. Clin. Endocrinol. Metab. 33:*980.

Kerdelhué, B., Jutisz, M., Gillessen, D., and Studer, R. O. (1973), Obtention of antisera against a hypothalamic decapeptide (luteinizing hormone/follicle stimulating hormone release hormone) which stimulates the release of pituitary gonadotropins and development of its radioimmunoassay, *Biochim. Biophys. Acta 297:*540.

Matsuo, H., Baba, Y., Nair, R. M. G., Arimura, A., and Schally, A. V. (1971a), Structure of the porcine LH and FSH-releasing hormone. I. The proposed amino acid sequence, *Biochem. Biophys. Res. Commun. 43:*1334.

Matsuo, H., Arimura, A., Nair, R. M. G., and Schally, A. V. (1971b), Synthesis of the porcine LH and FSH-releasing hormone by the solid-phase method, *Biochem. Biophys. Res. Commun. 45:*822.

Nett, T. M., Akbar, A. M., Niswender, G. D., Hedlum, M. T., and White, W. F. (1973), A radioimmunoassay for gonadotropin releasing hormone (Gn-RH) in serum, *J. Clin. Endocrinol. Metab. 36:*880.

Redding, T. W., Kastin, A. J., Gonzales-Barcena, D., Coy, D. H., Coy, E. J., Schalch, D. S., and Schally, A. V. (1973), The half-life, metabolism and excretion of tritiated luteinizing hormone-releasing hormone (LH-RH) in man, *J. Clin. Endocrinol. Metab. 37:*626.

Reeves, J. J., Arimura, A., Schally, A. V., Kraft, C. L., Beck, T. W., and Casey, J. M. (1972), Effects of synthetic luteinizing hormone-releasing hormone/follicle stimulating hormone-releasing hormone (LH-RH/FSH-RH) on serum LH, serum FSH and ovulation in anestrous ewes, *J. Anim. Sci. 35:*84.

Reeves, J. J., Harrison, P. C., and Casey, T. M. (1973), Ovarian development and ovulation in hens treated with synthetic (porcine) luteinizing hormone releasing hormone/follicle stimulating hormone releasing hormone (LH-RH/FSH-RH), *J. Poultry Sci.,* in press.

Reeves, J. J., Coy, D. H., and Schally, A. V. (1974), in preparation.

Rippel, R. H., Johnson, E. S., and White, W. F. (1973), Ovulation and serum luteinizing hormone in the cycling rat following administration of gonadotropin releasing hormone, *Proc. Soc. Exp. Biol. Med. 143:*55.

Schally, A. V., and Kastin, A. J. (1971), Stimulation and inhibition of fertility through hypothalamic agents, *Drug Therapy 1:*29.

Schally, A. V., Arimura, A., Baba, Y., Nair, R. M. G., Matsuo, H., Redding, T. W., Debeljuk, L., and White, W. F. (1971a), Isolation and properties of the FSH and LH-releasing hormone, *Biochem. Biophys. Res. Commun. 43:*393.

Schally, A. V., Arimura, A., Kastin, A. J., Matsuo, H., Baba, Y., Redding, T. W., Nair, R. M. G., Debeljuk, L., and White, W. F. (1971b), The gonadotropin-releasing hormone; one polypeptide regulates the secretion of luteinizing hormone and follicle stimulating hormone, *Science 173:*1036.

Schally, A. V., Nair, R. M. G., Redding, T. W., and Arimura, A. (1971c), Isolation of the LH and FSH-releasing hormone from porcine hypothalami, *J. Biol. Chem. 246:*7230.

Schally, A. V., Arimura, A., Carter, W. H., Redding, T. W., Geiger, R., König, W., Wissman, H., Jaeger, G., Sandow, J., Yanaihara, N., Yanaihara, C., Hashimoto, T., and Sakagami, M. (1972a), Luteinizing hormone-releasing hormone (LH-RH) activity of some synthetic polypeptides. I. Fragments shorter than decapeptide, *Biochem. Biophys. Res. Commun. 48:*366.

Schally, A. V., Kastin, A. J., and Arimura, A. (1972b), The hypothalamus and reproduction, *Am. J. Obstet. Gynecol 114:*423.

Schally, A. V., Arimura, A., and Kastin, A. J. (1973a), Hypothalamic regulatory hormones, *Science 179:*341.

Schally, A. V., Redding, T. W., and Arimura, A. (1973b), Effect of sex steroids on pituitary responses to LH and FSH-releasing hormone *in vitro, Endocrinology 93:*893.

Swerdloff, R. S., Jacobs, H. S., and Odell, W. D. (1972), Synergistic role of progestogens in estrogen induction of LH and FSH surge, *Endocrinology 90:*1529.

Vale, W., Grant, G., Rivier, J., Monahan, M., Amoss, A., Blackwell, R., Burgus, R., and Guillemin, R. (1972), Synthetic polypeptide antagonists of the hypothalamic luteinizing hormone releasing factor, *Science 176:*933.

Van Tienhoven, A., and Schally, A. V. (1972), Mammalian luteinizing hormone-releasing hormone induces ovulation in the domestic fowl, *Gen. Comp. Endocrinol. 19:*594.

Vilchez-Martinez, J. A., Schally, A. V., Debeljuk, L., Coy, D. H., Coy, E. J., Arimura, A., and Yanaihara, N. (1974), Development of a method to test anti-LH-RH activity in rats, *Neuroendocrinology, 14:*121.

Yanaihara, N., Yanaihara, C., Hashimoto, T., Kenmochi, Y., Kaneko, T., Oka, H., Schally, A. V., and Arimura, A. (1972), Syntheses and LH-RH activities of 8-position-substituted LH-RH analogs, *Biochem. Biophys. Res. Commun. 49:*1280.

Yanaihara, N., Hashimoto, T., Yanaihara, C., Tsuji, K., Kenmochi, Y., Ashizawa, F., Keneko, T., Oka, H., Arimura, A., and Schally, A. V. (1973a), Syntheses and biological evaluation of analogs of luteinizing hormone-releasing hormone (LH-RH) modified in position 2, 3, 4 or 5, *Biochem. Biophys. Res. Commun. 52:*64.

Yanaihara, N., Tsuji, T., Yanaihara, C., Hashimoto, T., Kaneko, T., Oka, H., Arimura, A., and Schally, A. V. (1973b), Syntheses and biological activities of analogs of LH-RH substituted in position 1 or 2, *Biochem. Biophys. Res. Commun. 51:*165.

Zanartu, J., Dabacens, A., Rodrigues-Bravo, R., and Schally, A. V. (1974a), Induction of ovulation with synthetic gonadotropin releasing hormone (LH-RH) in women blocked with contraceptive steroids, *Br. Med. J. 1:*605.

Zanartu, J., Dabancens, A., Kastin, A. J., and Schally, A. V. (1974b), Effect of synthetic hypothalamic gonadotropin-releasing hormone (FSH/LH-RH) releasing gonadotropic hormones in anovulatory sterility, *Fertil. Steril. 25:*160.

Zarate, A., Canales, E. S., Schally, A. V., Ayala-Valdes, L., and Kastin, A. J. (1972), Successful induction of ovulation with synthetic luteinizing hormone-releasing hormone in anovulatory infertility, *Fertil. Steril. 23:*672.

23

Induction of Ovulation with Various Regimens of Luteinizing Hormone-Releasing Hormone Administration

Carlos Gual

Department of Reproductive Biology
Instituto Nacional de la Nutrición
México, D. F., México

It has been shown that porcine luteinizing hormone-releasing hormone (LH-RH) as well as its analogous synthetic decapeptide induces a significant pituitary synthesis and release of both LH and FSH in the human after intravenous, intramuscular, or subcutaneous administration (Kastin *et al.,* 1969, 1970a,b, 1971a, 1972; Milhaud *et al.,* 1971). Furthermore, the porcine or synthetic LH-RH has proved to be an effective agent for gonadal stimulation and for induction of ovulation in amenorrheic women with normal pituitary gonadotropic function. Further attempts to use this compound for treatment of anovulatory sterility have been undertaken by a number of clinical investigators who have explored different regimens of LH-RH administration (Gual *et al.,* 1971; Kastin *et al.,* 1971b; Keller, 1973; Nakano *et al.,* 1973; Schneider and Dahlen, 1973; Zarate *et al.,* 1973; Zañartu *et al.,* 1974a). This chapter reports our experience using these and other combined regimens.

MATERIALS AND METHODS

Clinical Subjects

Ten women between 21 and 42 yr of age were treated for a total of 15 cycles with various doses and schedules of porcine and synthetic LH-RH. In four

This work was partly supported by Grant 650-025 from the Ford Foundation.

women with severe oligomenorrhea or amenorrheic periods of 3–12 months in length, a diagnosis of Stein-Leventhal's syndrome was fully established by routine diagnostic procedures, including ovarian visualization by laparoscopy or laparatomy. A positive gestagen-withdrawal bleeding was obtained in the four cases. Three other women had a syndrome of galactorrhea-amenorrhea for at least the previous 2 hr; one of them had a demonstrable pituitary tumor. In two of these patients a positive gestagen-withdrawal bleeding test was observed, but in the third one a negative response was found associated with severe hypoestrogenism (90% of basal cells in a vaginal smear). The remaining three women had primary or secondary amenorrhea, associated with normal pituitary reserve to intravenous LH-RH and a responsive ovarian tissue as demonstrated by a successful induction of ovulation and menstrual bleeding after sequential human menopausic gonadotropin (HMG) and human chorionic gonadotropin (HCG) therapy. These three patients with vaginal smears indicating discrete to severe hypoestrogenism did not respond to a gestagen-withdrawal bleeding test or to clomiphene therapy. On the basis of these clinical features and in the absence of an adrenal or polycystic ovarian disease (Stein-Leventhal's syndrome), a diagnosis of tonic hypothalamic amenorrhea was established (Gual, 1973).

Regimens of LH-RH Administration

Synthetic LH-RH was kindly provided by Hoechst, Frankfurt, Germany, in sterile ampules, each containing 100–500 µg of lyophilized decapeptide. Porcine LH-RH was supplied by Dr. Andrew V. Schally of the Endocrine and Polypeptide Laboratory, VA Hospital, New Orleans, Lousiana. The potency of these materials has been tested in previous clinical studies (Kastin et al., 1971a; Gual et al., 1970; Gual, 1973). Five different regimens of LH-RH administration were tested, as follows:

Regimen A consisted of repeated intramuscular (i.m.) injections of synthetic LH-RH in doses of 100 µg twice daily for 7–9 consecutive days. Forty-eight hours later, two doses of 200 µg of LH-RH each were injected i.m. 12 h apart. In one case, 300 µg of LH-RH was injected i.m. every other day for 2 wk with a final dose of 600 µg on day 14 of treatment.

Regimen B consisted of repeated daily i.m. injections of 400–500 µg of synthetic LH-RH for 8 consecutive days, followed by a single i.m. injection of 10,000 IU of HCG (Pregnyl, Organon) 48 h after the last LH-RH injection.

Regimen C consisted of HMG therapy (Pergonal, courtesy of Serono Laboratories, Rome, Italy) in doses of 150–225 IU for 8 consecutive days, followed 48 h later by a continuous intravenous (i.v.) infusion of synthetic LH-RH at a rate of 0.8 µg/min/6 h and 2.5 µg/min for a final extra hour. In a second patient, porcine LH-RH was infused i.v. for 24 h at a rate of 0.4 µg/min, with an extra dose after the first 8 hr of infusion of 20 µg/min for 30 min.

Regimen D consisted of repeated i.m. synthetic LH-RH injections in doses of

250 μg twice a day for 8 consecutive days, associated with clomiphene citrate (Clomid, Merrell) in doses of 50 mg twice a day for the same 8-day period. Forty-eight hours later, a single dose of 10,000 IU of HCG was also injected.

Regimen E consisted of a sequential administration of clomiphene (50 mg twice a day for 5 consecutive days), followed by repeated i.m. injections of synthetic LH-RH (250 μg twice a day for 5 consecutive days). Forty-eight hours later, a single dose of 10,000 IU was injected as in regimen D.

Criteria for Assessment of the Pituitary Response to LH-RH and Ovulation

Pituitary response to i.m. or i.v. LH-RH administration was measured by changes in circulating concentrations of serum LH and FSH as determined by radioimmunoassay (Midgley, 1966, 1967). In all cases, ovulation was assessed by daily or every other day urinary excretion of pregnanediol (Gual, 1966) and by basal body temperature (BBT). In one patient, pregnancy unequivocally confirmed ovulation. The ovarian secretion of estrogens was indirectly measured by evaluating the changes in the physicochemical properties of cervical mucus and the cerivcal os opening. In those patients with demonstrable hypoestrogenism, the changes in the vaginal cytology and its maturation value provided important data for estimating the ovarian responsiveness.

RESULTS

Attempts to Induce Follicular Maturation and Ovulation by Repeated Intramuscular LH-RH Administration (Regimens A and B)

Two patients with a diagnosis of Stein-Leventhal's syndrome and one with a galactorrhea-amenorrhea syndrome without sellar enlargement were submitted to LH-RH therapy described under regimen A.

As shown in Fig. 1, patient D. D., age 29, with Stein-Leventhal's syndrome, was given repeated i.m. injections of synthetic LH-RH in doses of 100 μg twice a day for 7 days. On day 10 of treatment, two doses of 200 μg each of LH-RH were i.m. injected every 12 h. The pituitary responsiveness to i.m. LH-RH was assessed on days 1 and 10 by radioimmunoassayable serum LH and FSH. In both instances, a significant increase of LH and FSH was sustained for a period of 2–4 h, thus confirming the expected biological effect of the injected decapeptide. In spite of the fact that this stimulatory effect was accompanied by increased amount and spinnbarkeit of cervical mucus and a positive ferning test, it was not possible to induce ovulation, as suggested by a monophasic BBT and persistently low urine pregnanediol values. No spontaneous menses was detected after 30 days of treatment.

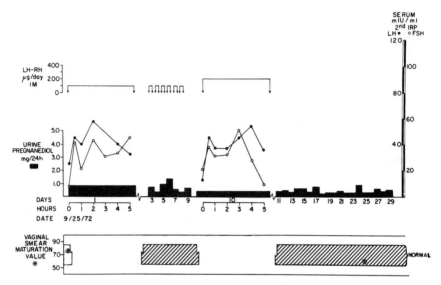

FIG. 1. D. D., age 29, with Stein-Leventhal's syndrome. Attempt to induce follicle maturation and ovulation by repeated i.m. LH-RH adminstration (regimen A). Note that ovulation
was not achieved with a total dose of 1800 μg LH-RH.

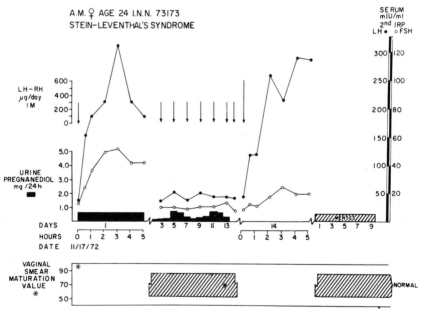

FIG. 2. A. M., age 24, with Stein-Leventhal's syndrome. Attempt to induce follicle maturation and ovulation by repeated i.m. LH-RH administration according to regimen A. Although the releasing hormone was injected every other day for a total of 3000 μg
throughout 14 days, ovulation was not achieved.

A second patient (A. M., age 24) with a diagnosis of Stein-Leventhal's syndrome (Fig. 2) was stimulated with doses of 300 μg of synthetic LH-RH, given in a different fashion consisting of i.m. injections every other day for a period of 14 days. On days 1 and 14, the pituitary responsiveness to LH-RH administration was assessed, confirming a significant serum LH and FSH increase. The following day after discontinuation of therapy, a prolonged menstrual bleeding was observed, but there was no evidence of ovulation.

A 39-yr-old woman (C. P. S.) with a galactorrhea-amenorrhea syndrome without sellar enlargement, and a positive gestagen-withdrawal bleeding test, had been submitted to clomiphene therapy to induce ovulation (100 mg/day for 5 days) 3 yr prior to the present LH-RH therapy. As shown in Fig. 3, a significant increase in urine pregnanediol excretion suggested ovulatory cycles. Continuation of therapy for another 3 months ended in pregnancy with a normal full-term delivery of a healthy 7-lb girl. The patient did not breastfeed the baby, and amenorrhea has persisted for the last 2 yr. The galactorrhea diminished, but did not completely disappear. Therefore, induction of ovulation was attempted again with repeated i.m. injections of synthetic LH-RH according to regimen A.

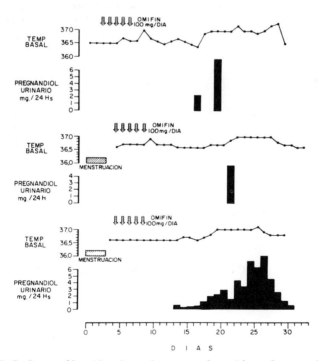

FIG. 3. C. P. S., age 39, with galactorrhea-amenorrhea without demonstrable pituitary tumor. Clomiphene therapy was given for three consecutive cycles. Note biphasic BBT and significant rise in urine pregnanediols. Pregnancy was achieved after three extra cycles of treatment not depicted in the figure.

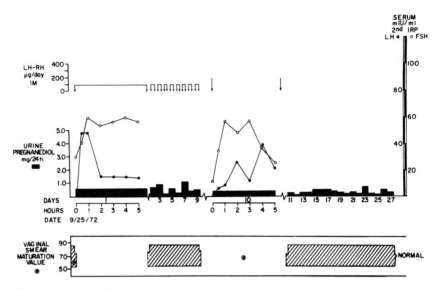

FIG. 4. *C. P. S., age 39, with galactorrhea-amenorrhea.* (Same patient as in Fig. 3.) Regimen A of LH-RH therapy did not induce ovulation. A total of 2200 μg LH-RH was injected i.m. twice a day through a 10-day period.

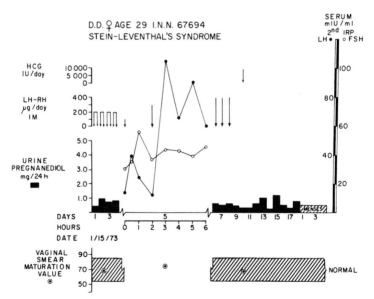

FIG. 5. *D. D., age 29, with Stein-Leventhal's syndrome.* (Same patient as in Fig. 1.) A total of 3200 μg of synthetic LH-RH was injected i.m. according to regimen B. Note that 10,000 IU of HCG was injected 48 h after LH-RH therapy without any ovulatory effects.

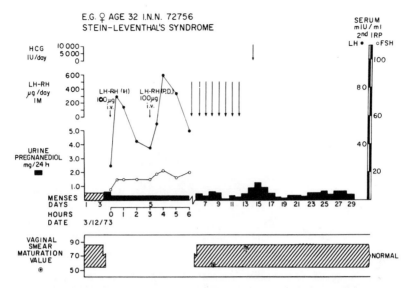

FIG. 6. E. G., age 32, with Stein-Leventhal's syndrome, previously submitted to ovarian wedge resection and clomiphene therapy without any ovulatory effect. Regimen B did not induce ovulation with a total i.m. dose of 4000 µg LH-RH.

Figure 4 shows that a significant LH and FSH response was obtained but ovulation did not take place, nor did menstrual bleeding within the following 30 days of therapy.

On the basis of these negative results, regimen B was tried in the same patient (D. D.) as in Fig. 1 and in a second woman (E. G., age 32) with ovarian polycystic disease, in whom bilateral ovarian wedge resection had been performed several years before without any ovulatory effect. In the last 2 yr, repeated courses of clomiphene therapy had consistently failed to induce ovulation. In these patients, high i.m. doses of LH-RH were given for 8 consecutive days in the attempt to achieve follicular maturation and subsequent ovulation by HCG administration. As shown in Figs. 5 and 6, a significant pituitary gonadotropin effect was obtained but ovulation was not observed, as suggested by a monophasic BBT and low levels of urine pregnanediol excretion. In patient D. D., a normal menstrual bleeding started 8 days after the 10,000 IU HCG injection.

Induction of Ovulation with Prolonged LH-RH Infusion, After Follicular Maturation by HMG Therapy (Regimen C)

Two patients with a presumptive diagnosis of hypothalamic amenorrhea, negative response to clomiphene therapy, and a negative gestagen-withdrawal bleeding test, but with a demonstrable pituitary gonadotropin reserve, were

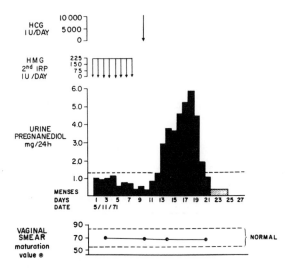

FIG. 7. J. S., age 33, with secondary hypothalamic amenorrhea, diabetes mellitus, previous negative response to clomiphene therapy, and positive response to a LH-RH pituitary reserve test. Note that sequential HMG/HCG induced ovulation.

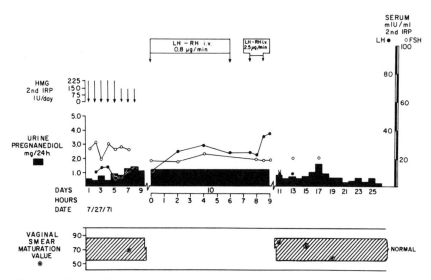

FIG. 8. J. S., age 33, with secondary hypothalamic amenorrhea and diabetes mellitus. (Same patient as in Fig. 7.) Attempt to achieve follicle maturation by HMG therapy as in the previous cycle depicted in Fig. 7. Note that HCG was replaced by i.v. infusion of LH-RH. Ovulation was not observed.

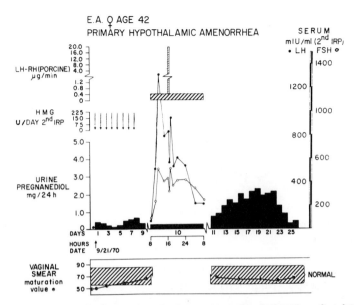

FIG. 9. E. A., age 42, with primary hypothalamic amenorrhea. Induction of ovulation after intramuscular administration of total doses of 1800 IU of HMG and 24-h intravenous administration of 1.4 mg porcine LH-RH according to regimen C. Note the initial brisk response to therapy and a noticeable decrease of serum LH and FSH after the first 4 h of infusion. From Gual (1973).

submitted to regimen C, consisting of sequential HMG and LH-RH. In patient J. S., age 33, several ovulatory cycles had previously been induced by sequential HMG and HCG therapy. Figure 7 depicts the established therapeutic schedule and the augmented urine pregnanediol excretion, which suggests an ovulatory cycle. Two months after this successful ovulation, follicle maturation was attempted by 8 days of HMG therapy for a total of 1525 IU. Forty-eight hours later, a continuous i.v. infusion of synthetic LH-RH was given. Details on this procedure are depicted in Fig. 8. No ovulatory response was observed with this particular treatment.

In spite of these disappointing results, in patient E. A., age 42, follicular development was achieved by 1800 IU of HMG and ovulation was induced by a continuous 24-h i.v. infusion of 1.2 mg of porcine LH-RH. As shown in Fig. 9, both LH and FSH reached very high levels with a noticeable decrease after the first 5 h of infusion. The stimulus of the pituitary gonadotropin secretion most likely resulted in ovulation, as suggested by increased urine pregnanediols during a 14-day period. Although a successful ovulation was obtained in this patient, the infusion of LH-RH was not responsible for the follicular maturation, since it was used only as a chorionic gonadotropin substitute according to the classical method of induction of ovulation with menotropins.

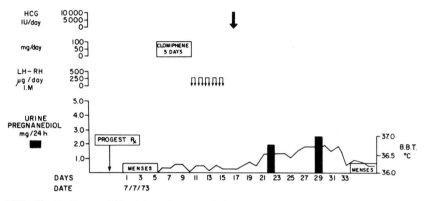

FIG. 10. E. G., age 32, with Stein-Leventhal's syndrome. (Same patient as in Fig. 6.) Regimen E induced ovulation. Pregnancy was obtained after two courses of a similar therapeutic schedule.

Induction of Ovulation by Sequential Clomiphene, LH-RH, and HCG Therapy (Regimens D and E)

The inability to induce ovulatory cycles in patient E. G. (Fig. 6) by bilateral ovarian wedge resection, by repeated clomiphene therapy, or by regimen B of LH-RH administration, suggested the possibility of using the sequential therapeutic procedure described under regimen E. Figure 10 depicts the therapeutic schedule as well as the results obtained. A biphasic BBT and high levels of urine pregnanediol suggested ovulation with a normal luteal phase and menstrual bleeding after 16 days of HCG injection. In this patient, a similar regimen was repeated for two consecutive cycles with ovulation demonstrated in both. In the last of these treatments, pregnancy was achieved.

A second patient (A. K. H., age 23) with Stein-Leventhal's syndrome without ovulation induced by ovarian wedge resection or clomiphene therapy, but with a positive response to sequential HMG/HCG therapy, was submitted to regimen D. Figure 11 shows an ovulatory response with a normal luteal phase of 14 days but no pregnancy.

A similar regimen was followed in one patient with galactorrhea-amenorrhea syndrome associated with a pituitary tumor (T. D. Z., age 31). As shown in Fig. 12, an ovulatory cycle was also induced with this regimen. It should be mentioned that both patients were resistant to clomiphene therapy alone and both had a noticeable estrogen secretion.

In two patients with diagnosis of hypothalamic amenorrhea and moderate hypoestrogenism, regimen D could not induce ovulation or menstrual bleeding within 1 month of treatment (Figs. 13 and 14).

Finally, patient R. M. G., age 21, with a diagnosis of galactorrhea-amenor-

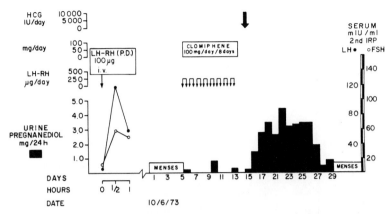

FIG. 11. A. K. H., age 23. LH-RH therapy according to regimen D induced ovulation, as suggested by biphasic urine pregnanediol excretion with high values for more than 10 days.

rhea but no demonstrable pituitary tumor, was treated with sequential HMG/ HCG prior to the initiation of the schedule described under regimen D. As shown in Fig. 15, the patient had severe hypoestrogenism, as suggested by a very low maturation value of the vaginal smear. Increased pregnanediols suggested ovulation with a 10-day luteal phase which was followed by a normal menstrual bleeding. In the following cycle, LH-RH associated with clomiphene therapy was

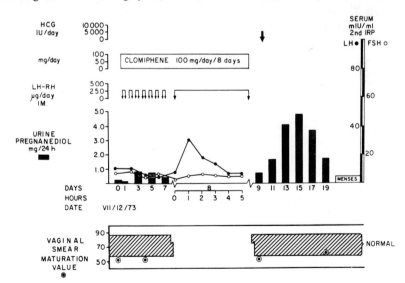

FIG. 12. T. D. Z., age 31. Ovulatory cycle after regimen D of LH-RH administration in a patient with galactorrhea-amenorrhea associated with a pituitary tumor.

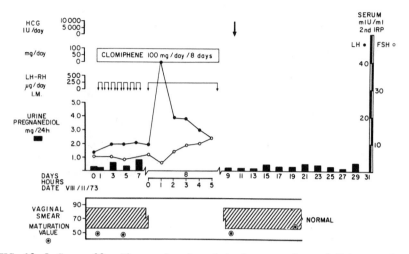

FIG. 13. J. S., age 33, with secondary hypothalamic amenorrhea and diabetes mellitus. (Same patient as in Figs. 7 and 8.) Note that regimen D of LH-RH administration did not induce ovulation.

initiated as described under regimen D. In spite of the ovulatory response obtained with the menotropin and HCG therapy, regimen D did not induce ovulation in this particular patient. It should be noticed that this patient and the previous two with hypothalamic amenorrhea did not respond to clomiphene therapy alone and all of them presented clinical features of hypoestrogenism.

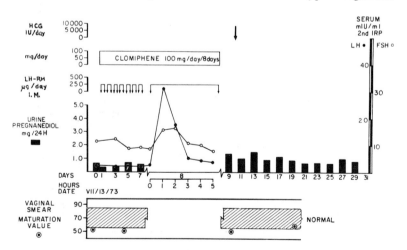

FIG. 14. C. V. G., age 22, with hypoestrogenic primary hypothalamic amenorrhea. Regimen D of LH-RH administration did not induce ovulation.

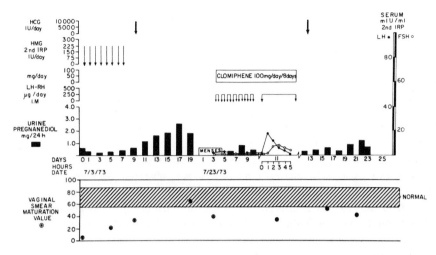

FIG. 15. R. M. G., age 21, with galactorrhea-amenorrhea without demonstrable pituitary tumor. Note severe hypoestrogenism in vaginal smears. Ovulation was induced by sequential HMG/HCG therapy but was not achieved by regimen D of LH-RH administration.

CONCLUSIONS

The first evidence of the ovulatory effects of LH-RH administration was reported by Kastin *et al.* (1971b) in a patient in whom follicular maturation had previously been achieved by an appropriate HMG therapy. In this particular case, LH-RH was infused throughout a 24-h period with the aim of inducing a brisk LH pituitary release and rupture of an already mature graafian follicle. Our present study confirms this initial report as well as that of Keller (1973). It should be pointed out that the therapeutic effect exerted by LH-RH may also be achieved with HCG, but LH-RH was administered with the idea of avoiding the overstimulation of the ovaries and multiple pregnancies which have been related to HCG therapy. Although only single pregnancies have been observed with the use of LH-RH in a similar fashion as our regimen C, it is not possible to establish any significant conclusion, since up to date only two cases have been reported. Triggering of ovulation after infusion of synthetic LH-RH in women with previously matured ovarian follicles has been reported by Nakano *et al.* (1973) in normal ovulating women in whom artificial insemination was tried in the preovulatory phase of the cycle. Although successful pregnancies were obtained in these patients, a causal relationship between LH-RH infusion and ovulation could not be proven since it is possible that ovulation took place independent of LH-RH therapy. In any case, from this and other reports (Akande *et al.*, 1972) it has been clearly established that a mature follicle should be obtained prior to a prolonged intravenous LH-RH administration.

Induction of ovarian follicle growth and ovulation with gonadotropin-releasing hormone in women with secondary amenorrhea has been successfully reported by a number of investigators (Keller, 1973; Schneider and Dahlén, 1973; Zarate *et al.*, 1973; Zañartu *et al.*, 1974a). In most of the reported cases, ovulation was obtained by therapeutic schedules comparable to our regimens A and B. Evidence presented by Zarate *et al.* (1973) indicates that repeated i.m. doses of synthetic LH-RH of at least 200 μg on each of 5 consecutive days induce ovarian response, as suggested by increased secretion of urinary estrogens in nearly 50% of treated women having secondary amenorrhea. It should be stressed that these patients gave a positive response to a gestagen-withdrawal bleeding test. Also an ovulation rate of 25% was observed with pregnancy in seven out of 42 patients so treated. Comparable results were reported by Zañartu *et al.* (1974a) in a group of seven lactating postpartum amenorrheic women and 15 with secondary amenorrhea diagnosed as idiopathic hypothalamic dysfunction. Successful ovulatory cycles have also been obtained after LH-RH therapy in amenorrheic patients secondary to long-term injectable progestational contraceptive therapy (Zañartu *et al.*, 1974b). In spite of these successful reports, we were not able to induce ovulation with similar regimens of LH-RH administration in three patients with Stein-Leventhal's syndrome and in one patient with galactorrhea-amenorrhea without demonstrable pituitary tumor. In all these patients, previous clomiphene therapy had induced ovulatory cycles. The small number of patients treated with regimens A and B in the present study makes it difficult to explain the differences found from results reported by others.

The use of regimens D and E of LH-RH administration in selected patients with Stein-Leventhal's syndrome and galactorrhea-amenorrhea with a positive gestagen-withdrawal bleeding test induced ovulatory cycles in all patients and even pregnancy in one. Although it is difficult to prove a causal relationship between LH-RH administration and ovulation, it should be taken into consideration that repeated cycles with clomiphene therapy alone had failed to cause ovulation.

It is interesting that regimens D and E were unable to induce ovulation in patients with hypothalamic amenorrhea or galactorrhea in whom ovulatory cycles had previously been induced by sequential HMG/HCG therapy. These three patients presented evidence of hypoestrogenism and did not respond to a gestagen-withdrawal bleeding test. For the time being, it is not possible to explain these failures, but it seems appropriate to point out that clear-cut differences in responses were found depending on the presence or absence of clinical hypoestrogenism. Therefore, it might be concluded that in some cases of primary or secondary amenorrhea and sterility some regimens of LH-RH administration have proved their potential and more experience is required to establish definitive conclusions.

REFERENCES

Akande, E. O., Bonnar, J., Carr, P. J., Corker, C. S., Dutton, A., MacKinnon, P. C. B., and Robinson, D. (1972), Effect of synthetic gonadotrophin-releasing hormone in secondary amenorrhoea, *Lancet 2:*112.

Gual, C. (1966), Pregnanediol studies in the detection of ovulation, in: *Ovulation: Stimulation, Suppression, Detection,* Sec. III, pp. 310–318. (R. B. Greenblatt, ed.), Lippincott, Philadelphia.

Gual, C. (1973), Clinical effects and uses of hypothalamic releasing and inhibiting factors, in: *Frontiers in Neuroendocrinology,* Chap. 4, pp. 89–131. (W. F. Ganong and L. Martini, eds.), Oxford University Press, New York.

Gual, C., Flores, F., Kastin, A. J., Schally, A. V., and Midgley, A. R., Jr. (1970), Valoración de la función hipofisiaria en el humano mediante el empleo de hormonas liberadoras hipotalámicas (LH-RH), in: *Proc. Annu. Meeting. Soc. Mex. Nutr. Endocrinol.,* Vol. 10, p. 331.

Gual, C., Kastin, A. J., Midgley, A. R., Jr., and Flores, F. (1971), Administration of LH-releasing hormone (LH-RH) as a clinical test of pituitary function, in: *53rd Meeting of the Endocrine Society, San Francisco,* p. 128 (abst.).

Kastin, A. J., Schally, A. V., Gual, C., Midgley, A. R., Jr., Bowers, C. Y., and Diaz-Infante, A., Jr. (1969), Stimulation of LH release in men and women by LH-releasing hormone purified from porcine hypothalami, *J. Clin. Endocrinol. Metab. 29:*1046.

Kastin, A. J., Schally, A. V., Gual, C., Midgley, A. R., Jr., Bowers, C. Y., and Gomez-Pérez, F. (1970a), Administration of LH-releasing hormone to selected subjects, *Am. J. Obstet. Gynecol. 108:*177.

Kastin, A. J., Schally, A. V., Gual, C., and Midgley, A. R., Jr. (1970b), Clinical studies with LH-releasing hormone, *Acta Endocrinol. Panam. 1:*147.

Kastin, A. J., Schally, A. V., Gual, C., Midgley, A. R., Jr., Miller, M. C., III, and Cabeza, A. (1971a), Dose–response relationship of luteinizing hormone to LH-releasing hormone in man, *J. Clin. Invest. 50:*1551.

Kastin, A. J., Zarate, A., Midgley, A. R., Jr., Canales, E. S., and Schally, A. V. (1971b), Ovulation confirmed by pregnancy after infusion of porcine LH-RH, *J. Clin. Endocrinol. Metab. 33:*980.

Kastin, A. J., Schally, A. V., Gual, C., and Arimura, A. (1972), Release of LH-FSH after administration of synthetic LH-RH, *J. Clin. Endocrinol. Metab. 34:*753.

Keller, P. J. (1973), Treatment of anovulation with synthetic luteinizing hormone-releasing hormone, *Am. J. Obstet. Gynecol. 11:*698.

Midgley, A. R., Jr. (1966), Radioimmunoassay: A method for human chorionic gonadotropin and human luteinizing hormone, *Endocrinology 79:*10.

Midgley, A. R., Jr. (1967), Radioimmunoassay for human follicle stimulating hormone, *J. Clin. Endocrinol. Metab. 27:*295.

Milhaud, G., Rivaille, P., Moukhtar, M. S., Binet, E., and Job, J. C. (1971), Response of normal, hypothyroid and hypothalamo-pituitary insufficient children to synthetic thyrotrophin-releasing hormone, *J. Endocrinol. 51:*483.

Nakano, R., Mizuno, T., Kotsuji, F., Katayama, K., Washio, M., and Tojo, S. (1973), "Triggering" of ovulation after infusion of synthetic luteinizing hormone releasing factor (LRF), *Acta Obstet. Gynecol. Scand. 52:*269.

Schneider, H. P. G., and Dahlén, H. G. (1973), Gonadotropin-releasing hormone induced ovarian follicular growth and ovulation in women with secondary amenorrhea, in: *Hypothalamic Hypophysiotropic Hormones: Physiological and Clinical Studies,* pp. 302–305 (C. Gual and E. Rosemberg, eds.), International Congress Series No. 263, Excerpta Medica, Amsterdam.

Zañartu, J., Dabancens, A., Kastin, A. J., and Schally, A. V. (1974a), Effect of synthetic hypothalamic gonadotropin releasing hormone (FSH/LH-RH) in anovulatory sterility, *Fertil. Steril. 25:*160.

Zañartu, J., Dabancens, A., Rodriguez-Bravo, R., and Schally, A. V. (1974b), Induction of ovulation with synthetic gonadotrophin-releasing hormone (FSH/LH-RH) in women with constant anovulation induced by contraceptive steroids, *Brit. Med. J. 1:*605.

Zarate, A., Canales, E. S., Soria, J., Kastin, A. J., Schally, A. V., and Gonzalez, A. (1973), Further observations on the therapy of anovulatory sterility with synthetic luteinizing hormone-releasing hormone, *Fertil. Steril. 25:*3.

24

Regulation of the Human Menstrual Cycle

Robert B. Jaffe

Department of Obstetrics and Gynecology
University of California
San Francisco, California

The temporal juxtaposition of several methodological and investigative advances in the area of reproductive endocrinology has furnished the impetus for a rapid proliferation of new information related to the regulation of the menstrual cycle. These advances have included the development of radioimmunoassay and other ligand-binding techniques for the precise, specific quantitation of hormones in very small quantities of blood and other body fluids; the isolation, identification, and synthesis of some of the neurohumoral substances of the hypothalamus which regulate pituitary function; and a greater understanding of the mechanism of hormonal action at the subcellular, cellular, and organ level. In this chapter, an attempt will be made to interweave a description of these advances into the matrix of currently held concepts of the endocrine regulation of the cycle.

THE HYPOTHALAMIC–PITUITARY SYSTEM AND ITS REGULATION

The synthesis and release of gonadotropins by the pituitary gland is regulated either by a single neurohormone (Schally *et al.,* 1971) or by two humoral factors, one regulating the synthesis and release of LH and the other those of FSH. This substance (or substances) has been variously referred to as gonadotropin-releasing hormone (GnRH), luteinizing-releasing hormone or factor (LH-RH or LRF), and follicle stimulating hormone-releasing hormone (FSH-RH) (McCann and Ramirez, 1964; Johansson *et al.,* 1973; Currie *et al.,* 1973; Bowers *et al.,* 1973). These substances are released by nerve fibers originating in the hypothalamus and are transported to the anterior pituitary via the hypophyseal portal system.

Substantiation of this concept was furnished by the demonstration that hypothalamic extracts from rats, domestic animals, and humans were capable of stimulating gonadotropin release (Schally *et al.*, 1972a). A substance capable of releasing LH, and to a lesser degree FSH, has recently been isolated from porcine hypothalami. This substance, referred to as GnRH, has been structurally characterized and synthesized (Matsuo *et al.*, 1971a,b). Porcine GnRH is a decapeptide containing glycine, histidine, arginine, tryptophan, serine, glutamic acid, proline, leucine, and tyrosine. Within months of the isolation of porcine GnRH, ovine GnRH was purified and its amino acid sequence determined. Although human GnRH has not been structurally identified, its chemical and biological characteristics appear similar to those of porcine GnRH. The observation that the human responds to porcine GnRH (Kastin *et al.*, 1969) further suggests a similarity of human and porcine GnRH.

In vitro experiments with GnRH have demonstrated the release of both LH and FSH from incubated pituitaries (Schally *et al.*, 1972b), demonstrating that GnRH acts directly on pituitary tissue. Further *in vitro* experiments suggested that GnRH stimulates both the synthesis and the release of LH and FSH (Redding *et al.*, 1972). Bio- and radioimmunoassays have been reported (Malacara *et al.*, 1972; Kerdelhué and Jutisz, 1972; Nett *et al.*, 1973; Keye *et al.*, 1973).

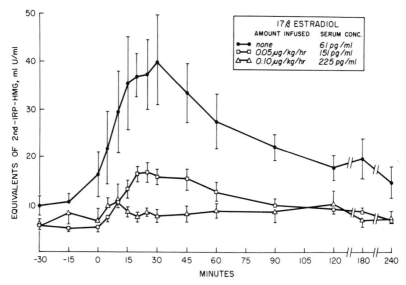

FIG. 1. *Luteinizing hormone (LH) response to intravenous bolus of 50 μg gonadotropin-releasing hormone in women receiving no treatment or infusions of 17β-estradiol during the early follicular phase of the menstrual cycle.* From Keye and Jaffe (1974).

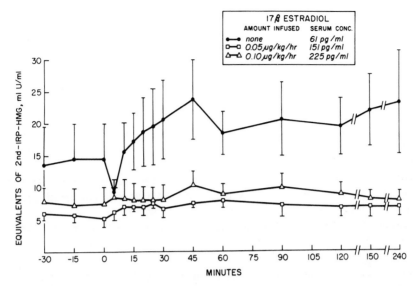

FIG. 2. *Follicle-stimulating hormone (FSH) response to intravenous bolus of 50 μg gonado-tropin-releasing hormone in women receiving no treatment or 17β-estradiol during the early follicular phase of the menstrual cycle.* From Keye and Jaffe (1974).

Several clinical studies with porcine, human, and synthetic GnRH have been reported. Kastin *et al.* (1969, 1970, 1971) studied the ability of porcine GnRH to release gonadotropins in 30 men and women. Some of the subjects were pretreated with estrogen alone, others with estrogen plus progestin, and others with clomiphene citrate. All of the subjects responded with the release of LH and FSH, except one subject with a pituitary tumor. In these experiments, the magnitude of the LH response was greater than that of FSH, and the peak response for both gonadotropins occurred between 16 and 32 min. A single case of pregnancy has been reported after a course of human menopausal gonado-tropins followed by a single dose of porcine GnRH (Gual *et al.*, 1971).

Studies with synthetic GnRH in women during the menstrual cycle have been reported (Yen *et al.*, 1972a). It was found that the sensitivity of the pituitary to GnRH progressively increases as the time of ovulation is approached. It was suggested that the midcycle surge of gonadotropins may be due to an increased sensitivity of the pituitary to endogenous GnRh brought about by increasing levels of circulating estradiol. We have recently studied the effect of 17β-estradiol on pituitary responsiveness to GnRH (Keye and Jaffe, 1974). Our initial studies examined the effect of 17β-estradiol on pituitary response to 50 μg of GnRh in 15 women on day 2 of the menstrual cycle. Three groups of women were studied: Group I did not receive exogenous estradiol. Groups II and III received 17β-estradiol in amounts which achieved circulating concentrations equal to those seen in the midfollicular and ovulatory phases of the menstrual cycle, respectively. The data from these studies are depicted in Figs. 1 and 2. As can be seen, a significant increase in circulating LH occurred following GnRH administration in group I. A diminished response occurred in group II, while LH concentrations failed to rise in group III. A significant increase in circulating FSH concentrations occurred only in group I. These data demonstrate a direct and inhibitory effect of estradiol on the pituitary.

The failure of 17β-estradiol to increase pituitary responsiveness may have been related to either the duration of the estradiol infusion or the temporal relationship between the increasing estradiol concentration and the administration of GnRH. A recent study utilizing the rhesus monkey suggests that the positive feedback effect of estradiol may be both dose and time related (Weick et al., 1972). Therefore, our more recent studies have involved bidaily intramuscular administration of estradiol benzoate to women on days 1–6 of the menstrual cycle, followed by administration of 100 μg GnRH on days 7 and 8. By use of this technique, a pronounced augmentation of the response to GnRH was observed, with the peak LH response reaching as much as tenfold the response seen in non-estradiol-treated control subjects during the follicular phase.

Other studies have focused on the possible clinical utility of GnRH. The ability of GnRH to induce ovulation has been established. Three women with secondary amenorrhea were given an 8-h infusion of 100 μg of GnRH with a bolus of 100 μg at the end of the infusion. Ten days later they received a second 8-h infusion of GnRH. Two of the women had presumptive signs of ovulation, but neither became pregnant. In this same study, ten women with secondary amenorrhea received intramuscular injections of 50 μg of GnRH each day for 10 days. Four had presumptive signs of ovulation, and two became pregnant. In another study, 15 amenorrheic women who were unresponsive to clomiphene citrate alone were given 100 mg of clomiphene citrate daily for 5 days. Six to seven days later, a 4-h infusion of 500 μg GnRH was performed. Presumptive signs of ovulation occurred in 12 women, and two became pregnant (Zarate et al., 1972; Keller, 1972).

It has also been suggested that GnRH may be useful in the practice of contraception. Four possible uses have been discussed by Schally et al. (1972a): (1) its administration once a month might induce and pinpoint the time of ovulation for those practicing the "rhythm method"; (2) once a month administration, if properly timed, might disrupt the normal events of the menstrual cycle, thereby interfering with ovulation or implantation; (3) interference with the function of endogenous GnRH might occur with the administration of an antiserum to GnRH; or (4) synthetic inhibitors, or analogues, of GnRH might be utilized. At present, no confirmation of the validity of these suggestions has been presented.

There is evidence, in a variety of species, that gonadotropin release is modulated, at least in part, by gonadal steroids. These steroids may exert either a positive or a negative feedback on gonadotropin release, acting either directly on the pituitary or indirectly via the hypothalamus. The concept of negative feedback, i.e., that the secretion of gonadotropins is inversely related to the levels of gonadal steroids, is supported by the observation that circulating gonadotropins decreased during the administration of estrogen to ovariectomized, postmenopausal, and premenopausal women during the follicular phase of the cycle (Bogdanove, 1964; Everett, 1969; Flerkó, 1970; Sawyer, 1969; Davidson, 1969; Tsai and Yen, 1971; Nilius and Wide, 1971; Monroe et al., 1972; Yen and Tsai, 1972). Similarly, the positive feedback of gonadal steroids resulting in a stimulation of gonadotropin synthesis and release has been suggested. The positive influence of estrogens is suggested by the midcycle surge of gonadotropins which, in general, follows the preovulatory peak of 17β-estradiol (Burger et al., 1968; Goebelsmann et al., 1969; Abraham et al., 1972). Evidence in support of the positive feedback effect of estrogens comes from studies in which (1) ovulation occurred in some anovulatory women after the administration of exogenous estrogens (Brown et al., 1953), (2) LH increased 36 h after the administration of intravenous Premarin (Swerdloff and Odell, 1969; Vande Wiele et al., 1970), (3) LH increased after the administration of 17β-estradiol in the early follicular phase (Monroe et al., 1972; Yen and Tsai, 1972), and (4) LH and FSH increased after the administration of 17β-estradiol in the midfollicular phase (Yen and Tsai, 1972). The stimulatory effect of progesterone on gonadotropins has also been noted (Odell and Swerdloff, 1968).

The question of whether prolactin plays a major, obligatory role in the menstrual cycle of women remains unanswered. Studies in which daily serum concentrations of prolactin have been measured in women with normal menstrual cycles (Hwang et al., 1971; Jaffe et al., 1973) demonstrate daily fluctuations; however, no significant consistent difference in values could be found in the various phases of the cycle. Further, no significant differences in prolactin concentration between menstruating and postmenopausal women have been observed (Friesen, 1971). These observations, as well as the ability to induce ovulation in hypophysectomized women, suggest that unlike in other species prolactin may not be essential to menstrual cycle regulation.

THE PITUITARY–OVARIAN AXIS AND ITS REGULATION

Utilizing daily blood sampling in women with normal menstrual cycles, Midgley and Jaffe (1968) (Fig. 3) found that the concentrations of LH rose sharply from 5.5 ± 0.6 milli-international units (mIU)/ml (mean ± SEM) on the day preceding the first day of menses to 9.3 ± 1.2 on the first day of menses. LH levels reached a plateau at an average concentration of 13 mIU/ml 10 days prior to a midcycle LH peak. This characteristic midcycle surge occurs over a 1–3 day

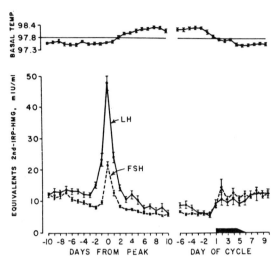

FIG. 3. *Composite curves of basal body temperatures and concentrations of LH and FSH in sera during the menstrual cycles of 37 women.* The data have been plotted in relationship to the number of days before and after the LH peak, the number of days before menses, and the day of the cycle. Vertical bars represent 1 SEM. From Midgley and Jaffe (1968).

interval and reaches a maximal concentration of 47.8 ± 2.2. Following this midcycle peak, LH concentrations fluctuate markedly throughout the luteal phase, gradually falling to reach a nadir on the day preceding the first day of the next menstrual cycle.

The mean serum concentrations of FSH showed a somewhat different pattern. From levels of 6.4 ± 0.5 mIU/ml on the day prior to the onset of menses, FSH concentrations rapidly increased, reaching a level of 14.4 ± 2.6 mIU/ml on the second day of menses. The levels fluctuated considerably during the first 5 days of the cycle, then stabilized and steadily fell to 8.1 ± 0.5 mIU/ml 2 days before the LH peak. Concomitant with the peak in LH, a peak of FSH of lesser magnitude (21.5 ± 1.3) and briefer duration than that of LH was observed. Following this peak, the levels of FSH gradually declined to a mean level of about 6 mIU/ml during the latter half of the luteal phase of the cycle. The marked fluctuations in serum concentrations of LH in the luteal phase were not observed for FSH.

The mean follicular phase LH/FSH ratios were lower than those seen in the periovulatory and luteal phases. The lowest daily ratio (0.73) occurred on cycle day 2, and the highest daily ratio (2.52) occurred 1 day before the LH peak.

Serum concentrations of gonadotropins, especially LH, do not seem to be maintained in a steady-state fashion. Hourly sampling during different phases of the menstrual cycle (Midgley and Jaffe, 1971) indicated that LH is secreted in a pulsatile fashion, especially at the time of the midcycle surge of LH and during the luteal phase (Fig. 4). The magnitude of the pulses was greatest during the midcycle surge and least during the late follicular phase. The pattern of these pulses also varies during the menstrual cycle. A periodicity of 1–2 h was observed during the early follicular phase, the early luteal phase, and the midcycle surge (Yen *et al.*, 1972b). During the mid and late luteal phase, the periodicity increased to 4 h.

Postmenopausal women, in contrast to menstruating women, had pulses of both gonadotropins which were usually coincident, but minor asynchrony between the LH and FSH patterns was seen. The frequency of pulses in postmenopausal subjects was the same as in women during the follicular phase and at midcycle, with the magnitude of the pulses resembling that of the midcycle surge.

Estradiol infusion diminishes the amplitude of the pulsatile pattern of LH and FSH secretion (Yen *et al.*, 1972b). Regardless of the dose of estradiol infused, pituitary gonadotropin secretion cannot be completely eliminated (Yen and Tsai, 1972). Gonadotropin concentrations therefore appear to be maintained both by continuous "basal" secretion and by superimposed episodic pulses of release.

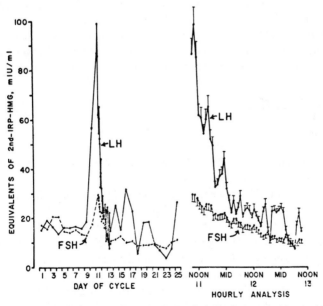

FIG. 4. Concentrations of LH and FSH obtained daily from a subject with a 25-day menstrual cycle. Samples obtained at hourly intervals during the descending phase of the LH peak observed at midcycle (days 11–13) are also shown on the right half of the figure on an expanded time scale. The vertical bars represent 1 SEM of duplicate determinations. From Midgley and Jaffe (1971).

REGULATION OF THE CORPUS LUTEUM

The role of LH in maintenance of the structural integrity of the corpus luteum and the capacity for steroid secretion, particularly of progesterone, have long been a subject of investigation.

LH has been employed to induce ovulation in hypophysectomized patients who have been pretreated with human menopausal gonadotropins (Vande Wiele et al., 1970). The ovulating dose of LH, if not administered repeatedly, results in an abnormally short luteal phase. Maintenance of the corpus luteum for the usual number of days requires repeated LH administration during the luteal phase. In such patients, continuation of LH administration beyond the expected life span of the corpus luteum does not prevent its regression around the eighteenth day of the luteal phase, as evidenced by falling progesterone and estrogen levels in blood. In contrast, ovulation induced by a single dose of HCG is followed by the formation of a corpus luteum which is maintained for its normal life span of about 13 days. This differing ability of HCG and LH to influence the human corpus luteum is thought due to the longer half-life of HCG.

Thus, in the absence of conception, the corpus luteum appears to be destined to regress. In the event of pregnancy, we have found that serum HCG concentrations begin to rise as early as 8 days after ovulation, presumably 1 day after implantation (Jaffe et al., 1969). This placental hormone maintains the corpus luteum and stimulates continued progesterone production until secretion from the developing trophoblast is adequate to maintain this function.

OVARIAN STEROIDS

The serum concentrations of estrone (E_1), estradiol (E_2), 17-OH-progesterone (17-OH-P), and progesterone during the menstrual cycle have been determined (Abraham et al., 1972; Baird and Guevara, 1969; Lloyd et al., 1971; Johansson et al., 1971; Ross et al., 1970).

Although serum E_2 concentrations found by use of radioimmunoassay techniques are somewhat lower than those reported previously using a double-isotope method, the profiles throughout the cycle are similar. A mean E_2 concentration of about 50 pg/ml is observed during the menses and early follicular phase. The estradiol levels then rapidly rise to about 250 pg/ml (range 130–400) just preceding, or on the day of, the LH peak. A sharp drop follows this midcycle peak to reach a mean concentration of about 80 pg/ml. One to two days later estradiol levels rise slowly, to about 120 pg/ml 4–10 days after the LH peak, and then fall to 30–50 pg/ml on the first day of menses. The plasma concentrations of estradiol are low in castrated (36 ± 13) and postmenopausal women (13 ± 2).

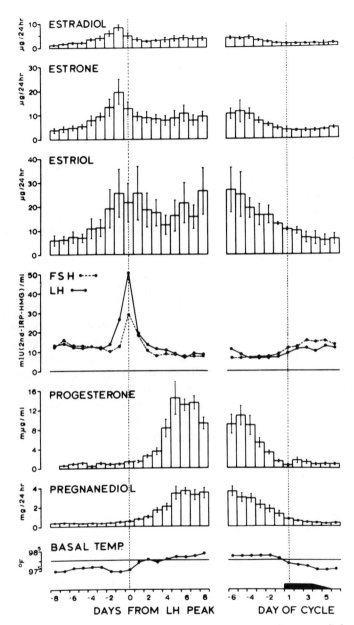

FIG. 5. Composite profiles of means of data of urinary estrogen and pregnanediol excretion and serum LH, FSH, and progesterone concentrations in five normally cycling women. Data are plotted in terms of both days from the LH and FSH peak at midcycle and days from the onset of menstruation. Vertical bars indicate SE. From Goebelsmann *et al.* (1969).

The ratio of E_2/E_1 changes significantly during the cycle. The mean ratio ± SE increases from 0.67 ± 0.13 in the early follicular phase to 1.90 ± 0.12 just prior to ovulation. The ratio falls to 1.32 ± 0.31 just after the LH peak and then rises to 1.03 ± 0.18 during the luteal phase of the cycle. In contrast, concentrations of E_1 are threefold higher than those of E_2 in castrated and postmenopausal women.

Plasma concentrations of 17-OH-P are relatively constant (approximately 0.2–0.5 ng/ml) during the follicular phase. Although there has been a significant rise 2–3 days prior to the LH peak in some cycles studied, this late follicular rise is inconsistent. A rise in 17-OH-P to a mean peak concentration of 2 ng/ml is seen on the day of the LH peak. Following a fall 1 day after the LH peak to a mean of 1 ng/ml, a subsequent rise is observed during the next 4–5 days to reach a second peak with a mean of about 2 ng/ml. Then plasma 17-OH-P levels decline progressively during the late luteal phase to reach levels between 0.2 and 0.5 ng/ml on the first day of menses.

The plasma progesterone concentration during the early follicular phase is about 0.8 ng/ml. A steady fall occurs to levels of approximately 0.3–0.4 ng/ml 8 days before the LH peak. This level is maintained until the day of the LH peak, when the progesterone concentration rises to 1–2 ng/ml. Using hourly sampling, we have shown that significant fluctuations of progesterone do not occur prior to the LH surge (unpublished data). On the third to fourth day following the LH peak a marked increase in progesterone occurs, reaching concentrations between 10 and 20 ng/ml 5–10 days later. Thereafter, the plasma concentrations decline to reach values of about 0.8 ng/ml on the first day of menses.

With the methodological techniques now available, further studies should elucidate the temporal and physiological interrelationships of the ovarian steroids and the gonadotropins which regulate their formation.

REFERENCES

Abraham, G. E., Odell, W. D., Swerdloff, R. S., and Hopper, K. (1972), Simultaneous radioimmunoassay of plasma FSH, LH, progesterone, 17-hydroxyprogesterone and estradiol-17β during the menstrual cycle, *J. Clin. Endocrinol. Metab. 34:*312.
Baird, D. T., and Guevara, A. (1969), Concentration of unconjugated estrone and estradiol in peripheral plasma in nonpregnant women through the menstrual cycle, castrate and postmenopausal women and in men, *J. Clin. Endocrinol. Metab. 29:*149.
Bogdanove, E. M. (1964), The role of the brain in the regulation of pituitary gonadotropin secretion, *Vitamins Hormones 22:*205.
Bowers, C. Y., Currie, B. L., Johansson, K. N. G., and Folkers, K. (1973), Biological evidence that separate hypothalamic hormones release the follicle stimulating and lutenizing hormones, *Biochem. Biophys. Res. Commun. 50:*20.
Brown, W. E., Bradbury, J. T., and Juncek, E. L. (1953), The effect of estrogens and other steroids on the pituitary gonadotropins in women, *Am. J. Obstet. Gynecol. 65:*733.
Burger, H. G., Catt, K., and Brown, J. B. (1968), Relationship between plasma luteinizing

hormone and urinary estrogen excretion during the menstrual cycle, *J. Clin. Endocrinol. Metab. 28:*1508.

Currie, B. L., Johansson, K. N. G., Folkers, K., and Bowers, C. Y. (1973), On the chemical existence and partial purification of the hypothalamic follicle stimulating hormone releasing hormone, *Biochem. Biophys. Res. Commun. 50:*14.

Davidson, J. M. (1969), in *Frontiers in Neuroendocrinology* (W. F. Ganong and L. Martini, eds.), Oxford University Press, New York.

Everett, J. W. (1969), Neuroendocrine aspects of mammalian reproduction, *Ann. Rev. Physiol. 31:*383.

Flerkó, B. (1970), in: *The Hypothalamus* (L. Martini, M. Motta, and F. Fraschini, eds.), Academic Press, New York.

Friesen, H. (1971), Human placental lactogen and human pituitary prolactin, *Clin. Obstet. Gynecol. 14:*669.

Goebelsmann, U., Midgley, A. R., Jr., and Jaffe, R. B. (1969), Regulation of human gonadotropins. VII. Daily individual urinary estrogens, pregnanediol and serum luteinizing and follicle stimulating hormones during the menstrual cycle, *J. Clin. Endocrinol. Metab. 29:*1222.

Gual, C., Kastin, A. J., Midgley, A. R., Jr., and Flores, F. (1971), *Endocrinology 88:*A-171.

Hwang, P., Guyda, H., and Friesen, H. (1971), A radioimmunoassay for human prolactin, *Proc. Natl. Acad. Sci (U.S.A.) 68:*1902.

Jaffe, R. B., and Keye, W. R., Jr. (1974), Estradiol augmentation of pituitary responsiveness to gonadotropin releasing hormone in women, *J. Clin. Endocrinol. Metab.,* in press.

Jaffe, R. B., Lee, P. A., and Midgley, A. R., Jr. (1969), Serum gonadotropins before, at the inception of and following human pregnancy, *J. Clin. Endocrinol. Metab. 29:*1281.

Jaffe, R. B., HoYuen, B., Keye, W. R., Jr., and Midgley, A. R., Jr. (1973), Physiologic and pathologic profiles of circulating human prolactin, *Am. J. Obstet. Gynecol. 117:*757.

Johansson, E. D. B., Wide, L., and Gemzell, C. (1971), Luteinizing hormone (LH) and progesterone in plasma and LH and oestrogens in urine during 42 normal menstrual cycles. *Acta Endocrinologica 68:*502.

Johansson, K. N. G., Currie, B. L., Folkers, K., and Bowers, C. Y. (1973), Biosynthesis and evidence for the existence of follicle stimulating releasing hormone, *Biochem. Biophys. Res. Commun. 50:*8.

Kastin, A. J., Schally, A. V., Gual, C., Midgley, A. R., Jr., Bowers, C. Y., and Diaz-Infante, A. (1969), Stimulation of LH release in men and women by LH-releasing hormone purified from porcine hypothalami, *J. Clin. Endocrinol. Metab. 29:*1046.

Kastin, A. J., Schally, A. V., Gual, C., Midgley, A. R., Jr., Bowers, C. Y., and Gomez-Perez, F. (1970), Administration of LH-releasing hormone to selected subjects, *Am. J. Obstet. Gynecol. 108:*177.

Kastin, A. J., Schally, A. V., Gual, C., Midgley, A. R., Jr., Miller, M. C., and Flores, F. (1971), Increased release of LH after administration of LH-RH to men pretreated with clomiphene, *J. Clin. Endocrinol. Metab. 31:*689.

Keller, P. J. (1972), Induction of ovulation by synthetic luteinizing hormone releasing factor in infertile women, *Lancet 2:*570.

Kerdelhué, B., and Jutisz, M. (1972), Development of a radioimmunoassay of a hypothalamic hormone which stimulates the release of pituitary luteinizing hormone and follicle stimulating hormone (LH-RH) using a synthetic decapeptide as antigen, in *IV International Congress of Endocrinology,* Abst. No. 352, p. 141, International Congress Series 256, Excerpta Medica, Amsterdam.

Keye, W. R., Jr., and Jaffe, R. B. (1974), Modulation of pituitary gonadotropin response to gonadotropin-releasing hormone by estradiol, *J. Clin. Endocrinol. Metab. 38:*805.

Keye, W. R., Jr., Kelch, R. P., Niswender, G. D., and Jaffe, R. B. (1973), Quantitation of endogenous and exogenous gonadotropin releasing hormone by RIA, *J. Clin. Endocrinol. Metab. 36:*1263.

Lloyd, C., Lobotsky, J., Baird, D. T., McCracken, J. A., Weisz, J., Pupkin, M., Zanartu, J., and Puga, J. (1971), Concentration of unconjugated estrogens, androgens and gestagens in ovarian and peripheral venous plasma of women: The normal menstrual cycle, *J. Clin. Endocrinol. Metab. 32:*155.

Malacara, J. M., Seyler, L. E., Jr., and Reichlin, S. J. (1972), Luteinizing hormone releasing factor activity in peripheral blood from women during the mid-cycle luteinizing hormone ovulatory surge, *J. Clin. Endocrinol. Metab. 34:*271.

Matsuo, H., Baba, Y., Nair, R. M. G., and Schally, A. V. (1971a), Structure of the porcine LH- and FSH-releasing hormone. I. The proposed amino acid sequence, *Biochem. Biophys. Res. Commun. 43:*1334.

Matsuo, H., Arimura, A., Nair, R. M. G., and Schally, A. V. (1971b), Synthesis of the porcine LH- and FSH-releasing hormone by the solid-phase method, *Biochem. Biophys. Res. Commun. 45:*822.

McCann, S. M., and Ramirez, V. D. (1964), The neuroendocrine regulation of hypophyseal luteinizing hormone secretion, *Rec. Progr. Hormone Res. 20:*131.

Midgley, A. R., Jr., and Jaffe, R. B. (1968), Regulation of human gonadotropins. IV. Correlation of serum concentrations of follicle stimulating and luteinizing hormones during the menstrual cycle, *J. Clin. Endocrinol. Metab. 28:*1699.

Midgley, A. R., Jr., and Jaffe, R. B. (1971), Regulation of human gonadotropins. X. Episodic fluctuation of luteinizing hormone during the menstrual cycle, *J. Clin. Endocrinol. Metab. 33:*962.

Monroe, S. E., Jaffe, R. B., and Midgley, A. R., Jr. (1972), Regulation of human gonadotropins. XII. Increase in serum gonadotropin in response to estradiol, *J. Clin. Endocrinol. Metab. 34:*342.

Nett, T. M., Akbar, M., White, W. F., Hedlund, M. T., and Niswender, G. D. (1973), A radioimmunoassay for gonadotropin releasing hormone (GnRH) in serum, *J. Clin. Endocrinol. Metab. 36:*880.

Nillius, S. J., and Wide, L. J. (1971), Induction of a midcycle-like peak of luteinizing hormone in young women by exogenous oestradiol-17β, *J. Obstet. Gynecol. Brit. Commonw. 78:*822.

Odell, W. D., and Swerdloff, R. S. (1968), Progestogen-induced luteinizing and follicle stimulating hormone surge in postmenopausal women: A stimulated ovulatory peak, *Proc. Natl. Acad. Sci. (U.S.A.) 61:*529.

Redding, T. W., Schally, A. V., Arimura, A., and Matsuo, H. (1972), Stimulation of release and synthesis of luteinizing hormone (LH) and follicle stimulating hormone (FSH) in tissue cultures of rat pituitaries in response to natural and synthetic LH and FSH releasing hormone, *Endocrinology 90:*764.

Ross, G. T., Cargille, C. M., Lipsett, M. B., Rayford, P. L., Marshall, J. R., Strott, C. A., and Rodbard, D. (1970), Pituitary and gonadal hormones in women during spontaneous and induced ovulatory cycles, *Rec. Progr. Hormone Res. 26:*1.

Sawyer, C. H. (1969), in: *The Hypothalamus* (W. Haymaker, E. Anderson, and W. J. H. Nauta, eds.), Charles C Thomas, Springfield, Ill.

Schally, A. V., Arimura, A., Kastin, A. J., Matsuo, H., Baba, Y., Redding, T. W., Nair, R. M. G., Debeljuk, L., and White, W. F. (1971), Gonadotropin releasing hormone: One polypeptide regulates secretion of luteinizing and follicle stimulating hormones, *Science 173:*1036.

Schally, A. V., Kastin, A. J., and Arimura, A. (1972a), The hypothalamus and reproduction, *Am. J. Obstet. Gynecol. 114:*423.

Schally, A. V., Redding, T. W., Matsuo, H., and Arimura, A. (1972b), Stimulation of FSH and LH release *in vitro* by natural and synthetic LH and FSH releasing hormone, *Endocrinology 90:*1561.

Swerdloff, R. S., and Odell, W. D. (1969), Serum luteinizing and follicle stimulating hormone levels during sequential and nonsequential contraceptive treatment of eugonadal women, *J. Clin. Endocrinol. Metab. 29:*157.

Tsai, C. C., and Yen, S. S. C. (1971), Acute effects of intravenous infusion of 17β-estradiol on gonadotropin release in pre- and post-menopausal women, *J. Clin. Endocrinol. Metab. 32:*766.

Vande Wiele, R. L., Bogumil, J., Dyrenfurth, I., Ferin, M., Jewelewicz, R., Warren, M., Rizkallah, T., and Mikhail, G. (1970), Mechanisms regulating the menstrual cycle in women, *Rec. Progr. Hormone Res. 26:*63.

Weick, R. F., Karsch, F. J., Butler, W. R., Dierschke, D. J., Krey, L. C., Weiss, G., Hotchkiss, J., and Knobil, E. (1972), Strength-duration characteristics of the estrogen stimulus for the LH surge in the rhesus monkey, *Physiologist 15:*300.

Yen, S. S. C., and Tsai, C. C. (1972), Acute gonadotropin release induced by exogenous estradiol during the mid-follicular phase of the menstrual cycle, *J. Clin. Endocrinol. Metab. 34:*298.

Yen, S. S. C., VandenBerg, G., Rebar, R., and Ehara, Y. (1972a), Variation of pituitary responsiveness to synthetic LRH during different phases of the menstrual cycle, *J. Clin. Endocrinol. Metab. 35:*931.

Yen, S. S. C., Tsai, C. C., VandenBerg, G., and Rebar, R. (1972b), Gonadotropin dynamics in patients with gonadal dysgenesis: A model for the study of gonadotropin regulation, *J. Clin. Endocrinol. Metab. 35:*897.

Zarate, A., Canales, E. S., Schally, A. V., Ayala-Valdes, L., and Kastin, A. J. (1972), Successful induction of ovulation with synthetic luteinizing hormone-releasing hormone in anovulatory infertility, *Fertil. Steril. 23:*672.

25

Electroencephalographic Changes in Women Treated with Contraceptive Steroids

J. P. Gautray, A. Eberhard, A. Jolivet, and F. Leygonie

Department of Obstetrics and Gynecology
Université de Paris Val-de-Maine
Centre Hospitalier Intercommunal
Créteil, France

Daily variations of gonadotropic or steroidal hormone levels, either during the normal menstrual cycle (Cargile *et al.*, 1969; Yussman *et al.*, 1970; Midgley and Jaffe, 1971) or during steroid contraceptive treatment (Swerdloff and Odell, 1969; Taymor and Levesque, 1971; Larsson-Cohn *et al.*, 1972), have been widely described during the last few years. Estrogens and progestogens, used as contraceptives, have demonstrated a negative feedback influence, usually preventing ovulation and suppressing the early FSH elevation and the midcycle ovulatory peak (Davidson, 1969; Nillius and Wide, 1970; Thomas and Ferin, 1972). On the other hand, electroencephalographic variations are now considered a possible reflection of neural activity correlated with endocrine events of the estrus cycle (Sawyer, 1970). Although several clinical investigations of EEG variations during menstrual cycle disorders (Koren *et al.*, 1963; Sharf *et al.*, 1969; Vogel *et al.*, 1971) or during contraceptive hormonal therapy (Matsumoto *et al.*, 1966; Ansari *et al.*, 1970) have been performed, the methodology did not demonstrate patterns of EEG variations associated with either normal cyclic function or stimulation or depression of the hypothalamogonadal axis. This chapter deals with the results of a study whose aim was to establish patterns of EEG correlates of the menstrual cycle.

This work was supported by grant DGRST 70.7.2480.

MATERIALS AND METHODS

Patients

Thirteen cycles were studied in eight volunteer patients. Cycles were either spontaneous or occurred during treatment with nonsequential contraceptive steroids. These patients were healthy eugonadal women, age 22–42 yr, who were selected because of their history of regular menstrual cycles.

Four patients were studied during one cycle only; one was a normal spontaneous cycle (patient 2442/71) and three were anovulatory cycles induced by

TABLE I. Number and Characteristics of the Cycles Studied

Patient	Age (yr)	Cycles Number	Cycles Characteristics
2442/71	42	1	Spontaneous ovulatory
2146/71	28	1	Anovulatory[a]
2283/71	30	1	Anovulatory[a]
113/72	24	1	Anovulatory[b]
1891/72	22	2	1. Spontaneous ovulatory 2. Anovulatory[a]
1790/72	22	2	1. Spontaneous ovulatory 2. Ovulatory, although treated[a]
1911/72	22	2	1. Anovulatory[a] 2. Spontaneous ovulatory
1860/72	24	3	1. Spontaneous ovulatory 2. Anovulatory[a] 3. Spontaneous ovulatory
Total: 8 Patients	Mean 27	13	Total: 7 Ovulatory cycles 5 Anovulatory cycles[a] 1 Anovulatory cycle[b]

[a]Treatment with 50 μg of ethinyl estradiol plus 0.5 mg of norgestrel.

[b]Treatment with 50 μg of ethinyl estradiol plus 2 mg norethisterone.

contraceptive steroids. In two of these anovulatory cycles, the patients (2146/71 and 2283/71) had taken 5 μg of ethinyl estradiol plus 0.5 mg of norgestrel daily for 21 days per cycle for more than 6 months; the other anovulatory patient (113/72) had taken the ethinyl estradiol plus norgestrel for 3 months (Table I). Two patients (1891/72 and 1790/72) were studied during one spontaneous ovulatory cycle and one cycle with ethinyl estradiol plus norgestrel treatment. One patient (1911/72) had been using the same contraceptive treatment for over 1 yr. She was studied during such an anovulatory cycle and during a following spontaneous cycle. One patient (1860/72) had three cycles investigated: a normal spontaneous one, an anovulatory one due to ethinyl estradiol and norgestrel treatment, and a normal spontaneous one.

Hormone Measurements

Blood samples were taken twice a week, between 8 and 10 A.M. on the same day as the EEG recording, and every day during the week presumed to encompass the ovulation date, or a similar period during anovulatory cycles. FSH and LH were measured according to previously described techniques (Rosselin and Dolais, 1967; Dolais *et al.*, 1968). Progesterone was measured by competitive protein binding (Pichon and Milgrom, 1973), and estradiol was measured by radioimmunoassay (Jolivet, unpublished).

Twenty-four hour urine samples were collected twice a week on the day before the EEG recording, and a GLC steroid profile technique was used for pregnanediol (Gautray *et al.*, 1970b).

EEG Recordings

Twice a week EEG recordings were performed between 10 and 12 A.M. Autocorrelation function and power spectra of the EEG signal from 0 to 25 Hz were calculated after analog to digital conversion. Two ratios were used to follow α-rhythm (8–12 Hz) and θ-waves (4–8 Hz) variations: (1) power spectrum area between 8 and 12 Hz/whole area of the spectrum for α-rhythm (Rα/PS) and (2) power spectrum area between 4 and 8 Hz/whole area of the spectrum for θ-waves (Rθ/PS). The different values of these ratios were assumed to be dependent on a periodic rhythm, and a periodic function was adjusted to these successive values. Its period was chosen according to the mean length of the menstrual cycle, i.e., 28 days, and its origin was set as the day of the LH peak, or day 14 in anovulatory cycles. According to this sophisticated mathematical methodology, the evolution of each ratio during the cycle describes a sinusoid, the amplitude of which is dependent on the EEG signal power (Gautray *et al.*, 1970a).

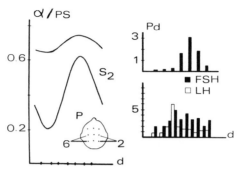

FIG. 1. Typical diagram of wide variations of Rα/PS observed in spontaneous ovulatory cycles. The scales are identical in all the following figures.

RESULTS

Spontaneous Ovulatory Cycles

The investigation did not reveal a typical pattern of EEG variations during spontaneous ovulatory cycles. Nevertheless, the Rα/PS was obviously high in all but one case (Fig. 1). The Rθ/PS was always lower. This is in agreement with the fact that slow waves are much less numerous than α-waves in a normal EEG recording. EEG and hormone variations during these ovulatory cycles were considered as controls and were compared to the same variations during cycles treated with contraceptive steroids.

Cycles During Treatment with Contraceptive Steroids

Anovulatory cycles induced by contraceptive steroids were ascertained by the lack of a LH peak and the low levels of LH and of progesterone in blood and/or pregnanediol in urine. Three different patterns of EEG variations were noted in such cases:

1. Among the patients who had been using ethinyl estradiol plus norgestrel for several months, two (2146/71, 2282/71) had a striking reduction in amplitude of variations of Rα/PS (Fig. 2) compared to most spontaneous normal cycles. However, one of them (1911/72) had a pattern of variation similar to tracings recorded during spontaneous ovulatory cycles. (Fig. 3).
2. Such a discrepancy was also noted but was of less importance, in a patient (113/72) who had initially used the same combination pill but had metrorrhagia and has used ethinyl estradiol plus norethisterone for the last 2 months at the time of investigation (Fig. 3).

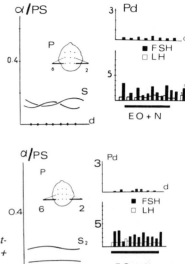

FIG. 2. Two anovulatory cycles induced by treatment with ethinyl estradiol plus norgestrel (EO + N). Decrease of Rα/PS is obvious.

3. One patient (1891/72) did not use any contraceptive steroid, except during her second cycle in this study. During treatment, the tracing variations were not reduced, but were no longer as homogeneous as before (Fig. 4).

One patient (1790/72) was studied during two ovulatory cycles (Fig. 5). The first one was a spontaneous ovulatory cycle; the second occurred during treatment with ethinyl estradiol plus norgestrel, but was nevertheless ovulatory. The EEG power spectra variations were identical in both cycles.

In two patients, we had the opportunity of recording the cycle which followed the cessation of contraceptive steroids. One (1911/72) had been using ethinyl estradiol plus norgestrel for 20 months (Fig. 6). She recovered an immediate, but severely impaired, hypophysiogonadal function: three successive LH peaks occurred during the first 22 days of this 37-day cycle, and the progesterone maximum was on day 25. The EEG power spectra variations were

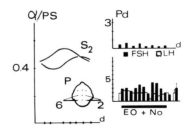

FIG. 3. Anovulatory cycle induced by ethinyl estradiol plus norethisterone (EO + No.). The decrease of Rα/PS is less than in patients using ethinyl estradiol plus norgestrel (Fig. 2).

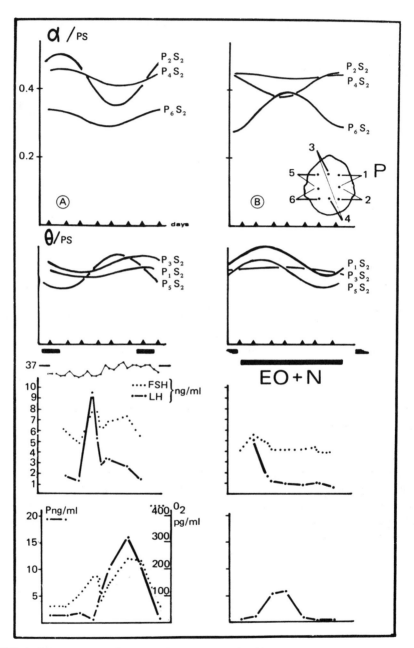

FIG. 4. *Spontaneous ovulatory cycle in patient 1891/72 and anovulatory cycle during treatment with ethinyl estradiol plus norgestrel (EO + N).* During the anovulatory cycle, EEG variations appear quite confused and discrepant from usual ones.

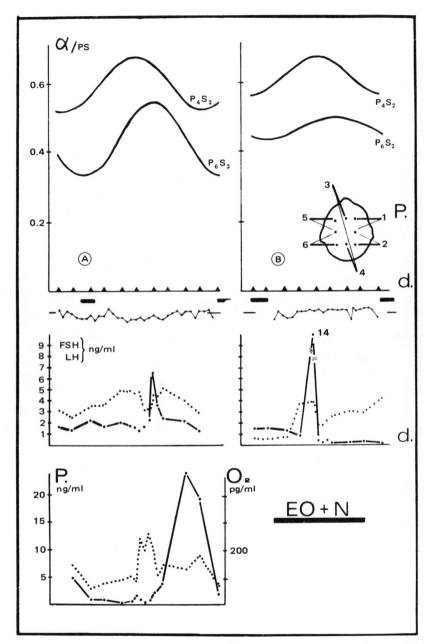

FIG. 5. Two ovulatory cycles in patient 1790/72. There is no discrepancy between EEG variations, even though the second cycle was treated with ethinyl estradiol plus norgestrel (EO + N), which did not impair ovulation.

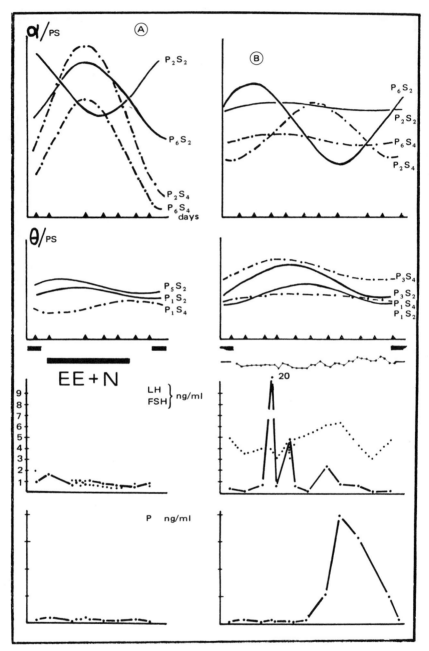

FIG. 6. An ethinyl estradiol plus norgestrel (EE + N) cycle in patient 1911/72 followed by a spontaneous cycle. Length of the cycle, LH secretion, and EEG variations are far from normal.

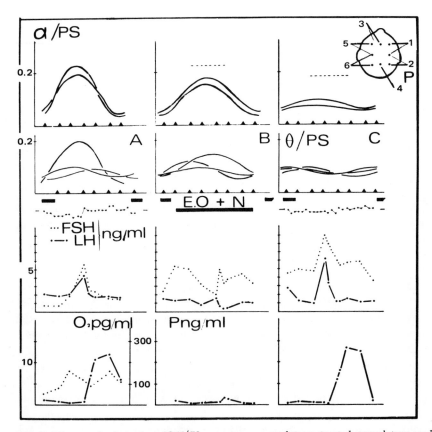

FIG. 7. Three cycles in patient 1860/72: spontaneous ovulatory, treated anovulatory, and another spontaneous ovulatory. The influence of contraceptive steroids on EEG variations is obvious not only during the treated cycle but also during the following spontaneous one; the amplitude and the level of variations are decreased.

quite discrepant from those previously observed in the same patient, or in patients with spontaneous ovulatory cycles. They can be described as appearing quite confused. The other patient (1860/72) was studied for 3 months; cycles 1 and 3 were spontaneous ones, and cycle 2 was treated with ethinyl estradiol plus norgestrel. The decrease of EEG power spectra variations was noticeable during cycle 2 and was even more obvious during cycle 3 (Fig. 7).

DISCUSSION

Mathematical analysis of EEG variations during normal menstrual cycles, during the cycles of patients treated with contraceptive steroids, and during the cycles of castrated patients treated with the same steroids has been performed

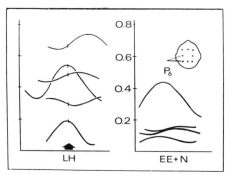

FIG. 8. The variations of the ratio α/PS are quite different, depending on whether the cycle is ovulatory (on the left) or whether anovulation is induced by ethinyl estradiol plus norgestrel (EE + N). P_6 is the only plug concerned in this diagram. Patterns of EEG variations are related to the LH peak.

(Gautray, unpublished results). This analysis has been correlated with endocrine parameters. Although individual discrepancies are to be expected, such a methodology may be of interest as a clinical neuroendocrine investigation. Tracings are rendered more meaningful by mathematical analysis and demonstrate the reactivity of the central nervous system to hormonal influences. The results may reveal neuroendocrine feedback mechanisms in human females.

The blockade of hypothalamic and hypophyseal activity, as demonstrated by anovulation, is associated with an important decrease in both α- and θ-rhythm power spectra variations (Fig. 8). Such a pattern, if confirmed by more data, might be typical of a negative feedback mechanism observed in patients using contraceptive steroids for an extended period of time. This pattern may be preceded by a confused state (Fig. 4) or may be dependent on the chemical structure of the steroid (Fig. 3). The lasting influence of ethinyl estradiol plus norgestrel after this treatment has been stopped (Fig. 7) might mean that the feedback mechanisms are more complex than usually admitted.

A 28-yr-old castrated patient was subjected to hypothalamic and hypophyseal stimulation by use of weak doses of ethinyl estradiol (Fig. 9). The EEG variations were strikingly increased. On the other hand, wide EEG variations were observed during all ovulatory cycles investigated. The same results were observed in another study of normal ovulatory cycles or clomiphene-restored cycles (Gautray *et al.*, 1970a). This pattern of wide variations and a high $R\alpha/PS$, and/or even $R\theta/PS$, might be typical of a positive feedback mechanism.

If confirmed by other data, the results of this correlative investigation may help to reveal the relationship between the human feedback mechanisms and the hypothalamogonadal axis. This may lead to a better understanding of clinical hypothalamogonadal dysfunction and to new therapeutic prospects.

FIG. 9. Studies of patient 2146/71. This patient was 28 yr old and had been castrated for 3 yr. (A) Investigation before any treatment. (B) Influence of a 21-day treatment with ethinyl estradiol (10 μg): variations of $R\alpha/PS$ are much wider and secretion of FSH is increased, the difference between the mean values being significant.

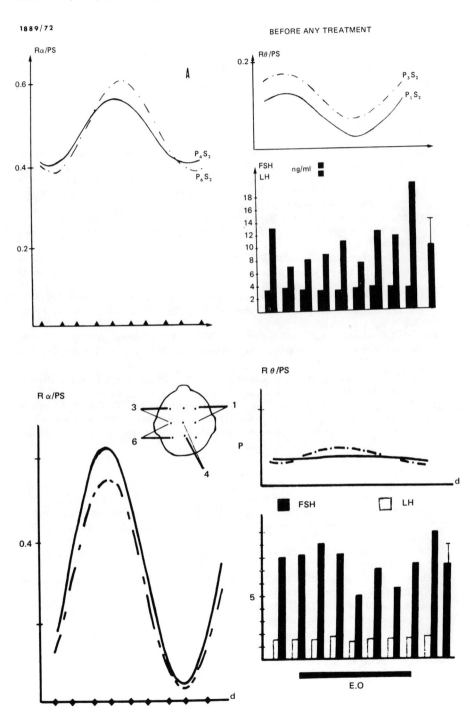

ACKNOWLEDGMENTS

Thanks are due to Miss Dolais, Ph.D., who carried out FSH and LH measurements, to A. Doussin, for pregnanediol evaluations, and to Roussel-Uclaf Laboratories, who kindly provided antibodies for estradiol assay.

REFERENCES

Ansari, A. H., Boyd, J. R., and Centa, C. J. (1970), Electroencephalographic recording during progestational treatment, *Fertil. Steril. 21:*873.

Cargile, C. M., Ross, G. T., and Yoshimi, T. (1969), Daily variations in plasma follicle stimulating hormone, luteinizing hormone, and progesterone in the normal menstrual cycle, *J. Clin. Endocrinol. Metab. 29:*12.

Davidson, J. M. (1969), Feedback control of gonadotropic secretion, in: *Frontiers in Neuroendocrinology*, p. 343 (W. F. Ganong and L. Martini, eds.), Oxford University Press, London.

Dolais, J., Freychet, P., and Rosselin, G. (1968), Dosage plasmatique de l'hormone lutéinisante humaine (H.L.H.) par la méthode radioimmunologique. Mise au point de la technique de dosage. *C.R. Acad. Sc. Paris, 267:*1105.

Gautray, J. P., Garrel, S., and Eberhard, A. (1970a), Electroencephalographic correlates of the human menstrual cycle I. Methodology. II. Results and discussion, *Acta Eur. Fertil. 2:*5.

Gautray, J. P., Chambaz, E. M., and Madani, C. (1970b), Urinary steroid gas chromatographic profiles in gynecology. Modifications following Nialamid therapy. *Excerpta Med. Int. Cong. Ser. 210, abst. 461.*

Koren, F., Bozezinski, A., Bental, E., and Amir, N. (1963), Electroencephalographic changes in amenorrhea, *Obstet. Gynecol. 22:*1.

Larsson-Cohn, U., Johansson, E. D. B., Wide, L., and Gemzell, C. (1972), Effects of continuous daily administration of 0.1 mg of norethindrone on the plasma levels of progesterone, and on the urinary excretion of LH and total oestrogens, *Acta Endocrinol. 71:*551.

Matsumoto, S., Sato, I., Ito, T., and Matsuoka, A. (1966), Electroencephalographic changes during long-term treatment with oral contraceptives, *Int. J. Fertil. 11:*195.

Midgley, A. R., and Jaffe, R. B. (1971), Regulation of human gonadotropins. X. Episodic fluctuation of LH during the menstrual cycle, *J. Clin. Endocrinol. Metab. 33:*962.

Monroe, S. E., Jaffe, R. B., and Midgley, A. R. (1972), Regulation of human gonadotropins. XII. Increase in serum gonadotropins in response to estradiol, *J. Clin. Endocrinol. Metab. 34:*342.

Nillius, S. J., and Wide, L. (1970), Effects of estrogen on serum levels of LH and FSH, *Acta Endocrinol. 65:*583.

Pichon, M. F., and Milgrom, E. (1973), Competitive protein binding assay for progesterone without chromatography, *Steroids 21:*335.

Rosselin, G., and Dolais, J. (1967), Dosage de l'hormone folliculostimulante humaine (H.FSH) par la méthode radioimmunologique. *Presse Med. 75:*2027.

Sawyer, C. H. (1970), Electrophysiological correlates of release of pituitary ovulating hormones, *Fed. Proc. 29(6):*1895.

Sharf, M., Sharf, B., Bental, E., and Kuzminsky, T. (1969), The electroencephalaogram in the investigation of anovulation and its treatment by clomiphene, *Lancet 1:*750.

Swerdloff, R. S., and Odell, W. D. (1969), Serum luteinizing and follicle stimulating hormone levels during sequential and nonsequential contraceptive treatment of eugonadal women, *J. Clin. Endocrinol. Metab. 29:*157.

Taymor, M. L., and Levesque, L. A. (1971), Levels of serum FSH, LH, and plasma progestin during microdose chlormadinone treatment, *Fertil. Steril. 22(1):*1.

Thomas, K., and Ferin, J. (1972), Suppression of the midcycle LH surge by a low dose mestranol lynestrenol oral combination, *Contraception 6:*1.

Vogel, W., Broverman, D. M., and Klaiser, E. L. (1971), EEG reponses in regularly menstruating women and in amenorrheic women treated with ovarian hormones, *Science 172:*388.

Yen, S. S. C., and Tsai, C. C. (1971), The biphasic pattern of the feedback action of ethinyl estradiol on the release of pituitary FSH and LH, *J. Clin. Endocrinol. Metab. 33:*882.

Yussman, M. A., Taymor, M. L., Miyata, J., and Pheteplace, C. (1970), Serum levels of FSH, LH, and plasma progestins correlated with ovulation, *Fertil. Steril. 21:*119.

26

Ovulation, Corpus Luteum Formation, and Steroidogenesis

A. V. Nalbandov and J. M. Bahr

Departments of Animal Science and Physiology and Biophysics
University of Illinois
Urbana, Illinois

Much of the research work dealing with ovulation, corpus luteum formation, and steroidogenesis involves the monitoring of these events in animals in which the appropriate hormones are of endogenous origin, or in which these hormones have been injected systemically and reach their target organ, the ovary, by the conventional route, the ovarian artery. The suspicion, for which there is a basis, arises that the hormones involved may be modified en route to the ovarian follicle in such a way that the substances impinging on the end organ are not actually the peptides synthesized and released by the pituitary gland or injected systemically; that is, the end organ may not be acted on by the original molecule released or injected. Accordingly, Jones and Nalbandov (1972) devised a technique by which hormones can be introduced directly into the lumen of antral follicles of rabbits. By this method, the substances injected bypass the normal avenues of entry into the follicle and act only on the follicle treated. Thus it can be shown that of two closely adjacent follicles only the one treated with a hormone responds (e.g., ovulates or luteinizes), while its immediate neighbor, treated with saline, remains unchanged (Fig. 1).

INTRAFOLLICULAR FSH AND LH

A variety of experiments were performed using this technique. First we explored the problem of whether ovulation is facilitated if both FSH and LH are present. This question arose because in the vast majority of animals studied

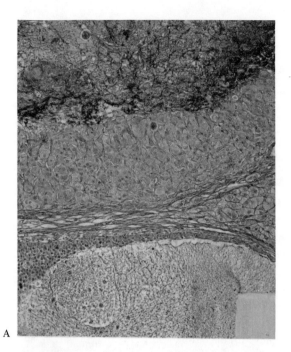

A

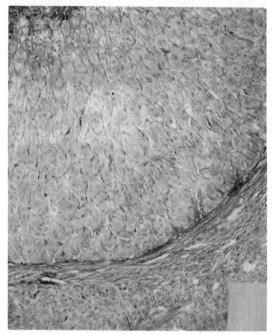

B

FIG. 1. Effect of saline or LH treatment of individual follicles. (A) The lower follicle was injected with saline and the upper one with 1.0 ng of LH (had FSH been used, the results would have been the same). Note partial luteinization of the granulosa layer in the upper follicle; the antrum persists. Normal granulosa layer in the lower follicle. (85×) (B) The luteinized layer consists of typical lutein cells. (298×.)

TABLE I. Induction of Ovulation in Rabbits After Systemic (i.v.) or Intrafollicular (i.f.) Injection of Hormones

Hormone	Route of adminis- tration	Dose	Number of treated or	Follicles present	Number of ovulated follicles	Percent
LH	i.v.	15 μg	58	$(7)^a$	50	86
FSH	i.v.	125 μg	101	(11)	83	82
LH:FSH	i.v.	10:25 μg	52	(6)	44	85
LH:FSH	i.v.	5:50 μg	38	(4)	31	82
LH:FSH	i.v.	5:25 μg	26	(4)	14	54^b
LH:FSH	i.v.	2:25 μg	19	(2)	2	11^b
Prolactin	i.v.	125 μg	51	(5)	0	0
TSH	i.v.	100 μg	59	(7)	0	0
Saline	i.v.	–	25	(4)	0	0
LH	i.f.	5 ng	10	(6)	0	0
LH	i.f.	10 ng	30	(15)	27	80
FSH	i.f.	50 ng	9	(4)	0	0
FSH	i.f.	100 ng	24	(5)	18	75
LH:FSH	i.f.	5:75 ng	23	(7)	18	78
LH:FSH	i.f.	5:50 ng	19	(6)	9	47^b
LH:FSH	i.f.	5:25 ng	20	(6)	0	0
Prolactin	i.f.	100 ng	11	(4)	0	0
TSH	i.f.	100 ng	13	(7)	0	0
Saline	i.f.	–	6	(3)	0	0

[a] Number of animals.

[b] Different from all other observations ($P > 0.01$).

(with the possible exception of the rabbit), the ovulatory peak of gonadotropins occurring prior to ovulation consists of both FSH and LH. Table I shows that either FSH or LH, when injected systemically, induces ovulation, although much higher doses of FSH (125 μg/kg) are required to cause follicular rupture than of LH (15 μg). Furthermore, when the two hormones are combined, it is seen that the dose of FSH can be reduced to 50 μg and that of LH to 5 μg to produce maximal efficiency of ovulation. In this and the experiment to be described next, the ovulation-inducing ability of FSH (NIH-S6) cannot be ascribed to its contamination with LH. In the lower half of Table I, the results of the injection of FSH or of LH directly into the antrum of the follicle are shown. Here 100 ng/follicle of FSH and 10 ng/follicle of LH were enough to cause maximal rates of ovulation. Just as in case of systemic injection, lower quantities of either hormone were required when the two hormones were combined. Maximal ovulation rates were induced by a mixture of 5 ng of LH and 75 ng of FSH per follicle. In both intrafollicular and systemic injection, the fact that the doses for maximal ovulation rate of the combined hormones were significantly lower than

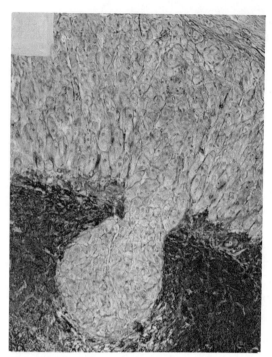

FIG. 2. Low doses of either FSH or LH will cause
luteinization of the granulosa layer and of the cells
supporting and surrounding the oocyte. Note that the
antrum persists. (80×.)

that of either hormone alone is interpreted as synergism of the two hormones.
Hence the conclusion is drawn that while either hormone alone can "force"
ovulation, under physiological conditions follicular rupture occurs more readily
when both FSH and LH are present. This and the fact that preovulatory peaks
include both gonadotropins inclines one to believe that the gonadotropic complex (FSH and LH) should be regarded as the "ovulation-inducing hormone"
rather than LH alone, as is commonly assumed.

All low levels of FSH or LH alone or in combination which are unable to
cause ovulation invariably cause luteinization of the unruptured follicles. The
type of luteinization is not that which typically occurs after ovulation. Although
the morphological appearance of the lutein cells is indistinguishable from that of
normal corpora lutea, lutenization usually involves only the granulosa cell layer,
leaving a large, fluid-filled cavity in the center (Fig. 2). Even low doses of either
hormone cause lutenization of the cumulus oophorus entrapping the egg. As
little as 1 ng/follicle of either gonadotropin produces this type of luteinization.
Jones and Nalbandov (1972) have shown that these partially luteinized "fol-

licles" are capable of synthesizing as much progesterone as are fully formed corpora lutea of pseudopregnant does ovulated by ovulatory doses of hormones.

This ability of either FSH or LH to cause rudimentary luteinization shows that even small doses of these hormones are able to overcome whatever luteinization-inhibiting properties the oocyte of the intact follicle may possess (El-Fouly *et al.*, 1970). The mechanism involved in this process remains unknown. To understand what changes occur in the steroid levels, we used either systemic or intrafollicular injection of FSH, LH, or of LH subunits and measured the steroids appearing in the ovarian affluent blood.

Figures 3 and 4 show what happens to estradiol (E_2) and progesterone (P_4) output in response to intrafollicular injection of FSH or LH. It is seen that FSH increases E_2 output by about 300%, while LH has no such effect. In contrast, either hormone raises P_4 output over 1000% within 5 min after injection. It should be noted that there is no change in hormone output in saline-injected control follicles. The main question that arises in connection with these experiments, as well as in those to be presented later, is whether the hormone treatment causes release of already synthetized and stored hormone or whether it causes *de novo* synthesis of the steroids, which are immediately released into peripheral circulation. Since in most cases illustrated, we noted a steep and immediate rise in steroid output in the affluent blood which was followed by a plateau of output, we tentatively interpreted our data to mean that the first effect of the tropic substances is to cause release of the steroids stored in one of the follicular compartments. This release is followed by a sustained synthesis

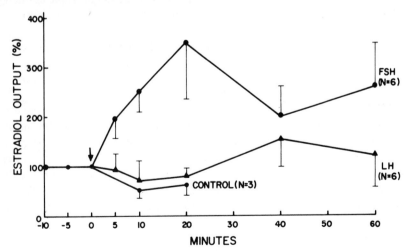

FIG. 3. Effect of intrafollicular injection of either FSH or LH on estradiol released into the ovarian vein. Control follicles were injected with saline. Note that LH had no significant effect.

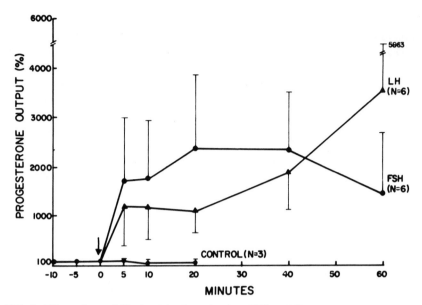

FIG. 4. *Effect of intrafollicular injection of either FSH or LH.* Progesterone output was measured in the same blood sample which was used for estrogen determination. Note that both FSH and LH causes an immediate increase in progesterone output which then levels off and is sustained for at least 60 min.

over at least the 60-min period following the single injection of tropic hormones during which ovarian blood was sampled. Whether this interpretation is correct is now being tested.

Of some interest is the fact that both FSH and LH cause release and synthesis of P_4 but only FSH is able to do this in the case of E_2.

SUBUNITS

We next tested the ability of LH α- and β-subunits to cause ovulations and steroid synthesis in rabbits. In these preliminary exploratory experiments, the effects of the subunits were compared to those of native LH, all of which were injected systemically. The results are shown in Table II. It was surprising that both LH-α and -β caused numbers of ovulations which were not significantly different from those produced by native LH. That the β-subunit has this ability had been previously shown in hamsters (Yang *et al.,* 1972). The ovulation-inducing ability of the α-subunit was surprising, and immediately raised the question of whether it could be ascribed to the contamination of the α-subunit with native LH. Since a dose of 50 μg/kg of the α-subunit was injected systemically and since it takes 10 μg/kg of native LH to produce comparable rates of ovulation, calculations show that a very major contamination of the subunit with LH would have to be present to account for this biological activity. Such a high degree of contamination would have to be detectable by other biological assay methods, and it was not. Furthermore, the subunits were prepared by Dr. Harold Papkoff by the method of countercurrent distribution. This method of preparation makes it seem highly improbable that LH contamination might be carried over to the subunit.

In addition to the study on the induction of ovulation, we investigated the ability of LH subunits to cause steroid synthesis by the ovary. As shown in Table II, the α- and β-subunits are able to increase the rates of output of both E_2 and of P_4 when compared to the base levels of output of these hormones. However, inspection of the data makes it clear that neither subunit is biologically as potent as the native LH molecule. Equally significant is the fact that 60 min after injection of LH the output of both E_2 and P_4 is still rising, and other data (not shown in Table II) indicate that even as late as 3 h after injection the steroid levels remain high. In distinct contrast, neither subunit is able to sustain steroid output for as long as the native LH, and by 60 min after injection the steroid levels have begun to revert to base levels of output. At present it is not clear whether the subunits have only the ability to release already synthesized steroids or whether they have the ability to cause *de novo* synthesis, as does native LH.

TABLE II. Ovulation and Steroid Secretion in Response to LH, LH-α, and LH-β

	LH (10 μg/kg)	LH-α (50 μg/kg)	LH-β (50 μg/kg)
Ovulations	10.8 ± 1.7^a	5.8 ± 0.4^b	8.8 ± 1.2^b
Ovarian E_2 output			
Basal level	100%	100%	100%
Post-treatment			
20 min	$252.5\% \pm 38.7$	$161.2\% \pm 44.1^b$	$252.7\% \pm 60.8^b$
60 min	$336.4\% \pm 60.7$	$116.4\% \pm 18.2^c$	$161.1\% \pm 56.0^d$
Ovarian P_4 output			
Basal level	100%	100%	100%
Post treatment			
20 min	$3432.0\% \pm 1260.7$	$1525.6\% \pm 283.7^b$	$705.3\% \pm 145.4^d$
60 min	$3599.2\% \pm 1469.8$	$1203.6\% \pm 281.9^b$	$283.0\% \pm 83.6^d$

^{a}Mean $\pm$ SEM.

^{b}Not significantly different from LH ($P > 0.05$).

^{c}Significantly different from LH ($P < 0.01$).

^{d}Significantly different from LH ($P < 0.05$).

DISCUSSION

Aside from the fact that this study furnishes additional information on the contention that either FSH or LH can cause ovulation, its most significant aspect is the demonstration that whereas ovulation requires a minimal effective dose of FSH or LH, or both hormones, luteinization of the follicle does not. Thus even picogram amounts of either gonadotropin injected directly into the follicle are able to trigger the events (whatever they may be) that are involved in the transformation of a follicular structure into a lutein one. Concomitant with this morphological transformation of the follicle wall is the switch in the endocrine system from the synthesis of predominantly estrogen to that of both estrogen and progesterone. It is also significant that while LH alone, or a mixture of LH and FSH, can cause ovulation much easier than FSH alone, there is no such disparity in the effectiveness of the two hormones in causing luteinization. Present data suggest that even minute quantities of either hormone injected into the follicle lumen are enough to trigger both the morphological transformation and the endocrine switch in hormone systems. Therefore, whatever luteinization-inhibiting mechanism is normally present in the follicle can be easily overpowered by either gonadotropin. It is possible to speculate that the preovulatory appearance of P_4 in follicle and blood may be caused by changes in either or both gonadotropins recognized by the follicle. In some animals, for instance, the mare, luteinized cells in the granulosa cell layer actually appear prior to ovulation.

The data presented on the role of FSH and LH in steroid synthesis and output strongly suggest it has dual components. One is the ability of either of the gonadotropins to cause an instantaneous and copious release of the steroids stored in the follicle. It is presently being determined whether this release occurs from the follicular fluid or from the cellular layers lining the follicle wall. The second component involves the very obvious ability of a single dose of either gonadotropin to cause a continuous and prolonged synthesis of steroids concomitant with their release into the bloodstream, which, however, differs from the initial precipitous release by being steady and sustained.

Preliminary experiments involved the α- and β-subunits of LH and their ability to mimic the physiological effects of the native LH. It was found that both subunits are able to cause ovulation as well as steroid release, with two apparently important differences between the subunits and the native molecule. First, it seems that either they are unable to cause steroid synthesis or, if synthesis does occur, it is of a very short duration with a distinct tendency for the steroid concentrations to decline rapidly toward base-level secretion. Second, both subunits are biologically far less potent than LH in their ability to cause ovulations or steroid output. It is of interest to note that attempts to cause steroid synthesis by use of LH β-subunits in cultures of cells which were originally derived from granulosa cells lining the follicle failed (Channing and Kammerman, 1974). The reason for this dichotomy of effects *in vivo* and *in vitro* is not clear.

ACKNOWLEDGMENTS

This study was supported in part by NIH grants T1-HD-181 and HD-3043 and by a Ford Foundation grant. NIH also furnished the purified LH and FSH preparations. We are grateful to Dr. Harold Papkoff for having provided the LH subunits used in this work.

REFERENCES

Channing, C. P., and Kammerman, S. (1974), Binding of gonadotropic hormones to ovarian cells, *Biol. Reprod. 10:*179–198.

El-Fouly, M. A., Cook, B., Nekola, M., and Nalbandov, A. V. (1970), Role of the ovum in follicular luteinization, *Endocrinology 87:*288–293.

Jones, E. E., and Nalbandov, A. V. (1972), Effect of intrafollicular injection of gonadotrophins on ovulation of luteinization of ovarian follicle, *Biol. Reprod. 7:*87–93.

Yang, W. H., Sairam, M., Papkoff, H., and Li, C. H. (1972), Ovulation in hamster: Induction by beta-subunit of ovine ICSH, *Science 175:*637–638.

Index

409

WARNER MEMORIAL LIBRARY
EASTERN COLLEGE
ST. DAVIDS, PA. 19087